is warmly appreciated. I am indebted to Mr A. Burn, Mr R. Smith and Mrs D. Human for the execution of the maps, and to Miss A. Flint for typing the manuscript. I am also grateful to countless planning authorities, government departments and regional organizations in France for the provision of data and for their willingness to give of their time for discussions. Finally, I am deeply indebted to my wife, Hélène, not only for assistance in correcting the manuscript, but more importantly for introducing me to the land of her birth.

Department of Geography,
Southampton University

Preface

This book seeks to portray France as a nation in a state of mutation in economy, society and landscape. In the course of teaching and research, the author has been made aware of the scarcity of literature available to students in English, attempting to analyse the structural and spatial changes which have transformed France since the Second World War. The preoccupation of most advanced texts remains that of regional description, with little reference to the fluidity of the underlying social and economic processes of change which, the author believes, impel a reappraisal of habitual ideas and attitudes concerning our nearest continental neighbour.

Like all Gaul, the text is divided into three parts. Part One, devoted to patterns of social development, seeks to analyse the manner in which demographic and economic resurgence has reacted upon the supply of manpower, the geography of population and the character of settlement. Part Two reviews in turn the institutional background to planned economic growth, the infrastructure of the economy and the sectors of production, followed by an assessment of regional disparities resulting from unbalanced growth. The book is concluded in Part Three by a series of essays which seek to integrate the first two parts of the text by analysing problems of economic and social development at the regional level.

The objectives of the book determined some measure of divergence from orthodoxy. In particular, the physical basis of regional differentiation is not elaborated. The consistent theme of the book is the exposition of problems of economic and social organization and the physical background is thus viewed as a variable resource base rather than as a matter for individual description. Similarly, the regional system employed may affront the scruples of the purist, whether of the traditional or regional science school. The author believes that the use of planning regions is a logical outgrowth of the central theme of the book and provides a more rational basis for the discussion of development problems than would a conventional regional framework.

Every author must entertain periodic reserve on the value of his labours, and at such times the encouragement received from relations and colleagues

Contents

ENGLAND
Butterworth & Co (Publishers) Ltd
London: 88 Kingsway, W.C.2

AUSTRALIA
Butterworth & Co (Australia) Ltd
Sydney: 20 Loftus Street
Melbourne: 343 Little Collins Street
Brisbane: 240 Queen Street

CANADA
Butterworth & Co (Canada) Ltd
Toronto: 14 Curity Avenue, 374

NEW ZEALAND
Butterworth & Co (New Zealand) Ltd
Wellington: 49/51 Ballance Street
Auckland: 35 High Street

SOUTH AFRICA
Butterworth & Co (South Africa) Ltd
Durban: 33/35 Beach Grove

First published 1970

ISBN 0 408 70016 5

Filmset by Siviter Smith Ltd, Birmingham

Printed in England by
Pitman Press, Bath

Modern France

A SOCIAL AND ECONOMIC GEOGRAPHY

I. B. THOMPSON, M.A., PH.D.

Department of Geography, University of Southampton

LONDON
BUTTERWORTHS

Dans la vie, il n'y a pas de solutions.
Il y a des forces en marche,
Il s'agit de les créer et les solutions suivent.
SAINT-EXUPERY

Modern France
France

A SOCIAL AND ECONOMIC GEOGRAPHY

Part One
PATTERNS OF SOCIAL DEVELOPMENT

I

Human Resources

The known physical resources of a nation are readily amenable to summary description[1] and an advanced industrial nation may make good deficiencies in its resource base by recourse to normal trading processes. On the other hand, the measurement of human resources involves certain intangibles that defy easy assessment. The numerical strength, quality and vitality of a population are critical elements in a nation's economic potential, while the institutional basis of a society must also be evaluated as a resource in so far as it impinges on the efficiency with which material and manpower resources are utilized. The question of national temperament and institutions can only be put to subjective judgement, and it is fitting to leave such matters to the perceptive regard of a Frenchman[2] The present chapter is concerned solely with those qualities of the French population which may be measured objectively and which directly affect patterns of social and economic organization.

MODERN POPULATION GROWTH

The population of France has been subjected to closer scrutiny than that of other west European country[3] in an attempt to explain certain anomalous

Table 1.1

TOTAL POPULATION GROWTH, 1861–1946

	1861	1881	1901	1911	1921	1936	1946
Total[a]	37,386	39,239	40,681	41,479	39,210	41,912	40,506
Index[b]	100	105	109	111	105	112	108

[a]In thousands.
[b]1861 = 100.
Source: Etudes et Conjoncture, 'L'Espace Economique Français', Fasc. 1, 1965, Tables R1–1, R1–2.

features in its demographic history. The most striking anomaly was the precocious decline in fertility levels, occurring half a century before the same phenomenon affected neighbouring nations, and condemning France to a century of demographic stagnation.

Between 1861 and the close of the Second World War, the French population increased by only 8 per cent (*Table 1.1*), as compared with a 30 per cent growth in the first 60 years of the nineteenth century. As a result, from a leading position in Europe in 1850, France had fallen behind Germany, Britain and Italy in terms of total population by 1939. This unfavourable trend was a consequence of declining fertility, the birth rate falling from 32 per thousand in 1800 to 14·6 per thousand in 1939. Between 1890 and 1936, the net reproduction rate exceeded unity in only four years.

Table 1.2

COMPARATIVE TRENDS IN FERTILITY, 1861–1939

	Crude birth rate per thousand				
	1861–70	*1881–90*	*1901–10*	*1930–34*	*1935–39*
France	26·4	23·9	20·6	17·0	14·8
Germany	37·2	36·8	32·9	16·3	19·4
England	35·2	32·5	27·2	15·8	15·3
Italy	36·9	37·8	32·7	24·5	23·2

Source: Etudes et Conjoncture, 'L'Espace Economique Français, Fasc. 2, 1965, p. 26.

Table 1.2 demonstrates that the reduction in fertility occurred much earlier and more emphatically in France than was the case in neighbouring nations with comparable base populations in 1860. By contrast, the decline in mortality rates associated with increased life expectancy did not gather momentum until the turn of the century. By the time that increased longevity became an established trend, the level of fertility was so low that the effect on natural increase was minimal. Between 1900 and 1936 life expectancy increased from 47 to 58·7 years, the median age progressed from 28 to 33 years and the mortality rate fell from 19·6 per thousand to 15·2 per thousand. Although increased life expectancy had the effect of adding to the total population, its combination with declining fertility had as a major consequence a progressive ageing of the national population.

Crude rates of vital statistics are notoriously generalized, but age specific and standardized rates, gross and net reproduction rates all point to the same conclusion, that by the middle of the nineteenth century France had lost her demographic vitality, and did not recover it until after the Second World War.[4] Numerous theories have been expressed to account for this phenomenon,[5] and the demographic determinants are unambiguous: a reduction in the marital rate, a high average age at marriage, and, above all, a reduction in the average size of completed family. However, precisely why these determinants should have changed course is open to speculation. Recurrent depressions in the agricultural economy, the desire to restrict property fragmentation by limiting the number of heirs, the effect of military service in postponing marriages and the effect of increased social capillarity in the middle classes have all been held to account for the reduction in family size. Similarly, the active participation of women in the agricultural economy was a factor conflicting with frequent childbearing. Late in achieving her industrial revolution, it is difficult to advance rapid urbanization, an acknowledged depressant of fertility, as a major factor in the reduced birth rate; moreover, differential fertility rates indicate a general decline affecting all social classes and residential groups.

To the social and economic causes of reduced fertility must be added the catastrophic demographic results of the First World War.[6] The cemeteries, so liberally distributed across rural and urban France, are eloquent testimony to the scale of loss of life, which may be estimated at 1·3 million servicemen and a total exceeding 2 millions including civilian losses.[7] The effect of the war was both direct, in terms of fatalities, and indirect, in terms of the distortion of the age and sex structure of the post-war population. The war thus curtailed marriages still in the reproductive stage, postponed other marriages, depressed the marital rate, and through war injuries rendered many combatants unable to support families. Moreover, this distortion occurred at a time when fertility was already abnormally low, and the 1921 population was marginally smaller than that of 1891.*

The extent of the demographic decline experienced by France during the nineteenth century and until the outbreak of the Second World War may be judged from figures presented by Sauvy[8] (Table 1.3).

Table 1.3

THE DEMOGRAPHIC BALANCE SHEET, 1801–1936

	Millions
Natural change	− 5
Increased life expectancy	+16
Losses of 1914–18	− 3
Immigration	+ 5
Net change	+13

Source: Sauvy A., op. cit.[8]

*Taking into account territorial changes.

Between 1801 and 1936 the population of France increased only by virtue of increased life expectancy and a very high level of immigration; on the basis of natural increase a net loss of five millions was registered. In the period between the world wars, the population increased by approximately three millions but this was very largely due to the large number of immigrants entering the country* By 1925 France had become the second most important nation in the world, after the United States, for the receipt of immigrants, and the leading nation in terms of the ratio of immigrants to native-born population. By contrast, the level of fertility continued to fall throughout the decade 1930 to 1940, reaching a record peacetime low of 14·8 per cent in 1938. This coincided with a decade of economic depression and with the arrival at the age of marriage of the age cohort born after the 1914–1918 war and consequently reduced in size. The Second World War thus struck a further blow at the population at a time when demographically it was at its lowest ebb. Armengaud[9] has calculated that the direct and indirect losses in population sustained during the period 1939–1945 totalled 1·4 million.

By 1946, the French population was smaller than in 1901 and only marginally larger than in 1881. The demographic balance, in terms of age structure and the ratio of births to deaths was completely distorted and the nation's productive fabric disrupted and in large proportion destroyed. Conditions could scarcely have been less auspicious in which to stage a demographic recovery and yet this is precisely what did occur. Between 1946 and 1954 the population increased by 5·6 per cent, and between 1954 and 1962 by 8·8 per cent.[10]

In the course of 17 years, between the close of the war and the end of 1962, the French population increased by over 7 millions, a complete

Table 1.4

THE DEMOGRAPHIC REVIVAL, 1946–1962

	Crude birth rate[a]	Natural increase[a]	Total population[b]
1946	20·8	7·4	40,125
1948	21·0	8·7	40,910
1950	20·5	7·8	41,647
1955	18·5	6·4	43,228
1960	17·9	6·6	45,465
1962	17·6	6·2	46,422

[a]Per Thousand.
[b]In thousands.
Source: Nizart, A., and Pressat, R., op. cit.[11] p. 1,116.

*Between 1921 and 1926 approximately one million immigrants entered France.

reversal of the trend between the wars. While immigration continued to play an important role, this demographic revival was largely due to an unprecedented upturn in fertility[11] (*Table 1.4*).

The causes underlying this resurgence of fertility were complex but the influence of public policy on population matters appears to have been undeniable. The principle of fiscal and financial aid to support families had been established before the war but the scale and conditions of payment were greatly modified in a series of reforms after 1946. Public policy was based on two objectives: to remove the financial obstacles to increased family size and to encourage an early start to families.

A further incentive to increased family size was the psychological change as compared with the inter-war depression years. The appearance of full employment, the assumption by the state of responsibilities formerly privately borne, the improvement in material living standards and greater leisure time all combined to reinforce the family as an image of well-being and security. The increase in the birth rate also coincided with a reduction in the age of marriage and an increase in the marital rate. Substantial although the recovery in the birth rate was, the magnitude must be kept in proportion. By 1962 the recovery in fertility was only to the level of the pre-depression year of 1931 and still considerably lower than the level of 1900. Furthermore, unlike the inter-war years, when fertility was uniformly low, certain differentials by social class and by region were apparent. The demographic recovery was a feature of urban residence and the more prosperous north and east, to a much greater extent than the under-developed parts of the country, sapped by a century of age-selective migration and sharing to a much lesser extent in the nation's post-war economic recovery. However, in conjunction with a declining mortality rate, achieved especially by reduced infant mortality, France regained its demographic equilibrium.

To the natural processes of growth must be added the substantial contribution made by immigration during the period 1946–1962. At the close of the war, manpower shortages caused the creation of the 'Office National d'Immigration' (O.N.I.), to regulate the flow of immigrants to the demands of the economy. Between 1946 and 1950, the O.N.I. introduced 271,000 permanent foreign workers, and a further 443,000 between 1950 and 1960. Recourse to immigrant labour was required in spite of the increased birth rate as a result of the time lag before this could have any effect on the labour force. Over half the immigrants were Italian, while large numbers of native Algerians, at this stage still French citizens, also entered the country. A high proportion of the foreign workers brought their families, giving further impetus to the reviving birth rate[12] By 1962, the foreign-born population had increased to 1·8 million, and including naturalized foreigners to over 2 million inhabitants.[13]

In 1967, Sibylle Lemoine was acclaimed as the 50 millionth inhabitant of France. However, the publication of the 1968 census[14] reveals this claim to have been somewhat premature, and by March 1968 the population of France had attained between 49·8 and 50 millions.*

Table 1.5

POPULATION CHANGE, 1962–1968

	Absolute	*Rate per cent*
Natural increase	+1,900,000	+4·1
Repatriation from North Africa	+800,000	+1·8
Other net immigration	+600,000–800,000	+1·2–+1·6
Total population increase	+3,300,000–3,500,000	+7·1–+7·5

Source: Recensement de 1968. Premiers résultats.

Table 1.5 reveals that the rhythm of total population increase has closely followed that of the previous inter-censal period. Some falling off has occurred in the level of the birth rate[15,16] in spite of the entry into the reproductive age group of the cohort produced by the post-war rise in fertility. Nevertheless, discounting the return of 815,000 Algerian repatriates, total population growth has averaged over one per cent per annum, of which two thirds is accounted for by natural increase and one third by foreign immigration.[17]

THE NUMERICAL STRENGTH OF THE LABOUR FORCE

Although the total population figure of 50 millions cited above is meaningless in itself†, the advance in the numerical strength of the population is nevertheless representative of an increased human potential. The trend in the total labour force since 1920 cruelly reveals the economic consequences of the general demographic trends outlined in this chapter. Between 1920 and 1954, the total labour force declined by approximately 5 per cent, while between 1954 and 1962 it remained stationary. This levelling out of the labour force, in spite of a rapid growth in total population, is accounted for by the rise in the birth rate, producing a large number of children whose

*The figures are the official preliminary results published three months after the census as a result of computer analysis.
†Figures of the labour force based on the 1968 census are not yet available.

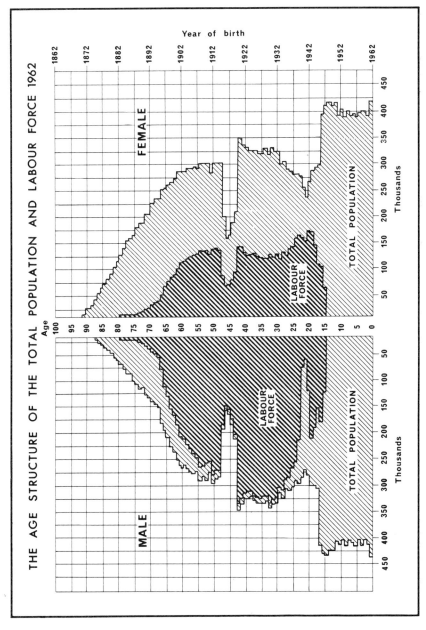

Figure 1.1

entry into the labour force is only just occurring. In addition, the increased
number of school leavers following some form of secondary education,
combined in the case of males with compulsory military service, means
that the full effect of the post-war increase in fertility will not be felt until
1969–1970.

A further reduction in the labour force has been brought about by the
retirement of many elderly farmers under the government scheme to
promote the rationalization of farm structures, and by the widespread
practice in mining and industry of the pre-retirement of older workers as
a means of avoiding unemployment among younger workers.*

The end result of the trends of a static labour force and a growing total
population has been to increase the dependency ratio. In 1936 the employed
labour force totalled 45·1 per cent of the total population whereas in 1954
the proportion had fallen to 43·4 per cent, and in 1962 to 40·1 per cent.†

The age structure of the total labour force is illustrated in *Figure 1.1*
superimposed on the conventional age pyramid. This reveals the enormous
gaps created in the male labour force by the First World War and the
subsequent loss of fertility, and by the Second World War. *Figure 1.1* also
shows that at the census of 1962, the post-war 'baby boom' was only just
entering into the work force and that the inflated base of the age pyramid
was still in a dependent status. Two conclusions may thus be drawn concerning the post-war period. The rapid increase in output and the related
rise in living standards have been achieved by increased productivity rather
than by additional manpower, and, secondly, the critical role of immigrant
labour at a time when natural replacement of the labour force was impossible cannot be exaggerated.

THE MOBILITY OF THE LABOUR FORCE

In its widest sense, the mobility of labour may be taken to imply sectorial,
geographical and international mobility. In all cases the ultimate objective
must be to concentrate labour in sufficient quantity and quality on to the
appropriate locations to maximize output. *Table 1.6* demonstrates that a
profound modification of the balance of the three major occupation
groups has taken place since 1921.

Between 1921 and 1954, the agricultural labour force diminished by 2·6
millions and from a leading position in the total labour force was overtaken by both industrial and service employment. Between 1954 and 1962

---

*Also permitting continued recruiting of trainees which, in the case of industries undergoing
contraction, would otherwise be impossible.

†In 1968 the total labour force attained 20 millions, growing by 5 per cent between 1962 and 1968,
but the proportion of the total population remained at 40 per cent.

the decline of agricultural employment became even more emphatic; in eight years the labour force declined by 20 per cent. During the same period, the tertiary category overtook manufacturing as the largest individual employment group. Although this pattern of evolution charac-

Table 1.6

THE EVOLUTION OF THE LABOUR FORCE, 1921–1962

	1921		1954		1962	
	Thousands	Per cent	Thousands	Per cent	Thousands	Per cent
Primary	8,997·4	43·4	5,193·6	28.0	3,897·7	21·0
Secondary	6,172·3	29·7	6,836·0	36·8	7,323·7	39·5
Tertiary	5,588·1	26·9	6,543·4	35·2	7,336·5	39·5
Total	20,757·8	100·0	18,573·0	100·0	18,557·9	100·0

Source: Etudes et Conjoncture, 'L'Espace Economique Français', Tome 11, Population Active, 1967.

terizes all advanced nations, the process was relatively slow in France and rapid change has been compressed in to the period since the Second World War.* The decline in agricultural employment is in part accounted for by the reduction in the number of females employed and by the withdrawal of elderly farmers above the normal age of retirement, but more particularly it reflects a universal drift from the land of younger male agricultural workers and their transfer to other occupational groups†.

At the crude level of the three main sectors, the French labour force has become increasingly mobile. However, this is just one aspect of mobility, and an inevitable and overdue adjustment in the fundamental structure of the work force of France. It represents an enforced shedding of labour by agriculture of its surplus manpower in an effort to rationalize its organization and increase productivity. True mobility of labour must be held to involve not only exchanges between sectors but also between individual branches of activity, and in this respect the degree of mobility in France has been less fluid. The position is most static in areas with high concentrations of unskilled workers, as in the coal basins, where mobility is limited by the problem of retraining, and in areas where the lack of diversity in the economic base is a structural barrier to mobility. In the latter case, the viticultural area of Bas-Languedoc may be cited as a monolithic structure within which mobility cannot be achieved without fundamental reforms. In two respects mobility has been greatly increased between 1954 and 1962. An 11 per cent decline occurred in the number of

*The industrial labour force did not exceed the agricultural labour force until the census of 1954.
†The preliminary results of the 1968 census reveal a further drop by 20·9 per cent in the agricultural labour force between 1962 and 1968.

self-employed and family-employed workers, adding to the labour pool an important number of persons previously employed in unremunerative work with low standards of productivity. Secondly, the position of female employment has been greatly modified by the expansion of light industries, offering opportunities for semi-skilled operatives, and by the advancement of women in professional occupations.[18]

In general mobility of labour has increased in direct proportion to improved educational levels, the structural reform of agriculture and increased urbanization. The changing balance between the three major employment groups has also involved a considerable spatial redistribution of employment opportunities. The expansion of industry has fostered the growth of urban agglomerations, and in turn the service functions are naturally intensified within the major population concentrations. Sectorial mobility has thus been paralleled by an increased geographical mobility reflected in complex patterns of rural-urban and inter-regional migration.[19] Although the drift from agriculture and from artisan industries is a long-standing phenomenon, Pinchemel has drawn attention to the deep-rooted sedentarism of the French population.[20] The sense of belonging to a particular region has remained strongly embedded in the national temperament and the French are not by nature nomadic in relation to employment. Mobility between areas of equivalent economic status has tended to be a weakly developed social phenomenon. In the past, therefore, geographical mobility tended to be based on relatively simple relationships; the expulsive forces exerted by an overpopulated and unremunerative agricultural sector and the attractive forces exerted by the large towns, and especially Paris, in terms of higher wages and better material opportunities.

The pattern of simple migration flows is now giving way to complex inter-regional exchanges of labour, due to a variety of social changes. Improvements in mass communications, the process of industrial decentralization, the increase in higher education and professional training, have all tended to widen the horizons of the labour force to encompass employment opportunities beyond the immediate locality.

Two factors must however be considered as limiting the full development of geographical mobility. The problem of housing shortages is a deterrent to a free circulation of labour. It is generally in the areas of economic bouyancy that the shortage is most acute and rents are the highest. Secondly, the level of geographical mobility is much higher within eastern France than within the western half of the country. In a more restricted sense of the term, geographical mobility has increased immensely in the form of daily commuting to urban employment. Statistically most important in the major agglomerations, the phenomenon has an even greater significance in predominantly rural areas. Whereas in the case of movements from the periphery to the centre of agglomerations commuting is an inevitable result of the physical expansion of residential suburbs, the daily movement of rural dwellers to the nearest town represents an alternative to permanent migration and eventual rural depopulation.

The degree of mobility between sectors of activity and between areas has thus greatly increased since the Second World War, and has become more complex in form. International mobility of labour, on the other hand, still retains specific traditional features. France is a heavy net importer of labour, and since the close of the colonial era the exodus of French workers abroad has rapidly diminished, being, at least temporarily, vastly outnumbered by returning repatriates. Within the context of the free movement of labour within the Common Market, France remains a net importer of permanent, seasonal and commuting* Italian and Belgian labour. Foreign labour constitutes the most mobile group geographically within the work force, since it is directed to specific activities and locations deficient in indigenous labour supply. However, the degree of mobility within branches of activity is low, since the majority of foreign labour is of a low professional qualification and is concentrated into the unskilled branches of mining, public works and agriculture.

THE QUALITY OF THE LABOUR FORCE

The measurement of the quality of the labour force is most meaningful in terms of the degree to which it equates with present and future needs of the economy.

In this respect France has urgent problems to solve in the interests of economic security. The most serious problem is the deficit of technically skilled industrial and commercial workers, stemming in part from the failure of the educational system to adjust to the rapid economic evolution which has taken place since the war, and partly from the difficulty of small firms to maintain expensive and long technical training programmes. The 1962 census revealed that the labour force as a whole has a low level of formal technical and professional qualification. The census indicated† that 1·3 million men and 500,000 women in the labour force possessed some form of professional or technical qualification in 1962, 10 per cent and 8 per cent respectively of the total labour force. Considerable variations occur by sector of activity, the degree of qualification being highest in

*The principal exceptions are French commuters from Alsace into West Germany, and from southern Alsace and Franche-Comté into Switzerland.
†Based on a 20 per cent sample.

industry—12·4 per cent of the work force—and office workers—11·8 per cent—while only 1·3 per cent of the agricultural labour force had received any form of advanced education.[21] The problem is likely to become more urgent in view of the increased demand for qualified workers in the future.[22,23] The Commissariat Général du Plan has forecast a demand for a 70 per cent increase in technicians, a 49 per cent increase in higher management, and a 17·7 per cent increase in skilled workers between 1960 and 1975.[24]

In the immediate future, the problem of adjusting labour supply to the character of demand is focussed most sharply in areas where staple activities are declining or subject to rationalization, creating large pools of labour in need of retraining to permit redeployment. The coalfields and textile areas are particularly exposed, as is the iron ore mining district of Lorraine. In the longer-term perspective, the more serious problem is to achieve a major redeployment of the working population into activities requiring higher standards of education and training.

Table 1.7

MANPOWER RESOURCES, 1965–1970

Increased manpower resources[a]		Increase in jobs[a]	
Natural population growth	325	Industry	350
Net immigration of workers	325	Tertiary	885
Reduction in agricultural employment	585		
	1,235		1,235

[a]Thousands.
Source: Fifth Plan of Economic and Social Development, 1966–1970.

Table 1.7 indicates that in the course of the Fifth Plan over 1·2 million new jobs will be created outside the agricultural sector, of which almost one half must be achieved by the redeployment of surplus agricultural labour, which has been shown to have a low professional qualification. Clearly the task of adjusting the economy cannot be achieved merely by increasing and improving the existing facilities of higher education but by extending in addition programmes of adult training and training within industry.

PROBLEMS OF MANPOWER RESOURCE USE

The preoccupation of successive French governments with domestic policies relating to population growth and labour supply has been shown to result from the demographic inheritance of the last hundred years. This inheritance may be restated in the form of a number of problems.

The fundamental problem is that of the distorted structure of the population resulting from declining fertility, the impact of wars and more recent resurgence of the birth rate. Three serious inconveniences result from this background: the high dependency ratio of elderly and young people in relation to the work force, the problem of the sudden appearance on to the labour market of the post-war bulge in the birth rate at a time of difficult adjustment in the economic structure of the country, and the problem of ensuring a continuation of high fertility to secure the future replacement of the work force. The latter problem may be rendered elusive since high fertility must be achieved within an increasingly urbanized society.

Secondly, although immigration in the past has enabled France to recruit necessary manpower, some of the traditional sources are now less abundant. The number of North African workers has diminished since Algerian independence and Italian workers are also less abundant, partly because of competition from high wage rates in West Germany and Switzerland, and partly as a result of buoyant expansion in northern Italy.

A third problem is to intensify further the present trend of increased mobility of labour and particularly to achieve a new balance between the sectors of activity and a strengthening of the productive advanced technology industrial workers. This demands a major reform of the infrastructure of training and also an effort to increase the 'transparency' of the labour market by increasing information levels on training and job opportunities. Increased geographical mobility must also be accompanied by strong policies for the dissemination of employment at the regional level, in order that mobility does not become a stimulus for renewed depopulation of the less developed areas. The latter problem raises the wider question of the geographical structure of the French population and the distribution of human resources, which forms the substance of the following chapter.

REFERENCES

[1] Pinchemel, P., *Géographie Régionale de la France*, Tome 1, p. 91, 1964, Paris, Armand Colin.
[2] Pinchemel, P., *op. cit.*, pp. 210–216.
[3] Huber, M., Baule, H., and Boverat, F., *La Population de la France, son évolution et ses perspectives*, 4th edn., 1965, Paris, Hachette.
[4] Bourgeois-Pichat, J., 'Evolution générale de la population française depuis le XVIIIe siècle', *Population*, 1951, p. 635.
[5] Beaujeu-Garnier, J., *Géographie de la Population*, Tome 1, pp. 85–91, 1956, Paris, Génin.
[6] Henry, L., 'Perturbations de la nuptialité résultant de la guerre de 1914–1918', *Population*, 1966, p. 273.
[7] Armengaud, A., *La Population Française au XXe Siècle*, p. 28, 1967, Paris, Presses Universitaires de France.

[8] Sauvy, A., *La Population*, p. 85, 1961, Paris, Presses Universitaires de France.

[9] Armengaud, A., *op. cit.*[7], p. 70.

[10] Clark, J., 'Demographic revival in France', *Geography*, 1963, p. 309.

[11] Nizart, A., and Pressat, R., 'Evolution générale de la population française', *Population*, 1965, p. 1,115.

[12] Nadot, R., 'Effet de l'immigration sur la natalité en France depuis 1953', *Population*, 1967, p. 483.

[13] Chevalier, L., 'La population étrangère en France d'après le recensement de 1962', *Population*, 1964, p. 572.

[14] INSEE, 'Premiers Résultats d'Ensemble du Recensement Général de la Population de Mars 1968', Paris, 1968.

[15] Pressat, R., 'Les aléas de la natalité française', *Population*, 1967, p. 611.

[16] Calot, M., and Hémery, S., 'La fécondité et la nuptialité en 1966 et 1967', *Population*, 1967, p. 983.

[17] Calot, M., *et al.*, 'L'évolution de la situation démographique française au cours des années récentes', *Population*, 1967, p. 629.

[18] Clerc, P., 'Changements dans la structure socio-professionnelle en France entre 1954 et 1962', *Population*, 1964, p. 683.

[19] Fielding, A., 'Internal migration and regional economic growth—A case study of France', *Urban Stud.*, 1966, p. 200.

[20] Pinchemel, P., *op. cit.*[1], p. 214.

[21] Vimont, C., and Baudot, J., 'Les titulaires d'une diplôme d'enseignement technique ou professionel dans la population active en 1962', *Population*, 1965, p. 763.

[22] Grais, B., 'L'évolution des structures de la population active', *Etud. Conjonct.*, No. 3, 1968, p. 1.

[23] Guelaud-Leridon, F., 'Perspectives sur la population active française par qualification en 1975', *Population*, 1964, p. 9.

[24] George, P., *La France*, pp. 63–70, 1967, Paris, Presses Universitaires de France.

2

The Geography of Population

Implicit in the preceding chapter was the observation that the population of France is unevenly distributed throughout the national space and that human resources are being replenished at varying rates in the different regions.

THE DISTRIBUTION AND DENSITY OF POPULATION

Just as the trend of population growth has been anomalous when compared with neighbouring industrialized countries, so also does the basic geography of population display certain anomalous features. Chief of these is the very low overall density of population, which in 1967 was 91 persons per square kilometre, as compared with values of 370 in the Netherlands, 313 in Belgium, 240 in West Germany, 224 in the United Kingdom and 173 in Italy. The general pattern of distribution and density is illustrated in *Figure 2.1*, within which five broad density zones are proposed. The greatest single concentration of the nation's population occurs within the rectangle enclosed by the middle and lower Seine axis, the Channel coast, the Belgian frontier, and a line approximately from Fontainebleau to Mézières passing through Reims (Zone 1 in *Figure 2.1*). Throughout most of this zone population densities exceed 80 per square kilometre. A second zone of uniformly high density occurs east of the Meuse valley, corresponding with the industrial regions of Alsace and Lorraine. In north-western France, a less coherent zone with moderately high densities, generally above 50 inhabitants per square kilometre, is enclosed within the rectangle based on Caen, Orléans, La Rochelle and Brest. A contrast exists between the higher densities found on the coastal margin of the Armorican Massif and along the Loire valley, and the interior, where densities fall below 50 per square kilometre. A fourth zone of high density has the form of an inverted letter Y, extending from Dijon via the Rhône valley to Arles where it bifurcates into Bas-Languedoc and Basse-Provence.

The four density zones described occupy less than 40 per cent of the national land area but contain over 75 per cent of the total population. The majority of the nation is constituted by a broad diagonal zone extending

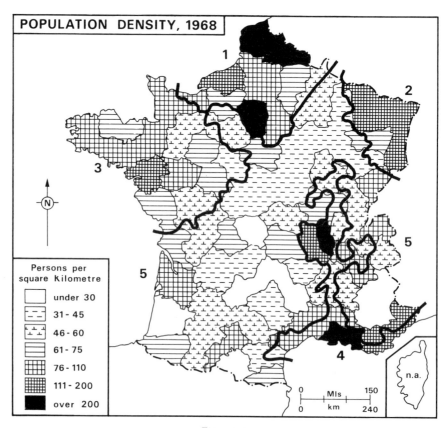

POPULATION DENSITY, 1968

Persons per
square Kilometre

under 30
31 - 45
46 - 60
61 - 75
76 - 110
111 - 200
over 200

Figure 2.1

from the Pyrénées to Champagne, characterized by very low average densities of below 49 persons per square kilometre and containing large tracts with less than 20 per square kilometre. The central and southern Alps, together with Corsica, may be considered as outliers of this 'under-populated' zone. Within this broad zone, a small number of cities and towns stand out as isolated centres of higher density.

Clearly the dominant influence on the general arrangement of population is the distribution of urban centres and only exceptionally does the intensity of the rural economy produce high population densities; the main instances being the intensive polyculture of coastal Brittany, the viticultural economy of Bas-Languedoc, the intensive fruit and vegetable growing of the Rhône valley and the productive arable farming of the Alsatian plain. Elsewhere, high rural population densities reflect an association with urban functions, as in the case of the rural–urban fringe of commuting population around the major agglomerations, or the existence of industrial villages, as in the Vosges and the Nord. The very low population densities of Zone 5 reflect two separate circumstances; the existence of large areas of unproductive land, coincident with infertile sands, badly-drained lowland or mountainous terrain, but, more generally, the history of rural depopulation brought about by the polarization of the French economy on to urban centres.

THE PROCESS OF REDISTRIBUTION

The situation in *Figure 2.1* is but one stage in a process of continuous evolution. The process of redistribution has been effected through two related mechanisms: internal migration and differing regional rates of natural increase. Since differential fertility is in large measure a function of distortions instigated by age-selective migration, it is logical to discuss redistribution by migration in the first instance. In modern times, internal migration has been characterized by three essential features; the dominant flows have been rural–urban in direction, economic motives have been the uppermost causative factors, and the national capital has been the overwhelming destination of migrants.

Throughout the nineteenth and early twentieth centuries, the major movements of population have been in response to the restructuring of the national economy, concomitant on industrialization, and the resultant concentration of the labour market on to urban centres. Specifically, the expansion of urban industry promoted rural exodus, not only of former agricultural workers and of artisans and traders whose activities were more rationally located within the expanding centres of industry and population, but also of young persons at the age of first employment.* The flow of migrants from the countryside has by no means been restricted to areas of mediocre land resources, but also included areas where farm mechanization made early progress, as in the northern Paris Basin, and areas where high human fertility and excessive fragmentation of holdings produced a pressure of rural population on land resources. Nor was the pattern of migration necessarily simple or direct. In the mountainous regions, seasonal migration, often to highly specialized urban employment, was a traditional means of supplementing a mediocre farming livelihood, and a precursor of

*Pinchemel terms this a distinction between 'professional' and 'non-professional' depopulation.[1,2]

.permanent migration. Similarly, rural exodus was commonly effected by stages, from the village to the national capital, through intervening opportunities in local and regional urban centres. Rural–urban migration often had a peripatetic character, as in the case of rural workers recruited for railway construction, leading to employment in a large number of towns, exposing the apparent advantages of urban living. A universal factor promoting migration was the improvement in education, exerting a double stimulus by qualifying rural dwellers for occupations other than farming and also increasing information levels concerning the outside world. Similarly, military conscription broke the continuity of rural life for males. In the case of 'professional' depopulation, the incidence of crop diseases, depressed agricultural prices, increased mechanization and the problem of fragmentation of holdings all acted as expulsive forces, while the existence of more remunerative and less arduous employment in towns, coupled with the greater comfort and wider distractions of urban living, were powerful attractive forces.

Until the outbreak of the Second World War, the greatest beneficiary of inter-regional migration flows was undoubtedly the Paris Region.* Clerc[3] has demonstrated that some evolution took place in the geographical origin of migrants to Paris. During the nineteenth century, the majority of the migrants were drawn from within the Paris Basin, Nord and Bourgogne, but at the turn of the century increasing numbers were drawn from Brittany, the south-west and the Massif Central. Detailed research by Pourcher[4] has indicated that the northern and south-western Paris Basin has consistently supplied large numbers of migrants to Paris, but that the former stream from eastern and south-eastern France was replaced in dominance by flows from Brittany and the Massif Central in the course of the present century (*Table 2.1*).

Table 2.1

THE ORIGIN OF IMMIGRANTS RESIDENT IN THE DÉPARTEMENT OF SEINE

Region	*1891* *Number of immigrants*	Region	*1954* *Number of immigrants*
Bourgogne	142,000	Bretagne	212,000
Centre	138,000	Centre	187,000
Picardie	106,000	Nord	160,000
Rhône-Alpes	92,000	Picardie	144,000
Lorraine[a]	84,000	Bourgogne	126,000

[a]Not including the département of Moselle.
Source: Pourcher, G., *op. cit.*, p. 23.

*Between 1861 and 1936, the population of the Paris region increased by almost four million inhabitants, a growth inconceivable without massive migration.

The draining of population from the Massif Central was particularly critical, since, unlike Brittany, the losses by migration were not offset by high levels of natural increase.

The second largest recipient of migrants during the nineteenth century was the Nord industrial area. The volume was modulated in part by the eccentric geographical location, but more especially by the ability of the Nord to fulfil its labour requirements by a very high rate of natural increase and by rural–urban migration within the region. The Lyon agglomeration was also a terminus of inter-regional flows, drawing population from the alpine valleys and the eastern flanks of the Massif Central. Apart from these movements between regions, intra-regional migration has been universal, taking the form of a general gravitation of rural population to those towns which were the sites of industrial and commercial development. Thus population descended from the 'Causse' and 'Garrigue' upland to the towns of the Languedoc plain, from the plateau of Lorraine to the expanding steel towns, from the mountains of Provence to Marseille, and from the bocage of Armorica to the Basse–Loire industrial region. The surplus rural population of the Massif Central was concentrated into the scattered mining and metallurgical centres, to be redistributed once again when these declined to Paris and Lyon. Conversely, those regions lacking in industrial towns, such as Brittany, Centre and Bourgogne, made the largest contribution of migrants to Paris.

Since the Second World War, certain changes have taken place in the pattern of internal migration. In quantitative terms the scale of mobility has increased,* stimulated by demographic and economic revival, rapid urbanization and by further reduction in the agricultural labour force.

Table 2.2

REGIONS EXPERIENCING HIGH LEVELS OF NET MIGRATION, 1954–1962

Regions of high net gain[a]		Regions of high net loss[a]	
Paris region	706·4	Bretagne	67·3
Provence	367·4	Basse-Normandie	55·5
Rhône-Alpes	219·3	Pays-de-la-Loire	42·1
Languedoc	77·0	Poitou-Charentes	26·9
Lorraine	50·4		

[a]Thousands.
Source: Recensement de 1962.

Table 2.2 demonstrates that movement towards Paris continued to dominate inter-regional migration between 1954 and 1962, but migration no longer played such an overwhelming role in the growth of the Paris

*Between 1954 and 1962, 3·27 million persons changed the region of their residence.

region. In proportionate terms, the scale of migration in total population increase was greater in Provence. *Table 2.2* indicates that north-western France had become the major region of exodus, losing almost 200,000 inhabitants by net migration. By contrast the regions of Auvergne and Limousin, formerly major sources of migrants, experienced a net exodus of only 7,000 inhabitants. This is a reflection of the extent to which past migration had sapped the demographic vitality of the heart of the Massif Central, thus reducing the number of potential migrants in the younger age groups. The recent publication of the 1968 census reveals some further evolution in the pattern of inter-regional movement.

Table 2.3

REGIONS EXPERIENCING HIGH LEVELS OF NET MIGRATION, 1962–1968

Regions of high net gain[a]		*Regions of high net loss*[a]	
Provence-Côte d'Azur-Corse	389·9	Lorraine	69·5
Paris region	339·7	Nord	47·7
Rhône-Alpes	210·0	Poitou-Charentes	19·0
Languedoc	122·4	Basse-Normandie	14·5
Aquitaine	96·0	Bretagne	12·7
Midi-Pyrénées	94·0	Pays-de-la-Loire	11·7

[a]Thousands.
Source: Recensement de 1968, Premiers résultats.

Table 2.3 indicates that Paris has relinquished its historic role as the nation's greatest recipient of migrants to the planning region of Provence-Côte d'Azur-Corse. During this period, the population of Paris grew by natural increase to a greater extent than by net migration. Secondly, as a result of the repatriation of Algerians and the rapid growth of Toulouse, Bordeaux and Montpellier, south-western France was established as an area of very substantial migrational gain. Although north-western France remains the largest area of consistent migrational loss, the scale has been much reduced and higher totals were lost by the depressed industrial regions of Nord and Lorraine. A more detailed illustration of recent changes is provided by *Figure 2.2*. This map indicates that emigration remains entrenched in an axis traversing western France from Brittany to the southern Massif Central, but that this has been joined by a second axis extending from the Vosges to the Pas-de-Calais, coincident with areas affected by the decline of old industries and as yet insufficiently compensated by the creation of new firms. *Figure 2.2* also demonstrates the trend of the départements surrounding the Paris agglomeration from being heavy donors of population to the metropolis to becoming a zone of net increase by migration, conditioned by the creation of decentralized industries in the effort to decongest Paris.

The causative factors underlying post-war inter-regional migration have been analysed by Fielding,[5] Chatelain[6] and by Girard, Bastide and Pourcher,[7] who establish a close correlation between the directions of

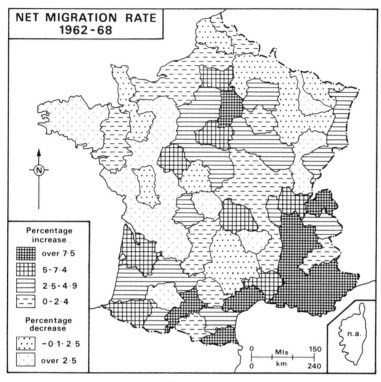

Figure 2.2

movement and differential rates of economic growth and salary levels. Inter-regional movement under-enumerates the true level of increased mobility since the Second World War; underlying the exchange of population between regions is the more intensive pattern of intra-regional movement consequent on the increased concentration of population into towns. The post-war demographic and economic revival is above all an urban phenomenon and has provided France with a network of urban centres capable, in varying degree, of intercepting rural exodus close to its source. This is particularly the case of towns located along transport arteries, provincial centres with expanding universities, and the many medium-sized towns which have attracted decentralized firms. While migration will remain a spontaneous reaction to differences in regional economic levels, government policy is now directed towards the strengthening of the industrial base of the regional and local centres as a means of rationalizing movement as compared with the anarchic pattern of the past. In particular, decisive action is necessary on behalf of western France if migration is to become a genuine mobility of labour as opposed to an enforced search for employment.

Migration must be considered an active form of population redistribution in that, through movement, additions and subtractions are made to

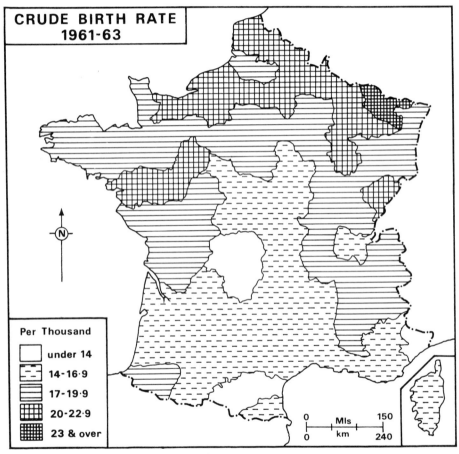

Figure 2.3

and from regional populations. The regional balance of population distribution is influenced in a more passive form by differential natural increase rates. *Figure 2.3* indicates that, on the evidence of the crude birth rate, the highest fertility in the nation is concentrated within an arc extending from the Gironde to Haute-Provence, sweeping round the

THE GEOGRAPHY OF POPULATION 25

northern margins of the Massif Central. Conversely, central, southern and south-western France is conspicuous as a homogeneous zone of low fertility. This basic contrast corresponds in part with traditional differences —the north and Brittany throughout modern history having experienced larger average completed family sizes—partly with differing levels of economic activity, but more particularly with the direction of past and present migration flows. The distortion of the age structure through decades of age-selective migration has undermined the demographic equilibrium of central and south-western France, while the arrival of

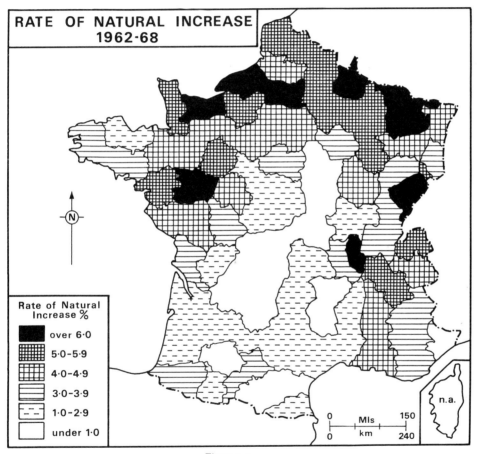

Figure 2.4

younger age-groups in the Paris region and the north-east has reinforced the areas of high fertility. The distortion of the age structure is also the major factor underlying differential mortality rates; the high average age of central and south-western France inevitably being reflected in mortality rates in excess of the national average.

The regional variations in fertility and mortality rates are compounded in the form of natural increase differentials, illustrated by *Figure 2.4*. Essentially the same arcuate pattern results, in which the nation's demographic vitality is seen to be concentrated north of the Loire, with extensions into north-eastern France and along the Rhône-Saône axis. Limousin, eastern Aquitaine and northern Midi-Pyrénées,* on the other hand, constitute the dead heart of the nation in a demographic sense. It is noticeable too that age-selective migration over the past half-century has reduced natural increase in Brittany to below the general level of northern France. The extent to which age-selective migration and differential natural increase have produced geographical distortions in age structure are summarized in *Figure 2.5*. In particular a downward spiral is apparent in central

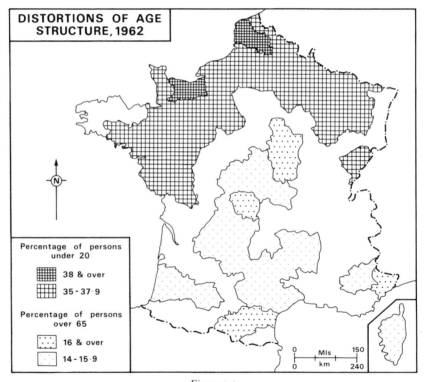

Figure 2.5

and south-western France where past selective migration has lowered the birth rate, in turn increasing the proportion of elderly and further supressing the birth rate.

The process of redistribution, as enacted by migration and natural

*In this area, constituted by the départements of Creuse, Corrèze, Haute- Vienne, Lot and Dordogne, natural increase had fallen below replacement level in 1962.

change, is expressed in the pattern of total change. *Figure 2.6* emphasizes that a line drawn approximately from Caen to Montpellier divides the nation into an eastern third, of positive growth at rates close to or in excess of the national average, and the western two-thirds of France, characterized by low rates of growth and containing large areas of absolute

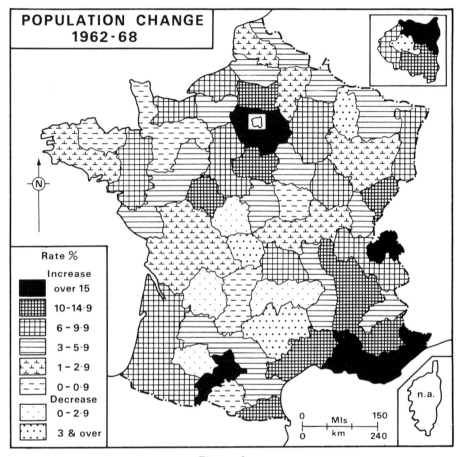

POPULATION CHANGE 1962-68

Rate %

Increase

over 15

10 - 14·9

6 - 9·9

3 - 5·9

1 - 2·9

0 - 0·9

Decrease

0 - 2·9

3 & over

n.a.

Mls 150
km 240

Figure 2.6

loss. Above all, *Figure 2.6* indicates the strict correlation between differential population growth and the distribution of urban centres.

This outline of the geography of population has of necessity been summary since many of the problems raised are discussed in more detail in the following chapters devoted to urban and rural population, and, in an areal context, in the concluding regional essays. It suffices to emphasize that regional demographic distortions also imply commensurate distortions in the distribution of labour supply and the location of internal markets. It is also clear that a stable pattern of distribution and density has not yet been achieved, but that a dual evolution of rural exodus and urban concentration is taking place corresponding with sectorial and locational changes in the labour force. At the two extremes of this evolution may be placed much of the Massif Central, where absolute depopulation results from both migrational losses and a negative balance of births and deaths, and the Paris region, where serious problems of excessive concentration exist. Many other regions of France are evolving towards one or the other of these two extremes. Thus interior Brittany has reached the stage of incipient depopulation attained by the Massif Central half a century ago, while many of the agglomerations of eastern France are faced with problems of congestion. In these conditions, the study of population matters is no longer a background element to social and economic problems but a vital determinant of planning decisions at all levels.

REFERENCES

[1] Pinchemel, P., *Géographie de la France*, Tome 1, p. 164, 1964, Paris, Armand Colin.
[2] Pinchemel, P., *Structures Sociales et Dépopulation Rurale dans les Campagnes Picardes de 1836 à 1936*, p. 204, 1957, Paris, Armand Colin.
[3] Clerc, P., 'Vue rétrospective sur la migration provinciale à Paris', Chapter 1 of Pourcher, G., *Le Peuplement de Paris*, p. 7, 1964, Paris, Presses Universitaires de France.
[4] Pourcher, G., *Le Peuplement de Paris*, 1964, Paris, Presses Universitaires de France.
[5] Fielding, A., 'Internal migration and regional economic growth—A case study of France', *Urban Stud.*, 1966, p. 200.
[6] Chatelain, A., La géographie des salaires en France et son incidence sur les migrations de population', *Revue Géogr. Lyon*, 1960, p. 381.
[7] Girard, A., Bastide, H., and Pourcher, G., 'Mobilité géographique et concentration urbaine en France—une enquête en province', *Population*, 1964, p. 227.

3

Rural Settlement

The veneer of urban civilization has been unevenly spread in France, failing to obliterate an underlying rural settlement of great complexity and diversity. The rural milieu has always evoked a strong response within the French geographer's awareness of landscape and the unravelling of its genesis still constitutes a lively and scholarly field of study. In the present context, greater relevance attaches to a functional rather than an academic standpoint, and emphasis is placed on the problems arising as patterns imprinted over centuries of gradual evolution adjust to a rapidly changing set of social and economic conditions.

THE SIGNIFICANCE OF RURAL POPULATION

At the census of 1962, 16,882,300 persons resided in the 35,000 rural* communes of France, forming 36·4 per cent of the total population. The distinction between urban and rural population is inadequately reflected in the census definition as many settlements of an industrial or suburban character fall within the census definition of rural communes but are more properly regarded as urban in function. A less arbitrary and more realistic assessment of the basic rural population is provided by eliminating all rural communes which form part of 'Zones de Peuplement Industriel ou Urbain'† and are thus functionally associated with urban agglomerations. The resultant totally rural population amounted to 11,995,600 in 1962, or 25·9 per cent of the total population. The significance of rural population is subject to considerable regional variation, both in absolute terms and in the proportion of the rural component in the total population. In an attempt to generalize this regional variation, *Figure 3.1* is based on data for rural communes located outside 'Zones de Peuplement Industriel ou Urbain' in an effort to eliminate the distorting effects of urban agglomerations. The association between two variables is portrayed in *Figure 3.1*;

*Communes of less than 2,000 inhabitants.
†This census designation is elaborated in Chapter 4, p. 50.

the proportion of the population resident outside urban industrial zones is a criterion of the regional significance of the basic rural population, while the density of this population indicates the absolute variations.

Figure 3.1 indicates that three broad types of rural population structure may be proposed; the types of Brittany, central and south-western France

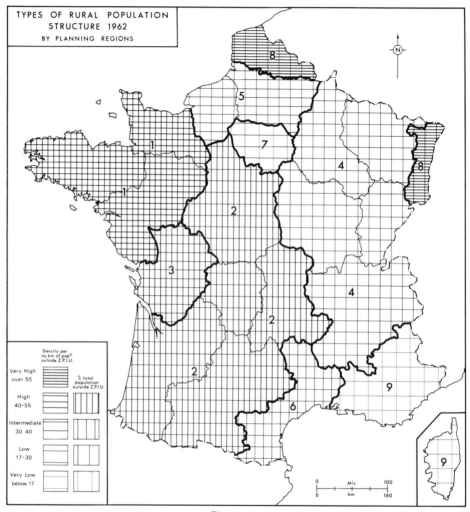

TYPES OF RURAL POPULATION
STRUCTURE 1962
BY PLANNING REGIONS

Density per
sq.km. of popⁿ
outside Z.P.I.U.

Very High
over 55

% total
population
outside Z.P.I.U.

High
40-55

Intermediate
30 40

Low
17-30

Very Low
below 17

Figure 3.1

and eastern France. The remaining structures may be regarded as either transitional between the three major classes, or are related to highly specific regional characteristics. The type of Brittany (1) extends into Basse-Normandie and the Basse-Loire region. It is characterized by a high density of the basic rural population and by high proportions of rural dwellers in the total population. The north-west may be considered as the most rural portion of the country in that it has the greatest absolute and relative concentrations.

The second dominant structure (Zone 2) extends in a broad belt from the south-west of the Paris Basin to the Pyrénées, encompassing much of the Massif Central and the Basin of Aquitaine. This zone is also characterized by a high proportion of basic rural population but is clearly differentiated from the type of Brittany by virtue of the great reduction in density. The reduction in rural density is related to a prolonged history of depopulation, the existence of large areas of marginal land, and, in the case of Aquitaine, the underdeveloped condition of the rural economy. The region of Poitou-Charentes (Zone 3) may be considered as being transitional between the two former classes.

In combination, the above types of rural population structure demonstrate very clearly that western France constitutes the rural domaine of the nation. By contrast, the majority of the area of eastern France (Zone 4) is characterized by a low proportion of basic rural population, reflecting the greater degree of urbanization, and by low rural densities, accounted for in part by the greater degree of mechanization in agriculture, but also is a function of extensive areas of high mountains and elevated plateaux. Two smaller zones are transitional in type between eastern and western France. Normandy and Picardy (Zone 5) have a low rural proportion, but a relatively high density. Conversely, Languedoc (Zone 6) has a low density of rural population but an intermediate proportion.

The remaining structures must be considered as being individual in type, possessing the general characteristics of neither eastern or western France. The Paris Region (Zone 7) is entirely anomalous, and only the outer fringes of this region are entirely rural in character. The regions of Nord and Alsace (Zone 8) share similar characteristics; a very low rural proportion but extremely high densities. The dominance of major industrial centres surrounded by densely settled tributary areas reduces the basic rural proportions to very low values, but the exploitation of extremely productive soil by advanced farming methods supports the highest rural densities in the nation. Finally, Provence-Côte d'Azur (Zone 9) is distinguished as having the lowest rural density in the nation, and, as a result of the contrast between a sparsely populated interior and an urbanized littoral, has the lowest rural proportion also.

RURAL SETTLEMENT FORM

Variations in the significance of rural population are accompanied by contrasts in the physical form of rural habitation. *Table 3.1* indicates that numerically France is a nation of small rural settlements.

Table 3.1

SIZE CATEGORIES OF COMMUNES OF UNDER 2,000 INHABITANTS (1962)

Commune size	Number of communes	Total population (thousands)	Percentage of total rural population
Under 100	3,415	227·7	1·5
100–199	7,361	1,097·8	7·0
200–299	5,941	1,458·6	9·3
300–399	4,287	1,481·1	9·4
400–499	2,951	1,313·1	8·4
500–999	7,248	4,994·7	32·2
1,000–1,999	3,670	4,999·5	32·2

Source: Recensement de 1962.

The table shows that of a total of almost 35,000 communes of fewer than 2,000 inhabitants, no less than 24,000 had fewer than 500 inhabitants and 21,000 had fewer than 400 inhabitants. However, communes of fewer than 500 inhabitants contained only 35 per cent of the total rural population, leaving approximately two-thirds of the remainder resident in equal proportions in communes of the 500 to 1,000 and 1,000 to 2,000 categories. The existence of 24,000 communes with populations of fewer than 500 inhabitants implies serious problems of administration. Such units have inadequate local financial resources to maintain public services at an optimum level while their small base populations hardly justify the maintenance of separate schools, health centres and other costly public utilities.

The problem of the provision of services is rendered more difficult by the great variations in the specific form of settlement concealed by the generalizations of total commune populations. The various particles of the settled area display a morphological arrangement measurable in terms of a tendency towards concentration or dispersion. Complete agglomeration and dispersion represent the extreme positions on a wide range of composite settlement patterns involving elements of both tendencies. These extreme positions are exemplified in the first instance by settlement on the chalk and limestone plateaux of the Paris Basin, which demonstrates a consistent tendency towards nucleation and a positioning of the key institutions—school, mayor's office, church, and postal services, together with commercial services—in the village nucleus. By contrast, the plain of maritime Flanders displays a remarkable degree of dispersion of farms and cottages, with the institutions and services tending towards the same random pattern of distribution. It is widely accepted that the former, nucleated pattern characterized the initial settlement of France and persisted until the tenth and eleventh centuries. Since that time, a secondary dispersal has occurred both within communes possessing an established nucleus and by the colonization of large areas previously lacking permanent habitation. The progress of dispersion was discontinuous in time and variable in character. Dispersion of settlement occurred in direct proportion to population growth, technological advance permitting reclamation of difficult environments, and the increased freedom of the individual in society. Conversely, periods of disease and political insecurity have tended to suppress the process of dispersion. Generally, areas of long-established nucleated settlement experienced the creation of tributary hamlets, often established on suppressed common land or by clearing on the margins of the commune territory. In other instances, large-scale reclamation of areas of formerly negative land has produced a widespread scattering of isolated farms and loosely agglomerated hamlets with an absence of coherent village centres.

In view of the complex evolution of the rural settlement pattern, it is not surprising that the census is unable to record meaningful data which can be directly related to settlement form. The census distinguishes between population agglomerated in the 'chef-lieu', and that which is dispersed in the remainder of the commune.* This distinction is deficient in that the 'chef-lieu' is not necessarily the largest agglomeration in a given commune, nor is any indication given of the character of the dispersed settlement. The infinite range of rural settlement form defies a summary description. Three brief case studies may serve to illustrate the degree of variation and are representative of distinctive regional patterns.

THE ALPINE PATTERN: PEISEY-NANCROIX COMMUNE[1]

Rural settlement patterns in the alpine environment are closely adjusted to vertical gradations in land-use potential. Accordingly, *Figure 3.2* seeks to portray settlement in the commune of Peisey-Nancroix, situated in the valley of the Ponturin, in relation to altitudinal zones. The Ponturin is a hanging, left-bank tributary of the Isère and its drainage basin constitutes the commune limits of Peisey-Nancroix, forming a self-contained and physically isolated administrative and economic unit. The 'chef-lieu', Peisey, is the largest settlement and contains over 70 per cent of the commune's 450 permanent inhabitants. The village is located at approximately 2,000 metres at a point where the Ponturin enters a constricted gorge plunging to the Isère corridor. Peisey thus controls the single point of entry into the valley, where, after a serpentine climb of almost 1,000 metres, the road encounters the relatively level surface of the Ponturin trough. Peisey controls the key institutions of the valley, dominates the

*The census defines the 'chef-lieu' as the agglomeration containing the mayor's office.

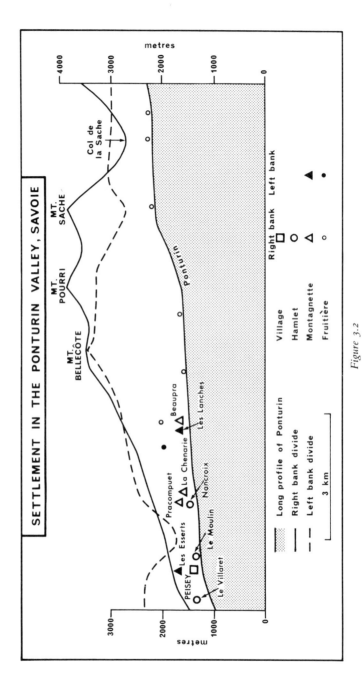

Figure 3.2

provision of commercial and personal services, and is the terminus of bus connections with the Isère valley. Although Peisey is centrally located in the zone of improved agricultural land, the farming economy is based on a chain of surrounding hamlets. Le Moulin is entirely agricultural in function, while the other hamlets, Nancroix and le Villaret, have been affected by the recent growth of tourism. Nancroix has a small general shop, a hotel and a youth centre but Le Moulin and le Villaret have no service provision beyond small chapels and are entirely dependent on Peisey. The dominant function of the hamlets is to provide the winter quarters of the valley's livestock.

Above 1,500 metres, improved land gives way to a 'montagnette' zone of open grazing, developed especially on the well-insulated right bank. Favourable aspect promotes an early clearing of snow and luxuriant grass growth in late spring, and thus provides a transitional zone, grazed during May, when the cattle move from the winter stalls and await the clearing of the high 'alpage' pastures. The exploitation of the 'montagnette' zone is directed from five temporary settlements occupied briefly during May, and again in September as the herds return towards their winter stalls. These settlements are linked merely by tracks to the valley floor and possess no services. Finally, a scattering of 'fruitières' (dispersed shelters) is distributed throughout the 'alpage' zone of summer pasture. These are occupied by a small number of herders responsible for the entire animal population during the grazing of the communal mountain pasture.

The settlement pattern of the Ponturin is distinctive from a number of points of view. The extremely specialized functions of the various components are strictly adjusted to the transhumant agricultural economy. A consistent gradation from service centre, agricultural hamlet, temporary 'montagnette' hamlet to isolated mountain shelters, is related to the successive exploitation of land resources which becomes progressively more extensive with increases in altitude and distance from the nucleus of Peisey. Also distinctive is the seasonal expansion and contraction of the effectively settled area in tune with the rhythm of climate. It is noticeable from *Figure 3.2* that aspect has a paramount effect on the distribution of settlement. The shaded left bank is predominantly wooded and only two very small 'montagnette' settlements occur.

The complex form of settlement is clearly related to the operation of a traditional economy. It is of interest, therefore, to observe the effects of recent economic change on this long-established structure. The commune has experienced more than a century of demographic decline[1] as evidenced in the landscape by abandoned terraced fields and the dereliction of houses in the 'montagnette' settlements. The recent growth of tourism has brought new life to the village of Peisey and to the hamlets of Nancroix and le

Villaret, where conversion of old property into holiday residences is widespread and new chalet construction is taking place. The 'montagnette' settlements, however, are continuing to decay. Clearly, the more accessible settlements have readily adapted to the intrusion of new functions, whereas the remote and highly specialized 'montagnette' habitations cannot easily be converted to a new role which imposes demanding conditions. Ephemeral camp sites are replacing the 'montagnettes' as the temporary residences in a new type of migrant economy. As the agricultural basis declines, the outposts of settlement are atrophying as the economy becomes even further concentrated into the zone immediately surrounding the 'chef-lieu'.

NUCLEATED SETTLEMENT IN THE NORTHEN PARIS BASIN

A completely different form of rural settlement characterizes the northern fringe of the Paris Basin related to environmental and economic conditions virtually the reverse of those described in the alpine case.

Figure 3.3 illustrates 14 rural communes located in Artois-Cambrésis, on the uptilted chalk rim of the Paris Basin, close to the industrialized Flanders Plain. All the communes in *Figure 3.3* are recorded in the last census as having their entire population resident in the 'chef-lieu'. The settlement pattern displays complete nucleation, there being virtually no secondary dispersion. Moreover, the degree of nucleation is enhanced by the compact rectilinear morphology of the individual villages. Four settlements dominate the area by virtue of their population size and the level of their service provision. Lécluse, Arleux, Ecourt St. Quentin and Oisy-le-Verger have populations of between 1,300 and 1,800 inhabitants, and all increased in population between 1954 and 1962. These villages have between twelve and seventeen shops, but a very limited range of personal services. Three of the villages have banks and two have recreational halls. The four villages may be cited as occupying the lowest grade of central place, possessing a service provision adequate for the daily needs of the indigenous population and that of two or three surrounding smaller villages. In all four centres the proportion of the population dependent on agriculture is less than 20 per cent. In part this is related to mechanized farming on consolidated land holdings but it also reflects the availability of alternative occupations in the tertiary sector and the practise of commuting to urban employment in the towns of the northern coalfield.

At the other extreme, the settlements of Dury, Recourt and Saudemont have only a skeletal service provision and more than 40 per cent of their population is dependent on agriculture. The remaining villages occupy an intermediate position, with 20 to 40 per cent of their inhabitants being

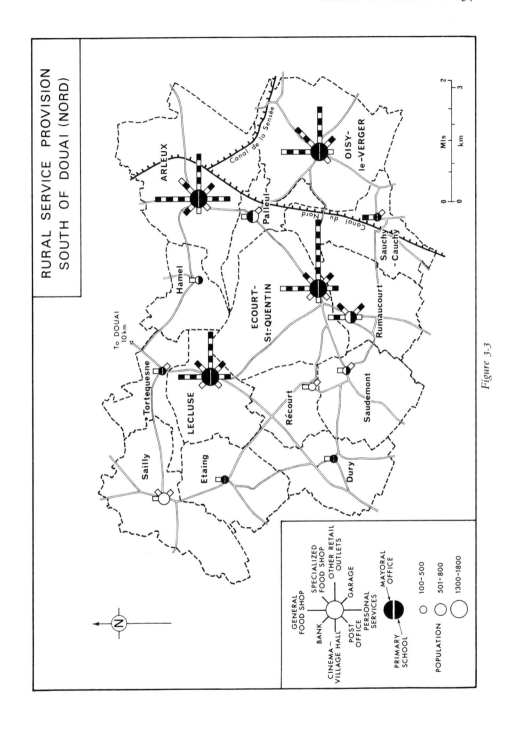

RURAL SERVICE PROVISION
SOUTH OF DOUAI (NORD)

Figure 3.3

dependent on agriculture, and an almost universal decline in population since 1954. Their meagre service provision is supplemented by itinerant tradesmen from larger centres.

The nucleation of settlement is an inheritance from the past, and in particular was confirmed by the communal organization of open-field farming, but contemporary economic trends are accentuating concentration even further. The modernization of agriculture is reducing employment on the land and the outlying villages are experiencing a contraction of their population and services, thus increasing their dependence on the rural service centres. The further decline in their population must ultimately compromise the maintenance of separate primary schools and mayoral offices and result in still further centralization on the larger villages. In turn, the large rural centres only maintain their equilibrium by virtue of commuting to outside employment.[2]

THE TYPE OF EASTERN BRITTANY: THE COMMUNE OF LANGROLAY

In contrast with the tendency towards nucleation in the settlement of the plateaux of the Paris Basin, the case of Brittany is commonly cited as showing a consistent tendency towards a dispersed settlement form. The character of this dispersion is far from simple and Le Lannou[3] has insisted on the composite nature of the Breton rural settlement pattern. The initial pattern consisted of small hamlets composed of small farms loosely grouped around the sites of the original gallo-roman fundi. The organization of ecclesiastical parishes and the choice of a particular hamlet as the site of a church marked the first significant differentiation of settlement. The practice of worship conferred a central function on the chosen hamlet within an otherwise ungraded settlement pattern. In time the parish centre became the location of other institutions and a rational location for commercial and artisan activities. However, the 'chef-lieu' seldom possesses a majority of the commune population, for, by process of reclamation and as a result of fragmentation of holdings, a further seeding of isolated farms has occurred. The end product is composite pattern in which the 'chef-lieu', containing a monopoly of services but a minority of the total population of a commune, is set in a matrix of unconsolidated hamlets and isolated farms linked to the 'chef-lieu' by a network of roads and tracks.

The commune of Langrolay,[4] situated on the western shore of the Rance estuary, 12 kilometres south of Dinard, in the département of Côtes-du-Nord, typifies the complex dispersion of rural settlement in eastern Brittany. The settlement is imprinted on the classic bocage landscape and is sustained by the traditional system of polyculture which in the past was combined with fishing. *Figure 3.4* differentiates three settlement forms within the commune. The 'chef-lieu', Langrolay, is located in the east of the commune and is the site of all administrative, commercial and religious services. It possesses the church, mayor's office and primary school, together

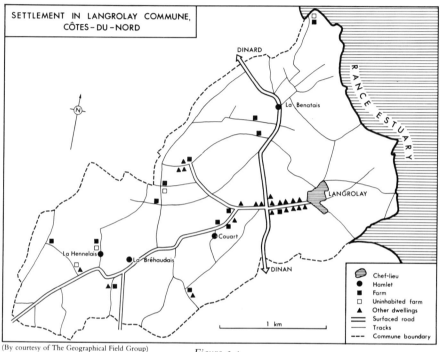

Figure 3.4

with four shops and a post office. In spite of this dominance in service provision, and the advent of some new construction linking the settlement in ribbon fashion to the main road from Dinard to Dinan, the 'chef-lieu' contains only 30 per cent of the total population. Secondly, four outlying hamlets contain much of the remaining population. These consist of cottages and small farms, characteristically aligned in south-facing terrace rows, and include many abandoned and derelict buildings. Finally, an irregular dispersion of farms and cottages occurs throughout the western half of the commune linked to the hamlets and village by a complex system of field tracks, many of which are overgrown and virtually impassable.

The census reveals a decline in population of 10 per cent since 1936 to the present total of 484. Evidence from the landscape indicates that it is in the outlying farms and hamlets that this depopulation has occurred.

Moreover, the hamlets are peopled by an elderly, predominantly female population and a further decay seems inevitable. Landscape and documentary evidence point to a more prosperous past during which subsistence agriculture combined with fishing enabled a relatively large population to be supported. The decline of fishing and the excessive fragmentation of holdings have precipitated a decline which the distorted age-structure, and the gradual regrouping of farmland with the elimination of submarginal holdings, seem likely to prolong. The outlying hamlets and farms are likely to decay further and the population will become increasingly concentrated along the axis of the main road to the west of the 'chef-lieu' and in the hamlet of La Benatais.

In addition to demonstrating the great diversity of rural settlement form existing in France, the case studies presented also serve as an indication of the mutations which have occurred as a result of economic changes during recent decades. The problems arising from forces of demographic contraction and economic concentration are seen to be variable in severity according to the precise form of rural settlement. The nucleated pattern best lends itself to the process of rationalization since the larger villages have already evolved as rural service centres and offer natural focal points for commercial and social reorganization. In the case of the complex alpine pattern, recent changes have called into question the survival of outlying settlements since their specialized functions have little relevance to the new economic currents generated by tourism. The problems of contraction appear to be most severe in areas of widely dispersed settlement where the isolation of scattered farms and hamlets is reinforced by the effects of depopulation and the consequent dilution of service provision in the commune centres.

It is important to establish that not all forms of rural settlement are currently experiencing problems associated with the reduction of employment, population and services. On the contrary, new forms of rural settlement are emerging which show every sign of growth as a result of their relationship to urban concentrations. Ribbon development radiating from towns and spilling out into the countryside adds to the population of the surrounding rural communes. Such development is more realistically viewed as being urban in function and inspiration and it is usually only a matter of time before such communes become absorbed into the parent urban agglomeration. Similar in function are the villages in proximity to large towns and cities which have assumed a dormitory role. In many instances they form detached suburbs and the original nuclei have become submerged in recent construction. Also related to the needs of a growing urban population is the transformation of many rural communes by the growth of tourism. Countless coastal and mountain villages have experienced a modification of their form and function and a revivification of their economy by this process. In many instances, especially in the less accessible mountain areas, entirely new resort settlements have been created, with an infrastructure and service provision out of all proportion to the needs of their permanent population.

The diminishing significance of rural population numerically and the modification of settlement form are the necessary accompaniments of social and economic transitions affecting the entire nation. While it is true that contemporary changes are basically an acceleration of tendencies already progressing at a more leisurely pace since the turn of the century, the magnitude of this acceleration is inevitably disturbing patterns of activity, settlement and psychology which had remained solid and stable throughout generations.

SOCIO-ECONOMIC CHANGE IN THE RURAL MILIEU

The scale and character of recent socio-economic evolution varies principally in accordance with the extent to which urban influences have pervaded the rural milieu. In areas remote from direct urban contact, the process of rural depopulation is already deeply ingrained and has produced a distorted age-structure as a result of past age-selective migration. In turn this carries the seeds of further depopulation through loss of demographic equilibrium due to the loss of the younger age-groups. It is in precisely the areas suffering from rural depopulation that the greatest dependence on agriculture exists, and these therefore face further losses as opportunities of employment in agriculture decline and land consolidation and mechanization advance. The modernization of agriculture, while rational and desireable in economic terms, and a valid national objective, cannot be accomplished without serious social problems which will fall very unevenly on the different regions of France. Regions like Brittany, with a high density of rural population and relatively high fertility level, are particularly vulnerable. Unless measures are taken to strengthen the network of rather weak local urban centres, no alternative to an exodus of the surplus rural population can be envisaged. The situation is even more extreme in wide areas of the Massif Central, where the low population densities reflect a region already deprived of vitality in the rural sector by the inroads of a century of depopulation. The depletion of rural population is invariably accompanied by an erosion of services as the reduced demand makes their economic operation impossible. In particular such trends promote the contraction of those amenities which tend to enrich the quality of life in areas with few outlets for social intercourse. The closure

(*Above*, By courtesy of J. Ferrand)

Plate 1. Changes in rural organization. Rural organization is becoming increasingly concentrated on the larger service centres to the detriment of outlying hamlets. *Above*, the rural service centre of Authon-du-Perche (Eure-et-Loire). *Below*, a decaying hamlet in the Grande Brière marshes of Loire-Atlantique

of primary schools, youth and social clubs, recreational amenities and personal services, as well as such essential public amenities as transport and medical provision, implies a reduction in the level of living and hastens the departure of the young element. The ultimate expression of rural de-population is thus an aura of decay, not only in the physical sense of abandoned buildings, but in the wider social sense of a deprivation of the services, distractions and comforts of twentieth-century living.

In rural areas in closer contact with large urban centres rather different trends are apparent. The decline in the population engaged in agriculture and artisan activities is commonly even more pronounced than in the purely rural communes, but the possibility of commuting to urban employment permits a diversification of employment opportunities and helps to restrain the rate of emigration. Furthermore, a return current of urban migrants, seeking cheaper homes and a more congenial environ-ment, often more than compensates the drift away of indigenous rural population. In such conditions, a new stratification of society may be created, the quality of social and service amenities may be enriched, and the importance of commuting may lead to an improvement in public transport. The amenities of the village may thus be readily complemented by access to the more elaborate provision of the urban centre.

The initial surge of urbanization gave rise to discrepancies in the level of opportunities and quality of life between the towns and countryside which subsequent trends have widened rather than narrowed. It cannot be denied that considerable progress has been made recently in raising the level of living in rural areas by the provision of electricity and main water supply. Similarly, the rural population is less isolated and more mobile than at any previous time in history. However, these advances have not been evenly conferred. In the areas closest to towns, a new, and apparently stable, rural–urban relationship is being established, giving to rural settle-ment many of the material advantages of urban residence. On the other hand, the regions furthest removed from large urban centres, currently experiencing a contraction of opportunities in the primary economy, have tended to lose further ground as compared with the rising quality of life in urban centres. It may be proposed that in addition to the original rural–urban dichotomy, recent trends have created a second discrepancy within the rural population. Two case studies serve to illustrate this observation.

A RURAL COMMUNE SUBJECT TO URBAN INFLUENCE:
LA RICHARDAIS, ILLE-ET-VILAINE

The commune of La Richardais is situated at the mouth of the Rance estuary immediately to the south of Dinard, and the influence of this town, together with the construction of the tidal power scheme on the Rance, has completely changed the socio-economic character of the settlement. Formerly a purely agricultural and fishing village, the population increased by over 22 per cent between 1954 and 1962 as a result of an influx of 200 migrants. Agriculture now supports less than 20 per cent of the population. Three major categories of inhabitants constitute the overwhelming majority of the population. Situated only three kilometres from the centre of Dinard, the village is within easy commuting range of urban employment. An important source of migrants is thus the urban population of Dinard, able to secure housing at lower cost than in the resort and in an agreeable waterfront situation. Secondly, the construction stages of the tidal barrage necessitated an influx of workers, drawn from all parts of France and abroad. Finally, the commune has an important retired element chiefly of local inhabitants, characteristically after a career connected with maritime activities, but also from other parts of Brittany and from Paris.[5] In addition, the commune contains almost 100 secondary homes, principally villas and converted cottages, occupied during holiday periods. As a result of these influences, the commune has experienced a transformation of both its physical appearance and social structure. The original settlement pattern, comprising the chef-lieu and a number of small hamlets, has been submerged beneath a ribbon development along the estuary-side road. The number of retail shops is small, but the commune has a relatively large number of personal service businesses reflecting the demands of a diverse, and generally prosperous, population. As building land in Dinard is particularly scarce, and as the new road over the tidal barrage has made the commune accessible to the St. Malo agglomeration, the dormitory and retirement function of La Richardais seems destined to be accentuated and the commune will become an annexe of the Dinard–St. Malo–St. Servan–Paramé conurbation.

DEMOGRAPHIC AND SOCIAL CONTRACTION: THE COMMUNE OF VITREY, MEURTHE-ET-MOSELLE

The commune of Vitrey is located on the liassic plain of Lorraine, 25 kilometres south of Nancy. The settlement is entirely agglomerated and conforms to the classic Lorraine form of 'street' villages. The commune has a wholly agricultural economy and occupies an isolated situation linked by small lanes to the canton centre of Vézelise. The commune formerly had an open-field system of arable farming and place-name evidence, such as 'Les Vignes' and 'Haut des Vignes', points to the past importance of viticulture. The excessive fragmentation of holdings, the decline of labour-intensive viticulture and the impact of the First World War were factors initiating depopulation, which has persisted until the present day. Remembrement has been completed in the last decade and has permitted the establishment of mixed farming on compact holdings. A majority of the land area is devoted to temporary pasture and feed crops and the change to a mechanized mixed farming economy has further reduced the amount of employment available in the commune.

Table 3.2

DEMOGRAPHIC AND SOCIAL TRENDS IN VITREY, 1911–1954

	1911	1921	1931	1954
Total population	308	238	241	203
Population under 14	59	32	66	61
Population 15–59	175	142	134	101
Population over 60	74	64	41	41
Men employed in agriculture	72	34	26	30
Number of families	93	83	75	60
Number of houses	98	94	92	65
Abandoned houses	9	13	18	20

Source: Listes Nominatives and Etat Civil documents in the mayor's office at Vitrey.

Table 3.2 emphasizes that the period from 1911 to 1921, including the war years, marked a catastrophic decline, specifically in the male population and in the number of births. A slight recovery was made by 1931, but since that date the decline has been reasserted.* The completion of remembrement and the emigration of young female population in search of employment are the most recent factors in the demographic decline revealed by the 1962 census.

Table 3.3

DEMOGRAPHIC TRENDS IN VITREY COMMUNE, 1954–1962

	1954	1962
Total population	203	162
Natural increase 1954–62	–	0
Net migration 1954–62	–	−41
Total change 1954–62	–	−41
Total number of houses	65	54
Abandoned houses	20	29[a]

Source: Recensement de 1962, Vol. 54, Meurthe-et-Moselle.
[a]Figure is for 1961 based on fieldwork.

*The figure of 61 children under age 14 shown in *Table 3.2* is an inflation due to the practice of fostering children on the part of older women and does not represent a permanent addition to the commune.

Table 3.3 demonstrates that in the period of eight years, the commune lost a fifth of its population and approximately half of the houses of the village had become disused. During the period concerned no natural increase took place, and in view of the migration of young people, a deficit of births as compared with deaths is inevitable in the future. The decline in population has been paralleled by a decrease in amenities. The church and one café represent the only permanent services other than those provided by itinerant tradesmen and a weekly bus service. The absence of young people, especially female, and the dereliction of buildings and streets combine with the absence of services to convey an atmosphere of decay and yet, ironically, the agricultural economy is now organized on a more sound and efficient basis than ever before.

RURAL SETTLEMENT AND TERRITORIAL
DEVELOPMENT PLANNING

The social and economic problems evoked in this discussion are not amenable to rapid solutions. On the contrary, the forces of inertia, bred alike by conservatism, remoteness and the weakness of local government resources, are still potent. A realistic approach to the resolution of rural problems can only be achieved in relation to long-term planning. Unless constructive measures are taken, an insidious process of a gradual diminution of the quality of rural life is inescapable over wide areas of France. The central problem is to reconcile a reduced level of employment in the primary sector with the maintenance of adequate standards of opportunity and amenity. To solve this problem a new framework for rural life must be created if regional depopulation is to be avoided. The responsibility for long-term planning of territorial development is vested in the Commission à L'Aménagement du Territoire,* which has defined certain objectives in relation to rural population. Three major principles have been proposed as a basis for long-term planning: the reform of local administration; the creation of additional employment in rural areas; and the introduction of a way of life closer to that of urban centres. Some elaboration of these principles forms a fitting conclusion since they represent an attempt to restructure the framework of rural life.

The reform of local administration implies the suppression of the system of rural communes in its present form. The commune, as has been demonstrated above, is too small a unit to provide a rational provision of services and an effective administration. The need for a reform of com-

---

*The constitution of this planning committee is described in Chapter 5, p. 80.

munes[*] has been widely urged for a considerable time.[6,7,8] To be effective, the reform must involve more than a simple re-grouping of communes. Gravier[9] has insisted on the sterility of amalgamating three communes of 300 inhabitants. Moreover, the reform must be accompanied by a planned adjustment in the centralization of services at appropriate focal points. Gravier[10] has suggested that a settlement of from 2,000 to 5,000 inhabitants is the minimum threshold at which collective services can be successfully established, and a radius of 15 kilometres as a practical tributary area. Such a restructuring demands not only administrative reform, but also a willingness on the part of the rural population to adjust to a new dimension in civic attitudes.[11] Long-term planning envisages the strengthening of the small towns of from 2,000 to 10,000 inhabitants, set in predominantly rural areas, to function as 'villages-centres'. These are intended to serve as focal points of the organization of rural France, within reformed administrative units. It is the function of the 'villages-centres' to act as 'anchor points', offering employment to rural dwellers and permitting the introduction of an urban form of living into the countryside.[12] The 'village-centre' is thus conceived as the base level in the urban hierarchy,[13] controlling the organization of a rural hinterland approximately 15 kilometres in radius for which it provides essential social services, together with commercial and cultural amenities. It is also intended that the establishment of light industries at this level should mitigate the effects of the decline in agricultural employment and provide alternative opportunities for displaced labour and for young rural dwellers entering the work force. The 'villages-centres' are also viewed as a mechanism to narrow the gap in material living standards and quality of life that exists between urban and rural France. In conjunction with agricultural reform, the creation of urban employment immediately accessible to rural dwellers is intended to raise rural income levels, enabling improvements in material conditions and also the possession of the private transport necessary to ensure that the benefits of urban living may be fully available to the outlying rural settlements. It is at this point that the creation of industrial employment becomes crucial, since an urban way of life can only be grafted on to the countryside if an equivalent degree of affluence is present.

As a long-term policy, the reform of rural communes around 'villages-centres' as nodes can hardly be criticized, since it is an attempt to redress the imbalance in the present distribution of economic and social opportunity. It is also an attempt to modernize rural areas both in terms of function and the outlook of their inhabitants. For the moment it remains only a

[*]The government introduced a substantial reorganization in 1968, but encountered much opposition at the local level.

policy, and the implementation is likely to prove difficult. In optimum economic conditions, in the 'developed' section of eastern France and along the major transport arteries of the rest of the nation, the conversion may be possible and relatively spontaneous. On the other hand, throughout western and central France, the evidence that sufficient new industry can be created in small towns to enable them to reanimate the countryside is far from convincing.

In the post-war years, France has made a major effort in the field of urban development. Considerable investment and imagination have been devoted to the task of equipping the towns as centres not only of economic activity, but also to fulfil the material and cultural needs of urban society. It may be suggested that a similar preoccupation with rural renewal is overdue and that this should involve not only the structural reform of agriculture, but also an effort in social renovation. The opportunities for social evolution must be extended to the countryside and not remain the prerogative of urban dwellers.

REFERENCES

[1] Thompson, I., 'Economic transition in a high alpine valley', *Tijdschr. econ. soc. Geogr.*, 1962, p. 215.

[2] Dewailly, J., 'Utilisation du sol et aménagement d'une vallée humide; la vallée de la Sensée', *Hommes Terres Nord*, 1967, p. 60.

[3] Le Lannou, M., *Géographie de la Bretagne*, p. 200, 1950, Rennes, Plihon.

[4] Thompson, I., 'The St. Malo Region, Brittany', *Geogr. Field Group Stud.*, No. 12, 1968, p. 63.

[5] Thompson, I., *op. cit.*[4], p. 71.

[6] Guichard, O., *Aménager la France*, p. 119, 1965, Paris, Laffont-Gonthier.

[7] Pinchemel, P., *La Géographie de la France*, Tome I, p. 275, 1964, Paris, Armand Colin.

[8] Riotte, A., 'La commune d'hier et d'aujourd 'hui, son évolution', *Expans. région.*, No. 36, 1965, p. 22.

[9] Gravier, J., *L'Aménagement du Territoire et l'Avenir des Régions Françaises*, p. 120, 1964, Paris, Flammarion.

[10] Gravier, J., *op. cit.*[9], p. 120.

[11] Pisani, E., 'Refaire la Commune', *Le Figaro*, April 16, 1968.

[12] Guichard, O., *op. cit.*[6], p. 119.

[13] Janrot, P., 'Du village-centre à la métropole d'équilibre', *Expans. région.*, No. 35, 1964, p. 15.

4

Urban Development

The popular image of eternal France, embodied in her farms and villages, punctuated at regular intervals by small, somnolent towns, is now an anachronism. The new France may be symbolized by apartment complexes, new office blocks and industrial estates, as a backcloth to an essentially urban civilization. Although less pleasing esthetically, this new image contains the elements of economic renewal and social transformation upon which modern France is based.

It is beyond the present scope to review in detail all the factors which have moulded the urban landscape. An immense and scholarly literature exists, encompassing both the evolution of urban civilization and the contemporary phenomena of expansion and renewal. The discussion which follows seeks to establish the essential characteristics of the urban structure of France as a preamble to an analysis of recent quantitative and qualitative changes in the process of urban development.

In the official census reports, the definition of urban population is essentially related to administrative units which do not necessarily coincide with any geographical, economic or social reality. The 1962 census defines as 'urban' any commune possessing an agglomeration of at least 2,000 inhabitants. While in the case of the smaller towns, the commune limit may adequately contain the physical extent of the urban structure, in the case of the larger towns and cities the urbanized zone extends beyond the immediate commune limits. Recognizing this deficiency, the census also records the populations of 'urban agglomerations'. These consist of contiguous urban communes defined according to a number of criteria of integration.[1] The criteria employed* may be regarded as arbitrary—as, for example, in comparison with the definition of urbanized areas in the United States census—and have been criticized on these, and other grounds by Pinchemel and Carrière.[2] Although the grouping of

*These are total population, density of population, rate of population growth and proportion of agricultural workers. Doubtful cases are verified by recourse to aerial photographs.

communes permits a more realistic appraisal of entire urban structures, the adherence to commune limits does not necessarily coincide with the physical extent of the built-up area. Both the above designations prove least realistic in the instance of complex urban-industrial zones constituted by a number of individual agglomerations set in a matrix of rural communes* functionally related to the urban economy. This structure is recognised by the census as a 'Zone de Peuplement Industriel ou Urbain', (Z.P.I.U.),[3] defined by the general homogeneity of population and employment characteristics and the importance of journey-to-work movements.

At the census of 1962, 29·5 million inhabitants resided in 2,539 urban communes, constituting 63·4 per cent of the total population. This urban predominance, modest in scale compared with neighbouring industrial nations, is an essentially recent feature.

Table 4.1

THE BALANCE OF URBAN AND RURAL POPULATION, 1851–1962

	Percentage urban	*Percentage rural*
1851	25·5	74·5
1881	34·8	65·2
1901	40·9	59·1
1921	46·3	53·7
1931	50·8	49·2
1936	52·0	48·0
1946	53·2	46·8
1954	56·0	44·0
1962[a]	61·6	38·4

[a]According to the 1954 definition of 'urban'.
Source: Annuaire Statistique, 1966, Table III, p. 23.

Table 4.1 indicates that the urban population did not exceed that of rural communes until 1931, and that the margin of this predominance did not widen greatly until after 1954. Although the urban population has grown at a more rapid rate than the population as a whole since 1851, the rate of urbanization cannot be considered rapid before 1945, seldom exceeding one per cent per annum. Against this background of steady growth, the increase by over 25 per cent between 1945 and 1962 is seen to be unprecedented in the nation's modern demographic history.

*As defined by the census definition of 2,000 inhabitants.

THE URBAN NETWORK

Two thirds of the inhabitants of France now live in towns and cities and 73·8 per cent live in urbanized zones. These national averages accord little with the realities of the urban network centres and conceal enormous regional variations in the degree of urbanization. In *Figure 4.1*, the distribution of individual towns and agglomerations, classified by size category,

Figure 4.1

has been superimposed on variations in the proportion of the population of each département resident in 'Zones de Peuplement Industriel ou Urbain'. The former indicates the specific distribution of the centres of the urban network, while the latter is indicative of the wider significance of urban functions in the total population.

Figure 4.1 reveals that in only five general areas does the degree of urbanization, as reflected by the proportion resident in Z.P.I.U., exceed the national average:—

1. The Paris agglomeration and Lower Seine Valley.
2. The départements of Nord and Pas-de-Calais.
3. Lorraine and Alsace.
4. Lyon–St. Etienne–Grenoble.
5. Basse-Provence.

The precise form of urban development varies considerably from one to another of these five concentrations. The Paris agglomeration and the Lower Seine Valley form in effect a single structure: the primate city of France together with an urbanized axis linking Paris to its maritime outlet. In the north, extractive and heavy industry are the basis of over one hundred urban centres which coalesce to form a linear agglomeration of over one million inhabitants. Lille–Roubaix–Tourcoing, by contrast, constitutes a discrete conurbation of over 750,000 inhabitants. In Lorraine, Nancy and Metz are the dominant centres of a linear zone of fragmented urban development consisting of small towns and industrial 'cités'. The situation is rather different in Alsace, where between Strasbourg and Mulhouse a regular network of towns and industrial villages has developed on the Rhine Plain and the flanks of the Vosges. Three contrasted forms of urbanization are found in the zone centred on Lyon and the lower Isère valley. Lyon is the archetype of a provincial capital which has retained, and even expanded, its historic role as a regional fulcrum of industry, commerce and culture, in spite of the rise of the national capital. St. Etienne, on the other hand, was born of the industrial revolution and is faced with the problem of converting industries with their roots in the nineteenth century. In sharp contrast, Grenoble is a product of the twentieth century and in particular of the science-based industries of the last 20 years. Finally, a chain of coastal agglomerations extends from Marseille to the Italian frontier in which the industrial and port complexes of Marseille–Berre may be differentiated from the almost continuous urban ribbon east of Fréjus, indelibly linked with tourism.

In the five concentrations outlined above, resided 17·7 million urban dwellers in 1962, or exactly 60 per cent of the urban population of the entire nation. If the urban population of the départements of Jura and Ardennes, which also have over 75 per cent of their total population resident in Z.P.I.U., is added, then approximately two thirds of the urban population of France is seen to reside on only 20 per cent of the national land area, all located to the east of a line from Le Havre to Marseille.

At the opposite extreme, *Figure 4.1* demonstrates that the majority of the Massif Central, eastern and southern Aquitaine, Vendée, Poitou, central Brittany, Cotentin and Basse-Normandie (6), all have less than

45 per cent of their population residing in Z.P.I.U. In an area equivalent to one third of the national territory, only Poitiers had a population exceeding 50,000 inhabitants in 1962. The degree of urbanization in the remainder of France falls between these two extremes, but again with a marked contrast between the east and west. A broad zone (7), encompassing the Paris Basin and the northern margins of the Massif Central, has a regular network of urban centres of varying size and importance. Conversely, in western France (8) the relatively high degree of urbanization of the Lower Loire, eastern Brittany and Maine, is seen to be a function of the existence of a few very large centres and a virtual absence of a network of medium-sized towns. The same is true of northern Aquitaine and the middle Garonne Valley.

A final zone where the degree of urbanization is intermediate in intensity has an arcuate distribution (9) extending from the northern Alps to Languedoc and the Pyrénées. Although the total urban population is not high, its significance is increased by the low overall rural densities. Corsica shares the characteristics of this zone.

In summary, *Figure 4.1* demonstrates the irregularity of the network of urban centres, both in the density of the net and in the relative weight of the points in the network. Marked variations also exist in the form of urbanization and in the grouping of centres by population size. From these observations it may be postulated that a complex pattern of urban hierarchy is present and that no consistent correlation exists between population size and the extent of spheres of influence of urban centres. Of the major regions, only the Paris Basin has a regular network of urban distribution and a harmonious pattern of towns in varied size categories.

THE URBAN HIERARCHY

The existence of a coherent hierarchical arrangement of urban centres in France is a modern feature, postdating the advent of mass communications. Prior to the construction of a dense railway network, relatively simple urban–rural relationships obtained. For centuries, the village had remained a largely autarchic unit and recourse to higher-order centres was largely for purposes of trading at fairs. Even after the increased centralization of administration during the Napoleonic era, the commune unit of organization fulfilled the purpose of mundane administration just as village artisans fulfilled the material needs of the rural population. The elaboration of a hierarchy of centres grew in direct proportion to the expansion of towns, since the middle of the nineteenth century, as centres of employment, administration, commerce and culture.

The task of describing the national pattern of urban hierarchy is rendered difficult by the scarcity of detailed definitive work in this field. Until quite recently, research centred on the interpretation of patterns within individual agglomerations and little comparative study embracing the concept of hierarchy appeared before 1950. Since this date, increased attention has been paid to the problem of defining the fundamental spatial patterns of urbanization in terms of the size, spacing and functions of town and cities. In a nation where local government is graded consistently in terms of administrative areas, it is tempting to base a classification of hierarchy on the network of préfectures, sous-préfectures and capitals of cantons. Similarly, in a nation where the distorting effects of nineteenth-century industrial urbanization are limited in areal extent, it is difficult to resist imputing hierarchical order according to the rank size of urban centres. In fact, neither of these criteria provides an infallible basis upon which to construct a hierarchy. The administrative capitals are frequently neither the largest nor most important centres within their départements. Frequently their status depends on historical continuity, unconfirmed by present-day conditions. The rank-size of urban centres has also ceased to be a reliable index of hierarchy order as a result of the growth of mono-industrial agglomerations in northern and eastern France, and the twentieth-century growth of dormitory towns. In both instances, towns of over 15,000 inhabitants are common but their central functions are no greater than those of a modest rural service centre.

Between 1952 and 1964, four systems of hierarchy were proposed by distinguished workers in the field of urban study (*Table 4.2*).

Table 4.2

PROPOSED HIERARCHY SYSTEMS, 1952–1964

1. George (1952)[4]	2. Gravier (1958)[5]
Centre local	Petit centre
Capitale régionale	Ville moyenne
Ville marchande industrialisée	Capitale secondaire
Ville industrielle	Capitale régionale
Grande agglomération	Métropole internationale
Paris	Paris
3. Coppolani (1959)[6]	4. Pinchemel (1964)[7]
Bourgade	Bourg
Centre local	Petite Ville
Ville maîtresse	Capitale régionale
Capitale régionale	Métropole provinciale
Paris	Paris

The system proposed by George is not a hierarchy in the strict sense, but rather a classification of types of towns. It is clear from their descriptions that the other three authors recognise similar gradations, differing only on the question of nomenclature. Gravier distinguishes an additional status, 'métropole internationale', exemplified by Lyon, as having strong direct international connections, chiefly in the sphere of commerce. It may be suggested that these four systems were supported by considerable familiarity and expertise on the part of their authors, but were unsupported by exhaustive documentation or empirical analysis. Recent work, directly or indirectly relating to the question of hierarchy, has attempted to eliminate arbitrariness by a more rigorous statement of the criteria of classification and by recourse to detailed documentation. Three main lines of approach may be distinguished. Hautreux and Rochefort[8] established, in 1965, a hierarchy of 74 centres demonstrated as possessing a regional service function from an analysis of the quality and sphere of influence of their tertiary activities. Although the work was conducted within an established conceptual framework, the thoroughness and objectivity of the inquiry has cast new light on what the authors term 'l'armature urbaine française'. Parallel work, directed by Chabot,[9] in which geographers from 16 universities participated, approached the question in terms of the physical extent of the spheres of influence of agglomerations of over 50,000 inhabitants. By the employment of a wide range of criteria, three separate zones of influence were mapped: the zone of direct social and economic dominance, the larger extent of commercial dominance, and the wider sphere of intellectual influence. Chabot did not propose a formal hierarchy, but cross-reference with the work of Hautreux and Rochefort permits integration between the ordering of regional centres and the varying extent of their spheres of influence.

In contrast to the above approaches, essentially based on compilation methods, Boudeville[10] has adopted the statistical approach of the space economist in the form of regional operational models. In particular, his work on the definition of polarized regions is of direct relevance to the establishment of hierarchy systems. Boudeville defines a polarized region as 'the set of neighbouring towns exchanging more with the regional metropolis than with other cities of the same order in the nation'.[11] Such structures are close in concept to the term 'city regions' more commonly employed by British geographers. The basis of the polarized region model is the measurement of traffic flows, commercial currents and the deployment of labour and capital around a strong focal point. This method has the advantage of demonstrating spheres of influence as active, functional, organic structures and has perhaps greater analytical value than the largely descriptive methods employed by Hautreux and Chabot.

A completely documented representation of the hierarchy of all places designated as urban in the census is not available, but as a result of the works cited above, and the evidence of a large number of regional studies, certain conclusions may be presented. An undisputed fact is the complete dominance of Paris at the head of the national hierarchy. The gap between Paris and the second-order cities, the regional metropolises, is larger than that between any subsequent orders. This dominance is a reflection not only of the concentration of population and the economic and cultural fabric of France in the national capital, but also of its monopoly of the power of decision and direction, vested in both government agencies and in the head offices of industry and commerce. It is impossible to attribute a sphere of influence to Paris other than that of the entire national space. Boudeville[12] has demonstrated that the polarized region of Paris—that is, the area throughout which the direction from Paris is unchallenged—occupies over one third of the national space. It is noticeable that no regional metropolis has developed in the vast Paris Basin. Only Rouen is equipped with high-order services, the remaining regional centres serving to transmit the influence of Paris rather than to exert a strong direction within their spheres of influence.*

As a corollary, it is notable that the regional metropolises, Lyon, Marseille, Lille, Nantes, Nancy, Strasbourg, Bordeaux and Toulouse, all have peripheral locations. With the exceptions of Lyon and Marseille, Guichard[13] attributes their elevation to this status as a function of their great distance from Paris.† They are located at points where the economic and cultural currents generated by Paris become most attenuated, allowing them to exercise some measure of direction within their tributary regions.

The irregularity of the urban network inevitably complicates the spatial pattern of hierarchy. Hautreux and Rochefort[14] insist on the discontinuity of the French hierarchy and point to the frequency with which lower-order centres are dependent directly on Paris, even for low-order services, rather than on an intervening series of centres. Gravier[15] has drawn attention to the regional contrasts in the pattern of the hierarchy, comparing the situation in Alsace, where a coherent grading from Strasbourg to small local centres is present, with Basse-Normandie, where no semblance of an orderly hierarchy exists. A further complication results from the close juxtaposition of cities of comparable size and importance, with overlapping spheres of influence and the lack of a clear dominance of one centre over another. Examples are afforded by Tours and Orléans, Le Mans and Angers, Rennes and Nantes and Nancy and Metz.[16]

The urban hierarchy is not static, but rather permits of evolution. In the

---

*Most are road and rail junctions on routes radiating from Paris and many possess industries decentralized from Paris but still controlled from the capital. Most are agricultural collecting centres of goods destined for the Paris market.

†The closest metropolis to Paris is Lille, some 200 kilometres distant.

case of France, this evolution is related both to spontaneous forces and, less importantly, to government action. Spontaneous evolution is most pronounced at the base of the hierarchy pyramid where a great sensitivity exists in the smaller towns to minor adjustments of their central functions. Pinchemel[17] points to the vulnerability of the small town in the face of increased centralization of higher-order services, the closure of branch railway lines, the construction of by-pass roads and the closure of small-scale industries. The factor of government intervention is more important towards the apex of the triangle. Government intervention stems from the observation that the factors by which hierarchy order is determined are, to some extent, amenable to artificial manipulation, especially in the case of high-order administrative and commercial services. It is possible to argue that a harmonious hierarchy, possessing a continuum of graded centres finely adjusted to the distribution and density of population, offers advantages and economies over a discontinuous and irregular system. The growth of regional planning and long-term planning of territorial development has demonstrated the inadequacies of the French network of regional centres from a functional viewpoint. Centuries of centralization on Paris have stifled the capacity of the regional capitals to exert a directional influence commensurate with the extent of their spheres of influence and their new-found economic growth. Accordingly, the 'Commissariat National de l'Aménagement du Territoire', the government body concerned with long-term territorial development, has nominated eight centres as 'métropoles d'équilibre', occupying a hierarchical position immediately below Paris and destined to counterbalance the present dominance of the capital. In turn, ten regional capitals have been designated as 'centres-relais' (regional relay centres), of which the function is to transmit the influence of the 'métropoles d'équilibre'. To achieve this restructuring of the national hierarchy, priority investment is proposed in transport, universities and research institutions, together with some decentralization from Paris of government agencies. In addition, state encouragement is being given to the decentralization of tertiary activity in the private sector.*

The question of hierarchy has thus moved, in a short period of time, from an academic plane to being a basis for planned development and a guideline for investment. As in the case of the regional concept, geographical theory on the size, spacing and functions of towns has become part of the debate concerning the desirable organization of the national space.

*For a fuller description of these proposals see Chapter 5 and *Figure 5.3*.

RECENT QUANTITATIVE CHANGES IN URBAN DEVELOPMENT

The post-war resurgence of the French population has been above all an urban phenomenon, affecting all but the smallest towns.

Table 4.3

THE GROWTH OF URBAN POPULATION, 1954–1962, ACCORDING TO SIZE CATEGORIES

Size category	Population 1962 (thousands)	Increase 1954–1962 (per cent)
Paris agglomeration	7,694	15·5
200,000–1,000,000	5,996	15·2
100,000–199,999	3,089	19·0
50,000–99,999	2,832	18·6
20,000–49,999	3,457	15·6
10,000–19,999	2,014	14·7
5,000–9,999	2,148	12·3
Less than 5,000	2,247	9·3
Total urban population	29,477	15·3

Source: 'L'Espace Economique Français', I.N.S.E.E., 1965, Table V, p. 36.

Table 4.3 shows that between 1954 and 1962 the urban population of France increased at a rate almost double that of the nation as a whole, and the preliminary results of the 1968 census indicate that this relationship has been maintained. A significant deceleration has recently occurred in the growth rate of the Paris agglomeration. *Table 4.3* indicates that between 1954 and 1962 the Paris agglomeration grew by 15·5 per cent, and the increase by approximately one million included a net gain of 700,000 by migration. Between 1962 and 1968, the rate of increase was reduced to 7·9 per cent and the net gain by migration was only 222,000. Thus in spite of a high numerical gain in the last 15 years of 1·6 million inhabitants, the Paris agglomeration has not increased its proportion of the nation's total urban population, and, since 1962 has only expanded at a rate comparable to that of the nation as a whole. Several factors may account for this trend, among them being the effect of decentralization policies, the slowdown in the rate of growth in the national economy in very recent years, and the fact that since 1962 the birth rate in the nation as a whole has tended to fall.

In the case of the remaining large agglomerations of over 125,000 inhabitants, certain differentials may be indicated by reference to size categories and the part played in urban growth by migration.

Table 4.4

RECENT POPULATION GROWTH IN AGGLOMERATIONS OF OVER 200,000 INHABITANTS

	Population 1968 (thousands)	Growth rate per cent		Percentage of growth due to net migration	
		1954–62	1962–68	1954–62	1962–68
Lyon	1,083·0	18·5	14·5	72·2	59·2
Marseille	964·4	16·4	14·9	74·9	73·6
Lille–Roubaix–Tourcoing	881·3	8·4	7·3	23·8	30·0
Bordeaux	555·2	5·8	11·4	45·6	70·0
Nantes	393·7	14·1	12·7	44·0	47·8
Nice	392·6	19·1	12·9	100·0	100·0
Toulouse	370·8	21·0	14·5	76·6	75·8
Rouen	369·8	16·3	12·7	48·7	40·6
Toulon	340·0	21·9	18·1	70·7	75·0
Strasbourg	334·7	14·1	10·5	57·8	47·0
Grenoble	332·4	44·5	27·1	77·6	64·9
St. Etienne	331·4	10·3	5·2	51·7	12·5
Nancy	257·4	14·8	10·9	45·0	34·9
Le Havre	247·4	14·1	9·5	39·6	38·1
Cannes	213·4	19·7	25·4	95·0	95·5
Clermont-Ferrand	204·7	18·8	18·9	66·2	73·0
Mulhouse	199·0	13·4	9·8	60·7	55·5

Source: Calculated from Recensement de 1962 and Recensement de 1968, Premiers Résultats.

The agglomerations over 200,000 inhabitants, including all the major regional capitals, are listed in *Table 4.4*. It is clear that most of the regional metropolises, such as Lyon, Marseille and Toulouse, have expanded at rates approximately double the national average, and that over two thirds of the population increase was as a result of migration. The main exception is Lille–Roubaix–Tourcoing, where due to a lack of growth in the industrial sector the rate of growth was reduced to the national average, mainly as a result of the weaker power of attraction of migrants. It is also clear that certain cities show highly individual trends. Thus Cannes and Nice owed their rapid growth entirely to migration, especially involving retired persons. Grenoble holds the distinction of being the most rapidly expanding city of France, related to the location of scientific research institutes and advanced technology industries in the city, together with the continued growth of tourism. It is noticeable too that in almost all the major agglomerations a deceleration of growth has occurred since 1962 in consonance with the reduction in the national population growth rate. Nevertheless, most of the agglomerations in spite of this continued to grow at approximately twice the rate of the nation as a whole. The main exceptions are agglomerations such as Lille, Mulhouse and St. Etienne, where staple industrial activities occupy a high proportion of the work force.

Although the largest agglomerations have advanced rapidly, Mols[18] and Charlet[19] have demonstrated that their growth rate was surpassed by that of the smaller regional and industrial centres in the category from 125,000 to 200,000 inhabitants, and it is in this category that recent trends diverge most markedly from those of the past.

Table 4.5

RECENT POPULATION GROWTH IN AGGLOMERATIONS OF 125,000 TO 200,000 INHABITANTS

	Population 1968 (thousands)	*Growth rate per cent*		*Percentage of growth due to net migration*	
		1954–62	*1962–68*	*1954–62*	*1962–68*
Rennes	192·8	24·9	19·5	70·0	55·0
Dijon	184·0	24·3	17·8	65·2	57·3
Montpellier	171·5	25·5	37·7	81·9	83·0
Brest	169·3	25·3	12·8	48·1	36·8
Reims	167·8	13·7	16·8	39·7	41·7
Orléans	167·5	23·0	18·7	61·3	61·6
Metz	166·4	20·4	10·7	45·8	7·7
Le Mans	166·2	21·9	14·0	56·0	45·0
Angers	163·2	18·4	13·3	50·8	47·4
Caen	152·3	35·2	25·8	65·3	64·8
Limoges	148·1	12·1	13·7	86·3	83·5
Dunkerque	143·2	26·3	13·4	50·0	70·8
Avignon	139·1	19·4	20·3	79·0	78·5
Amiens	136·7	17·1	12·7	62·2	60·0
Nîmes	125·0	15·8	23·5	78·9	79·0

Source: Calculated from Recensement de 1962 and Recensement de 1968, Premiers Résultats.

It is evident that almost all the agglomerations in *Table 4.5* increased their populations by an average rate of over three per cent per annum over the period 1954 to 1968, and that the contribution of migration was uniformly high. Almost all the towns possess university or technical institutions, most have attracted decentralized industry, and, with the exceptions of Dunkerque and Metz, are discrete regional centres rather than components of heavily industrialized urban regions. The growth of these regional centres, together with the equally rapid growth of towns in the size category of from 50,000 to 100,000 inhabitants, constitutes a trend of great significance. It implies the urbanization of what has been termed the 'désert français', the vast expanse of territory from which Paris has drained population over the last century and a half. The new-found dynamism of the medium-sized and smaller regional centres represents the appearance of a network of poles of development, capable of diverting at least a proportion of the flow of rural migrants from their habitual destinations in Paris and the largest provincial capitals.

RECENT QUALITATIVE CHANGES IN URBAN DEVELOPMENT

The expansion in urban population since 1945 is inevitably echoed in the landscape of towns and cities as they adjust to new dimensions, functions and social needs. The most outstanding individual developments have taken place in the largest cities, but it is in the smaller agglomerations, where recent construction is starkly juxta-posed with a more harmonious historic urban landscape, that changes in the quality of urban development are most striking. The historic French towns, as opposed to the major provincial capitals and nineteenth-century industrial agglomerations, were characterized by their compactness. The essential elements of such towns were confined within the limits of their fortifications or the natural defensive features which conditioned the initial choice of site. Annexed to these medieval nuclei, were small suburbs, commonly associated with railway development and the growth of industry on the periphery of the old town. The post-war surge of population growth has caused such formerly compact towns to spill out into the countryside in the process of rapid suburban extension.

Although most striking visually in the case of the historic towns, the rapid expansion of the physical extent of the built-up area is a universal trend, as a consequence of the low absorptive capacity of the core of most French towns and cities. Densely settled, with little available unbuilt land, the urban centres existing in 1945 were incapable of accommodating the large post-war increase in population. On the contrary, in many instances, reconstruction of war-damaged property and slum clearance schemes implied the reduction of population in town centres. The process of suburban extension has progressed by chain reaction. The initial consequence of physical expansion was the increased separation of place of work from place of residence, with a commensurate increase in the volume of commuting. In turn the problems of congestion and high land values in the centre of towns have led industries to locate in new industrial estates on the periphery of built-up areas. This represents a shift to a location closer to the work force, to a cleaner environment and to sites capable of further expansion directly linked to transport arteries. The process of suburban industrialization in turn sows the seeds of further residential development on the periphery of towns.

Plate 2. Urban expansion. *Above*, urban and industrial expansion along the Basse-Seine axis at Rouen. In the middle distance, the oil refinery of Petit Couronne. *Below*, the encroachment of Paris into the countryside—the 'grand ensemble' of Sarcelles

(*Above*, By courtesy of Paris Normandie; *below*, By courtesy of Institut Géographique National)

The mushroom growth of suburbs has followed a consistent pattern of evolution in terms of the resultant urban structures. In the immediate post-war years, emphasis was placed on the restitution of housing destroyed during hostilities. In some instances, as at Le Havre,[20] St. Nazaire and Lorient, the destruction was total and whole towns were rebuilt. The problem of reconstruction, not only of housing but of bridges, railways and port installations, was soon overshadowed by the greater task of housing the growing urban population, stemming from the nation's demographic revival and the high volume of rural–urban migration concomitant on the expansion of industry. Severe technical and financial difficulties impeded a rapid solution. The building industry had been run down between the wars, partly because of the small demand, heightened by the effects of the depression, of a population growing only at a slow rate of increase, and partly as a result of high taxes on rents which discouraged speculative building. In strength, organization and construction methods, the building industry was inadequate to fulfil the needs of the acute post-war housing shortage. Equally severe were the problems of financing new construction, since France lacked private and municipal funds for the financing of low-cost housing. Both these problems were approached by the creation of collective housing in the form of apartment blocks, which in the decade 1950 to 1960 transformed the physical appearance of the large towns. These low-rent apartment blocks, 'habitations à loyer modéréll' (H.L.M.), proliferated as a result of the adoption of industrialized building techniques and by the creation of government funds to finance their construction. Whereas the number of houses built in 1950 totalled only 71,000 units, a figure of 320,000 was achieved in 1959, of which 101,000 were H.L.M. dwellings. Since 1959, the volume and form of state assistance have been increased and diversified. In 1965, out of a total of 411,000 units completed, 120,000 were H.L.M. apartments and a further 227,000 new dwellings, mostly in collective schemes, benefited from state aid.[21]

The profusion of apartment blocks, virtually indistinguishable one from another in architectural style, has introduced a note of uniformity and monotony into the suburban landscape of France: While even the most modest towns have acquired a number of blocks of H.L.M. flats or similar constructions, huge complexes have burgeoned on the periphery of the larger cities, forming the so-called 'grands ensembles'* [22] The dominant architectural form of the 'grands ensembles' is the grouping of low blocks of flats, usually four or five storeys high, but often several hundred metres

*The term 'grands ensembles d'immeubles collectifs' is strictly applied to very large complexes possessing a number of amenities specifically for the use of their inhabitants. The term is applied more loosely to other large, but inorganic groups of apartments possessing no collective amenities.

long; the form to which industrial building techniques are most economic-ally applied. In some instances tower blocks and open spaces diversify the landscape, but too often the 'grands ensembles' correspond to the econom-ist's dream and the urbanist's nightmare. That the 'grands ensembles' responded most rapidly to the exigencies of the housing shortage is undeniable, as is the factor of low-cost construction and the proportionately small amount of building land required relative to the housing density. On the other hand, critics of the system point to the inhuman environment of the less well-planned complexes, the hazards to mental health of such high density and uniform living conditions, and the vast contribution which the 'grands ensembles' make to the problem of commuting.[23] Sociologists have decried the discrepancy between the pace of apartment construction and the addition of social amenties, with a consequent absence of com-munity development* Of great concern too is the destruction of open spaces by a form of housing which nevertheless demands exceptional recreational amenities to offset the pressures of collective living.[24] The problem is intensified by the high proportion of children and young families housed in this form of residence and recent research has revealed a unanimous preference on the part of the inhabitants of 'grands ensembles' for individual residences.[25] By 1969 it is estimated that 350 major apart-ment complexes will have been built, comprising almost one million dwellings. However, the experience gained from the first wave of H.L.M. construction has led to an improvement in the design of recent complexes and projected schemes. The need to preserve open spaces and to vary both style of architecture and the composition of dwelling units is appreciated and has been incorporated into ambitious comprehensive schemes in the major agglomerations.

A period of reconstruction was thus followed in the decade 1950 to 1960 by a period of incessant suburban expansion. Not only was the building industry forced to reform but the process of town planning was ill-adjusted to the unprecedented demands. The mistakes in urban design during this period may be attributed in part to the strain imposed on a planning structure ill-prepared conceptually, and in terms of organization and legal powers, for the task imposed on it. Although the principle of adhering to town development plans has been adopted, too often the pace of growth has entailed frequent revision and a lack of perspective necessary to achieve a balanced and coordinated use of urban land. Organizational problems arose from the outward growth of agglomerations into adjacent communes subject to different local authority control. The need to plan agglomerations in their functional entirety led to the establishment

*The 'grand ensemble' of Sarcelles near Paris increased the population of the commune from 8,397 in 1954 to 35,430 in 1962.

of 'groupements d'urbanisme', consultative groupings of local authorities, to coordinate planning measures in the context of multi-commune units. A further constraint on integrated urban planning was the limited legal powers of local authorities in the matter of land acquisition for comprehensive development. Since 1955, the powers of expropriation have been increased progressively. This is an important factor in a nation characterized by housing built on very small plots, and unbuilt land consisting of small parcels with fragmented ownership. Comprehensive developments were thus delayed by the problem of obtaining land on a piecemeal basis and the need for 'remembrement' before extensive construction of roads and buildings could be attempted.[26] This problem has been substantially reduced by legislation of 1958 introducing powers for the creation of 'Zones à Urbaniser par Priorité' (Z.U.P.) and, in 1962, of 'Zones d'Aménagement Différé' (Z.A.D.). Z.U.P. are designated as areas where powers of expropriation may be enforced so as to enable comprehensive development of large sections of urban terrain. Z.A.D., on the other hand, are areas on which a right of pre-emption exists for a period of twelve years, enabling municipal authorities to create reserves of land for future development and, incidentally, combating speculation.

Considerable progress has thus been made in the sphere of physical planning, replacing the anarchy of the past. Emphasis is increasingly being placed on the need for coordinated planning of entire urbanized regions. Study groups were constituted, in 1966, charged with the task of creating master plans for the economic and urban development of a number of metropolitan areas. In addition to the central Paris Basin, these 'aires d'études métropolitaines' include Nord, the Lower Seine Valley, Nancy–Metz–Thionville, Nantes–St. Nazaire, Lyon–St. Etienne, and Marseille–Aix–Berre–Fos. The study groups, linking research workers from several disciplines, are of particular interest in that their areal framework is that of the city region.

It has been suggested that the post-war evolution of urbanization has consisted of three stages: an immediate phase of reconstruction leading on to a second stage of accelerated expansion, during which concessions were made in the planning of the urban environment to the short-term housing problem, and a third stage, during which, in spite of continued pressure, a stricter planning control has been applied. The recent history of urban development has been different in kind from that of the past not only in terms of the rate of growth but also in the form and quality of physical expansion. In particular, the sudden appearance of large suburban accretions on the margins of towns upon which history seemed to have set its seal, points to a new vitality which is not confined merely to the major cities. It is noticeable that the growth in urban population has been accommodated within the pre-existing network of towns. No substantial new towns have been added, in contrast with the practise adopted in Britain and the Netherlands. This stems from two principal considerations which have rendered the new towns concept of less relevance to French conditions. In the first instance, with the exception of Paris, France suffers less from the problems associated with massive industrial conurbations than is the case in Britain. It is of interest that Pinchemel[27] has argued in favour of the establishment of new towns less as a means of redistributing overspill population from cities, than for the purpose of intercepting rural migrants closer to their point of departure and alleviating regional de-population. Secondly, the rapid expansion of urban population during the decade 1950 to 1960 took place during the period of financial stringency. The relative cost of expanding existing towns, taking advantage of an established infrastructure, and the creation of completely new towns, argued strongly in favour of the former course. Mourenx, with a popu-lation of 11,000 in 1964, remains the chief exception. Built to house the labour force required to exploit the Lacq natural gas, the decision to build a new town was a case of 'force majeure' rather than an acceptance of the principle of new town construction.

The basis of urban growth has been suburban extension rather than the creation of new or autonomous units. The physical extension of towns has, unfortunately, rarely been accompanied by a parallel dispersion of commercial and cultural amenities throughout the new urban terrain. On the contrary these functions, together with the tertiary employment that they generate, have remained firmly rooted in the centre of towns and cities. Three predictable consequences result from this circumstance: the congestion of central business districts, the problem of high levels of commuter traffic and the existence of suburban tracts with a service provision disproportionately small in relation to their populations. Realization of these problems has led to an attempt to secure a more balanced suburban growth in recent years, with emphasis placed on the location of industry and the provision of services close to the major new concentrations of population. Such, in fact, is the French concept of new towns,[28] a concept which in time will tend to produce polycentric or multicellular cities in which the initial nucleus will be surrounded by self-contained annexes, progressively less dependent on the services and employment opportunities of the original centre.

A further consequence of post-war trends is that the distinction between urban and rural terrain is becoming increasingly blurred. The cities are surrounded by wide aureolas of rural terrain which have become functional extensions or urban civilization. The growth of commuting, the change-over from rural settlement to dormitory village, the proliferation of secondary residences in rural areas, and, latterly, the establishment of regional parks, all represent a spilling out of urban influences into the surrounding countryside. It is imperative therefore that planning should not be restricted to the contiguous built-up areas of cities, but should also strive to preserve the recreational and amenity value of the sensitive rural area around the agglomerations. This conservation aspect of planning is of the utmost importance as the tide of urban expansion is still swelling. It is estimated that by 1985, the urban population of France will have doubled.[29] The experience of the past 25 years must be used to ensure that the towns of the future are not only efficient in function but also offer an environment compatible with the strains and pressures or urban living.

In a comparatively short period of time, France has undergone a mutation in the scale and character of her urban landscape.[30] It seems paradoxical that France, least lacking in space among West European nations, should experience an increasing concentration of her population and adopt high-density forms of urban residence. It is tempting to attribute this to a national characteristic of individuality in temperament but gregariousness by instinct. A more convincing argument would be based on the sectorial movement of labour from agriculture to industry and services, in combination with the technical difficulties that France has experienced in adjusting her urban structures to this change.[31]

REFERENCES

[1] Le Fillatre, P., 'Nouvelle définition des agglomérations utilisées par l'INSEE', *Etud. Statist.*, 1961, No. 1.

[2] Carrière, F., and Pinchemel, P., *Le Fait Urbain en France*, pp. 23–24, 1963, Paris, Armand Colin.

[3] *Les Zones de Peuplement Industriel ou Urbain*, 1962, Paris, INSEE.

[4] George, P., *La Ville*, 1952, Paris, Presses Universitaires de France.

[5] Gravier, J., 'Réalité de la Région', *Urbanisme*, No. 58, 1958.

[6] Coppolani, J., *Le Réseau Urbain de la France*, p. 13, 1959, Paris, Editions Ouvrières.

[7] Pinchemel, P., *Géographie de la France*, Tome 2, pp. 600–608, 1964, Paris, Armand Colin.

[8] Hautreux, J., and Rochefort, M., 'Physionomie générale de l'armature urbaine française', *Annls. Géogr.*, 1965, p. 660.

[9] Chabot, G., 'Carte des zones d'influence des grandes villes françaises', *C.N.R.S. Mém. Docums*, Tome 8, 1961, p. 141.

[10] Boudeville, J., *Problems of Regional Economic Planning*, 1966, Edinburgh, Edinburgh University Press.

[11] Boudeville, J., *op. cit.*[10], p. 10.

[12] Boudeville, J., *Les Espaces Economiques*, p. 14, 1961, Paris, Presses Universitaires de France.

[13] Guichard, O., *Aménager la France*, p. 65, 1965, Paris, Laffont-Gonthier.

[14] Hautreux, J., and Rochefort, M., *op. cit.*[8], pp. 672–673.

[15] Gravier, J., *L'Aménagement du Territoire et l'Avenir des Régions Françaises*, pp. 137–140, 1964, Paris, Flammarion.

[16] Verrière, J., 'Réflexions sur la région dite du "Centre" ', *Norois*, 1968, pp. 512–515.

[17] Pinchemel, P., *op. cit.*[7], p. 601.

[18] Mols, Rev. P., 'L'accroissement de la population de la France selon les régions et l'importance des agglomérations', *Population*, 1963, p. 262.

[19] Charlet, J., 'Les agglomérations urbaines françaises de plus de 100,000 habitants; quelques aspects de leur croissance', *Hommes Terres Nord*, 1967, p. 49.

[20] Damais, J., 'La nouvelle ville du Havre—Reconstruction et repopulation', *C.N.R.S. Mém. Docums*, Tome 9, 1963.

[21] 'Le financement de la construction en France', *Notes Etud. docum.*, No. 3,301, 1966.

22 Lacoste, Y., 'En France, un type nouveau d'habitat urbain; les "Grands Ensembles" ', *C.N.R.S. Mém. Docums*, Tome 10, Fasc. 2, p. 77.

23 Lacoste, Y., 'Un problème complexe et débattu: les grands ensembles', *Bull. Ass. Géogr. fr.*, 1963, p. 40

24 Kaes, R., *Vivre dans les Grands Ensembles*, 1963, Paris, Editions Ouvrières.

25 Delouvrier, P., 'Urbanisation et habitat', *Expans. région.*, No. 35, 1964, p. 21.

26 Bastie, J., 'Le sol, élément primordial du paysage urbain', *Annls Géogr.*, 1965, p. 708.

27 Pinchemel, P., 'L'interdépendance des villes et des campagnes et les problèmes des niveaux optima', *Revue Econ.*, 1960, p. 339.

28 Susquet-Bonnard, A., 'New towns for France', *Tn Ctry Plann.*, 1962, p. 288.

29 Massé, P., 'Réflexions pour 1985', *Documn fr.*, 1964, p. 71.

30 *L'Urbanisation Française*, 1964, Paris, Centre de Recherche d'Urbanisme.

31 'La croissance urbaine et les problèmes d'urbanisation', *Notes Etud. docum.*, No. 3,210, 1965.

Part Two
PATTERNS OF ECONOMIC ACTIVITY

5

State and Regional Economic Planning

The completion of five national plans since 1945 has established economic planning as an institutional feature which permeates all aspects of life in France. Accordingly, some discussion of the character of planning is a necessary preliminary to any analysis of economic activity. The birth of economic planning in 1945 may be attributed to several separate circumstances, which, in conjunction, created the appropriate economic and political atmosphere for such an initiative.

The most pressing factor was that of the material and economic destruction caused by the Second World War. It was apparent that a speedy economic recovery could best be attained by a strict direction of capital and resources towards priority objectives. The post-war shortage of manpower and essential raw materials was a cogent argument for central direction of resources and investment. Irrespective of the war damage, the economic structure of France was ripe for reform and renewal by virtue of the relative stagnation of the pre-war decade. After the economic depression of 1930, France failed to modernize its industrial fabric and organization, and fell behind some West European rivals, not only in the growth of output, but also in the efficiency and productivity of her industrial structure. Similarly, French agriculture, bedevilled by problems of fragmentation, a slow rate of mechanization, and above all a lack of efficient commercial organization, produced only a proportion of its real potential yet absorbed an excessive amount of manpower. The catastrophe of the war served to highlight the fact that economic weakness engenders political hazard, and that a return to the pre-war economic pattern would not ensure the future security of the country or restore France as a leading European state.

If logic argued some form of central direction of economic affairs, this would not have been achieved so rapidly had not the political circumstances been propitious. The war had suppressed the traditional political institutions and in its train brought into power a provisional government of predominantly socialist orientation. Although certain key sectors of the economy were subjected to nationalization, the idea of widespread reform was less a question of doctrinaire beliefs than an expression of a determination not to return to the discredited status quo ante bellum.

Finally, the necessity of substantial aid from the United States, under the terms of the Marshall Plan, called for the establishment of a plan for economic recovery indicating the nation's financial needs and priorities. The initiation of economic planning in France was thus a combination of economic and political reality called into being by the shock of war and occupation.

THE STRUCTURE OF STATE ECONOMIC PLANNING

The detailed structure of French planning is extremely complex and only the major administrative and consultative organs are included in the following summary. Since the inception of state planning in 1946, the major administrative body has been the 'Commissariat Général du Plan'. This is a permanent body, attached to the Ministry of Finance and Economic Affairs, charged with the task of preparing the national plan for government approval and, subsequently, supervising its implementation. Contrary to the popular image of France as a bureaucratic nation, this commission was deliberately restricted in size. This feature reflects its function as a coordinating agency, working with the existing government departments, rather than interposing rival administrative machinery. The responsibility of the Commissariat is to produce an integrated analysis of national economic and social objectives with the degree of impartiality and objectivity permitted by its separation from narrow departmental interests and its lack of executive power[1].

The Commissariat Général is composed of experts who must establish the guiding priorities at a national level and design appropriate plans for each sector of the economy and for each branch of activity. This complex process is aided by the assistance of modernization commissions. These consist of groups, with from 30 to 50 members, who are appointed on a voluntary basis by virtue of their special knowledge and experience. In general, the members are drawn from government departments, industry, the professions, trade unions and academic life. The modernization commissions fall into two distinct groups, referred to as 'vertical' and 'horizontal' commissions. The vertical commissions are specialized by sectors of activity; for example, agriculture, energy production and manufacturing industry. The horizontal commissions consider problems relating to all activities, such as manpower, investment and regional development. Thus, while the vertical commissions can report on the prospects for expansion of individual industries, the horizontal commissions review the implications for the entire economic structure of the nation.

The creation of the national plans normally consists of three stages; an initial draft of general objectives, a stage of discussion in the modernization commissions, and a final stage of synthesis. The initial draft, produced by the Commissariat Général, is of necessity based on certain assumptions concerning the desirable rate of economic growth to be achieved by the plan. This choice is established by the government and is the maximum growth rate compatible with a secure equilibrium of employment, investment and savings, internal financial stability and a sound balance of payments position. On receiving this directive, the Commissariat Général is able to produce an outline of objectives to be discussed in the appropriate modernization commissions. It is the purpose of these commissions to translate general objectives into detailed programmes. Finally, the Commissariat Général has the task of synthesising the report of the modernization commissions into an integrated blueprint for parliamentary consideration. In particular, a close accordance must be achieved between the plans submitted by the vertical commissions for individual activities, with the resources of manpower, energy and finance as appraised by the horizontal commissions.

Once the published plan has received parliamentary approval the blueprint is ready for implementation. It is at this stage that the distinctive feature of French planning—its 'indicative' rather than 'directive' approach—must be made effective. To achieve this the government relies partly on cooperation, partly on direct intervention and partly on indirect measures of control. Since the plan is established with the participation of the private sector, it is logical that its recommendations should be accepted as a guideline for investment and production targets by individual private enterprises. Moreover, in the preparation of the plan, the projected sales and purchases between each sector of activity are calculated. Thus the supply and demand situation in different markets is best kept in balance by a strict adherence to the targets of the plan. Each branch is thereby given some reassurance as far as supply of raw materials and availability of markets are concerned provided that all producers cooperate. In this manner, there are powerful psychological factors, founded on self-interest, which assure the government of some measure of cooperation from the private sector.

In addition to this voluntary cooperation, the government can exercise a direct control over approximately one third of gross investment through the nationalized industries and public expenditure. The investment in energy production is very largely directed by the government, as is investment in telecommunications, the railways and public works. The government also controls a large section of the automobile industry, and by virtue of loans and defence contracts, the aerospace industries. The level of investment established by the government in these industries inevitably helps to regulate the level of activity in the related dependant sectors of the economy.

Finally, indirect government control is exercised through a large number of media which are at once both effective but flexible in their application. Fiscal means can be employed to stimulate those programmes which conform with the objectives of the plan. In particular, credit controls, equipment premiums and state-guaranteed loans are used to stimulate investment in particular industries and selected regions, and offer a more supple control than general taxation policies. Such indirect methods permit the government to take regulatory action within the period of a plan to meet short-term or localized problems as they arise.

The First Plan,* 1946–1953, was termed a 'plan for modernization and equipment'. Set against the background of the post-war emergency situation, the plan was an instrument of reconstruction and also aimed at the rehabilitation of the economy by equipping it for rapid growth. Priority was given to six key sectors—coal, steel, electricity, transport, agricultural machinery and cement—which were regarded as motivating activities for the remainder of the economy. By the end of 1952, almost all the targets in the key sectors had been attained, but recovery in the other branches of the economy was less impressive.

In contrast to the selective priorities of the First Plan, the Second Plan (1954–1957), introduced investment and production targets for virtually all activities, and notably for manufacturing industry, agriculture and housing. Recognizing that the size of the labour force was unlikely to increase during the plan, and that foreign competition was likely to harden in both the home and export markets, emphasis was placed on increased productivity, reduction of costs and technical research and training. During the Second Plan, the French economy became a victim of its own success. To sustain the rapid growth a massive rise in imports was necessary, shortage of labour resulted in a rising wage bill, while the buoyant home demand diverted goods from the export drive. The inevitable results were internal inflation and a severe balance of payments problem.

The overwhelming preoccupation of the Third Plan (1958–1961) was

*Frequently termed the 'Monnet Plan', after M. Jean Monnet, the architect of French planning in its formative years.

to restore the financial situation and at the same time to prepare the economy for entry into the Common Market. A period of restraint, during which the franc was devalued, was followed by a phase of accelerated expansion in 1960 and 1961. Priority was accorded to activities with a high export potential, as automobiles and aircraft manufacture, while export substitution was encouraged by investment in natural gas exploitation and the petrochemicals branch.

In each successive plan, the content became more complex. Freed for the first time from the distorting effects of either the post-war emergency or acute financial problems, the Fourth Plan (1962–1965) contained proposals affecting the entire economic and social life of the country. The keynote of the plan was expansion, and a target of a 24 per cent increase in gross domestic production was adopted. In addition, the plan contained definitive proposals in the sphere of integrated national and regional planning. In general terms the Fourth Plan achieved its growth target, but at the expense of renewed signs of inflation. The threat to the competitive position of France in the Common Market led to the introduction of legislation to control wages and prices and the Fourth Plan thus ended on a more subdued note, with certain tasks in the sphere of social development incomplete.

France is currently completing her Fifth Plan (1966–1970), which emerged as being more detailed in content and more regional in context than any of the preceding plans. In addition to an enlarged social programme, the plan contained measures favouring greater competitiveness in agriculture and industry to coincide with the complete liberalization of trade in the Common Market. In both agriculture and industry, incentives were offered towards consolidation into larger production units, necessary for modernization and to meet international competition. Progress under the plan was rudely interrupted by the social and political disturbances of the summer of 1968. From the geographical standpoint, however, the chief interest of the Fifth Plan was the strengthening of the regional sphere of operation. To appreciate the significance of this far-reaching development, it is necessary to trace the evolution of regional planning from its spontaneous origins to its present status as a framework for medium-term and long-range planning.

THE DEVELOPMENT OF REGIONAL PLANNING

French regional planning has developed in a pragmatic fashion and is characterized by great administrative complexity.[3] When state economic planning was initiated at the close of the Second World War, responsibility for the development of the territory was given to the Ministry of Reconstruction. Wholly preoccupied with the critical task of restoring the nation's productive fabric, the question of regional disparities was not of immediate government concern. The chief administrative subdivision of the state remained the département, while each government department had its own system of administrative 'regions', few of which coincided in terms of areal definition.

The germs of regional planning were not to be found in government initiatives, but rather in the spontaneous efforts of private committees and groups concerned with the future of their respective cities, départements or regions. These committees were ad hoc associations of representatives of local government, business, industry, trade unions, farming and universities among others. This 'grass roots' impetus to regional action did not pass unobserved by the government, and in 1955 they were encouraged to constitute themselves according to new regional divisions proposed by the government, at which stage they were officially recognized as 'regional expansion committees'. This status did not vest any powers in the committees, and not until 1961 was their consultative role formally integrated into the planning structure. Their chief activity has been in the sphere of documentation, research and coordination of development within their respective regions.

During the course of the Second National Plan, the need for regional action was increasingly appreciated in government circles. In particular, the period of 1954 and 1955 may be signalled as a turning point during which a number of significant regional policies were introduced and the first regional plans proposed. A law passed in 1951 had authorized the constitution of development companies for the execution of major schemes in some of the most underdeveloped regions of the country. This came to fruition in 1955 when the 'Compagnie Nationale du Bas-Rhône-Languedoc' was established, charged with the task of converting the monocultural system of the vineyards of the Languedoc plain into a more profitable system of mixed farming. This company was constituted with the formula of 'économie mixte'; a blending of state direction and financing with the participation of private enterprise. The same basic formula was extended shortly afterwards to the eastern plain of Corsica, to Provence, Gascony and the heathlands of eastern France.[4] In all cases the function of the company was to sponsor and coordinate land reclamation and conversion on a scale beyond the resources of private companies or local government*

---

*This system of state participation in regional development had a precedent in the 'Compagnie Nationale du Rhône', created in 1934 to execute the integrated development of navigation and power production in the Rhône valley.

A second policy initiated in 1955, which had strong regional implications, was the granting of state assistance to industry to facilitate projects involving conversion, modernization and decentralization.[5] The regional aspect of this policy was twofold. In the first instance, special provision was made for the needs of areas suffering from a low level of industrial development, or where the decline of traditional industries produced unemployment. Secondly, associated legislation was enacted to restrict new industrial growth in the Paris region and thus stimulate decentralization to the areas benefiting from government aid. The type of aid granted by the government was both financial, in terms of grants and loans, and fiscal, involving tax and licence concessions. Areas of high unemployment, designated as 'zones critiques', were given the maximum assistance, especially in the form of 'primes spéciales d'équipement'. These were grants of up to 20 per cent of the capital investment costs of new installations where more than twenty new jobs were created. In addition to this direct aid to problem areas, indirect aid was given to certain municipalities towards the construction of industrial estates and associated housing schemes. Similarly, aid for retraining programmes and disturbance grants for workers obliged to change their place of residence were designed to ease the problems of declining areas. The administration and financing of this aid was provided by a new government agency, created in 1955, the 'Fonds de Développement Economique et Social'.

The first formal acceptance of the principle of integrated regional planning also came in 1955 with the adoption of 21 'circonscriptions d'action régionale'. These embryonic regions, defined territorally in 1956, were designed as a framework within which the various government departments would coordinate their efforts to achieve the overall objectives established by the national plans. The regions were formed by groupings of départements with common broad development problems, the number varying from two to a maximum of eight, as illustrated in *Figure 5.1*. Apparently delimited so as to coincide as closely as possible with the boundaries most commonly employed by government agencies in the past, a certain arbitrariness inevitably results. A more rigorous choice of criteria indicative of functional association might well have produced a substantially different framework.[6] For each region, a programme of long-term development was to be proposed and submitted as white paper for government approval. The first programme, that of Brittany, was approved in 1956, but more than a decade elapsed before all the plans were prepared.* In fact, very little immediate action stemmed from the 'programmes d'action régionale'. With few exceptions they

*The plan for Brittany appeared promptly largely due to the background work already achieved by the regional expansion committee, C.E.L.I.B.

remained as inventories of resources and outlines of necessary developments, but with inadequate reference to the means of financing and implementing the proposals. That rapid results were not obtained was also due to the lack of a strong regional administration and the under-representation of private regional interests in the drafting of the plans.

The period from 1956 to 1959 witnesses no outstanding new measures

Figure 5.1

of regional policy; rather it was a stage of consolidation during which the major decisions of 1955 were put into operation. New legislation was introduced in 1958 restricting office construction in the Paris area and giving further incentives to decentralization. The chief advances were achieved in industrial decentralization, the establishment of new industries in problem areas, and the continued activities of the regional development companies, the latter mainly in Bas-Rhône-Languedoc, Provence and Corsica. During this period, the first seven 'programmes d'action régionale' were published but the amount of associated action was comparatively small.

By contrast, the period from 1959 to 1965 witnessed an unprecedented strengthening of the structure of regional planning. It was a phase when great urgency was attached to the task of simplifying, rationalizing and integrating the machinery of planning at the regional level. It may be suggested that this increased commitment to the regional framework was based on three main circumstances. Firstly, it was becoming increasingly clear that many of the national problems, which featured prominently in the state economic plans, were essentially regional in context. This applied with particular emphasis in the case of land reform, the modernization of agriculture, the drift of population from the land, changes in the balance of energy sources and the problems of urban renewal. The solution of each of these national problems implied a concentration of action in certain specific regions where their incidence was particularly severe. Secondly, the magnitude of the tasks undertaken by the regional development companies and by certain of the largest cities, demonstrated the lack of effective administrative machinery at an intermediate level between the central government and the département. In the case of the development companies, conflict arose from the profound economic and social effects of these major schemes planned in isolation from their wider consequences outside the areas directly involved. Similarly, the growth of cities such as Marseille and Lyon had an impact throughout their city regions for which no planning machinery existed to control. Finally, the overriding consideration was the growing regional disparity in economic growth, income levels, living standards and quality of life. First denounced by Gravier in 1947,[7] this discrepancy between the standards and opportunities afforded east and west of a line approximately from Le Havre to the middle Loire and along the Rhône valley had progressively widened. Although the greater prosperity enjoyed by eastern France could be attributed to superior resources and strong economic forces, it could be argued that the widening of this disparity owed much to a planning approach concerned too much with gross production targets and the performance of the total economy, while taking insufficient cognizance of the distribution of new economic growth over the national space. A compelling argument in favour of regional planning became, therefore, the need to diminish regional inequalities by raising the level of activity in the less-developed parts of the country.[8]

As a consequence of these intransigent problems, the period from 1959 to 1965 witnessed a spate of administrative reforms and institutional creations designed to provide effective regional direction to the nation's economic life. The process began in 1959 with the constitution of 'conférences inter-départementales' for each of the 21 planning regions. These were coordinating committees drawn from the existing administrations of the départements within each planning region. Their task was to coordinate public investment within their respective regions and to supervise the execution of the priorities established in the 'programmes d'action régionale'. In practice, these committees tended to meet in the most important préfecture, and the prefect of that particular département presided over deliberations with the title of 'préfet coordonnateur'. The regional administration thus consisted entirely of civil servants, subject to strong central government control, and the only private regional interests involved were the 'comités d'expansion régionale', which acted purely on a consultative basis.*

A significant development in the course of 1959 was the practice, on the part of the Prime Minister, of holding discussions with government ministers on the general theme of regional economic development. From this informal initiative was created a permanent 'Conseil Interministériel de l'Aménagement du Territoire', which met at regular intervals to survey, at the highest level, the spatial effects of government policies. In turn, this practice led to the institution of two further bodies, the 'Délégation à l'Aménagement du Territoire' and the 'Commission Nationale de l'Aménagement du Territoire' (C.N.A.T.), created in 1963. The former is a small body of approximately 30 members, directly responsible to the Prime Minister, and charged with the task of providing a driving force and coordination to the government's regional plans and policies. To facilitate this task, the delegation administers a special budget, the 'Fonds d'Intervention pour l'Aménagement du Territoire' (F.I.A.T.), which it allocates to priority developments throughout the country, complementing other sources of investment. The C.N.A.T., however, is a much larger body and forms one of the permanent horizontal commissions of the Commissariat Général du Plan. Its purpose is to establish the long-term perspective of regional economic development 20 years ahead and marks the inauguration of a new concept in French planning—the prospective planning of territorial development.[9]

Accompanying these administrative reforms were practical measures without which the new institutions would have been of little value. In 1962, the practice was introduced of subdividing the national budget into 'tranches opératoires', annual 'slices' of public investment accorded to each

*Also in 1959, a decree enforced the harmonization of the subdivisions of government departments so as to conform territorially with the planning regions, permitting greater coordination between the central government and the regional administration.

of the planning regions.[10] This system makes known to each region the amount of subventions and credit allocated to it from the national budget, the amount being determined by the Commissariat Général du Plan in accordance with the evidence of needs submitted to it by the 'conférences inter-départementales'.[11] A further practical measure, introduced in 1964, replaced the status of 'préfet coordonnateur' by 'préfet de région', with greatly increased powers to represent regional interests.* The chief role in the economic field of the 'préfets de région' is that of preparing and executing the regional sections of the national plan and administering public investment towards this end within their respective regions. The préfet is aided in this task by a general staff of experts and consultation with the 'conférence inter-départementale'.[12] In addition, the former regional expansion committees, the advisory bodies representing private regional interests, were reconstituted as 'Commissions de Développement Economique Régional' (C.O.D.E.R.), with enlarged consultative responsibilities.

In 1964, far reaching changes were made in the procedure of granting state assistance to private industry. The allocation of these funds was placed under the control of the 'Délégation à l'Aménagement du Territoire', which clarified the specific areas qualifying for such assistance and systematized the purpose and value of the grants.[13] The system of defining 'zones critiques' was replaced by a division of France into five zones for which differential assistance was allocated. These are illustrated in *Figure 5.2*. The first zone constitutes the whole of the under-industrialized western and central France encompassing over one third of the total national land area. Within this broad area, 'primes de développement' and fiscal exonerations were made automatically available for the creation of new factories and, on a moderated scale, for expansions of existing firms. Eight localities, Cherbourg, Brest, Lorient, Nantes–St. Nazaire, La Rochelle, Limoges, Bordeaux and Toulouse, qualify for the maximum grant of up to 20 per cent of investment costs. The planning region of Bretagne, together with the adjacent départements of Manche, Loire-Atlantique and Vendée, qualifies for grants of up to 12 per cent, and the remainder of the area for grants of up to 10 per cent. The second zone, termed a 'conversion zone', is a discontinuous and fragmented zone of eastern France, where traditional industries are in a state of contraction notably in the case of the textiles and mining industries. In this zone 'primes d'adaptation' of up to 20 per cent and fiscal concessions are payable to new firms helping to diversify the industrial structure. The third zone is again fragmented and includes many of the secondary towns

*This reform did not apply to the Paris region, which has a more complex planning machinery, discussion of which is deferred to Chapter 12.

of eastern France where the pace of industrialization has been slow. In these cases, no direct grants are accorded but fiscal exonerations are applied to new firms. The fourth zone includes the rest of France, with the exception of the Paris region, for which fiscal exonerations are made in certain cases only. Finally, in the Paris region no state assistance is given to

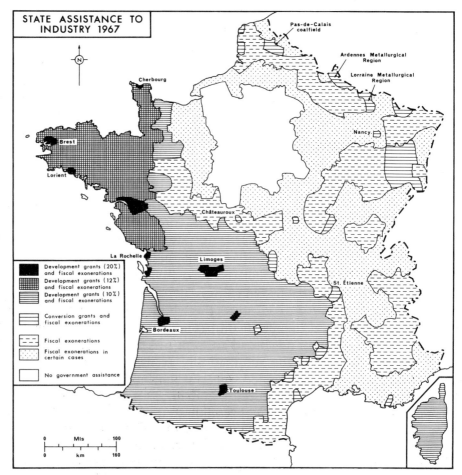

Figure 5.2

new industry and the major incentives are for decentralization rather than expansion* The purpose of this reform was clearly to stimulate the industrialization of the west in an effort to bring new jobs to an area where traditionally population growth has exceeded increases in employment and where improvements in agriculture will release further labour

*For this purpose the Paris region extends beyond the planning district and includes the central Paris Basin from Rouen in the north, to Soissons in the east, and Blois in the south-west.

supply in the future.* Elsewhere, maximum government assistance is restricted to limited areas where extreme dependence on a narrow range of declining industries threatens problems of unemployment.

By the close of the Fourth Plan, the government had largely attained the objective of 'regionalising' the national planning structure. From modest beginnings, an elaborate machinery had been created, which ensured that regional needs were considered in the preparation of the national plans, and that the regional administrations had technical and financial resources to implement approved regional action. It may be claimed that by the time the Fifth Plan was being prepared, machinery existed for the first time to integrate national and regional planning, and that some measure of decentralization had been achieved through the creation of regional prefects.

The Fifth Plan introduced a further concept in planning which is both national and regional in application and which represents a new dimension in both time and space: the prospective development of the territory. This rather stilted translation of the more graceful phrase 'l'Aménagement du Territoire', implies the long-term planning of the environmental, social and economic fabric of France.[14] The basis of this planning is the long-term projection, made by the 'Commission Nationale de l'Aménagement du Territoire', of the decisions made during the preparation of the national plans. It is the task of the C.N.A.T. to consider the effect of government decisions on the entire nation over a period of 20 years ahead. The commission can thus produce guidelines on such matters as demographic trends, employment needs, population distribution, trends in the distribution of industry and urbanization, and recreational needs. Such research permits the formulation of long-term objectives for the future remodelling of the country and builds a high degree of continuity into the national and regional plans. As a result, the Fifth Plan contained some important principles and decisions which relate not merely to the period 1966 to 1970, but to the France of 1985.[15]

As an example, the case may be cited of the long term policy affecting urban development. The problem of the excessive development of Paris has concerned the government for some time, as reflected in policies favouring the decentralization of industry and tertiary employment. The dominant position of the national capital is a result not only of its own dynamic growth but also of a fundamental lack of balance in the hierarchy of urban centres, both in terms of size and spatial arrangement. The government has thus proposed the creation of eight 'métropoles d'équilibre', for preferential expansion in terms of their industrial, com-

*The Commissariat Général du Plan has established as a target that 40 per cent of all new jobs created between 1962 and 1985 should be located in western France.

Plate 3. Urban expansion. Rapidly growing regional relay centres: *above*, Rouen; *below*, Grenoble
(*Above*, By courtesy of Paris Normandie; *below*, By courtesy of French Government Tourist Office)

mercial and cultural functions.[16] The role of these regional metropolises will be two-fold; to counterbalance the excessive concentration of the nation's economic and cultural substance on the Paris region, and also to act as poles of development within their respective city regions. This second function is seen as crucial in the future of western France, where

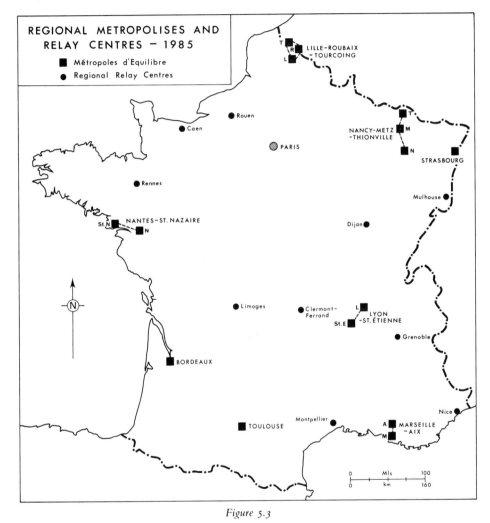

REGIONAL METROPOLISES AND
RELAY CENTRES – 1985
■ Métropoles d'Equilibre
● Regional Relay Centres

Figure 5.3

the creation of positive growth points could act as levers to lift economic development on a regional scale. To achieve this diffusion process, it is anticipated that intermediate regional centres, termed 'centres-relais', will act as transmitters of economic forces emanating from the regional metropolises. Ten such centres, illustrated in *Figure 5.3*, have been proposed. These long-term projections are clearly of great importance as a guideline to shorter-term investment in communications, the expansion of educational and research institutions, decentralization policies, and a great number of other matters where decision-making requires long term perspective and coordination.

French planning has evolved by stages, culminating in a highly elaborate machinery. State planning remains the supreme institution and thus perpetuates the tradition of centralization. Nevertheless, a regional framework has been established which serves both as a reference in the drafting of the national plans and as a medium for their execution. While the regional approach permits an attack on basic disparities of development, regional planning is not merely an equalizing force. Guided by the long-term view of prospective planning, the fundamental objective of the regional apparatus is to allow each region to reach the maximum level of development consonant with the optimum utilization of the nation's human and physical resources. The next logical stage must be in the direction of greater coordination within the structure of the Common Market and the formalization of international regions which already exist as economic realities.[17,18] The main criticism of the present system is that in spite of an elaborate structure, allocation of budget funds and the power of decision on their use remains vested in the central government. The regional reforms, under discussion at the time of writing, foreshadow a greater degree of autonomy vested in regional administrations, with an effective participation of representatives of regional interests.[19]

REFERENCES

[1] Massé, P., 'Economic Planning in France', *P.E.P. Rep.*, Vol. XXVII, No. 454.
[2] Commissariat Général du Plan, 'Fifth Plan-Economic and Social Development, 1966–1970', *Documn fr.*, 1966.
[3] Robertson, B., *Regional Development in the European Economic Community*, p. 49, 1962, London, George Allen and Unwin.
[4] Clout, H., 'France renovates her rural areas', *Tn Ctry Plann.*, 1968, p. 312.
[5] E.E.C. Commission, *La Politique Régionale dans la Communauté Economique Européenne*, pp. 102–108, 1964, Brussels.
[6] Labasse, J., 'La portée géographique des programmes d'action régionale français', *Annls Géogr.*, 1960, p. 371.
[7] Gravier, J., *Paris et le Désert Français*, 1947, Paris, Flammarion.
[8] Thompson, I., 'Some problems of regional planning in predominantly rural environments; the French experience in Corsica', *Scott. geogr. Mag.*, 1966, pp. 120–123.
[9] Guichard, O., *Aménager la France*, p. 217, 1965, Paris, Laffont-Gonthier.
[10] 'La régionalisation du budget de l'état et l'aménagement du territoire', *Notes Etud. docum.*, No. 3,243, 1965.
[11] Phliponneau, M., 'Le budget régionalisé de 1964 et la loi-programme', *Vie bretonne*, No. 72–73, 1963, p. 5.
[12] Stirn, A., 'Le préfet de region', *Vie bretonne*, No. 102, 1967, p. 13.
[13] Délégation à l'Aménagement du Territoire et de l'Action Régionale, *Aides au développement régional*, 1966, Paris.
[14] *France—Town and Country Environment Planning*, 1965, New York, French Embassy.
[15] Massé, P., 'Réflections pour 1985', *Documn fr.*, 1964.
[16] 'Métropoles Régionales', *Documn Photogr.*, No. 5-244, 1964.
[17] Hirsch, E., 'French planning and its European application', *J. Common Market Stud.*, Vol. 1, 1962, p. 117.
[18] Maclennan, M., 'The Common Market and French planning', *J. Common Market Stud.*, Vol. III, 1965, p. 23.
[19] Elkins, T., 'France and its regions', *New Society*, 13 February, 1969, p. 240.

6

The Production of Energy

The level of consumption of energy is an accepted index of the economic status of a nation and the rate of increase in consumption correlates directly with the rate of economic growth and rise in living standards. The fact that French energy consumption has doubled in the past two decades and currently increases at approximately six per cent per annum, is evidence of a rapid economic and social evolution which imposes certain strains on the power industry. The insatiable rise in demand, coupled with the need to adjust the infrastructure of production to a new balance between the various sources of energy, has called into existence a profound revolution in the power industry since the Second World War, and will continue to transform its character during the next decade.

THE CONDITIONS OF ENERGY PRODUCTION[1,2,3]

The most fundamental problem confronting French energy policies is the overall deficit of domestic resources. At the present time domestic sources yield approximately 60 per cent of the nation's needs and it is estimated that this proportion will fall to 55 per cent by 1985. This adverse balance poses problems of assuring access to increasing amounts of imported fuel sources, the growing cost in foreign exchange, and, in the case of petroleum, the need to control a substantial portion of the refining industry in the interests of national security. The deficit in domestic power resources is compounded of inadequate coal supplies and the realization of the greater proportion of the hydroelectric potential. Although France possesses large reserves of coal, the factors of inferior quality, expensive extraction and geographical maldistribution have encouraged substitution by petroleum products, which are more cheaply obtained and more easily distributed, both in physical and cost terms. Technical advances are yielding greater efficiency in the production of hydroelectricity, but suitable sites for new

87

construction are limited and the growth in output will increase at a modulated rate in future.

The deficit at the level of the national energy budget is an aggregate of profound regional variations in supply and demand. The peripheral concentration of domestic power resources poses problems of transfer to the major consuming areas and to those regions with a total lack of indigenous resources. The location of 75 per cent of coal production in the north-east, coupled with the concentration of hydroelectric capacity on, and east of, the Rhône, renders western France particulary weak in energy resources (see *Figure 6.1*). Similarly, the enormous demand of the Paris city region

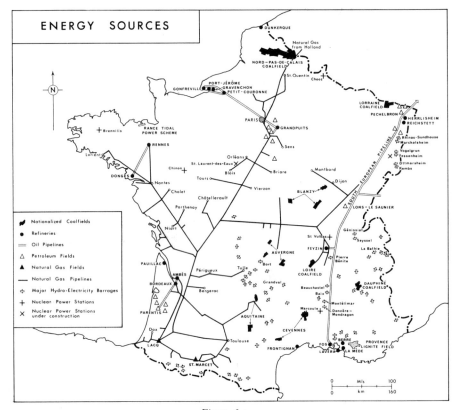

Figure 6.1

must be met by resources derived from outside the Paris Basin. The deposits of natural gas at Lacq, in the foothills of the Pyrénées, complete the overall peripheral distribution of domestic power resources. Imported fuels, chiefly petroleum, only partially offset the maldistribution of internal resources. The navigational requirements of large petroleum tankers have concentrated refinery capacity at a limited number of deep-water sites, while the economies of scale vital to this industry have encouraged the construction of large complexes rather than a widespread distribution of small refineries. The peripheral distribution of both domestic and imported energy resources creates two serious problems: the increased cost brought about by inter-regional transfer of minerals, gas and generated current to the major consuming areas, and the lack of a strong impetus to industrial growth in western France. In this latter respect, the development of the Lacq natural gas field has brought only partial relief (see *Figure 6.1*).

THE COMPOSITION OF ENERGY PRODUCTION

From 1850 to 1900 coal dominated energy supply as the motive power of the industrial revolution, the railway system and source of electricity. After the turn of the century, petroleum began to turn the wheels of private and ultimately public transport, while the techniques of hydraulic electricity generation became more fully understood and applied. The period since 1918 has witnessed an increased diversification of sources of power culminating in the development of atomic and tidal energy. The

Table 6.1

THE ENERGY RESOURCES OF FRANCE, 1964

1. Domestic resources:	
Coal production	55·3 million tons
Crude petroleum	3·0 million tons
Natural gas	5·0 milliard cubic metres
Hydroelectricity	34·7 milliard kilowatt hours
2. Imported resources:	
Coal	19·6 million tons
Crude petroleum	49·3 million tons
3. Total energy balance:	
Percentage of total consumption:	
Solid mineral fuels	45·2
Petroleum products	40·6
Natural gas	5·0
Hydroelectricity	9·2

decline of coal has been relative rather than absolute; the amount of coal consumed in 1965 was 69·2 million tons, compared with 63·9 million tons in 1950, but the proportion of the total energy supplied by coal fell from nearly 75 per cent to 40·5 per cent in this same period. While the volume of energy derived from coal has remained relatively stable in the past 20 years, the increase in the national demand has been met in large measure by an unprecedented expansion in the consumption of petroleum products.

In 1950 only 17 per cent of the power consumed in France was derived from petroleum, while in 1965 the proportion had risen to 43 per cent. While less spectacular, the contribution of natural gas has risen from one per cent in 1950 to over five per cent at the present time. After a rapid post-war expansion, the contribution made by hydroelectricity has remained relatively stable since 1957, representing approximately nine per cent of the annual energy consumption. Finally, France is on the threshold of a great expansion in the production of nuclear energy, which by 1985 is planned to supply over 30 per cent of the total electricity generated.

The conditions described above relate to patterns of gross energy production and consumption. When specific forms of energy are considered rather different trends appear. In this respect, the case of electricity generation is crucial, since this represents the most universal, most flexible and the most rapidly expanding form of energy consumed[4] (see *Table 6.2*).

Table 6.2

THE GENERATION OF ELECTRICITY IN FRANCE
(milliard kilowatt hours)

	1955	1960	1964	1965	1967
Thermal[a]	24·0	31·8	59·1	55·0	66·7
Hydro	25·5	30·6	34·7	45·3	45·0

[a]Including all kinds of thermal electricity sources: coal, lignite, natural gas, fuel oil and blast furnace gas.

After a period of approximately 30 years, in which the proportions of hydro- and thermal electricity generated were almost equal, thermal generation has established a substantial dominance since 1960. The abrupt divergence from earlier post-war trends reflects a combination of circumstances. The most cogent factor has been the enormous rise in the demand for electric current localized especially in the major industrialized agglomerations. The inexorable annual increase in demand can only be met, in the short term, by immediate increases in capacity located close to the sources of the demand. For this reason, thermal power stations, which can be built more quickly, with less capital investment and with flexible location factors operating, are better equipped to meet current increases in demand than hydraulic schemes. Moreover, since the most accessible sites have now been equipped, hydroelectricity schemes tend to demand elaborate engineering, a formidable amount of investment, require several years to complete, and in most instances are subject to seasonal fluctuations in output. In total, coal still remains the largest individual source of thermal

electricity, and in 1965 provided almost three quarters of the total produced. This is related to the continued importance of coal-fired power
stations on the northern and Lorraine coalfields, using relatively abundant
resources of low-grade coal. Elsewhere, the use of fuel oils is increasing
substantially, as it offers high efficiency and is accessible by pipeline to
several of the major urban–industrial agglomerations.

THE ORGANIZATION AND DISTRIBUTION OF ENERGY PRODUCTION

COAL

The large-scale commercial exploitation of coal took place in the middle
of the seventeenth century in the scattered fields of the Massif Central, and
for the next hundred years production was dominated by the fields of St.
Etienne, Le Creusot, Montceau-les-Mines, Alès, Graissessac, Carmaux and
Decazeville. Output remained modest until, in the middle of the nineteenth century, a transformation occurred both in the volume of production and the geographical distribution. The development of steam power,
the use of coke in the iron and steel industry and the discovery of the
Gilchrist-Thomas process for the use of phosphoric iron ores stimulated an
increase in production from 4·4 million tons in 1850, to 34·5 million tons
in 1900. The discovery of the western extension of the Nord field into
Pas-de-Calais, and of the Lorraine deposits, produced a movement north-
eastwards in mining activity, and by 1900 over 60 per cent of the national
output was extracted in these two basins. From 1900 until the outbreak of
the Second World War production increased more slowly, punctuated by
declines during the First World War and the depression years* By 1938
output reached 46 million tons, of which approximately 60 per cent was
produced in the Nord, Pas-de-Calais basin. At this time domestic coal
supplied 56 per cent of all the energy produced in France, while imported
coal swelled the proportion to 83 per cent.
  Wartime disruption and the post-war energy shortage were major
factors in the nationalization of an industry which had long laboured under
structural deficiencies of organization which undermined its efficiency. The
system of awarding concessions had established a large number of companies free to control their output and marketing, whereas joint invest-
ments and cooperation in marketing would have made for greater
efficiency and cheaper production. Although 11 large companies controlled

*The pre-war record figure was in 1930 at 55 million tons, an output unequalled until 1952.

92 per cent of the production in 1938, their concessions were heavily fragmented, especially in the Nord, Pas-de-Calais field. The existence of large companies represented a high degree of horizontal concentration but vertical integration with steel manufacture, power generation and the chemical industry was little developed. The industry, prior to nationalization, was based on strongly individual companies whose activities were based on general market conditions, with production increasing during periods of sustained economic growth and declining during recessions. Long-term planning of investment was exceptional, and indeed difficult, in view of the lack of integration with the major consuming industries. When the industry was nationalized, in 1946, it was characterized by an irrational organization, generally outmoded equipment and a relatively low level of productivity.*

Confronted with a critical shortage of coal after the war and with little possibility of importing because of currency deficiencies and the lack of surplus production in western Europe, the Monnet Plan selected the coal industry as one of the sectors for preferential expansion and a modernization plan was put into operation. The new unit of organization was that of the 'Houillères de Bassin', representing the entire coalfields in the case of Nord, Pas-de-Calais, Lorraine[5] and St. Etienne,[6] and groupings of the smaller scattered fields† (*Table 6.3*).

Table 6.3

THE HOUILLERES DE BASSIN OF THE NATIONALIZED INDUSTRY

1. Nord, Pas-de-Calais
2. Lorraine
3. Centre-Midi
   (a) Loire: St. Etienne
   (b) Cevennes: Alès, Graissessac
   (c) Blanzy: Montceau-les-Mines, Le Creusot, Decize, Epinac
   (d) Aquitaine: Carmaux, Decazeville
   (e) Provence: Gardanne lignite field
   (f) Auvergne: St. Eloi, Messeix, Brassac
   (g) Dauphiné: La Mure

Each Houillère de Bassin has a decentralized administration but overall control is exercised by the 'Charbonnages de France', responsible to the government for the coordination of activities between the different fields

---

*The Nord, Pas-de-Calais field had been taken into government control in 1944 by edict of the provisional government of General de Gaulle.

†A substantial number of small mines, chiefly in the Alps and the northern fringe of the Massif Central, producing for purely local needs, were left in private ownership. Before the war their output was two per cent of the national total and remains approximately the same at the present time.

Plate 4. Conventional sources of energy. *Above*, opencast coalmining at Decazeville, Basin of Aquitaine. *Below*, a modernized mine at Bruay, on the northern coalfield

(By courtesy of Charbonnages de France)

and the integration of the coal industry within the structure of the national plans. The questions of investment, production targets and price control are determined by the Charbonnages de France and accord directly with government policy on energy matters. In this latter respect a distinct change of emphasis in relation to coal production was formally instituted in 1960 and it is necessary to review trends before and after this date.

The immediate policy adopted after the nationalization was one of rationalization and modernization. This policy had multiple objectives: to swell output during a period of a universal shortage of coal in Europe and to increase productivity, which had suffered due to insufficient investment in advanced machinery, and which was rendered all the more vital because of labour shortages. Finally, the policy aimed to reduce the volume of imports, which had exceeded 20 million tons per annum immediately prior to the war, and thus reduce the drain on foreign currency reserves. The rationalization involved the suppression of the concession boundaries and reorganization of the mines into integrated groups with unified direction. This was accompanied by a policy of concentration, which eliminated uneconomic and obsolete mines, concentrating extraction at a reduced number of points located on the most productive sites. Because of its large extent and the high degree of fragmentation of the pre-nationalization companies, the Nord, Pas-de-Calais coalfield underwent the most drastic reorganization.[7,8]

Stimulated by the modernization plans, by the post-war fuel shortage and by a rapid rate of economic growth in the nation, coal production increased from 49 million tons in 1946 to approximately 60 million tons per annum between 1957 and 1960. During the same period productivity doubled and the number of miners was reduced from 213,200 to 132,300.[9] The increased output was not evenly distributed between the various Houillères de Bassin (*Table 6.4*).

The output of the Northern coalfield, hampered by labour shortages, disturbed seams and the need for extensive rebuilding and re-equipment, remained stationary at approximately 28 million tons. The Centre-Midi fields increased their production only marginally overall. The growth in output was sustained largely by the Lorraine field.

The year 1960 marked a watershed in the post-war coal industry. In this year the government introduced a 'Plan d'Adaptation', a policy designed to adjust coal production to changes in the nation's energy needs and sources of supply. The plan envisaged a reduction in output to 53 million tons in 1965, a decline of 10 per cent over the 1959 total. The greatest reductions, over 20 per cent, were applied to the Centre-Midi basins, and reductions of 4·3 per cent and 10·8 per cent respectively for the Northern and Lorraine coalfields. The reduction of the production target

Table 6.4

THE OUTPUT OF THE HOUILLERES DE BASSIN, 1946–1960
(million metric tons)

	1946	1950	1954	1958	1960
Nord, Pas-de-Calais	28·4	27·6	28·7	28·8	28·9
Lorraine	6·1	10·3	13·0	14·9	14·7
Loire	4·0	3·6	3·3	3·5	3·0
Cevennes	2·4	2·7	2·8	3·1	2·6
Blanzy	2·3	2·6	2·6	2·7	2·6
Aquitaine	1·7	1·9	1·9	2·2	2·1
Auvergne	1·1	1·0	1·1	1·2	1·1
Dauphiné	0·4	0·4	0·5	0·3	0·7
Provence	1·1	1·0	1·1	1·5	1·3

Source: Rapports de Gestion, 'Charbonnages de France'.

represented a reversal of the policy expounded since 1946 and reflected a change in the criteria by which energy production was evaluated. The prior emphasis, on an increased volume of domestic output, conditioned by fuel shortages and lack of foreign currency, was replaced by a qualitative appraisal of the relative cost of the various alternative resources, both domestic and imported. This reappraisal was made possible by virtue of a much improved foreign trading position, the discovery of Saharan oil, the exploitation of the Lacq natural gas, the reduced price of coal in international trade and the prospect of atomic power at a price competitive with conventional sources. Viewed against these developments, and taking into account the likely long-term perspective, a reduced output of coal was judged desirable. The substitution of cheaper and more efficient fuels, already an established trend, implied a declining demand for coal, while, by corollary, the coal industry could only remain competitive on price by further closures of the less productive mines. The national output realized in 1967 was 49·2 million tons; slightly below the target established by the policy of the Plan d'Adaptation.

The present activities of the Charbonnages de France must be viewed in the perspective of the Fifth National Plan, which has established a target of 48 million tons for 1970, a continuation of the rhythm of a reduction of one million tons per annum established during the Fourth Plan. On the other hand, the processing and manufacturing sector of the industry will be substantially strengthened. The ancillary industries account for approximately half of the organization's activity, and since these offer an assured market for coal their expansion is of direct interest. In 1966, the Charbonnages de France operated 27 power stations, and its 12 coking plants supply more than half the metallurgical coke consumed by the steel industry. In association with private companies, Charbonnages de France control a major portion of the chemical industry. The scope of these industrial interests will be enlarged during the Fifth Plan by the development of a petroleum-coal complex on the Lorraine coalfield at Carling, linked by pipeline to German plants, and producing ammonia, plastics and fertilizers. In addition, a heavy-water plant has been established at Mazingarbe, on the Northern Coalfield, to supply the needs of the atomic energy industry.

The role of the coal industry is still evolving, from a pre-war emphasis merely on extraction towards an industrial complex producing power and a wide range of base materials and finished products. It will supply a declining proportion of the nation's energy but is enlarging the output of processed commodities for which there is a growing demand.*

PETROLEUM

Prior to the Second World War, France occupied a leading position in the European petroleum refining industry. This had been achieved by government protection in the form of customs and licence restrictions, and by virtue of an ambitious programme of refinery construction by both French and foreign interests. The capacity of the 15 refineries in operation in 1938 was eight million tons, which substantially exceeded the demands of the home market. Production was completely disrupted by the war and at the close of hostilities capacity had been reduced by over 80 per cent.† The post-war fuel and foreign currency shortages dictated an urgent programme of refinery construction, an intensified search for petroleum resources in France and her overseas territories, and an increased use of Middle East oil to conserve dollar and sterling currency.

In 1938, the only domestic source of petroleum was the small field at Pechelbron, in Alsace. Exploited since 1866 and refined locally at Merckwiller, the output was steadily declining and yielding a mere 37,000 tons of refined produce when production ceased in 1963. At the close of 1949, the Société Nationale des Pétroles d'Aquitaine discovered an oilfield at Lacq, in the foothills of the Pyrénées. The quality and yield were mediocre and were soon overshadowed by more substantial discoveries of natural gas at the same site in 1951. The major domestic source of petroleum was struck in 1954 at Parentis, in the Landes, by the French subsidiary of Esso-Standard. Subsequent discoveries led to the establishment of the Parentis-

*The Charbonnages de France constitutes the largest single business enterprise in France after the nationalized railways (S.N.C.F.).

†The refineries at Dunkerque and Pauillac were totally destroyed, and the remainder suffered damage through lack of maintenance and Allied bombing.

Born oilfield, situated around the Etang de Biscarosse and linked by pipe-line to the refineries of Bordeaux and Bec d'Ambès. In 1956, the search was intensified in the Brie region of the Paris Basin, where the first major strike was made in 1958 at Coulommes, followed by discoveries at Châteaurenard, Chailly, Brie-Chartrettes and at Saint-Martin de Bossenay. The total domestic output of petroleum in 1965 amounted to 2·9 million tons, of which the Parentis-Born field supplied 2·3 million tons.

In spite of the new discoveries, domestic resources supply only six per cent of the petroleum refined in France. The post-war surge in demand has been met by an unprecedented rise in imports and enlargement of refinery capacity[10] In 1966, France had 17 refineries with a total capacity of 62 million tons. Distinct changes in the pattern of refinery location have taken place since the war, related to specific developments in the bulk transportation of crude oil. Two major trends have occurred: the con-centration of refining at a limited number of deep-water sites and the recent construction of major inland refineries. The advent of super-tankers in excess of 100,000 tons has favoured sites with deep draughts and ease of manoeuvring. Additionally, the greater volumes discharged from single vessels have necessitated expansions in refinery and storage capacity to permit the rapid turn-around of super-tankers necessary for their economic utilization. In this context, the Seine estuary and the Etang de Berre have enjoyed advantages. Both can accept large vessels and the former is close to the major market, Paris, with which it is connected by pipelines, while the latter has an ideal location for importing Middle East and North African oil, which now provide the bulk of French supplies of crude oil[11] Expansion of the other coastal refineries has been on a more modest scale, with the exception of Dunkerque. Here, the French subsidiary of British Petroleum built a refinery which is being enlarged to a capacity of six million tons per annum. A deep water terminal has been built for tankers of up to 80,000 tons. The expansion at Dunkerque and lesser developments on the Loire estuary and the Gironde are completely over-shadowed by the Seine and Etang de Berre complexes, which now account for approxi-mately 60 per cent of the nation's output of refined products.

The selection of inland sites for refinery construction is a recent trend facilitated by the development of pipelines[12] Specifically, the completion of the South European Pipeline,[13] in 1962, linking Lavéra with Karlsruhe, in West Germany, supplies crude petroleum to the new refinery at Feyzin, near Lyon, and to two new refineries at Strasbourg, Reichstett and Herrlisheim.* The cheap bulk transport of crude petroleum by pipeline has permitted the movement of the point of refining towards the market, which in the case of Strasbourg is potentially international in scope.

*The pipeline had a capacity of 25 million tons per annum in 1965.

Since 1950, the consumption of petroleum has doubled every five years, and in the single year of 1964 refining capacity increased from 51 to 61 million tons. The certain continuation of the upward trend in demand implies the need for additional refineries and involves decisions on the location of future capacity. The separation of terminal facilities from refineries by the use of connecting pipelines has permitted a greater flexibility in location. While deep water will become increasingly vital for the construction of terminals, economic arguments favour the location of refineries as close as possible to the areas of consumption.

Table 6.5

PRODUCTION OF REFINED PRODUCTS, 1964

	Net production[a]	Capacity[b]
Lower Seine		
Gonfreville (C.F.R.)	6,658	10,200
Port Jérôme (Esso)	3,956	4,000
Petit Couronne (Shell Berre)	4,876	5,500
Gravenchon (Mobil Oil)	951	1,100
Etang de Berre		
La Mède (C.F.R.)	5,771	6,400
Berre (Shell Berre)	3,677	6,000
Lavéra (B.P.)	3,522	4,400
Fos-sur-mer (Esso standard)[c]	–	3,000
Gironde		
Pauillac (Shell Berre)	303	500
Ambes (U.I.P.)	1,679	1,750
Bordeaux (Esso)	2,183	2,000
Strasbourg		
Reichstett (R.de.R.)	2,705	3,700
Herrlisheim (R.de.S.)	3,244	3,300
Other		
Dunkerque (B.P.)	3,253	5,500
Donges (Antar)	3,339	3,850
Feyzin (U.G.P.)	718	2,000
Frontignan (Mobiloil)	1,432	1,730
Rennes (Antar)[3]	–	1,200
Total	48,267	66,130

[a]Thousand metric tons.
[b]Thousand metric tons at the end of 1964.
[c]Refinery completed in 1965.
C.F.R. —Compagnie Française de Raffinage.
U.G.P. —Union Générale des Pétroles.
U.I.P. —Union Industrielle des Pétroles.
R.de.R.—Compagnie Rhénane de Raffinage (Shell).
R.de.S. —Société de Raffinage de Strasbourg (C.F.R.).

New refineries were completed in 1965 at Fos and at Rennes, the latter being connected to the oil port of Donges on the Loire estuary. In the course of the Fifth Plan a refinery will be built at Porcheville, near Paris, with a capacity of 3·6 million tons and at Grandpuits* in Seine-et-Marne, with a capacity of 2·8 million tons. New refineries are proposed for the Valenciennes area, linked by pipeline to Dunkerque, for Metz in Lorraine, and for Vernon, midway between Paris and Rouen.

NATURAL GAS

The strike of natural gas at Lacq in 1951 constituted the largest individual discovery of primary power resources made in the last hundred years. It had been preceded by exploitation in 1941 of gas found at St. Marcet in Haute-Garonne, which was fed by pipeline to Tarbes and Toulouse. The discovery of the Lacq deposit, some 20 kilometres west of Pau, followed the strike of a small oilfield, 'Lacq Supérieur', at the end of 1949. The continuation of borings to a depth of 3,550 metres revealed the existence of a natural gas field 15 kilometres long and seven kilometres wide with recuperable reserves of 200 milliard cubic metres†. The conditions of extraction are extremely difficult since the gas occurs under very high pressure, at extreme temperatures of 140°C. and has a highly corrosive composition‡. Prior to distribution, the gas is treated to remove the acid constituents and to recover sulphur, propane, butane and petrol. Over four milliard cubic metres of treated gas are produced per annum; equivalent to the energy derived from seven million tons of coal.

The marketing of the Lacq gas required the resolution of conflicting opportunities.[14,15] The location in south-western France, lacking in major fuel resources, argued in favour of a distribution within the region to act as a springboard for industrial development. Alternatively, the transfer of the gas to the Paris region offered a simple distribution that was capable of absorbing the entire output. Both of these proposals had counter-arguments. The restriction of distribution to the south-west would not have afforded a large enough market to permit low-cost operation. Similarly a disgorgement of the entire production in the Paris region alone would have disrupted the established pattern of fuel supply. A compromise policy was adopted which afforded a relatively widespread distribution at a volume of consumption consonant with fully economic operation. The gas is distributed by two pipeline systems. Within Aquitaine the distribution is achieved partly by the existing pipelines of the St. Marcet field and partly by new pipelines serving especially the needs of Toulouse,

---

*The Grandpuits refinery is now in production.
†The nature of the strike was spectacular. The boring triggered off a serious explosion and escape of gas which was not controlled until two months later.
‡Exploitation of the gas was not possible until special steels had been developed to construct pipelines resistant to corrosion.

Tarbes, Pau, Bayonne and Bordeaux. Secondly, the area north of the Garonne is reached by a trunk artery to St. Benoit, south of Châteauroux, from which regional pipelines branch off. The principal branches serve Nantes, Lorient and Rennes, Clermont-Ferrand, Lyon–St. Etienne, Châlon-Sur-Saône, Dijon and Besançon, and the central Paris Basin.

Less than half the gas is retained in the south-west. Approximately one third is consumed by Electricité de France for use in the power stations at Artix on the gas field, Bordeaux, Nantes and Paris. Gaz de France buys a rather smaller amount for public distribution in the major agglomerations. The largest individual consumer is manufacturing, especially the chemical sector. From a position of insignificance in 1956, natural gas has now become an important source of power, contributing five per cent of the nation's energy budget. The nation's indigenous supply is supplemented by imports of gas by pipeline from the Netherlands, which since the end of 1967 has reached the Nord region and Paris, and by methane tanker from Algeria.

HYDROELECTRIC POWER

The conditions of her physical geography have favoured the development of hydroelectricity schemes in France, and in recent years over one third of the electricity consumed has been of hydraulic origin. The Alps and Pyrénées have afforded numerous sites with large heads of water and high-altitude catchment areas nourished by abundant precipitation and glacial melt water. Frequent breaks of slope and narrow defiles inherited from a history of intense glaciation have afforded natural sites for barrage construction and water storage. The Massif Central is the virtual water tower of France and has the specific virtue of a surface run-off regime complementary to that of the Alps and Pyrénées. Finally, the Rhône and Rhine provide large volumes of water permitting the construction of power barrages allied to the regulation of these rivers for navigation. The combination of propitious landforms, interlocking climatic regimes and great engineering skill have enabled France to draw the maximum advantage from her powerful rivers and mountain streams.[16,17] Nevertheless, certain difficulties impose limitations on the present and future utilization of hydraulic electricity.

The fundamental control is that of climate as affecting the total discharge and seasonal regime of rivers. Annual variations and seasonal fluctuations in precipitation and temperature are reflected in reciprocal variations in the amount of electricity generated. Severe and prolonged winters cause losses of production while increasing the demand, and prolonged dry spells in

Plate 5. New sources of energy. *Above*, the Roselend barrage (Savoie), which nourishes the La Bathie power station. *Below*, the Lacq natural gas field (Basses–Pyrénées)
(*Above*, By courtesy of Electricité de France; *below*, By courtesy of French Government Tourist Office)

summer reduce the output of the Massif Central stations. Implicit in the complementary regimes of the rivers of the Alps and Pyrénées with maximum discharge in summer, and the Massif Central with maximum discharge in winter, is the fact that at no single period can the maximum installed capacity be fully utilized. In fact, the various types of power scheme fulfil different roles related to contrasted patterns of demand. Thus the Rhône and Rhine plants, free from problems of storage, are capable of almost continuous output. On the other hand, the Alps, Pyrénées and Massif Central experience seasonal fluctuations in output, and during their most active season require time for refilling of the reservoirs. The process of refilling has been shortened by the use of pumping to supplement natural flow, but the periodic mode of operation necessitates generation to be coordinated with the hours of peak demand. The most serious handicaps as far as the future expansion of hydroelectricity generation is concerned are the shortage of further suitable sites and the increased investment necessary to equip difficult sites. Present expansion of capacity is thus tied to major integrated schemes, as those of the Rhône and Durance basins, involving multipurpose development to secure an economic return on high investment costs. Elsewhere the trend is towards the construction of complexes with very large power stations using water diverted from a number of basins rather than small-scale individual schemes. This latter trend is especially the case in the northern Alps,[18] where Tignes, on the Isère, and Randens, on the Arc, were early examples of this system. Other complex developments have been built on the Drac at Le Sautet, the Romanche at Chambon and at Bissorte on the Arc. Similarly, the La Bathie power station, near Albertville on the Isère, utilizes the waters retained by the St. Guérin, La Cittaz and Roselend dams. This pattern of complex development is being continued in the Mont Cenis scheme, a joint construction by the French and Italian electricity authorities. A new dam has been built on the French side of the frontier, supplying power stations at Modane in France and Venous in Italy. Although the alpine region contributed 50·8 per cent of the hydraulic energy generated in France in 1965, the high cost and difficult engineering involved in equipping the remaining potential sites ensures that an increased proportion of future production will be of fluvial rather than mountain origin, and especially from the Rhône, Rhine and Durance schemes*

NUCLEAR ENERGY [19, 20]

The French effort in harnessing atomic energy dates from the immediate post-war period when the 'Commissariat à l'Energie Atomique' was

*In 1965 the Massif Central provided 22 per cent of the total hydroelectricity generated, the Pyrénées 13·4 per cent, and the Rhône and Rhine schemes 13·8 per cent.

Plate 6. New sources of energy. *Below*, the nuclear power station of Chinon (Indre-et-Loire). *Above*, the tidal power scheme on the Rance estuary near St. Malo (Ille-et-Vilaine)
(By courtesy of Electricité de France)

established. Prior to the last war, France held a prominent position in the field of fundamental research into nuclear science.* The initial activities of the Commissariat were concentrated on further fundamental work in research centres and an intensification of the search for uranium in France and the dependent overseas territories. Since 1947 deposits of uranium have been exploited at Lachaix (Puy-de-Dôme), St. Symphorien-de-Marmagne and La Faye (Allier), la Crouzille in Limousin, and Clisson and Mortagne (Vendée). Overseas the major discoveries have been in Madagascar. The first large reactor was inaugurated at Marcoule near Orange, in 1957, commissioned essentially for the production of plutonium for military uses. Two further reactors have been built at Marcoule and although their purpose remains primarily military, the feed substantial amounts of electricity into the national grid. Commercial atomic electricity production by Electricité de France began on an experimental basis at Chinon, near the confluence of the Loire and Vienne rivers. The site was selected because of the large amounts of water required for the natural uranium–graphite–gas system and its location in an area lacking alternative power sources. The reactor EDF 1, with a capacity of 70 megawatts, fed power into the grid in mid-1963. A second reactor, EDF 2, was commissioned at Chinon in 1964, with a capacity of 200 megawatts, and EDF 3 in 1966 with a capacity of 480 megawatts. The experience obtained at Chinon provided the technological knowledge for the design of a larger reactor being built at St. Laurent-des-Eaux, between Orléans and Blois, which had a capacity of 500 megawatts when completed in 1968. A small reactor of 70 megawatts was commissioned at Brennilis, in the Monts d'Arée in central Brittany in 1966. A further plant, built at Chooz in the Ardennes, was built under the auspices of EURATOM; the capacity of 266 megawatts will be shared by France and Belgium. Other new nuclear power stations under construction are at Fessenheim on the Rhine and at St. Vulbas, 35 kilometres upstream from Lyon on the Rhône. The latter is scheduled for completion in 1971 and will have a capacity of 540 megawatts, the largest individual installed capacity of any reactor in France. Preliminary studies are being carried out for a plant at Golfech, on the Garonne.

The future expansion of the industry is assured in view of the rising demand for electricity, the need to diversify sources of energy and the possibility of location in areas deficient in power resources. For the most efficient operation, plants of the future will need to be in the 1,000 megawatt class which will almost certainly lead to the adoption of enriched uranium fuels.

*At the time of the German occupation, many of the leading nuclear scientists escaped to Britain, taking with them the largest amount of heavy water produced at that time in the world.

TIDAL POWER

The sole example of commercial production of electricity from the tides, not only in France but in the world, is the Rance scheme,[21] located five kilometres south-west of St. Malo. The specific advantages of this location are the extreme tidal range, which at the equinox reaches 13·5 metres, and the vast storage capacity of the ria of the lower Rance. Construction of a barrage 750 metres long began in 1961 and the first electricity was generated in 1966. The scheme was inaugurated in 1967 by which time 16 of the eventual 24 horizontal turbines had been installed. The turbines require a minimum head of water of 4 ft 8 in., conditions which are fulfilled for eight hours per day on average, with a maximum of 12 hours at spring-tides and only four hours at neap tides. However, at night and at weekends off-peak current is used to activate the turbines as hydraulic pumps to increase the head of water behind the barrage and thus reduce the non-productive periods. The scheme is extremely flexible and can generate power during both the filling and emptying of the storage basin; it has a capacity of 5·4 milliard kilowatt-hours, and together with the atomic power station at Brennilis★ brings power to northern and central Brittany, otherwise lacking in domestic energy resources. A similar scheme has been studied for the Bay of St. Michel but the formidable engineering difficulties of constructing a barrage on insecure foundations 35 kilometres long and in face of an even greater tidal range preclude such a development for the foreseeable future in view of the technical and financial obstacles.

REFERENCES

[1] Chardonnet, J., *Géographie Industrielle*, Tome I, 1962, Paris, Sirey.
[2] Gamblin, A., *L'Energie en France: étude de géographie*, 1963, Paris, CDU.
[3] Mainguy, Y., 'Eléments d'une géographie économique de l'énergie en France; Généralités', *Revue fr. Energ.*, No. 136, 1962.
[4] Laigroz, J., 'Perspectives nouvelles de l'énergie électrique en France, l'inventaire du potentiel de production', *Annls Géogr.*, 1955, p. 17.
[5] Haby, R., *Les Houillères Lorraines et leur région*, Vol. 1, 1965, Paris, SABRI.
[6] Schnetzler, J., 'Le bassin houiller de la Loire', *Inf. géogr.*, 1966, p. 110.
[7] Thompson, I., 'A geographical appraisal of recent trends in the northern coalfield of France', *Geography*, 1965, p. 252.
[8] Thompson, I., 'A review of problems of economic and urban development in the northern coalfield of France', *Southampton Res. Ser. Geogr.*, No. 1, 1965, pp. 38–9.
[9] 'Evolution de la productivité globale dans l'extraction française de charbon', *Etud. Conjonct.*, 1960, No. 11, p. 887.
[10] Anon., 'Fiches techniques des raffineries françaises', *Pétrol. Inf.*, No. 435, 1967, pp. 67–70, 73–80, 83–88.
[11] Hoyle, B., 'Oil refineries and oil pipelines in France', *Scott. Geogr. Mag.*, 1959, p. 172.
[12] Fischer, A., 'Oléoducs et gazoducs dans le Marché Commun', *Inf. géogr.*, 1966, p. 191.
[13] Debrabant, H., 'Le pipeline Sud-européen, aspects techniques et économiques', *Revue Navig. intér. rhén.*, 1963, p. 377.

★The Brennilis reactor is as yet only experimental.

[14] Fouchier, J., 'Considérations économiques sur Lacq', *Revue fr. Energ.*, 1955.

[15] Brunet, R., 'Lacq, le pétrole et le Sud-Ouest', *Revue Géogr. Pyrénées S.-Ouest*, 1958, p. 361.

[16] Nicod, J., 'Types d'installations hydro-électriques', *Inf. géogr.*, 1963, p. 1.

[17] Kish, G., 'Hydro-electric power in France. Plans and projects', *Geogrl Rev.*, 1955, p. 81.

[18] Ritter, J., 'L'aménagement hydro-électrique du bassin de l'Isère', *Annls Géogr.*, 1959, p. 34.

[19] 'Le développement nucléaire français depuis 1945', *Notes Etud. docum.*, No. 3,246, 1965.

[20] Ginier, J., 'L'énergie nucléaire en France', *Inf. géogr.*, 1965, p. 9.

[21] Jones, I., 'The Rance tidal power station', *Geography*, 1968, p. 412.

7

Transport

Space without adequate transport facilities presents a barrier; it is transport which breathes economic life into space. This axiom is particularly apt in the case of France. As late as the mid-nineteenth century, stonemasons walked from Creuse to Paris to seek work, while throughout rural France, horses, mules and oxen formed the most universal form of transport. A century later, France has reached out into space, tunnelled under Mont Blanc, has the most rapid long-distance trains in Europe and is participating in the construction of a supersonic airliner. The density of the transport network and the level of private car ownership are among the highest in the world, and yet certain large regions are inadequately integrated into the national space as a result of deficiencies in the transport system.

The increased mobility of population and goods is the greatest single social and economic change of the past century and, as such, has created both opportunities and strains. The most striking repercussions have been the impetus to urbanization and the breakdown of the isolation of rural France. Paradoxically, the ability to move further and more freely than ever before throughout the national space has produced a greater concentration of population into limited areas. This trend has progressed to such a degree that movement within the large cities is becoming increasingly difficult, at the precise points where the network is most elaborate. The expansion and diversification of transport has transformed rural France in equal measure, breaking down the simple rural–urban relationship between the countryside and market towns and swelling the importance of the regional capitals as centres of economic, social and cultural activity. The static pattern of rural life, undisturbed for centuries, has given way before new opportunities and aspirations extending beyond parochial confines. The 'disenclavement' of rural areas inevitably found its response in rural–urban migration and rural depopulation, to such a degree that the public transportation developments which permitted this movement are no longer warranted by the residual demand of a greatly reduced rural population. Above all, the modern expansion of communications has reinforced the centripetal strength of Paris, the regional capitals and the major industrial nodes. Thus far economic forces have moulded the transport system, with resultant centralizing effects. The advent of long-term prospective planning envisages the creation of new transport links as a force directing economic growth, in concert with policies of decentralization.

The tasks for the future development of the transport network are those of adaptation and integration. The French transport system must be adapted to the scale and standards of the European Economic Community if she is to gain the maximum advantage from the increased size of the market. The former interest in maintaining the security of frontiers has been superseded by penetration of international boundaries along new rail, motorway, canal and pipeline arteries linking the member countries. Secondly, if the peripheral regions of western France are to benefit from membership of the Common Market, they must, in the first instance, be more effectively integrated into the national network.

ROAD TRANSPORT

The road network of France is the end product of a complex evolution since Celtic times.[1,2] This inheritance provides France with the densest road network in Europe, over 775,000 kilometres in length (*Table 7.1*), but one which has severe deficiencies in terms of present and future needs. The period since 1945 has witnessed an unprecedented rise in road traffic leading to severe congestion in urban centres and an inadaptation of the main inter-urban roads to the present volume of traffic.

Table 7.1

THE FRENCH ROAD NETWORK, 1967

	kilometres
Routes nationales	80,000
Routes départementales	280,000
Routes communales	415,000
Routes urbaines[a]	45,000
Autoroutes[b]	788

[a]This figure is also included in the category 'routes communales'.
[b]Completed motorway at the end of 1966.

Three serious deficiencies in the road transport system may be elaborated: the inadequacy of the network structure, the problem of congestion, and the need to coordinate international motorway links.

The deliberate focusing of 'routes nationales' on Paris, from the sixteenth century onwards, has left lacunae in the network in terms of inter-regional links. This is particularly the case in the western half of the nation, where the lack of heavy industry excluded the play of economic forces sufficiently strong to overcome the political forces of centralization. In the past, the needs of a predominantly agricultural economy in the west were adequately met by the network of secondary and local roads, together with main road and railway connections to Paris, the chief market for surplus produce. Although a remodelling of the basic network is not feasible, a priority need is to improve the capacity of the existing inter-regional connections both within western France and transversally to the Mediterranean and the north. Such improvements would integrate the major ports of the west more effectively with their hinterlands and create situations for new industries that would have access to the major urban markets of eastern France.

The problem of congestion does not apply to the entire network, but is localized in the major conurbations and to the inter-urban highways linking the industrial regions of eastern France. The problem is thus two-fold: the decongestion of urban centres throughout the nation and the improvement of trunk routes linking the manufacturing centres and ports of eastern France. In turn, these problems stem from two basic causes: the vast rise in private car ownership and the use of private transport in commuting, and the transfer of goods traffic from canals and railways to the more flexible road system.* In addition to the failure of the road-building programme to keep pace with these trends, it may be suggested that uneven distribution in the growth of employment since the war has added to the strain placed on the network of eastern France and, above all, that of the Paris city region. The saturation of the roads in and between the major manufacturing cities must be attributed to the small proportion of multiple-land highway and motorways in the total network. At the end of 1966, the 788 kilometres of motorway completed were essentially distributed along a single axis from Lille to Marseille via Paris. No inter-urban motorways are to be found in the western two thirds of France, nor do any east–west motorways exist.

The problem of congestion becomes most severe in the major urban agglomerations, where through-traffic competes with business and commuter traffic for the use of the same road system. With the exception of Paris, and to a lesser extent, Lyon, Marseille and Lille, intra-urban motorways are absent from the road network. To some extent by-pass roads and

*Private car ownership has risen from 4·4 million vehicles in 1955 to 10·5 million at the present time.

diversions for heavy traffic solve the problems of through traffic, while the establishment of 'zones bleues' eases the circulation and parking of business traffic in the centre of towns, but neither of these expedients solves the problem of the growing volume of commuter traffic*

A final problem, less serious as far as internal circulation within France is concerned, is the need to improve links with other European neighbours, especially in the form of motorways. This particularly applies to the coordination of motorway development within the Common Market, where agreement on the alignment and specifications of motorways will greatly ease the international flow of traffic. Since 1966, the member countries have adhered to a consultation agreement which, as in the case of inland waterways, will shape the outlines of future links.[3]

The development of the road system in the course of the Fifth Plan must be assessed against the three deficiencies outlined above. The Fifth Plan called for a rate of motorway construction of 200 kilometres per annum. The details of the programme are illustrated in *Figure 7.1*. This rate would permit the completion of the Paris–Lille motorway and the greater proportion of the Paris–Lyon–Marseille motorway. This axis, from the Channel to the Mediterranean, is clearly to be the spine of the future motorway system, from which a number of spurs will diverge. During the Fifth Plan spurs will be completed from Lille to the Belgian frontier, from Lyon to St. Etienne and from Lyon to Voreppe. Work will also begin on new spurs from the Nord motorway towards Valenciennes, from the Lyon–Marseille motorway towards Aix-en-Provence, and also on the Grenoble and Chambéry spurs. The Nancy–Metz and Mulhouse–Basle motorways are also due for completion by 1970. The remaining programme consists of extensions to existing 'autoroutes' and the initiation of new ones on the basis of discontinuous sections. Sections of intra-urban motorway are to be completed in Paris as part of the overall remodelling of the transport system in the region encompassed by the master plan,[4] and at Marseille, where motorway connections are to be made from the city to the expanding industrial area of the Etang de Berre.

Road improvements have been sanctioned affecting over 5,000 kilometres of 'routes nationales'. In general the works consist of local diversions and by-passes, realignments and renewal of engineering works. Credits have also been authorized for the widening of 1,700 kilometres of highway to three or four lanes. Main roads radiating from the 'métropoles d'équilibre' are to be subject to integral improvement, consonant with the policy of strengthening their role as regional capitals. Integral improve-

*In many of the older towns and cities, the external boulevard along the lines of former fortifications has provided a partial ring-road by-pass for through traffic, though still necessitating the traversing of suburban areas generating large volumes of commuter traffic. 'Zones bleues' are areas, usually confined to the central business district, where parking is restricted by time limits.

ments are also to be carried out in tourist areas where the existing roads
are saturated in the summer months.

The Fifth Plan deals solely with developments to which the state is
committing budget funds and does not concern the myriad of local
developments. As a matter of principle, these funds are allocated to road

THE MOTORWAY PROGRAMME

—————— Motorway completed 1968.
■ ■ ■ ■ ■ Motorway to be completed during the Vth Plan.
▯▯▯▯▯ Motorway to be commenced during the Vth Plan.
═══════ Longer term projects, 1975.

Figure 7.1

schemes which, in the short term, will yield the greatest economic benefit,
which explains the concentration of new road construction east of a line
from Le Havre to Marseille. The construction of motorways represents an
example where conflict between short-term and prospective planning is
particularly difficult to reconcile. The concentration of motorway building
in eastern France, where congestion is greatest and where economic

advantage will accrue most rapidly, conflicts with the longer-term policy of industrializing western France. The motorways will enhance the economic strength of the Marseille–Lyon–Paris, Paris–Le Havre and Paris–Lille–Dunkerque axes, together with the internationally orientated industrial outliers of the Rhine and Moselle valleys*

The structure of the road network will be little modified by the programme. The pattern of motorway construction will do little to offset the relative isolation of western France or to open up the Massif Central. No new lateral inter-regional connections will be completed during the Fifth Plan in western France, where the improvements in the routes nationales could easily be overtaken by the inexorable annual increase in road traffic. The programme will bring some relief to the more saturated trunk roads of eastern France but the problem of congested city centres will remain critical. In the latter case, a long-term programme of intra-urban expressways with substantial remodelling of the functional zones of the major agglomerations constitutes the only permanent solution. During the Fifth Plan, international motorway connections will be established between Lille and Belgium and from Mulhouse to Switzerland. Work will begin on a second link to Belgium via Valenciennes and from Nice towards the Italian frontier. Of these, only the Lille–Belgium link can be considered a genuine international connection since the other routes will involve only short stretches of motorway within France for a number of years to come.

By 1970, the road system will be substantially improved. Given a limited budget, and the adoption of criteria involving an immediate economic benefit, the selection of projects is realistic. The criticism could be made, nevertheless, that insufficient use is made of road planning as a method of creative prospective planning on behalf of the less-developed portions of the country.

THE RAILWAY SYSTEM

The early growth of the French railway system followed in outline the pattern established in Britain, being initiated on coalfields and spreading rapidly to the capital city.[5] From the outset, however, state influence was much more in evidence, in the planning of routes, financing of construction, and the regulation of prices. In very large measure, the present network is the result of government decisions during the nineteenth century, founded on political and egalitarian criteria rather than commercial viability.

*All of these motorways are paralleled by electrified railways, and over much of their extent by inland waterways. By contrast, the 'métropoles d'équilibre' of western France have neither motorways nor major canals.

The year 1842 marked a turning point in the development of French railways. Up to this time, the network consisted of uncoordinated fragments, mainly of short distance. A law of 1842 established the alignment of future routes and defined the organizational structure of construction and operation. A national railway plan was drawn up, and, reflecting the centralization of government, was firmly based on Paris as the focus of the network. The only transverse lines planned were from Dijon to Mulhouse and from Marseille to Bordeaux. The network was designed to link Paris with the major provincial capitals and the railways paralleled the routes nationales created a century earlier.[6] The legislation initiated a wave of railway construction, and between 1841 and 1851 the network grew from 573 kilometres to 3,554 kilometres. The proliferation of private companies led to financial failures and a series of compulsory amalgamations took place between 1852 and 1857, resulting in the constitution of six main-line companies, each having a compact regional sphere of operations. The second half of the nineteenth century witnessed the rapid construction of the secondary network, especially under the impetus of the Freycinet Act of 1878. This called for the addition of 150 new lines, assuring the linkage of every préfecture and sous-préfecture with Paris. Construction under the Freycinet Act was largely designed to serve predominantly rural areas, and a tertiary network of purely local lines, often narrow-gauge, was built concurrently, linking the smallest towns to the national system.

In the space of little more than half a century, the system had expanded from a limited number of main lines to a dense network reaching into every recess of the national space. Only in the Alps and the Massif Central was the density of the network more attenuated.[7] The railways broke down the isolation of rural France to a greater degree than the improvement of the road network, but the small volumes of freight handled, especially in western France, and the low level of passenger travel scarcely justified the creation of such a comprehensive network*. The unprofitability of the branch lines, rising operating costs, the depression years and the spread of motorized transport precipitated the nationalization of the private companies in 1937 and the creation of the 'Société Nationale des Chemins de Fer' in 1938. The period of the Second World War marked a clear break in the evolution of the French system by consequence of the vast scale of wartime destruction†. Since the war, the major trends have been modernization of equipment and infrastructure, further rationalization of the

*Schnetzler[8] is of the opinion that had the development of motor transport been anticipated, much of the network created by the Freycinet Act would never have been built.

†The number of locomotives was reduced from 15,000 pre-war to 3,000 at the time of the liberation. The destruction of the infrastructure amounted to 4 locomotive works, 24 marshalling yards, 1,965 bridges, 27 tunnels, 115 large stations and almost 2,000 miles of track.

network and an increased effort to meet competition from road transport. The modernization programme has involved much new construction of stations, depôts and marshalling yards, but the most pronounced changes have occurred in the form of motive power. The post-war decades have witnessed the progressive withdrawal of steam trains and the growth of

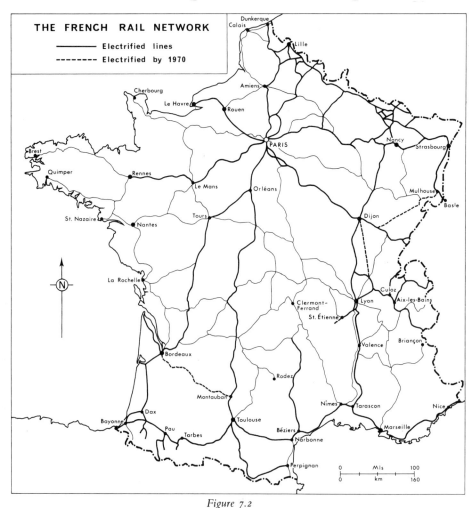

Figure 7.2

electric and diesel traction.[*] Prior to the war, electrification had been achieved on 3,340 kilometres of track; by 1965 this had been increased to 8,420 kilometres; and at the close of the Fifth Plan it will total 9,350 kilometres.

The pattern of electrification consists of four elements *Figure 7.2*. The dominant feature is the electrification of trunk arteries radiating from

[*]The total elimination of steam traction will be achieved in 1972.

Paris to major industrial cities and international boundaries. This permits swift passenger travel on the most heavily-travelled routes at a speed competitive with air travel, taking into account the relative cost. Secondly, in contrast to the axial pattern radiating from Paris, more elaborate networks have been electrified to serve the industrial and mineral districts of Nord and Lorraine. Regional networks occur too in areas producing large volumes of hydroelectricity, notably the Jura, the northern Alps and the western Pyrénées. Finally, there are two transversal electrified links, from Strasbourg to Rennes and from Marseille to Bordeaux. The economies, in terms of operating and maintenance costs, afforded by electric traction are well established, in addition to which the increased speed increases line capacity and enhances the quality of service.[*] These advantages are most fully exploited on routes where traffic volumes are high and accordingly the effort has been concentrated on inter-city, commuter and industrial routes. On the remainder of the network diesel traction has substantially replaced steam since 1950 for passenger traffic. The operating economics of diesel haulage are particularly favourable over routes where high-capacity trains are not required. Diesel railcars operate omnibus services throughout France and multiple units operate fast services over medium distances, linking with the main lines at important junctions. Whereas 70 per cent of the freight traffic is hauled by electric locomotives, as measured in ton-kilometres, diesel traction accounts for only 12 per cent.

The present network of passenger lines is illustrated in *Figure 7.2*. Local branch lines have been omitted in order to show the major long-distance routes and inter-regional connections. The map highlights the under-priviledged position of certain regions and the paucity of transversal routes. Brittany has only two principal lines west of Rennes, the rest of the region being served by narrow-gauge track and branch lines threatened with closure. Similarly, the Massif Central[9] has no major through artery, while the majority of Normandy and southern Lorraine has a skeletal network of main lines. The only direct transversal line is from Marseille to Bordeaux via Toulouse. This link, which by 1970 will be entirely electrified, represents a genuine inter-regional connection between the Rhône corridor, Languedoc and Aquitaine, and links the three southern 'métropoles d'équilibre'. The remaining major transverse routes all involve a change of line at Paris. In 1966, the S.N.C.F. proposed the withdrawal of passenger services from over 5,000 kilometres of tracks in an attempt to reduce losses[10]. The proposed measures affect particularly central Brittany, the Massif Central, Champagne and southern Lorraine, and

[*] The operating and maintenance economies of electric trains are considered to be in the order of 50 to 60 per cent over steam traction.

involve for the most part short branch lines. While current commercial criteria amply justify such action, longer-term economic and social criteria are less persuasive. Against the argument for a reduced network in order to produce a viable commercial system can be ranged the social needs of areas with uncertain connections in winter, and areas seeking, with official encouragement, to develop tourism and new industries.

The third major trend since 1945—the diversification of services and the application of tariffs—results from the growing strength of competition from road and pipeline transport. Greater success has been achieved in the case of passenger traffic than with freight. The introduction of additional sleeper accommodation, improved coaches, continuous welded rails and expanded electrification, has increased the comfort of passenger travel on the main lines. The introduction of sleeper coaches, with provision for the transport of private cars, has stimulated traffic on routes to tourist areas, while a network of Trans-Europe express connections permits rapid journeys to all the principal capitals of western Europe. The major effort in freight traffic has been concentrated on container handling and on the encouragement of homogeneous train loads of raw materials and manu-factured goods. In this respect, the provisions of special sidings for large industrial concerns and the employment of preferential tariffs have been particularly significant. The question of tariffs is a delicate issue as a result of the implications for regional economic development.[11] Reduced tariffs bring substantial returns only where the potential volume of traffic is high. In practice, this implies offering advantages along the main lines, especially of eastern France. The initial tariffs, introduced in 1947, gave concessions to customers producing full train loads and utilizing private sidings. A revision in 1951 introduced tariffs based on the point of origin and destination, with the greatest concessions applying to the cheapest routes from an operational standpoint. A reform in 1961 introduced a weighting of the various parts of the network. This system was in turn revised in 1962 and a complex system is now in operation involving the type of commodity, the distance travelled and the volume of the consign-ment. The aim of recent developments, in both equipment and tariffs, has been to establish a competitive position in the sphere of bulk handling and rapid transit.

While the general decline in freight traffic may be attributed to the greater speed and flexibility of road transport, characteristics which a modernized rail service may expect to acquire, certain specific develop-ments represent a permanent loss of traffic. The construction of waterside steel works, the reduced output of the Lorraine iron ore field and the reduced demand for domestic and imported coal have deprived the rail-ways of much traffic in basic raw materials. The canalization of the Moselle and the construction of oil pipelines represent a further diversion of trade. In the longer term, the construction of motorways parallel to the most heavily used main lines is improving the direct competitive position of road transport.

In spite of the problems which confront the railways, their importance is modified rather than diminished. Since the war, a changed role has emerged, from being a universal form of transport, with services to every small town, to a more restricted network adjusted to present demands. To some extent, this policy has resulted in a lack of coordination with other transport media[12] and with the broader aspects of the planned development of the national territory.

PORT DEVELOPMENT

The expansion of port activity in the last two decades is a direct response to the nation's rapid economic growth with its associated increases in imports of fuels and raw materials and a vigorous export effort to maintain a satisfactory trade balance. The increased maritime activity has by no means been evenly shared between the ports of France. As in other aspects of economic activity the trend has been one of concentration. The largest ports have increased their dominance, while the smaller ports have expanded at a much slower rate or even declined.[13] This trend, already apparent before the Second World War and intensified since, reflects the changed conditions of port development as compared with those of the previous century.

THE CONDITIONS OF PORT DEVELOPMENT

France has few very large ports in relation to her population and the length of her coastline. Only Marseille could be listed among the highest-ranking European ports and, even so, has handled less than half the tonnage of Rotterdam in recent years. Similarly, France's second port, Le Havre, handles less than half the tonnage of Antwerp, and Dunkerque less than half the volume of cargo handled by Genoa. In part, this phenomenon is explicable by the possession of over 3,000 kilometres of coastline, with Atlantic, Mediterranean and Channel façades, and a consequent dispersion of maritime activity. More important was the fact that even after the industrial revolution and the acquisition of overseas territories, France did not become a great maritime trading nation on the basis of her own merchant marine. As compared with the economies of Britain, Belgium and the Netherlands, the need to import great volumes of foodstuffs and raw materials was more limited, as was the volume of export goods. The natural outlet to the African and Asian colonies was the Mediterranean, where only Marseille offered an adequate site for large-scale development and access to the interior. Similarly, Le Havre was admirably positioned to dominate transatlantic trade. This bifurcation of the nation's two main trading streams has precluded the establishment of a single national port on the scale of Rotterdam or London. Moreover, unlike Britain, the continental situation of France permitted overland trade with European partners, even in bulky commodities, by canal and rail. These same conditions allowed France to utilize the ports of neighbouring countries. The canal links between north-eastern France and the Scheldt, Meuse and Rhine systems have enabled Antwerp and Rotterdam to compete successfully with the channel ports for French trade.

The expansion of the secondary ports of France was made particularly difficult by the situation of the majority of the nation's industry in the north and east. This effectively isolated the ports of Brittany and the Atlantic coast from the regions generating the largest volumes of external trade. Although a proliferation of small ports punctuates the coast between Le Havre and Bayonne, their hinterlands are small, difficult of access and do not generate return cargoes to match their imports of fuel, tropical produce, timber and chemical products. In 1937 only 11 ports handled more than one million tons of cargo, and only Marseille, Le Havre and Rouen handled over five million tons.

Since 1945 the conditions under which port activity has developed have greatly changed. The most obvious changes were those brought about in the train of the war itself in terms of destruction of port installations. Destruction of certain ports was almost total, especially in the cases of Dunkerque, Le Havre, St. Nazaire and Cherbourg. Bordeaux and Marseille also suffered heavy damage. Although this posed a critical problem of post-war reconstruction, it had the beneficial result of producing modern installations and infrastructure and an opportunity to remodel the port complexes. The reconstruction of the French ports coincided with a trend towards larger ships and the development of specialized vessels and container traffic requiring appropriate terminal facilities for bulk handling. In combination, these trends have multiplied the advantages of the large ports and caused extensions to be built specifically to the requirements of large vessels with homogeneous cargoes. This has favoured the deep-water ports with spacious berths, room for expansion and possessing a high-capacity transport network within their hinterlands. Conversely, the smaller ports, with difficult approaches and small, shallow basins have been excluded from these developments, in

Plate 7. Port development. *Above*, the port of Le Havre. In the right foreground the new oil terminal, capable of accepting tankers of over 200,000 tons. In the right background, reclaimed land for industrial development. *Below*, the new oil terminal at Le Verdon, an outport of the Bordeaux port complex

(*Above*, By courtesy of Port Autonome du Havre; *below*, By courtesy of Port Automone de Bordeaux)

most instances permanently. The growth in vessel size relative to pre-war standards applies especially to petroleum tankers* In particular, the use of super-tankers implies navigational facility and terminal capacity which can only be provided at a limited number of sites, both because of physical limitations and the heavy investment costs involved. By 1960, over 75 per cent of French petroleum imports was concentrated on two major port refinery complexes, the Le Havre–Rouen and Etang de Berre groups. The dramatic growth in petroleum imports has been matched by a reciprocal decline in coal imports. This has been most severely felt by the ports of western France, traditionally associated with coal imports from Britain and the United States. Bulk handling involving large shipping units is not restricted to petroleum; it is equally a feature of ore transport. The recent expansion of the trade of Dunkerque is in part due to the reception of ore carriers supplying the new coastal integrated iron and steel works.[14]

Significant changes have occurred in the character of port hinterlands in the past two decades, which again have tended to confirm the supremacy of the largest ports. These changes have been quantitative as a result of the differential rates of economic expansion between the regions of France, and qualitative as determined by post-war improvements in inland communications. The rapid industrial expansion of the Paris city region constitutes a huge quantitative growth in the hinterland of the Seine ports, while the development of the Rhône valley and the Lyon agglomeration has given a similar advantage to Marseille. The major effort in road improvement and railway electrification has also benefited the same ports, while those of the Brittany and Atlantic coast have witnessed few comparable developments in the transport infrastructure. The implementation of the Common Market agreements is a further factor affecting port hinterlands.[15,16] The expansion of trade with Common Market partners and the proportionate decline of trade with the former colonial territories have increased the volume of trade carried by overland routes. The liberalization of customs barriers has enabled the Benelux ports to consolidate their hinterlands in France. Antwerp currently exports as much French produce as does Dunkerque and includes the Lorraine metallurgical region in its hinterland. The completion of the Moselle Canal is likely to stimulate further Rotterdam's share of French trade. This competition is based partly on relative costs of port services, but more particularly on accessibility and frequency of shipping lines. The ports of Brittany and the Atlantic coast are particularly handicapped by their situation to participate in the additional trading within the Common Market. Their peripheral location in France becomes further

*Of the 17 tankers on order by French companies in 1967, only four were under 100,000 tons and six were of 200,000 tons.

exaggerated in relation to the land mass of the Common Market.[17]

A feature common to most French ports is the downward trend in passenger traffic. This applies with greatest emphasis in the case of long-distance lines susceptible to competition from air transport. This has been partially offset by an increased volume on the shorter routes, across the English Channel, and from the mainland to Corsica, associated with the general expansion of tourism in western Europe. Marseille, France's leading passenger port in terms of the number of lines operating regular services, has suffered heavy losses of traffic as a result of Algerian independence and the repatriation of approximately one million French nationals.

Table 7.2

VOLUME OF CARGO HANDLED BY MAJOR FRENCH PORTS, 1965

		Thousand metric tons[a]
1. Marseille Complex	Marseille–Etang de Berre	54,958
2. Seine Complex	Le Havre–Rouen	37,298
3. Channel Group	Dunkerque–Calais–Boulogne	18,316
4. Loire Complex	St. Nazaire–Donges–Nantes	10,399
5. Bordeaux Complex	Bordeaux–Pauillac–Bec d'Ambès	7,003
6. Mediterranean Group	Sète–La Nouvelle–St. Louis–Nice–Toulon–Ajaccio–Bastia–Antibes	6,606
7. Atlantic Group	La Rochelle–Bayonne–Tonnay Charente–Rochefort–Royan	4,703
8. Brittany Group	Brest–Lorient–St. Malo–St. Brieuc–Quimper–Granville–Pontrieux–Concarneau	3,567
9. Normandy Group	Caen–Dieppe–Honfleur–Le Tréport–Cherbourg	3,349

[a]Statistics refer to maritime trade only, excluding fish. All ports handling over 100,000 tons of cargo are listed.

Finally, changes in the administration of French ports and the effects of government planning decisions are active factors in port development. Since Napoleonic times the majority of the ports of France were government owned and their operation was the responsibility of a number of government departments in collaboration with the local chambers of commerce. Only Le Havre, Bordeaux and Strasbourg had achieved the status of 'port autonome', permitting a large measure of decentralized control. Since June 1965 the status of autonomy has been extended to Dunkerque, Rouen, Nantes–St. Nazaire and Marseille, in addition to Le Havre and Bordeaux, giving a greater representation of local interests on the governing boards. This reform has delegated the operation of the ports autonomes to the local councils, and the chambers of commerce and industry and the governing bodies retain port dues and tolls to finance the running of the ports. The government, however, controls and finances major improvements in port infrastructure and can coordinate the activities of ports with overall objectives established in the national and regional plans. The reform is clearly designed to improve the efficiency of the major ports by integrating their operation more closely with local commercial, industrial and transport developments, while ensuring budget resources for large expansion schemes. The process of concentration, already established by the play of economic forces, has thus been formally recognized, and is a key factor in the competition with strong rivals in the other Common Market countries.[18,19]

Table 7.2 summarizes the activity of French ports according to their geographical grouping. The activity of individual major ports is discussed in the appropriate regional chapters.

INLAND WATERWAYS

In 1965, France possessed a network of 7,900 kilometres of canals and navigable rivers, along which 89 million tons of cargo was transported, representing 17·5 per cent of all goods transported overland. The network is very irregular both in its distribution and in the capacity of its components. In part this reflects the influence of physical conditions as affecting canal construction, but, more particularly, the existence of a large demand for the cheap transport of heavy bulk cargo is a prerequisite for a dense canal network.[20] This latter factor has confined elaborate canal systems to the north-east quadrant of France, where the provision of Paris in fuel, raw materials and foodstuffs, and the extractive and heavy industry of Nord and Lorraine have stimulated waterway traffic. The limited capacity of the majority of the network is a function of the date of construction, chiefly in the first half of the nineteenth century, and the subsequent failure to enlarge canal dimensions to meet modern requirements* This is particularly severe in view of the adoption of 1,350 tons as the 'European' gauge. Thus far, only the Lower Seine, Moselle[21,22] and Rhine waterways conform to this standard.

In spite of its deficiencies, the inland waterway system plays a vital role in the French economy. In 1964, 11 million tons of coal and coke, 37·8 million tons of ores and building materials and 16 million tons of petroleum and refined products were transported by inland waterway. During the Fifth Plan, major developments include the deepening and improvement of the lower Seine system, the construction of a new port at Metz linked

*Most canals were built to standards established by the Freycinet Act of 1879, which conformed with the requirements of the Flemish 'péniche', a vessel of approximately 300 tons. Almost 75 per cent of the present network can only receive barges of less than 400 tons. In 1965, out of a total of approximately 10,000 barges, only 118 were over 1,500 tons capacity.

to the Moselle canal and the completion of the Dunkerque-Valenciennes canal to European gauge. It is anticipated that canal traffic will increase from 89 million tons in 1965 to 110 million tons in 1970. Considerable interest attaches to the proposal to link the Rhône and Rhine as a high-capacity waterway traversing western Europe.[23] In view of the high cost involved only limited works will be undertaken during the Fifth Plan, chiefly in the Doubs valley and in the middle Rhône valley. The existing canal network is illustrated in *Figure 7.3* and *Table 7.3* indicates the tonnage handled by the major inland ports.

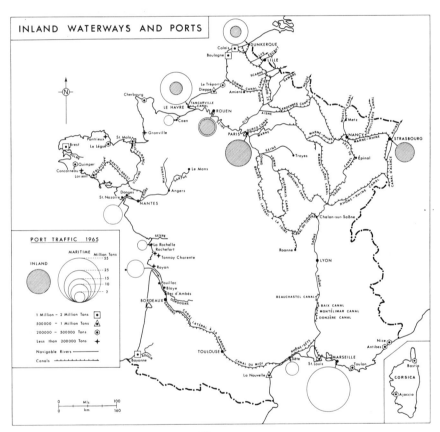

Figure 7.3

The provision of energy, the characteristics of transport and the institutional basis of economic planning or the essential infrastructure to the patterns of economic activity which are now to be discussed. An arbitrary distinction between the primary, secondary and tertiary sectors of activity is employed in the belief that this permits the definition of problems at the national level. The integration of these three sectors into

more complex economic structures is deferred until the discussion of
regional problems which forms the concluding section of the book.

Table 7.3

TRAFFIC HANDLED BY THE MAJOR INLAND PORTS, 1965

	Thousand metric tons
Paris group	21,843
Strasbourg	9,512
Rouen	6,726
Le Havre	3,817
Gonfreville–Orcher[a]	2,889
Dunkerque	2,568
Moisson	2,541
Bordeaux	2,375
Lyon	1,877
Nantes	1,621
Port Jérôme[a]	1,461

[a]Petroleum and refined products.

REFERENCES

[1] Cavaillès, H., *La Route Française, son Histoire, sa Fonction*, 1946, Paris, Armand Colin.
[2] 'Les transports routiers en France', *Notes Etud. docum.*, No. 3,146, 1964.
[3] *European Community*, July–August, 1967, p. 8.
[4] 'Les transports en région de Paris', *Cah. Inst. Aménagement Urban. Rég. Paris.*, Vols. 4 and 5, 1966.
[5] Lartilleux, H., *Géographie Universelle des Transports*, Tome 1, 1956, Paris, Chaix.
[6] Caralp, R., 'L'évolution des relations ferroviaires; les exemples de Toulouse–Paris et Toulouse–Lyon', *Revue Géogr. Pyrénées S.-Ouest*, 1957, p. 141.
[7] Bird, J., 'Road and rail in the Central Massif of France', *Ann. Ass. Am. Geogr.*, 1954, p. 1.
[8] Schnetzler, J., 'Chemin de fer et espace français', *Revue Géogr. Lyon*, 1967, p. 81.
[9] Wolkowitsch, M., *Economie régionale et des transports dans le Centre-Ouest*, 1960, Thesis, Paris.
[10] Schnetzler, J., *op. cit.*[8]
[11] Caralp, R., 'Les tarifications ferroviaires de marchandises et les économies régionales' *Annls Géogr.*, 1967, p. 305.
[12] Wolkowitsch, M., 'Le problème actuel du rail et de la route en France', *Annls Géogr.*, 1950, p. 269.
[13] Pollier, R., 'Quels ports pour la France?', *Transmondia*, No. 144, 1966, p. 49.
[14] Bruyelle, P., 'Dunkerque, 1964–1970', *Hommes Terre Nord*, 1966, p. 76.
[15] 'Situation des ports français dans le Marché Commun', *Journal Officiel*, No. 13, 1962.
[16] Vigarie, A., 'L'attitude des ports continentaux de la Mer du Nord devant le mouvement d'européanisation', *Cah. Sociol. écon.*, 1963, p. 177.
[17] Bird, J., 'Seaports and the European Economic Community', *Geogrl J.*, 1967, p. 302.
[18] Chapon, J., 'The recent changes in French port administration', *Dock Harb. Auth.*, No. 545, 1966, p. 345.
[19] Clout, H., 'Expansion projects for French seaports', *Tijdschr. econ. soc. Geogr.*, 1968, p. 271.
[20] Jouanique, M., and Monce, L., 'La Navigation Intérieure', 1951, Paris, Presses Universitaires de France.
[21] Gourdon, A., 'The Moselle ship canal and the port of Thionville', *J. Inst. Transp.*, Vol. 31, 1965, p. 44.
[22] Michel, A., 'The canalisation of the Moselle and West European integration', *Geogrl Rev.*, 1962, p. 475.
[23] 'L'axe de transport par voie d'eau entre le nord-est de la France et la Méditerranée', *Notes Etud. docum.*, No. 2,874, 1962.

8

Agriculture

The attachment of the French peasant to his land throughout history is proverbial and the image of the country as a bounteous land, richly endowed by nature, is deeply rooted in the nation's literature and popular imagination. The opulence and regional variety of French cuisine testifies to the abundance and diversity of the product of the soil. Less disturbed by the industrial revolution than were some of her neighbours, and sheltered by protective tariffs, French agriculture persisted as a way of life rather than a commercial system until comparatively late in the nation's economic history. Although modern attitudes and practices permeated certain regions of France during the nineteenth century, it is only since 1945 that a rigorous attack has been made on archaic structures and low productivity in much of the nation's farming. Prompted by government measures, the agricultural landscape and economy are currently in a phase of rapid evolution. To appreciate the significance of these changes it is necessary to review the structure inherited from the past.

THE EVOLUTION OF FRENCH AGRICULTURE[1,2,3]

The paradox of an advanced nation populated by an industrious and inventive people, located close to the cradle of the industrial and agricultural revolutions, yet until recently possessing a stagnant rural economy in which archaic systems of production persisted, is central to an understanding of present problems. Certain stages in the evolution of agriculture may be regarded as being crucial in determining contemporary characteristics.

Modern French agriculture has its roots in the abandonment of the cereal-based system, prevalent since antiquity and perpetuated in its essentials until the beginning of the eighteenth century. In this system, the basic rotation consisted of two years of cereal cultivation alternating with one year of fallow, during which livestock were grazed and manured the land. In the drier Midi, the rotation was shortened to a single year of cereals alternating with fallow. This practice was characterized by low yields, a low livestock carrying capacity, an autarchic economy and extreme vulnerability to natural hazards of drought and disease. The replacement of the fallow period by leguminous and root crops, which at once preserved the soil quality and afforded an increase in fodder, was diffused through France in the early eighteenth century. Thus was established the classic 'polyculture', characterized by a wide variety of crops integrated with livestock rearing, which remains a fundamental trait of the agriculture of wide areas of France. The essential features of polyculture became the diversification of land use with the introduction of artificial grasses and fodder root crops, permitting a much longer rotation cycle and assuring a continuous supply of feedstuff. Natural and artificial pasture supported dairy and veal production, while skimmed milk, grain and root crops were fed to pigs. The new variety in the crop range accompanied the rearing of a miscellany of fowl, together with rabbits, in a 'basse-cour' system of production, largely for domestic use. The establishment of polyculture represents a major watershed in French agrarian history, which transformed not only the economy and landscape, but also the way of life and thought of the peasantry. The new developments confirmed the viability of the small-scale farm unit, since the variety of production afforded security against individual crop failure. The establishment of polyculture also represented an intensification of production which permitted commercialization, even if of a sporadic nature initially. Above all, the new developments stamped an individualist outlook on the peasant farmer. Freed from insecurity and communal dependence, the peasant life and economy revolved around the family as an operative unit.

By 1750, France had adopted a mixed farming system, and the two centuries which have since elapsed may be regarded as a period of effort to elaborate and perfect this basic pattern. The process has been marked by varying rates of advance, both in time and between the different regions of the country. The first century was one of slow development, during which the agricultural output increased only marginally. In part this was due to momentous political upheavals and international warfare, but it was also related to the slow growth of population. As in agriculture, so in industry, the technological advances made elsewhere in Europe were slow to be transmitted to France, so depriving agriculture of the stimulus of rapidly growing urban markets.

After a century of stagnation, the period from 1840 until the close of the Second Empire in 1871 was one of rapid expansion in output in response to the belated surge of industrialization in north-eastern France.

This increased food production was achieved by an extension of the cultivated area rather than by an intensification of farming methods. It was a period of active land reclamation, during which clearing and draining extended agriculture to former marshland and pushed up the limit of cultivation on the flanks of the uplands.* Increased production was also facilitated by the rapid extension of the railway network into rural areas. From the point of view of agriculture, this extension had a multiple significance. The railways permitted the cheap transport of lime, critical for the colonization of new farm land, and assurance of rapid and cheap transport connections with the expanding urban markets was a stimulus to regional specialization and marked the onset of inter-regional competition. This stimulus was applied most directly to the regions closest to the industrial concentrations. The early mechanization and increase in farm size in the Paris Basin relative to the remainder of the country, was in response not only to an accessible large market but also to the drift of agricultural workers from the land to competing employment opportunities in industry.

The expansionist atmosphere of the Second Empire received a severe setback at the creation of the Third Republic in 1871. A series of bad harvests had necessitated large grain imports from the American prairies and the spectre of low price competition agitated the peasantry, who pressed for protective tariffs.[4] In 1884, customs duties were imposed on imported foodstuffs, largely inspired by political expediency and without regard to the possible long-term consequences. Secure from foreign competition, agriculture sheltered behind tariff protection, insulated against the stimuli towards greater regional specialization and increased efficiency. For half a century, the traditional polyculture, wasteful of both labour and land resources, was perpetuated over the majority of the nation. This implied a tolerance of low yields, a deficiency in the application of fertilizers and a very slow rate of mechanization. This inertia was permitted by the tariff protection and encouraged by the political mystique of the traditional rural way of life as a symbol of the nation's strength and solidarity. Advances in mechanization were most marked in the Paris Basin and Nord, where contact with industrialized Europe was more pronounced and where favourable soil conditions and access to markets combined to reward the progressive farmer. Elsewhere, substantial achievements in mechanization were delayed until the manpower shortages occasioned by the First World War.

At the opening of the twentieth century, France was still a predominantly rural nation, having over 40 per cent of the active labour force engaged in agricultural employment. In spite of its numerical importance, the farming

*In 1862 the largest area of arable land in the nation's history was achieved, 65 million acres.

community was but imperfectly integrated into the national economy. With the exception of a few regions, the basis of commercialization was haphazard and depended on the activities of a large number of middlemen. The intervention of middlemen and wholesale merchants effectively isolated the farmer from direct contact with the market, while the sale of produce in small quantities at irregular intervals made for low prices and slow capital accumulation, in turn discouraging investment in machinery and fertilizers. The middlemen were frequently the only source of credit, placing the farmer in a extremely weak bargaining position for marketing his produce. In these conditions, any surplus capital tended to be diverted into the purchase of additional land rather than to improving efficiency. This was seen as affording further security and a tangible asset. The commercial weakness of the individual farmer was the prime factor in the growth of the cooperative movement at the close of the nineteenth century. Originally founded as a means of collective purchasing, the cooperatives gradually extended their activities to embrace the marketing and processing of produce. The movement did not, however, become a driving force for reform and technical innovation. The independence of the farmer was not compromised by a movement designed to safeguard, rather than merge, individual liberty.

The mobilization of agricultural workers, and subsequent need to replace the killed and maimed, acted as a stimulus towards increased mechanization during and after the First World War. Nevertheless, at the outbreak of the Second World War, only 40,000 tractors were in use; a ratio of one tractor to every 1,500 acres of farmland. In 1938, the entire production of tractors totalled only 1,700 units. By 1945, 36 per cent of the national labour force remained employed in agriculture, which absorbed 4·2 million men. The period between the wars was thus one of slow development during which only halting progress was made to correct the fundamental weaknesses of the organizational structure of agriculture. The failure to exploit fully the rich farming potential available accounted for the widening discrepancy between urban and rural living conditions. The post-war reappraisal of the entire economy, in the course of the preparation of the First National Plan, revealed the full extent of the deficiencies of agriculture and the need for reform became a major preoccupation of the government. The agricultural situation in 1945 was critical, both in terms of the level of output and of productivity. To the problems stemming from a century of inertia were added the disruptive effects of the war and occupation. At the close of the war, the central problem may be summarized as having been too many farmers exploiting holdings that were too small and fragmented by methods that were both inefficient and extravagant of labour. The results were low yields per capita and per acre and thus high-cost production and the absorption of large amounts of labour at a time of critical manpower shortages nationally.

That comprehensive reforms were necessary was undeniable. The most immediate priority was that of technical reform, involving a modernization of the processes of production. This was a problem of many facets, including not only the need to stimulate productivity by intensifying mechanization, but also to achieve fundamental transformations of the traditional systems of crop and livestock husbandry. In 1946, at a conservative estimate, increased mechanization was capable of replacing one million farm workers together with a million horses and half a million draught oxen. This represented a valuable potential redirection of labour into more productive employment and the release of large amounts of pasture and cropland supporting draught animals for commercial use. Equally urgent was the need to change the attitudes embedded in traditional polyculture. The emphasis on a variety of crops giving security but yielding only marginal returns had to be replaced by increased specialization and the maximization of yields in accordance with directly commercial principles. This process involved the selection of new crop and livestock combinations, the increased use of fertilizers, the adoption of new varieties of seeds and improved strains of livestock. Above all the problem was to convert a peasant outlook into that of a businessman, versed in commercial management and attuned to the dictates of a market now bereft of tariff protection in the Common Market. For many farmers the situation called for a revolution in thought and practice for which three prerequisites were essential. In the first instance, a system had to be devised by which the farmer might take advantage of the technological and scientific development which formed no part of his heritage or professional experience. Secondly, improvements in the system of distribution and marketing were necessary to achieve competitive production and secure an adequate cash return to the farmer as an incentive to modernization. Thirdly, the greater use of machinery was dependent on a major effort in the consolidation of fragmented holdings, both for obvious practical reasons and to achieve economic utilization. As a corollary to these preconditions, two inevitable consequences complicated the task of modernization. The necessary reforms demanded a massive injection of capital investment, especially in the form of loans. Secondly, agriculture had to continue to shed its surplus manpower. The post-war effort in the field of agricultural reform and the present day characteristics of farming in France must be viewed against the inheritance described above, and in the context of the rapid social and economic evolution of the country as a whole.

THE SIGNIFICANCE OF AGRICULTURE

The importance of a particular sector within the total economy may be measured in several objective ways, of which the level of employment and value of the output may be considered the most significant. Out of a total employed civilian labour force of 19,419,000 in 1965, agricultural occupations employed 3,534,000 or 18·2 per cent of the work force. By contrast, agriculture contributed only 7·8 per cent of the gross domestic product (at market prices), reflecting a far lower value of output per capita employed than obtained in other sections of the economy. To some extent this is explicable by the structure of the agricultural labour force (*Table 8.1*).

Table 8.1

THE STRUCTURE OF THE AGRICULTURAL LABOUR FORCE, 1962

	Operators	Family help	Paid workers	Total
Men	1,450,000	394,300	732,300	2,577,000
Women	223,000	944,000	97,300	1,214,000
Total	1,673,000	1,338,300	829,600	3,791,000

From the table it is noticeable that little more than 20 per cent of the agricultural labour force is supplied by paid workers,[5] the remainder being constituted by farm operators with the assistance of their family, notably the female members. Increases in mechanization have tended to diminish the amount of paid labour employed but the importance of family assistance has remained high. French agriculture thus contains a large working segment whose activity is part-time, and in the case of females largely restricted to simple manual tasks. Secondly, the family basis of operation is often accompanied by a high level of direct consumption, especially in the case of small and marginal farms.

Further measures of the significance of agriculture are the contribution made to the nation's food supplies and to the export drive. In recent years France has had an unfavourable trade balance, by value, in agricultural commodities, although the margin is comparatively small for an advanced industrial nation* One third of imports are of commodities which, for climatic reasons, France is unable to produce. The majority of the remaining imports are of animal fibres and meat products in which domestic output is deficient, or arise out of trading agreements within the franc zone. In the field of exports, French performance is handicapped by the

*In 1963, 81 per cent of agricultural imports were covered by exports of farm produce.

lack of adjustment to market demands. Major surpluses are of wheat, dairy products and wines. Whereas dairy produce and quality wines find ready markets, grains and inferior wines are less easily disposed of. French agriculture is at present maladjusted to exploit the growing export possibilities for fruit, vegetables and meat within the Common Market.

The agricultural sector clearly absorbs an unwarranted proportion of

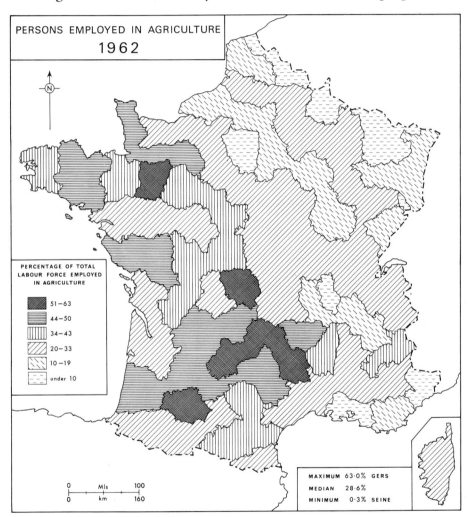

PERSONS EMPLOYED IN AGRICULTURE
1962

PERCENTAGE OF TOTAL
LABOUR FORCE EMPLOYED
IN AGRICULTURE

51–63
44–50
34–43
20–33
10–19
under 10

MAXIMUM 63·0% GERS
MEDIAN 28·6%
MINIMUM 0·3% SEINE

0 Mls 100
0 km 160

Figure 8.1

the nation's manpower resources but the degree of concentration varies spatially, as summarized by *Figure 8.1*. The data plotted are restricted to the male labour force and thus represents full-time agricultural employment. The variables underlying the pattern of distribution are analysed more fully in a later section but three very prominent characteristics may be cited. The proportion of the male labour force employed in agriculture should be viewed not as a measure of the dominance of agriculture in the economy, but rather of the degree of dependence on farming as a result of the lack of alternative employment. Thus, western France has a high degree of dependence, especially in Brittany and the Massif Central, as a direct result of the low level of industrial and urban development. Throughout north-eastern France, values are consistently below the median for the nation as a whole. This results not only from the greater possibilities of non-agricultural employment, but also coincides with a high average farm size, consolidated holdings, a high level of mechanization and therefore a low per acre labour application.

THE CHARACTERISTICS OF PRODUCTION

Over 90 per cent of the land surface of France may be considered as fulfilling some agricultural function. The characteristics of agricultural production may be classified as spatial, in the sense of the physical arrangement of land-use zones, and quantitative, in terms of the volume of output.

The land uses depicted in *Figure 8.2* generalize a highly varied agriculture which covers the entire spectrum of farming from the extreme diversification of the classic polyculture of Brittany to the equally extreme specialization of viticulture, where localized variations occur in response to minute differences of soil and microclimate.[6] Between these two extremes, the majority of French agriculture may be considered mixed farming, in that some degree of integration of crops and livestock is practised. Over much of the country, the mixed character of farming is less in response to flexible environmental conditions than a cultural inheritance of polyculture, a system designed to give maximum economic security. *Figure 8.2* indicates the major contrasts in land use. It is inevitably generalized, and, especially in the northern half of the nation, the boundaries between zones are ill-defined in reality.

Analysis of *Figure 8.2* suggests a broad threefold division into latitudinal provinces of dominant types of land use. An arcuate band, varying in width from 100 to 200 kilometres (represented on the map by vertical shadings), extends from Brittany to the northern flanks of the Massif Central and thence north-eastwards into Lorraine and Champagne. This central province forms an axis of mixed farming 'par excellence', separating the predominantly arable north-east from the varied and fragmented land use types of the Midi.

Differentiation within the central province of entirely mixed farming may be made by reference to the degree of intensity as measured by the

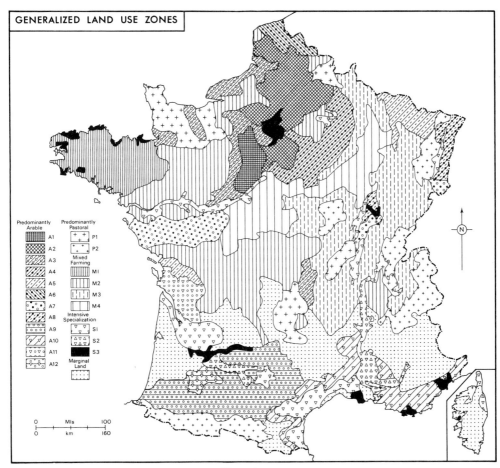

Figure 8.2

PREDOMINANTLY ARABLE
A1. Intensive cereals
A2. Cereals–sugar-beet
A3. Cereals–pasture
A4. Cereals–root crops
A5. Cereals–fodder crops
A6. Root crops–sugar-beet
A7. Root crops–pasture
A8. Root crops—fodder–cereals
A9. Maize–pasture
A10. Vines–cereals
A11. Vines–pasture
A12. Vines–maize–pasture

PREDOMINANTLY PASTORAL
P1. High-quality pasture
P2. Mountain grazing

MIXED FARMING
M1. Intensive polyculture
M2. Medium intensity, predominantly arable
M3. Medium intensity, predominantly pastoral
M4. Low intensity

INTENSIVE SPECIALIZATION
S1. Viticulture
S2. Fruit and vines
S3. Market gardening
Rice (Camargue)
Flowers (Côte d'Azur)

average farm size, density of population dependent on agriculture and the amount of non-agricultural land. Thus Brittany constitutes a zone of high-intensity mixed farming, with small farms, high rural population densities, little woodland and high crop yields compared with the rest of the province. Progressing south-eastwards into Maine, Poitou and the northern margins of the Massif Central, mixed farming of medium intensity prevails. Arable land predominates in the total acreage, but much is devoted to feed crops for livestock. To the east of the Allier, medium-intensity mixed farming extends to the contact with the Vosges, Jura and northern Alps, but with pasture occupying a greater proportion than arable land. Finally, a zone of low-intensity mixed farming, with considerable areas of woodland and low rural population density extends from the Sologne to the Plateau de Langres and southern Lorraine.

To the north of the central mixed farming province, the proportion of arable land increases substantially, and although livestock remain important the Paris Basin is the prime cropland region in the nation. The core of the province is constituted by the 'limon'-covered plains extending from Beauce in the south-west to Artois in the north-east. This is the great grain belt of France, with cereals grown in association with sugar-beet, except in Beauce. Historically, the zone has functioned as a generator of advanced farming in that land consolidation, mechanization and heavy use of artificial fertilizers have been successfully applied by a progressive farming community. To the west of the grain belt, the proportion of fodder crops and pasture increases in Haute-Normandie, Bray and the Boulonnais, while to the east, in Champagne and southern Brie, the intensity of arable production declines in the absence of a 'limon' cover. To the north of the chalk rim of Artois, the Flanders Plain, devoted to the cultivation of root crops, sugar-beet and market garden produce, and the small dairy region of Thiérache, supply the demands of an urban market of over two million inhabitants in the Nord, Pas-de-Calais industrial region. The dairy region of Basse-Normandie forms a separate sub-region, different in character from both the provinces described so far. Here high-grade natural pasture forms the basis of a highly organized dairy industry supplying both domestic and export markets.

The Midi agricultural province defies orderly description, since land resources vary from virtually barren mountain surfaces to deep fertile alluvial deposits, amenable to irrigation and supporting intensive horti-culture. Moreover, the pattern is not static, for while the agricultural area is contracting on the marginal lands, irrigation schemes are revitalizing Languedoc, the Rhône and Durance valleys and eastern Corsica, and the introduction of hybrid maize has transformed the potential of the Basin of Aquitaine. The rapid lateral and vertical variation in land use is in part a reflection of the extended crop range permitted by the Mediterranean climate, but more particularly is a response to a bewildering array of contrasts in landforms and soils. As compared with the central and northern agricultural provinces, large expanses of cropland are restricted and are interrupted by extensive areas of marginal land and mountain grazing. The northern Alps support a pastoral economy based on the alternate use of the valleys and mountain pasture in a system of trans-humance. Moving southwards, the summer drought becomes pro-gressively more emphatic and the quality of grazing deteriorates. The southern Alps thus support extensive sheep grazing with arable farming restricted to irrigation schemes in the major valleys. On the plateaux of Quercy and the Causse, limestone bedrock combines with low summer rainfall to limit agricultural activity to extensive grazing, and only on the valley floors and structural depressions does a patchwork of arable land support a more intensive farming. The high, crystalline Cévennes support extensive sheep grazing, and the agricultural population density is extremely low. The high Pyrenean valleys have a similar pastoral economy to that of the northern Alps and a parallel transition to poorer grazing as the Mediterranean is approached. Marginal conditions are not restricted to the uplands, the infertile sands are largely forest-covered, while the Crau and Camargue are areas of formerly negative land where reclamation has made possible rice cultivation, cattle rearing and fruit growing.

The areal importance of marginal land and extensive grazing confines intensive arable farming to clearly defined lowland corridors. In Aquitaine, the Bordelais vineyards give way inland to an integration of viticulture, market gardening and fruit growing in the middle Garonne and lower Aveyron valleys. To the north of this axis, the importance of vines diminishes and pasture assumes greater importance in Charente, while vines, maize and pasture characterize the general farming of the plateaux of southern Aquitaine. The second lowland corridor, the plain of Bas-Languedoc, is the largest individual area of viticulture in France, and until recently had a system of monoculture yielding low-quality wine. It is now the scene of a regional development scheme involving major irrigation works as a means of achieving diversification of agriculture. The low plateaux of the Garrigue region of Haute-Languedoc support the classic Mediterranean dry farming complex of vines, cereals and olives, but land resources are mediocre and the value of production low. The third lowland, the Rhône corridor has a more rational farming system; irrigation facilitates intensive vegetable and fruit production while viti-culture is concentrated in favourable conditions for the production of quality wine. Lowland in Basse-Provence consists of valleys and basins rather than plains. Intensive arable farming is restricted by water shortage to areas where irrigation is available, notably in the lower Durance and Verdon valleys, while a marked attenuation occurs on the dry-farmed areas.

The problems of land utilization are distinctly contrasted between the

Figure 8.3   *Figure 8.4*

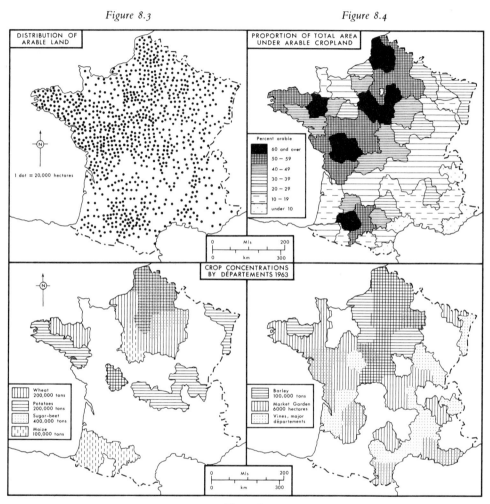

Figure 8.5

three major agricultural provinces. The northern province may claim to have the most evolved and stable system. Favoured both by environmental conditions and access to the major consuming areas, farming has acquired a rational structure and achieves a high level of production. By contrast, the central mixed farming province has a deficient structure of small, fragmented farms, exacerbated in Brittany by pressure of population. Land use is imperfectly adjusted to market demands and an increased emphasis on animal production, supported by sown pasture and fodder crops, seems desirable. Such a transition in land use will require a major effort in land consolidation, mechanization and market organization and a profound psychological readjustment to the necessity for specialization and abandonment of polyculture. Although polyculture offered security in a largely autarchic situation in the past, logic dictates that a wide variety of crops cannot be produced in optimum economic conditions on small farms in the intensely competitive situation now existing. The problems of the Midi are altogether different in kind for this province is one of difficult physical environments which can only be mastered by long-term integrated hydraulic developments, for which massive capital investment is required. Conversely, the Midi has a great potential for products with an increasing demand and high price elasticity, in the form of citrus and soft fruit, vegetables and flowers.

The second aspect of production, the volume and composition of agricultural output, is amenable to more precise definition. *Figures 8.3* and *8.4* indicate that in absolute and relative terms arable production is concentrated north of a line from the Gironde to the Low Vosges. In the Midi only the Garonne Basin stands out as an arable concentration and the secondary concentrations are outweighed by proportionately larger expanses of non-arable land uses. Within these broad contrasts, detailed variation in the level of production occurs in response to differences of soil quality and farming practice.

Table 8.2

THE PRODUCTION OF MAJOR CROPS
(100,000 metric tons)

	1939	1950	1955	1960	1964
Wheat	73·0	77·0	103·6	110·1	138·4
Barley	13·6	15·7	26·7	57·2	67·9
Oats	52·7	33·1	36·4	27·4	23·1
Rye	7·5	6·1	4·4	4·2	3·6
Maize	6·1	4·0	10·9	28·1	21·1
Potatoes[a]	144·1	129·4	137·5	148·9	114·2
Vegetables[a]	15·2	19·1	19·6	23·2	28·5
Sugar-beet	115·7	135·8	109·8	190·2	162·4
Edible oils	0·08	1·6	1·3	1·0	2·8
Wine[b]	49·4	65·1	61·1	63·1	62·4

[a]Field production only, excluding private and market garden.
[b]In millions of hectolitres.
Source: Statistique Annuaire, 1966.

Table 8.2 indicates the dominant position of cereals in the crop output, and profound changes have occurred in the composition of grain production. Production of wheat has doubled in the past 15 years in response to considerable improvements in yields; the area cultivated in 1964 being smaller than that of 1950. Soft wheat is the most widely cultivated crop in France, but *Figure 8.5* shows that highest production is concentrated in the northern and central Paris Basin—a function of very high yields rather than excessive dominance in the area of cropland* In recent years, surplus production has placed France among the major exporters of wheat, notably to her Common Market partners and eastern Europe. The production of barley shows an equally striking increase related to its expanded use as a feed grain for beef cattle, pigs and poultry. Concentration of production is similar to that of wheat but extends further south in the Paris Basin. In recent years France has been the world's largest exporter of barley. The production of maize has also expanded dramatically with the introduction of hybrid species but production totals vary considerably due to the crop's susceptibility to the degree of dryness during the growing season. The major concentrations occur in the Basin of Aquitaine but it has a wider distribution as a green fodder. By contrast, the production of oats and rye has declined progressively. Rye survives only on the poorer soils and the decline of oats parallels the reduced use of animal traction and the substitution of feedstuffs with a higher conversion value.

The production of sugar-beet fluctuates with climatic variations and price levels, but the general trend is upwards as a result of higher yields rather than an extension of the acreage. The output of fruit and vegetables has doubled during the last decade in response to increased urbanization and improvement of purchasing power. Increased output has been particularly the result of specific schemes in the Rhône valley, Languedoc, eastern Corsica and the Durance valley. The production of wine has remained relatively stable in recent years†. The emphasis has been placed on improving the quality of production and the reduction of the output of 'vin ordinaire' as a result of decreased demand and low market prices.

The widespread distribution of livestock in France gives a misleading impression of the importance of animal farming. A high proportion of the livestock is reared as an adjunct of polyculture and specialized animal farming is limited to relatively few areas. The distribution of grassland, as shown in *Figure 8.6*, reveals concentrations in Normandy, the Vendée, Cantal, Limagne and Charolais and in the département of Isère. Elsewhere, livestock farming is associated with leguminous and root fodder crops in

*Hard wheat production exceeded one million quintaux in 1964, but France imports between four and five million quintaux per annum.

†France, nevertheless, still produces approximately a quarter of the world's wine.

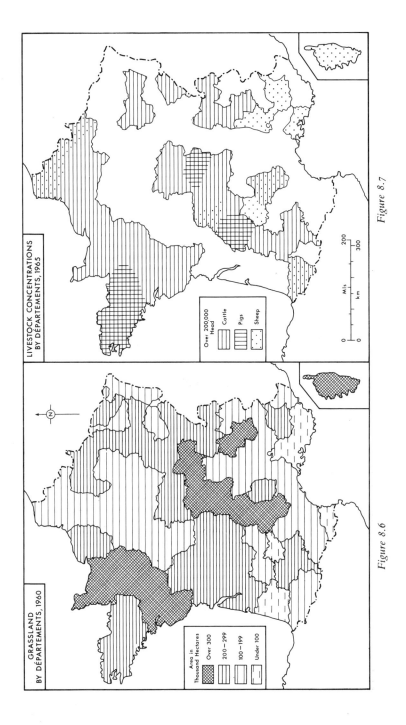

LIVESTOCK CONCENTRATIONS
BY DÉPARTEMENTS, 1965

Over 200,000
Head

Cattle

Pigs

Sheep

Mls
km

0   200
0   300

Figure 8.7

GRASSLAND
BY DÉPARTEMENTS, 1960

Area in
Thousand Hectares

Over 300

200 – 299

100 – 199

Under 100

Figure 8.6

a system of mixed farming, or is based on the extensive grazing of mountain pasture. Animal products currently account for approximately 65 per cent of agricultural cash receipts, but deficiencies in certain commodities still exist. Output of whole milk, pork and veal are adequate for domestic consumption and high-quality dairy produce is exported. Output of beef remains below national requirements, partly due to high guaranteed prices for cereals, which have orientated farming away from intensive stock rearing. The sheep population is relatively stable but the present total of 8·8 millions compares with 32 millions a century ago. (See *Figure 8.7*.)

The potential of animal farming would seem to be great in view of the rising demand for quality meat in the Common Market as a whole. The best prospects for increased output exist in north-western France where cereals find neither their physical nor economic optimum conditions. Here the conversion of feed grains and fodder crops to meat would increase the value of agriculture and bring higher cash returns to the farming population.

THE STRUCTURE OF AGRICULTURE

The fabric of French agriculture as expressed in systems of land holding is summarized in *Table 8.3*.

Table 8.3

SYSTEMS OF FARM OPERATION, 1963[a]

Type of holding	*Number of farms (thousands)*	*Percentage of total*
Owner operator	865·9	45·6
Tenancy	352·7	18·5
Métayage	39·6	2·1
Variations of tenancy[b]	641·0	33·8
Total	1,899·2	100·0

[a]Based on a 10 per cent sample.
[b]In this category 518,400 operators owned their farm buildings.
Source: Ministry of Agriculture.

It is apparent from *Table 8.3* that rather less than half of the farms of France are owner-operated, and this involved approximately half of the agricultural land area. *Figure 8.8* demonstrates that this system is particularly dominant south of a line from the Vendée to Lake Geneva.[9] This coincides with farming characterized by small units of under 25 hectares, family operation and a high average age of farm operator, and where subdivision and fragmentation have reduced the size and efficiency of holdings. Tenant farming of all kinds accounts for 52 per cent of farm holdings but only in the case of 18·5 per cent does the tenant rent the entire farm. This latter system is characteristic of the large units and rich

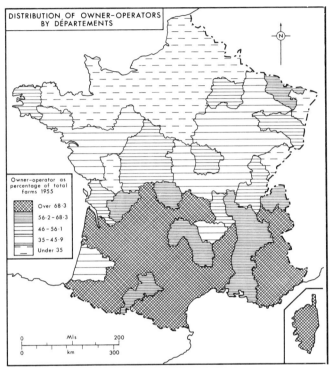

Figure 8.8

farming land of the Paris Basin. More widespread is the variation of tenancy where the operator owns some land but supplements his holding by renting additional fields. Since the 'Statut de Fermage' of 1946, tenant farmers have enjoyed a greater degree of security, since an automatic renewal of lease is guaranteed except in certain limited circumstances.* In general, tenant farming has tended to propagate advances in agriculture, since the tenant is able to invest in machinery and fertilizers rather than in the fixed capital of land and buildings. Moreover, the need to secure an annual cash rent places a premium on the maximum commercial achievement.

The system of 'métayage' is of declining importance, and accounts for approximately two per cent of land holdings. It is a system of share

*For example, when poor management compromises the value of a farm.

cropping in which the proprietor provides the land and buildings and the necessary investment in machinery, livestock and seed. The 'métayer' provides the labour under the supervision of the proprietor or his agent. Since 1946, the cash returns are divided in the proportions of two thirds to the 'métayer' and one third to the proprietor.* The 'métayage' system has generally been conducive to wasteful and inefficient farming practices, since the 'métayer' has little incentive to conserve the quality of the land or maintain farm buildings, but rather to reap the maximum short-term returns with the minimum of paid labour. The division of profits restricts capital accumulation on the part of the owner and in turn precludes necessary investment in machinery. Because of the possibility of abuse, 'métayage' has always encouraged polyculture with a high level of self-sufficiency and the restriction of commercial production to a limited number of commodities amenable to a controlled division of profits. In view of these problems, the system has steadily declined in favour of conversion to tenancy. Its distribution is limited to the poorer environments of the Massif Central and the Basin of Aquitaine, where shortages of labour stemming from depopulation, the lack of suitable tenants and the advanced age of many proprietors have been factors in its survival.

The average farm size in France as a whole is 14·5 hectares, but 75 per cent of holdings are less than 20 hectares (see *Table 8.4*).

Table 8.4

THE COMPOSITION OF FARM HOLDINGS BY SIZE, 1963

Size category (hectares)	Number of holdings (thousands)	Percentage of all holdings
0–4·9	547·9	28·9
5–9·9	364·0	19·2
10–19·9	485·0	25·5
20–49·9	393·9	20·7
50–99·9	84·9	4·5
Over 100	23·5	1·2
Total	1,899·2	100·0

Source: Annuaire Statistique, 1966.

At first sight, France would appear to be a land of very small farms, since over 28 per cent are less than five hectares and 48 per cent less then ten hectares. In fact, farms of under ten hectares occupy only 16 per cent of the agricultural area, and in many instances are not farms in the full sense. Many of the smallest farms consist of a few parcels of land operated part-time by operators whose main occupation is as a paid farm worker

*Prior to this date, the profits were customarily shared in equal proportions.

or is outside agriculture altogether. Other small holdings belong to retired farmers and are little more than large gardens, yet others represent land attached to secondary residences serving recreational rather than productive functions. Most of the operative farms under ten hectares produce specialized intensive crops such as market garden, flowers, fruit and vines.

The essence of French farming is contained in the size category of 10–50 hectares, accounting for 46 per cent of the total holdings and 56 per cent of the agricultural land area. This corresponds with the family unit of operation, supplemented in the case of farms of over 30 hectares by some recourse to hired labour in many instances. Farms of over 50 hectares

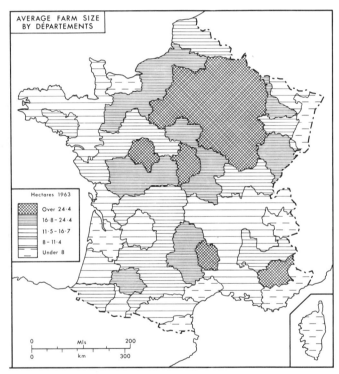

Figure 8.9

account for less than six per cent of the total but occupy over 25 per cent of the agricultural land area. These large farms are concentrated especially in the Paris Basin, are highly capitalized in machinery and buildings, and, for the most part, are operated on a tenancy basis. Very large units also characterize extensive grazing systems, especially in the départements of Lozère and Basses-Alpes. A generalized impression of the regional variations in farm size is presented in *Figure 8.9*.

Except in the case of very small units on marginal land, the modest size of the majority of French farm holdings is not in itself a barrier to progress. It does, however, imply a degree of dependence on collective activity in the spheres of mechanization, bulk purchasing and marketing. The slow capital accumulation from small units also implies the necessity of access to credit and the acceptance of a material standard of living below that of other occupations. Too frequently, small farm size is associated with fragmented holdings and a high average age of operator. The effort of modernization since 1945 has thus been marked by a greater association of farmers in collective schemes and also by strenuous government efforts to rationalize the basic structure of farm operation.

THE MODERNIZATION OF AGRICULTURE

The concerted attempt to give French agriculture an efficient structure dates from the First Plan. Since that date considerable improvements have been effected and the volume of output has reached record levels. However, further improvement is necessary in three directions: structural reform, technical development and the reorientation of production in relation to market demands.

The need for structural reform springs from two basic characteristics of the agrarian landscape: the division of land into very small fields and the fragmentation of land holding into widely scattered fields.[10] These features result especially from the application of the Napoleonic Code Civil, providing for equal inheritance between heirs at the death of a landowner. Successive generations of subdivision has resulted in the creation of minute fields and excessive fragmentation of holdings. Obvious problems result in the form of obstacles to rational mechanization, while in the open-field areas the narrow strips and lack of enclosure impede the integration of crops and livestock. Prior to the policy of official 'remembrement'* in 1941, some consolidation was achieved by voluntary exchanges of land and by the purchase of additional land adjacent to existing holdings†. A further spontaneous trend has been the passing of ownership of land to a single heir and the payment of compensation to the remaining heirs. Such unofficial action has only been a palliative, leaving the core of the problem untouched. The present system of official remembrement was instituted in 1941, at which time approximately 14 million hectares were in need of the reform, and by 1965 over four

*The redistribution and consolidation of property.
†More commonly the desire to increase farm size has led farmers to purchase land irrespective of its contiguity to their existing fields, thus increasing fragmentation.

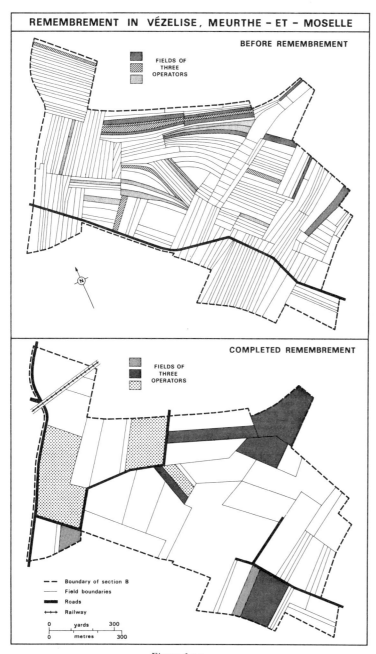

REMEMBREMENT IN VÉZELISE, MEURTHE – ET – MOSELLE

BEFORE REMEMBREMENT

FIELDS OF
THREE
OPERATORS

COMPLETED REMEMBREMENT

FIELDS OF
THREE
OPERATORS

– – Boundary of section B
Field boundaries
Roads
Railway

0   yards   300
0   metres   300

Figure 8.10

million hectares had been consolidated.[11] The operation of remembrement is the subject of an abundant literature and a brief example serves to illustrate the practical effects.[12–15]

The commune of Vézelise,[16] situated 30 kilometres south of Nancy, has 1,200 inhabitants and prior to remembrement had a land use dominated by cereals on a basis of unenclosed field strips. Remembrement was completed in 1960, reducing the number of fields from over 2,500 to 358. The increase in field size together with the improvement of access roads has permitted mechanization, while the enclosure of the fields by wire fencing permits the integration of crops and livestock. *Figure 8.10*, illustrating the south-eastern section of the commune, reveals that not all of the narrow parcels have been eliminated. The obligation to provide holdings under the new structure equivalent in productive value to that of the former holdings means that a complete consolidation is seldom possible, especially where marked variations in soil quality and aspect are present. In Vézelise, a weak system of cereals, orchards and water meadow grazing has been replaced by integrated arable and livestock farming involving the rotation of grains, artificial pasture and fodder crops, with a high level of mechanization.

A number of problems interpose obstacles to a rapid extension of remembrement to all the land which requires it. Since it is a voluntary reform requiring the support of 75 per cent of the farmers in a given commune, much depends on the initiative of groups of farmers and the breakdown of barriers of conservatism. Once initiated, the reform tends to be slow in completion in view of the complex evaluation of land resources, the need in bocage areas to dismantle hedges and banks, and the time consumed in ancillary works such as road building and drainage. The most widespread problem is the divergence between land ownership and farm operation. The fact that most holdings consist of land tenanted from one or more owners poses complex practical and legal problems. The effect of the above obstacles is expressed in the differential distribution of completed remembrement operations, illustrated in *Figure 8.11*. Most progress has been made where farms are relatively large, with a high proportion of young and progressive farmers and a high level of tenancy. Conversely, least progress has occurred in regions characterized by small units, traditional systems, a high level of owner-operation and a high average age of the farm population. *Figure 8.11* demonstrates the high concentration of completed remembrement in the Paris Basin in contrast to the modest results obtained in Brittany, Aquitaine and the Massif Central. It is thus the areas with the most favoured environmental conditions and the strongest commercial basis which have benefited most from the reform.

Plate 8. The changing agricultural landscape. *Above*, the diversion of the Rhône at Donzère to power the Bollène hydroelectricity station also permits irrigated farming in the valley. *Below*, remembrement in the Paris Basin. Completed remembrement in the commune of Puisseau (Loiret) contrasts with the fragmented field pattern in the adjacent commune of Grangermont.

Official remembrement represents a final reform, in that once completed a stable structure results which yields permanent benefits. However, it has been indicated that the progress of remembrement has been most hesitant in the areas where structural reform is most seriously needed—in western and central France. Accordingly, recent government legislation has attempted to complement remembrement with more

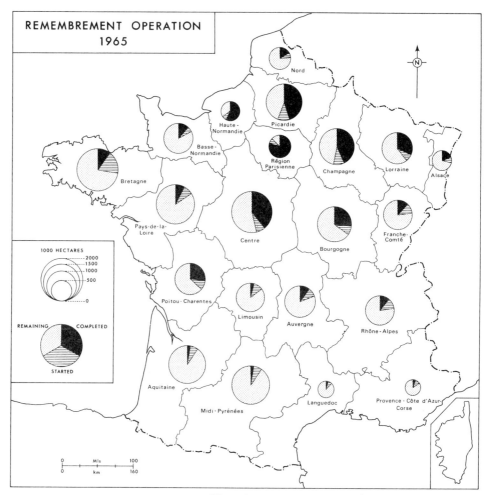

Figure 8.11

flexible procedures, which, while not achieving complete consolidation of entire communes, promote increases in the size of holdings that are too small for viable operation. An act of 1960 created 'Sociétés d'Aménagement Foncier et d'Etablissement Rural' (SAFER).[18,19] The function of these bodies is to buy land offered for sale on the open market and to use the land to enlarge farms that are too small for efficient operation. The societies may also acquire abandoned land, and after suitable improvement use it for the same purpose.* In addition to the enlargement of uneconomic farms, the SAFER can combat speculation in land values by the exercise of rights of preemption on uncultivated farm land. In practice, the limited budgets of the SAFER have inhibited the scope of their activity†, while their intervention represents an additional purchaser on the land market and may tend to increase prices. Moreover, the SAFER commonly purchase large farms and split them up to enlarge tiny farms, a policy which many critics regard as paradoxical.[20]

Further efforts to encourage the concentration of land holdings were contained in legislation introduced in 1962, creating the 'Fonds d'Action Social pour l'Aménagement des Structures Agraires' (FASASA). This fund is devoted to promoting the retirement of elderly farmers in order to free land for redistribution to younger operators. At the age of 60, farmers in certain, predominantly western, regions may receive an annuity on voluntary retirement. In addition, the FASASA provides for the award of installation grants to farmers leaving areas of land shortage in order to settle in designated reception zones with a lack of young farm operators. The fund also provides for the retraining of operators leaving non-viable holdings in order to take up alternative employment. As in the case of the SAFER, effective action commensurate with the scale of the problems is hindered by budget limitation. Moreover, the greatest concentration of farms owned by elderly farmers without heirs to continue operation is located in the poorer agricultural areas, where opportunities for creating a modern intensive farming are extremely limited. Constructive although the efforts of the SAFER and FASASA organizations may be, the limits imposed by the availability of funds ensure that natural economic forces will continue to be the strongest factors in the future evolution of the agricultural property structure.

The second prerequisite for the further modernization of agriculture is an improvement in the level of technology applied to farming. The task of technical improvement in management and production methods receives considerable government encouragement but is basically a matter of individual initiative and competence on the part of farmers.[21] The principal organ of direct state assistance to modernize not only farming but the whole rural environment is the 'Service du Génie Rural et de l'Hydraulique'. This corps of highly qualified administrators, agronomists

---

*Government research has established the minimum farm size, for each agricultural region, capable of viable operation by two full-time workers. Priority is accorded in the granting of loans and subsidies to the creation of units of these dimensions through the activity of the SAFER. The aim is clearly to strengthen the family unit of operation on a sounder commercial basis.

†In 1964, the SAFER acquired only 53,250 hectares of land for redistribution; the target established by the Fifth Plan, for 1970, is 1·85 million hectares.

and engineers is responsible for agricultural and rural developments in which the state is the major source of investment. Principal responsibilities are for remembrement, regional agricultural development programmes, rural electrification and water supply schemes and the SAFER organizations. The full list of activities is extremely wide, ranging from the promotion of mechanization to the equipping of cooperative storage and processing plants. Considerable success may be claimed in the spheres of improving the basic infrastructure of rural life, in the coordination of regional development schemes, and in liaison with unofficial organizations devoted to agricultural advancement.

Table 8.5

INDICES OF THE MODERNIZATION OF FRENCH AGRICULTURE

1. *Trends in crop yields (quintaux per hectare)*					
	1939	*1950*	*1955*	*1960*	*1964*
Wheat	15·9	17·8	22·8	25·2	31·5
Barley	16·6	16·3	20·3	27·0	28·8
Sugar beet	333·0	334·0	293·0	445·0	382·0
2. *Chemical elements consumed as fertilizers (thousand tons)*					
	1939–40	*1949–50*	*1955–56*	*1960–61*	*1964–65*
Nitrates	177	229	370	569	847
Phosphates	250	440	717	975	1,270
Potassium	70	323	550	728	971
3. *Machinery employed (thousand units)*					
	1946	*1950*	*1955*	*1960*	*1964*
Tractors	59·9	137·4	305·7	680·4	952·8
Combine harvesters	–	4·9	17·7	47·9	92·8
Milking machines	–	46·0[a]	79·9	124·0	165·6

–Data not available.
[a]1951.
Source: Annuaire Statistique, 1966.

Table 8.5 presents an impressive picture of post-war achievements and an accelerating rate of modernization.* The problem remains, however, of the wide discrepancy which exists between the best and worst levels of French farming and consequent regional disparities in standards of farm management.[22] *Figures 8.12* and *8.13* demonstrate the regional contrast in the level of application of fertilizers and machinery as indices of progress in modernization, and point to the vicious circle of circumstances existing in the more backward regions; namely that modernization is only possible with considerable investment, but capital accumulation for investment requires high productivity which in turn can only be achieved by modern practices.

*Production of tractors, for example, totalled 62,900 units in 1960 and 89,500 units in 1965.

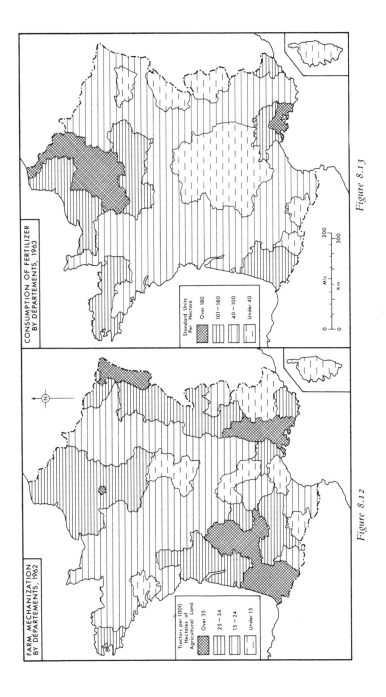

CONSUMPTION OF FERTILIZER
BY DÉPARTEMENTS, 1963

Standard Units
Per Hectare
Over 180
101—180
40—100
Under 40

Mls
km
0
0
200
300

Figure 8.13

FARM MECHANIZATION
BY DÉPARTEMENTS, 1962

Tractors per 1000
Hectares
of
Agricultural Land
Over 35
25—34
15—24
Under 15

Figure 8.12

The third aspect of modernization is the reorientation of production in accordance with market conditions. This is a complex problem in which the main ingredients are the necessity of increased productivity in order to maintain a competitive position within the Common Market structure,[23] the need to improve the machinery of marketing and wholesaling, and the difficult problem of attuning specialized production to the specific demands of the market. The question of productivity is of vital importance in view of the generalization of common price policies within the Common Market. Such a system can only work equitably where production costs are brought into equilibrium and at present the system discriminates against the small and inefficient producer, unable because of the lack of capital and because of fragmentation to maximize output. The problem of improving marketing and distribution has been attacked by the establishment of marketing boards for particular commodities, such as grain and wine, the proliferation of cooperative marketing bodies, and especially through the creation of a network of 'Marchés d'Intérêt National', major regional markets serving the principal producing and consuming areas.

The problem of adjusting the type of production to specific demands is proving intractable and is posed in two general forms in France. In some instances, as in the viticultural area of Languedoc, the extreme dependence on a single item for which demand is falling emphasizes the need for diversification and the introduction of new cash crops. Conversely, throughout much of western and central France, the practice of inefficient polyculture must be replaced by a greater degree of specialization. The problem of conversion is aggravated by the large amount of investment involved, leading to large burdens of debt to amortize and the necessity for high market prices. This problem is particularly severe in the case of the conversion of viticultural and general farming in the Midi to intensive irrigated production of soft fruit, which has produced gluts of supply but at price levels which suppress demand and encourage the consumer to prefer less perfect, but cheaper fruit produced by traditional methods.

A sign that the farming community is shedding its entrenched individualism is the striking growth of the cooperative movement. At the present time, approximately 75 per cent of all farm operators participate in the 19,000 cooperatives established for group purchasing, processing and marketing. These are supplemented by 'Sociétés d'Intérêt Collectif Agricole' (SICA), federations of cooperatives operating over a broader field, and by 'Centres d'Etudes Techniques Agricoles' (CETA). The latter are local groupings of farmers, devoted to the discussion of common problems.* In turn, the local groups collaborate in order to engage the

* This movement began on the initiative of a single farmer and now forms a network over the entire country of over 1,000 branches.

services of technicians and research workers to study specific production problems. The CETA have been a vital spontaneous factor in modernization by virtue of their appeal to the more progressive farmers.

The cooperative and professional organizations present both an opportunity and a certain element of danger for the modernization of French agriculture. On the positive side, their contribution to modernization, especially through the purchase of equipment beyond the investment capabilities of individual farmers, is undeniable. Their activities have brought modern means of production to the small farmer without the attendant risk of overcapitalization. A certain risk, however, attaches to the tendency for cooperative movements to prolong the survival of small inefficient farms.[24]

The three aspects of modernization—structural reform, technical advance and adjustment to market demands—are inextricably interlinked. Agriculture must rid itself of archaic structures and traditional ingrained attitudes, at a time when the advance of the Common Market places a premium on rapid evolution. In the less advanced farming regions, such an adjustment will not be made without a certain amount of social strain.*[25]

French agriculture has reached a critical point in its evolution, when changed economic circumstances demand the rapid transformation of a sector where the forces of inertia are still strong. The need is for structural and technical revolution rather than piecemeal renovation.[26, 27]

REFERENCES

[1] Bloch, M., *Les Caractères Originaux de l'Histoire Rurale Française*, 1931, Paris, Les Belles Lettres.
[2] Dion, R., *Essai sur la Formation du Paysage Rural Français*, 1934, Tours, Arrault.
[3] Sourdillat, J., *Géographie Agricole de la France*, pp. 27–40, 1959, Paris, Presses Universitaires de France.
[4] Gervais, M., Servolin, C. and Weil, J., *Une France sans Paysans*, pp. 27–45, 1965, Paris, Seuil.
[5] Langlois, F., *Les Salariés Agricoles en France*, 1962, Paris, Armand Colin.
[6] Klatzmann, J., *La Localisation des Cultures et des Productions Animales en France*, 1955, Paris, INSEE.
[7] Fischer, A., 'L'élevage bovin en France', *Inf. géogr.*, 1965, p. 164.
[8] Rieucau, L., 'Le cheptel francais au 1ᵉ janvier 1964', *Inf. géogr.*, 1964, p. 171.
[9] de Farcy, H., 'La répartition géographique des modes de faire-valoir en France', *Revue Géogr. alp.*, 1951, p. 229.
[10] Sargent, F., 'Fragmentation of French farm land', *Land Econ.*, 1952, p. 218.
[11] Baker, A., 'A modern French revolution', *Geogrl Mag.*, 1968, p. 833.
[12] Lambert, A., 'Farm consolidation in Western Europe', *Geography*, 1963, pp. 38–40.
[13] Baker, A., 'Le remembrement rural en France', *Geography*, 1961, p. 60.
[14] Dumas, A., *Le Remembrement Rural*, 1967, Paris.
[15] 'Le Remembrement Rural', *Documn fr. illustr.*, No. 68, 1964.
[16] Thompson, I., 'Le remembrement rural en France—a case study from Lorraine', *Geography*, 1961, p. 240.
[17] Rieucau, L., 'Où en est le remembrement rural en France?', *Inf. géogr.*, 1962, p. 161.
[18] Butterwick, M., and Rolfe, E., 'Structural reform in French agriculture; the work of the SAFER', *J. agric. Econ.*, 1965, p. 548.

*The Fifth Plan anticipates a reduction by 3·7 per cent in the agricultural labour force between 1965 and 1970.

[19] Clout, H., 'Planned and unplanned changes in French farm structures', *Geography*, 1968, p. 311.

[20] Gervais, M., Servolin, C., and Weil, J., *op. cit.*, pp. 101–102.

[21] Colson, R., *Motorisation et Avenir Rural*, 1950, Paris, CNER.

[22] Pautard, J., *Les Disparités Régionales dans la Croissance de l'Agriculture*, 1965, Paris, Gauthier-Villars.

[23] Baker, A., 'Agricultural policy in the European Economic Community during 1967', *Geography*, 1968, p. 310.

[24] George, P., *La France*, pp. 74–85, 1967, Paris, Presses Universitaires de France.

[25] Leroy, L., *Exode ou Mise en Valeur des Campagnes*, 1958, Paris, Flammarion.

[26] Wright, G., *Rural Revolution in France; the Peasantry in the Twentieth Century*, 1964, Stanford University Press.

[27] Boichard, J., 'Perspectives de l'agriculture française', *Revue Géogr. Lyon*, 1968, p. 99.

9

Manufacturing

That classic imprint of the industrial revolution, the sprawling industrial conurbation, is largely absent from the landscape of France. The full vigour of the industrial revolution came late and in an incomplete manner. Tied closely to coal and ore deposits, industrial conurbations equal in scale and complexity to those of Britain and Germany developed only on the northern periphery of the nation. If the term 'revolution' is taken to imply a radical transformation of the technique, output and distribution of industry, and the transfer of labour from rural to urban functions, then, in a real sense, the vital industrial revolution in France has been a twentieth-century feature and, in particular, a phenomenon of the last two decades. In an analysis of the contemporary industrial geography, the modern technological revolution is of greater consequence than the events of the nineteenth century.

THE SIGNIFICANCE OF MANUFACTURING*

The present importance of manufacturing in the national life may be measured by its contribution to the total economy, employment opportunities and external trade. In 1965, manufacturing and extractive industries contributed 42·1 per cent of the gross domestic product. At the 1962 census 6,475,369 persons were employed in these same sectors, representing 34·2 per cent of the employed labour force. Manufactured goods provided 73·4 per cent, by value, of French exports in 1965, which exceeded imports of manufactures by 40 per cent.

France may be placed in the second rank of the industrial nations of western Europe as measured by the absolute and relative strength of her manufacturing labour force (*Table 9.1*).

*In the present context, building and public works are excluded from the manufacturing category. Extractive industry is included only where specifically indicated.

Table 9.1

MANUFACTURING EMPLOYMENT IN SELECTED WEST EUROPEAN NATIONS, 1964[a]

	Thousands employed		Per cent labour force employed in manufacturing
	Total labour force	Manufacturing	
West Germany	26,523	10,095	38·1
United Kingdom	25,007	9,016	36·0
Italy	19,389	5,586	28·8
France	19,037	5,554	29·2
Holland	4,310	1,331	30·9
Belgium	3,566	1,257	32·3

[a]Excludes extractive industries.
Source: Annuaire Statistique, 1966 Partie Internationale.

On a numerical basis France occupies an intermediate position, with Italy, below the larger manufacturing labour forces of West Germany and the United Kingdom but substantially above the levels of Belgium and Holland. It is noticeable, however, that among the leading industrial nations of Western Europe, only Italy has a lower proportion of the labour force in the manufacturing sector.

THE CHARACTERISTICS OF MANUFACTURING INDUSTRY

The interplay of four sets of circumstances has played a decisive role in establishing the present characteristics of manufacturing: the heritage of the industrial revolution, the impact of the modern technological revolution, the factor of state intervention, and the growth of concentration. Some elaboration of these four circumstances is a necessary prelude to the classification of industrial regions.

THE HERITAGE OF THE INDUSTRIAL REVOLUTION

'In the course of the nineteenth century most French industries were remodelled, but it might be said that France never went through an industrial revolution. There was a gradual transformation, a slow shifting of her economic centre of gravity from the side of agriculture to that of industry, and a slow change in the methods of industrial organization.'[1]

Many reasons may be advanced to account for the tardy and incomplete onset of the industrial revolution. The deep-rooted attachment to agriculture, exigent of labour by reason of the persistence of irrational polyculture, acted as a restraint on regional movements of population implicit in the transition from the cottage to the factory unit of organization. The secondary importance of maritime trade, the lack of large amounts of disposable private capital, and the barrier of protectionism, combined to weaken the impact of technical innovations emanating from Britain, Germany and Belgium. Of critical significance too were the size and disposition of energy and mineral resources. The known coalfields were scattered and, until the second half of the nineteenth century, weakly linked by rail and canal to the major centres of population. The 'minette' iron ore deposits of Lorraine were little exploited before the introduction of the Gilchrist-Thomas process. The first half of the nineteenth century thus witnessed only the initial stage of industrial concentration; the gradual decay of cottage and rural artisan industry and the growth of centres on water power sites or with immediate access to coal. The nation's largest coalfield, that of Nord, Pas-de-Calais, played only a minor part in the initial stages of the industrial revolution, and only in the St. Etienne area did the exploitation of coal create an embryonic industrial region.* In the nation as a whole, industrial activity remained widely dispersed on the basis of small production units, the degree of integration within branches of activity was weak and the modification of the pre-existing pattern of distribution was much less pronounced than in Britain or Germany.

By contrast, the period from 1850 until 1914 was one of rapid evolution as improvements in transport permitted the widespread use of steam power. The peripheral distribution of the coalfields, nevertheless, imposed a differential growth between north-eastern France and the remainder of the country. The strongest growth occurred on the larger coalfields and in the area linked to them by the rail and canal network focusing on Paris. Elsewhere, industry expanded on a more restricted scale, on the scattered coal and iron deposits of the Massif Central, on the basis of imported coal at the ports of western France, or on the basis of traditional skills, where the existence of labour pools was of greater importance than direct access to abundant power sources. The growth of heavy industry on the coal and ore fields called into existence an entirely new urban structure, completely alien to the existing urban landscape; industrial agglomerations, characterized by large areas of undifferentiated housing juxtaposed with factories, canals and railways. Although such agglomerations represented the most striking innovation of the latter half of the nineteenth century, the pre-existing large urban centres were also beneficiaries of the advances in industrial technology and transport systems. The greatest advantages accrued to large cities like Paris, Lyon

*The full extent of the deposits of the northern coalfield was not known until 1846 with the discovery of the extension of the Nord field into the Pas-de-Calais.

and Lille, with easy access to coal, and also to the major ports, benefiting from the trading currents generated by increased industrial activity and able to intercept flows of raw materials on which textiles, refining and food processing industries were established. With the development of the Lorraine iron and steel industry at the turn of the century, the industrial revolution, in the classic sense of the application of steam power to basic heavy industry, textiles, engineering and transport, came to an end. Henceforth, the distribution of industry was to be characterized by greater complexity, as the internal combustion engine and the long-distance transmission of electricity ushered in a more intricate pattern of location factors.

Certain specific attributes of the contemporary geography of manufacturing may be directly related to the events of the nineteenth century. A major legacy of the industrial revolution is the existence of few regions of heavy basic industry. Only on the northern coalfield, the Lorraine iron ore field, and, to a much lesser extent, the Loire coalfield, did substantial urban–industrial agglomerations develop based on the primary transformation of coal and metals. Even in these instances, the establishment of heavy industry did not provide an adequate impetus towards more diverse industrial development. Their function became defined as the furnishers of energy and base materials to be consumed elsewhere. The result was the formation of mono-industrial urban aggregates which now pose urgent problems of conversion, adaptation of the industrial structure and renewal of the urban fabric.

The late development of the Lorraine iron and steel region explains the inheritance of a dispersed metallurgical industry? The growth of metallurgy during the nineteenth century was based on a persistence of the location pattern of the former charcoal centres, to which new sites on the scattered ore and coal deposits of the Massif Central were added, together with a second generation of blast furnaces, built at certain ports, using imported ore. Not until the latter part of the century did Nord and Lorraine become established as the core areas. While the charcoal centres, in the Meuse and Marne valleys especially, have long since disappeared, the momentum created by fixed investment and labour pools has perpetuated a large number of small metallurgical centres which now operate with great difficulty. Their combined output, measured against national production, is insignificant, but their local importance in terms of employment opportunities is often critical. In many instances, closure has been inevitable, especially in the case of plants located far from coal supplies and markets, or where the local minerals are now exhausted. In the latter instance, survival has been based on the elimination of blast furnaces and a reliance on the production of special steels.

During the nineteenth century, the most widespread technological advances were made in the textiles branch, and although theoretically these developments could be applied wherever motive power was available, factors of availability of capital, access to imported raw materials and abundant labour, together with the element of initiative, were potent factors in the concentration of this formerly most ubiquitous of industries. Thus Lille–Roubaix–Tourcoing and Lyon grew rapidly to a dominant position by virtue of the easy application of steam power to new machinery, the recruitment of large amounts of female labour, and the existence of a commercial class possessing capital and versed in international developments. Certain other provincial centres, notably Rouen and Reims, possessed similar advantages. From the nineteenth century has been inherited a number of centres where employment in textiles forms a substantial proportion of the labour force, and where ancillary industries swell further the number of establishments dependent on textiles. The post-war rationalization of the industry has thus weighed heavily on centres such as Lille, and more particularly on a number of disseminated zones of textile manufacture, such as the Vosges, which due to special circumstances escaped the concentrations which took place during the nineteenth century.

The decline of cottage and artisan industry, which paralleled nineteenth-century urbanization, inevitably produced a geographical concentration of industry. This was not accompanied, however, by an equivalent structural integration or financial concentration. Most branches of industry were characterized by small companies, lack of integration of processes, vulnerability to cyclic variations in the economy and inability to benefit from economies of scale and increased productivity. The industrial revolution produced few giant companies or cartels, but rather a proliferation of family and private concerns, ill-equipped to meet the modern conditions of industrial growth and thus preparing the ground for the present surge of concentrations.

Finally, the industrial revolution sowed the seeds of the regional disparities in economic activity which characterize contemporary France. The north-east quadrant of the country became indelibly stamped as the body of the nation's industry. A small number of limbs were grafted on to this body, notably the Lower Seine and Rhône–Isère axes, but elsewhere, manufacturing consisted of small cells, loosely attached to the main body and to each other, and many in peril of decaying. The growth of north-eastern France may in large measure be attributed to the favourable distribution of natural resources, but by the close of the century to this advantage had been added the existence of a dense transport system, the accumulation of a massive labour force drawn from the countryside and the concentration of the national consumer market, which crystallized the advantages of the past century and assured future dominance.

THE MODERN TECHNOLOGICAL REVOLUTION

It may be suggested that France played a comparatively passive role in the initial stages of the industrial revolution, absorbing new ideas hesitantly and with substantial prompting from foreign initiative and capital. Not until the second half of the nineteenth century did the structure of industry submit to the trends long since established among her industrial neighbours. The trauma of the First World War marked a turning point in the nation's industrial history and heralded the modern technological revolution. This phase, marked by the relative decline of steam and mechanical power and the evolution of more complex and fluid location factors, took root between the World Wars, but has only come to fruition since 1945 and still continues to mould the industrial geography of France.

The experience of the First World War was a triumph for the national spirit, but the cost in lives and destruction of a war fought very largely on French soil was incalculable. In addition to the physical damage sustained by industry, the nation had been deprived of a substantial proportion of its labour force and the future nourishment of the labour supply was compromised by the depression of the marital and birth rates. In spite of these difficulties, a rapid recovery was made in the output of coal and steel, while in the fields of automobile and aircraft engineering and the generation of hydroelectricity, French technology gained a leading position in Europe.* The adoption of mass production techniques, the formation of professional industrial organizations and the introduction of new sources of power were factors in the general expansion of manufacturing to record levels by 1928. The world economic recession and its aftermath, closely followed by renewed hostilities and occupation, ensured that the full impact of technological advances were delayed for two decades. Since the alleviation of the immediate post-war emergency, French industry has experienced continuous growth although with marked variation between the different branches. The spectacular expansion of certain activities as compared with the more restrained cadence of others has inevitably reacted on the regional balance of industry, with severe social repercussions. Similarly, as was the case in the nineteenth century, certain regions have proved unable to provide the necessary conditions for industrial growth in the context of modern industry.

*The recovery in basic heavy industry was greatly aided by the return of Alsace-Lorraine to French possession.

The character and effects of the modern technological revolution are best expressed by changes brought about in location factors. Initially, such changes gave the impression of an increased freedom and fluidity as compared with the relatively simple forces operating in the latter half of the nineteenth century. At the present time, however, the new set of location factors are beginning to solidify and, while more complex, are no less rigorous than those of the past, as efforts by the government to influence the distribution of industry have demonstrated.

The greatest single change is in the significance of power as a location factor. Since the development of the transmission of high-tension electricity and the substitution of diesel-powered machinery for steam power, direct access to primary sources of energy no longer exerts an overriding influence on industrial location. The declining proportion of the national energy budget provided by coal and the commensurate increase in the significance of petroleum, hydroelectricity and natural gas, all of which are readily transferred, has liberated industry from a rigid association with the distribution of energy sources, except in special circumstances. The chief exceptions occur where the primary energy source also forms a raw material, as in the use of coal in the chemical and steel industry, the linkage of petrochemical industries with refineries and the chemical industry based on natural gas distillation. Secondly, where very large volumes of energy are consumed and form a high proportion of the total production costs, a site close to the centre of generation, benefiting from the lowest tariffs, is desirable. This applies in particular to electrometallurgy, where the demand for very high-tension electricity predisposes a site close to abundant and inexpensive hydroelectricity.

The second major change has been the reversal of the balance between the heavy and light sectors of industry. The most sustained growth in the last two decades has occurred in the lighter branches of industry, ranging from everyday consumer goods to elaborate precision engineering. These form the types of industry where the new location factors are most potent and the simple factors of access to raw materials and energy sources relatively weakest. In these industries, factors of transport, labour supply and market take on a new significance. No longer tied to the bulk movement of heavy raw materials, modern light industries demand speed, flexibility and low cost for the assembly of a very varied range of raw materials and distribution to widespread markets. These conditions are best fulfilled in most instances by road transport, and locations strategically positioned with respect to major road transport arteries have been favoured* The new balance in favour of light industry has also transformed

*Road transport has been particularly attractive to large firms with a volume of production sufficiently large to justify investment in a fleet of vehicles.

the pattern of labour demand. Three categories of employee in particular have assumed enormous importance: the skilled technician, capable of operating and maintaining highly complex machinery, semi-skilled labour, often female, needed for repetitive work demanding considerable dexterity and precision, and administrative workers needed not only for commercial transactions but also for the administration of the increasing burden of social charges made against firms on behalf of their employees. In addition, the scientific basis and mass market conditions of modern light industry increase the importance of research workers, market researchers and managerial staff in the branch of cost and quality control.

Until recently, shortages have existed in the nation as a whole of these kinds of labour, and the traditional areas of surplus workers—the more backward rural areas and the declining coal basins—provide labour unsuitable for such employment without expensive retraining. New light industries have thus attracted to locations with abundant sources of female labour, a steady replenishment of well-qualified school-leavers and graduates of higher institutions, and with an existing pool of skilled labour. In this respect, the major cities, such as Paris, Lyon, Marseille, Rouen, Strasbourg and Grenoble, have exerted a strong attraction. The changing balance between the heavy and light sectors of industry has also modified the importance of market accessibility, both in quantitative and qualitative terms. Modern light industry, in the consumer goods category, depends on a mass market, and, in order to effect economies of scale, an expanding market. In the case of many branches, such conditions are not provided by the national market alone but must be supplemented by access to export markets. The same applies with particular force to the automobile, engineering and aircraft industry. In qualitative terms, the level of purchasing power influences the effective size of the market and areas with an income level above the national average attract certain types of industry. The increased importance of access to densely populated markets has again increased the attraction of the eastern half of the nation, the most densely populated and most prosperous section of the country, advantageously located with respect to the Common Market and possessing the major outlets for overseas trade.

The above trends represent a reordering of priority and certain qualitative changes in a series of location factors which have always been important. In addition a completely new factor, that of the environmental setting of factories, is assuming great importance. Modern industry shows a preference for clean atmosphere and an agreeable natural environment. In situations where all other aspects of location are comparable, the question of environment may exercise a determining influence on the selection of a specific site from a list of possible alternatives. However, the ideal of 'une usine dans la chlorophylle' is uncommonly achieved, since the importance of an appropriate infrastructure, the existence of industrial linkages and the need to establish close to commercial currents cannot be overruled on aesthetic grounds alone. In addition to physical attributes, the social and cultural environment plays an important role in the attraction of new industry. The existence of university and research institutes, professional organizations, commercial institutions and the drive and initiative of local government authorities are features of importance to the undustrialist. Finally, the increased complexity of modern industry, the internationalization of organization, the process of merging and coordination of firms, all place emphasis on the need for frequent direct contact at executive level and the rapid displacement of sales staff. Locations situated close to airports and fast motorways are thus attractive to firms consisting of dispersed production units or where export trade constitutes a large proportion of total sales.

The changes in the relative importance of location factors during the modern technological revolution may be restated in terms of changes in the pattern of costs. In the case of capital costs, the proportion invested in buildings and infrastructure works has tended to decline while the proportion invested in machinery, research and staff training facilities has increased. In the case of operating costs, the amount involved in raw materials and energy has increased less than the cost of labour, transport, research, promotion and social charges. The general effect of these trends has been to increase the importance of access to appropriate labour supplies and markets. Any barrier, physical or economic, which impedes the rapid movement of manufactured goods to the point of consumption, represents an obstacle to growth.

The changes brought about by the modern technological revolution are not unique to France but have applied to all advanced economies in recent decades. Their effect on the distribution of industry within France has been profound. The new location factors have stimulated growth in the largest cities, above all Paris, but also in the major provincial capitals of eastern France. Factors of assured markets, good communications, the development of new industrial linkages and the existence of qualified labour, stimulated fast growth after the war. A momentum was established by which industrial growth attracted additional labour by rural–urban migration, further swelling the regional market and in turn supporting more industrial growth. By this process, the major cities have become poles of development which have initiated secondary growth within their tributary polarized regions. The growth of Paris has reanimated the smaller towns of the central Paris Basin, close enough to the metropolis to share many of its advantages, but lacking its problem of congestion.

More commonly, secondary waves of industrial growth have occurred along transport arteries, especially those leading to ports; for example, the Paris–Rouen–Le Havre and Lyon–Marseille axes. The operation of new location factors has depressed industrial growth in two specific types of location and in a broad zone of western France. The heavy industrial regions of the northern coalfield, Lorraine and St. Etienne are faced with the problem of creating new employment at a rate equivalent to the run-down in the traditional sectors. The possession of an infrastructure geared to the bulk transport of heavy raw materials and the existence of an urban environment in urgent need of renewal have been factors discouraging the attraction of new industry. Secondly, the smaller isolated nineteenth century centres of heavy industry suffer from the particular disadvantage that their initial resource base is now extinguished while their strength of attraction in terms of modern location factors is particularly weak. Finally, throughout much of western France new industrial development has been restricted to a small number of growth points. The problem is especially severe in view of the need for the redeployment of surplus labour from the agricultural sector but, lacking an industrial tradition and handicapped by distance from large markets and underprivileged in terms of communications, an adequate impetus for rapid industrialization is absent. In the two extreme situations—industrial senescence in the case of the coalbasins and industrial immaturity in the case of western France—the achievement of an adequate level of new manufacturing employment is difficult without the creation of artificial incentives.

GOVERNMENT INTERVENTION IN INDUSTRIAL LOCATION

The factor of state intervention in industrial location springs from the operation of a mixed economy. The simple distinction between public and private sectors bears little relationship to the scale of government influence in industrial activity. In fact, over half the annual investment in industry is directly or indirectly subject to government control. Direct control applies in the case of the nationalized industries and those in which the state is a majority shareholder. Indirect intervention is afforded by the placing of government contracts, allocation of budget credits to regional and local authorities, the allocation of premiums, grants and loans to private industry, the control of industrial building permits, and by a wide range of fiscal methods.

The application of the whole spectrum of direct and indirect methods of intervention has, in recent years, been guided by a number of both short- and long-term policies which may be listed summarily. Short-term policies have included the preservation of strategically important industries in the advanced technology group, the alleviation of areas of severe unemployment and incentives for industries with a high export potential. Longer-term policies have included the encouragement of financial and technical concentrations[3] with a view to the creation of enterprises appropriate to the scale of the Common Market. In the same long-term category may be placed the attempt to achieve a more balanced distribution of industry in accordance with the objectives of regional planning and prospective territorial development as enunciated by the 'Délégation Nationale à l'Aménagement du Territoire'. This latter policy is worthy of elaboration since it has become an active and controversial factor in industrial location.

The term 'industrial decentralization' is surrounded by a certain ambiguity and its usage may embrace three separate circumstances. Total decentralization refers to the transfer by firms of all their manufacturing activity from the Paris area to a new location. Partial decentralization implies the creation of new factories in the provinces by firms which nevertheless continue to operate their Paris works. This category embraces the majority of decentralizations executed thus far. Finally, the creation of new, extended or converted factories in the provinces, independent of any reference to Paris, is regarded as a form of decentralization, since any such operation promotes a lessening of the dominance of Paris.* Decentralization, in all its forms, is a response to two basic problems. The over-concentration of economic activity in the Paris area has led to congestion, inflated land values and the social problems associated with an excessive rate of population growth. Conversely, decentralization is designed to favour regions lacking growth in industrial employment, and especially those where the contraction of staple industries or the shedding of excess agricultural workers presents serious immediate problems. As a corollary, it should be noted that decentralization is not aimed at a stifling of economic growth in Paris, but rather as a means of achieving a better balance between Paris and the provinces. A marked change in policy has occurred in relation to the basis of this balance. Initial legislation was designed to promote a widespread dispersal of new industrial growth. More recently, emphasis has been placed on the creation of 'pôles de développement', or growth points, capable of attracting a range of decentralized industries and with a long-term function as springboards for the further diffusion of industry to smaller towns at present ill-equipped to sustain manufacturing.

The official government programme of decentralization was initiated

---

*These three categories represent an oversimplification. A recent study[4] has defined seven types of decentralization and takes into account the location of head offices. The compilation of consistent data on decentralization is rendered difficult by the variety of definitions.

during the period 1949 to 1954. During this time, a system of building permits for new factory construction was introduced, the 'Fonds National d'Aménagement du Territoire' were created for the purpose of stimulating decentralization and 'Comités d'Expansion Régionale' were established to coordinate efforts within regions to attract new industry. However, no restrictions were placed on the expansion of industry in Paris during this period and over one third of the building permits granted applied to the Paris area. Although only 55 firms were decentralized, many were large enterprises and an important precedent had been established.

A second period, from 1955 until 1961, witnessed an upsurge in the number of decentralizations (see *Table 9.2*).

Table 9.2

NUMBER OF INDUSTRIAL DECENTRALIZATION OPERATIONS COMPLETED, 1955–1961

1955	72	Creation of F.D.E.S. and S.D.R.
1956	103	
1957	140	
1958	85	Economic crisis
1959	140	Regional planning reformed
1960	178	Restrictions on industry in Paris strengthened
1961	289	

Source: 'Expansion Régionale', No. 38, 1965, p. 19 with annotations.

This phase of increased decentralization coincided with a period of rapid economic growth, with the exception of the set-back in 1958. It also corresponds with the reconstitution of available government funds into a 'Fonds de Développement Economique et Social' (F.D.E.S.) which were disbursed for new industrial development outside the Paris region and especially on behalf of the 'zones critiques'* Similarly, the creation of 'Sociétés de Développement Régional' (S.D.R.) was aimed at combining financial resources within each region with a view to stimulating industrial investment through loans. These measures, together with the reform of regional planning and the imposition of restrictions on new industrial growth in Paris, swelled the tide of decentralization. It was noticeable, however, that until 1959 the majority of decentralized factories remained within a 200 kilometre radius of Paris†. After 1958, the combination of labour shortages in the towns closest to Paris, the establishment of well-

*The application of these funds is discussed in Chapter 5 (State and Regional Economic Planning), pp. 81–83. The 'zones critiques' were redefined as 'zones spéciales de conversion' in 1959. Figure 5.2 illustrates the present distribution of financial aid to industry.

†At the close of 1958, the eight départements closest to Paris had obtained over one third of the total number completed; 200 out of 550 operations. The literature relevant to planning during this period makes constant reference to the '200 kilometre wall'.

equipped industrial estates in the more distant centres, the application of substantial grants to the 'zones spéciales de conversion' and the imposition of more severe restraints on industrial growth in Paris, stimulated an increase in the number of long-distance decentralizations*

Since 1962 a double trend has emerged. In total, the number of decentralizations has decreased markedly, from 289 in 1961 to only 150 in 1965. The decline is particularly marked in the engineering industry, with 60 decentralizations in 1965 as compared with 132 in 1962.[5] Secondly, a return to the pattern of relocation as close as possible to Paris has been experienced in spite of the ineligibility for state assistance. The reasons for this abrupt departure from previous trends are complex, but a fundamental cause may have been the slackening of private industrial investment as compared with the high levels of the Third Plan and the early years of the Fourth Plan. A reason for the renewed preference for the area encircling Paris may be that the plan for the development of the Paris Region, published in 1965, outlining improvements in transport and the establishment of new towns, has persuaded firms to remain in Paris or to decentralize sufficiently close to keep contact with these planned developments. In addition, many firms consider the existing scale of state assistance inadequate to offset the costs of decentralization and complain of delays in payment.

It is important to keep the scale of state assistance in true perspective. Between 1961 and 1966, the total state aid accorded to new industry in Brittany amounted to only one fifth of the annual defecit of the Paris transport system.[6] The majority of decentralizations executed latterly have qualified for state assistance only on a minor scale and indicate the spontaneous rather than induced mechanism which underlies the operation. Industrialists have become wary of inherent locational disadvantages, resulting from geographical situation or deficiencies of the intrastructure, in the problem areas of western and southern France. Although state assistance offsets initial investment costs, such problems as high operating costs, labour retraining and distance from markets are less easily resolved. It is noticeable that many of the most recent decentralizations have involved the cities nominated as 'métropoles d'équilibre' by the government, and scheduled for priority investment in transport, industrial estates, educational and research facilities and housing†.

The degree of effectiveness of legislation designed to influence the location of industry may be measured by the distribution of new factories

---

*Between 1959 and 1962, 53 per cent of decentralizations were located over 200 kilometres from Paris.
†Examples are the choice of Toulouse by Motorola for a factory eventually employing 2,000 workers, and Metz by Peugeot.

(*Figure 9.1*) and the distribution of growth in industrial employment *Figure 9.2. Figure 9.1* indicates the factories constructed under building permits between November 1958 and May 1966; a period during which government policy encouraged decentralization and the industrialization of western France. A heavy concentration of new factory construction can be seen in an arc to the north and west of Paris. A second concentration

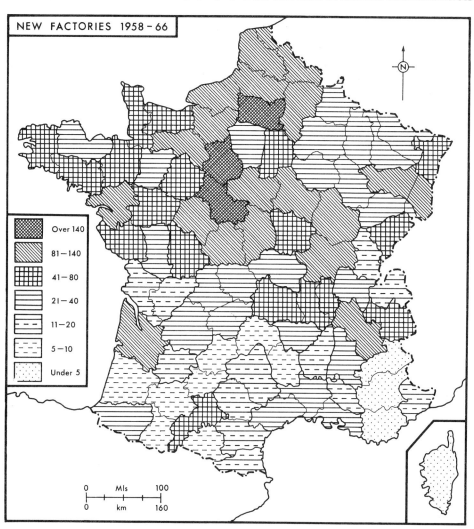

Figure 9.1

occurs in the middle Rhône and Isère corridors. Of the underdeveloped areas, only Brittany gained a substantial number of new factories. *Figure 9.2* reinforces the impression of a growing disparity between eastern and western France.[7] In spite of the acquisition of new factories, Brittany gained only marginally in terms of industrial employment, as the older-established industries continued to be run down. The northern Paris Basin, the Seine axis and the Isère–Rhône–Marseille axis, all made dispropor-tionate gains. The départements of Seine and Seine-et-Oise, with a net increase of over 80,000 industrial jobs, gained more industrial employment

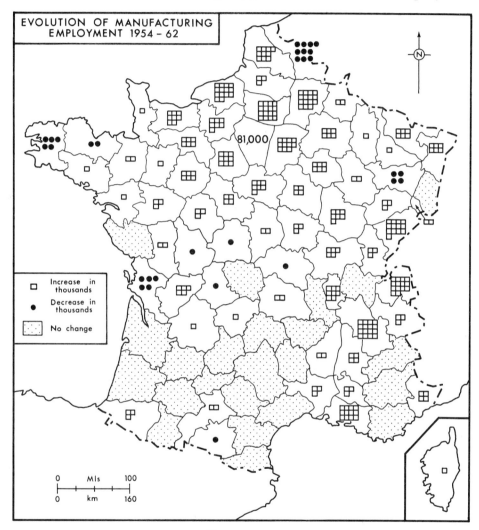

EVOLUTION OF MANUFACTURING EMPLOYMENT 1954 – 62

81,000

Increase in thousands

Decrease in thousands

No change

0   Mls   100

0   km   160

Figure 9.2

than the combined total of over 50 départements in western and central France.

The policy of decentralization has evolved in two stages. Initially it served as a means of decongesting central Paris before embracing the wider perspective of a regional redistribution of industry to redress the severe imbalance. Clearly it has best succeeded in the former context,[*] but as a lever for the regional expansion of underdeveloped areas and the conversion of declining industrial zones the policy has proved less effective.[8] The wider phenomenon of decentralization, including spontaneous as well as state-assisted operations, has resulted in a strengthening of the position of the Paris city region, through the reviving of the towns of the central Paris Basin. Clearly, a continuation and strengthening of present policies are essential. It would be invalid, however, to belittle the effects of what has been achieved so far. Whereas some decentralized firms have subsequently closed their new plants on economic grounds, others have exerted a pronounced multiplier effect on employment opportunities; the creation of new factories provides work in the construction and tertiary sectors and in some instances has attracted linked and ancillary industries.

THE GROWTH OF CONCENTRATION

French industry, like agriculture, is characterized by a predominance of small production units. The survival of a multitude of small family and private firms, and the lack of rationalization in heavy industry before 1945, is a complex matter. It stems from the particular character of the industrial revolution, the effects of protectionism, the survival of artisan and small workshop methods and the strong spirit of individualism. France lacks numerous giant coporations on the scale of those of Britain, Holland and Germany[†]. In 1962, only 32 industrial units employed more than 5,000 employees[‡].

From *Table 9.3*, which excludes self-employed artisans, it is apparent that firms of less than 50 employees numbered 409,870 and firms of over 500 employees only 1,458. However, in terms of total employment, the significance of the small firms is much reduced. Whereas 2·9 million workers were employed in factories of less than 100 employees, 3·6 million were employed in factories of over 100 workers.

France is currently in a stage of rapid reorganization in which concentrations of firms are almost daily events. The motivation of concentration is the growth of international competition, especially resulting from the dismantling of tariffs within the Common Market. In this context, many

[*]Between 1950 and 1960, Paris increased by approximately 1·3 million inhabitants. Many writers are of the opinion that without the decentralization policy the increase would have been almost double the amount.

[†]France's largest firm, St. Gobain, ranks only tenth in the Common Market by annual turnover, and the second largest, Rhône-Poulenc, ranks seventeenth.

[‡]Of these, 11 were steelworks, nine were automobile factories, three were shipyards, two textile factories and two coal mines.

Table 9.3

SIZE OF INDUSTRIAL ESTABLISHMENTS, 1962

Size	Number of firms	Total employment
1–5	309,933	559,232
6–10	44,585	340,835
11–20	28,875	427,237
21–50	26,467	855,462
51–100	10,100	713,181
101–200	5,500	776,759
201–500	3,328	1,015,840
501–1,000	928	855,462
1,001–2,000	371	713,181
2,001–5,000	127	367,271
Over 5,000	32	279,136

Source: Annuaire Statistique, 1966.

French firms are at a disadvantage in competition with larger foreign companies, benefiting from economies of scale, an international sphere of operation, high capacity to meet large orders and greater financial resources for research, development and sales promotion. In these conditions the smaller French firms have a limited number of possible options: closure, merging of interests, association with other firms or reduction to the status of subcontracting and production under licence for larger firms. Factory closures have been widespread in the last decade on the part of smaller firms engaged in traditional activities—chiefly textiles, metallurgy and engineering—lacking capital for re-equipment and placed in locations unsuitable for expansion. The complete merging of firms has also been widespread and has offered advantages to firms in a sound basic position but needing to pool resources for research, development and enlargements of capacity. Commonly, the merging of firms has been followed by rationalization leading to the closure of the weaker factories.★ The process has created a number of firms of truly European dimensions. In the textiles sector, the merging in 1966 of Lainière de Roubaix, Filatures Prouvost, with 6,000 employees, and François Masurel Frères of Tourcoing with 2,500 employees, has created one of the largest textile firms in Europe. The iron and steel industry has long witnessed amalgamations but without the creation of giant corporations. However, in 1967, the fusion of USINOR with Lorraine Escaut created a major complex of five iron ore mines, 24 blast furnaces and 16 steelworks. The new company controls one third of French crude steel production, half the national

★The merger of the engineering firms of Fives-Lille and Maison Bréguet led to the immediate closure in 1965 of the Douai factory of Maison Bréguet. This was one of the three largest factories of that town and represented a serious loss of employment.

production of steel tubes, and, with an annual output of 6·3 million tons of crude steel, ranks as the fifth producer in western Europe.*

As an alternative to complete merging of interests, various forms of association are increasingly common, although in many instances this forms a prelude to ultimate fusion. Association in the fields of research, marketing and joint investment are commonplace. Recent examples are the association of the Renault and Peugeot car firms which, combined with the association between Citroën, Panhard and Berliet, concentrates French automobile production into two very large groups†. A further example is the 'Union Textile de Lorraine', which associates 14 textile firms in the Vosges whose independent survival would otherwise have been jeopardized. An example of association for the purpose of joint investment in new plant is afforded by the grouping of four major chemical firms for the construction of a new ammonia plant at Grand Quevilly, Rouen‡. Industrial association has also taken place on an international basis. An accord exists between Rhône-Poulenc and the German chemical firm of Bayer, while Michelin and Goodyear are collaborating in the construction of a synthetic rubber plant at Le Havre. Similarly Sud-Aviation, SNECMA and the British Aircraft Corporation are collaborating in the field of supersonic air transport.

Government policy has favoured concentration as a means of improving the competitive position of French industry. This is particularly the case in such sensitive sectors as aircraft construction and computer building, where advanced technology implies enormous research costs. The national market alone is insufficiently large, and American competition strong.

It is important to distinguish between financial concentration and geographical concentration, as the two do not necessarily coincide. In many instances, financial concentration, through mergers and associations, has brought about a geographical concentration of activity through rationalization programmes involving the closure of uneconomic factories. This has applied particularly in the textiles[9] and metallurgical industries. On the other hand, financial concentration in the more active branches, such as electronic and precision engineering, automobile manufacture and petrochemicals, has promoted a certain dispersal of activity through the creation of new factories and subsidiary firms.

*This amalgam has now been surpassed in scale by the merger announced at the end of 1967 of de Wendel, SIDELOR and Mosellane de Sidérurgie, with a annual capacity of 7¼ million tons of crude steel.
†The much smaller firm of Simca is associated with the Chrysler corporation. In 1968, Citroën announced technical collaboration with the Italian firm of FIAT.
‡The firms are St. Gobain, Pechiney, Pierrefitte and ONIA.

THE DISTRIBUTION OF MANUFACTURING

The pattern of distribution of manufacturing activity is summarized in *Figure 9.3* in terms of the major structures involved. A distinction is made between industrial regions consisting of large concentrations of manufacturing, and individual centres where manufacturing is restricted to a single urban agglomeration in an otherwise non-industrial setting. Further subdivision between these two categories has been attempted.

INDUSTRIAL REGIONS

METROPOLITAN REGIONS

Metropolitan industrial regions are formed by very large industrial and commercial cities with associated industrial annexes in suburbs and

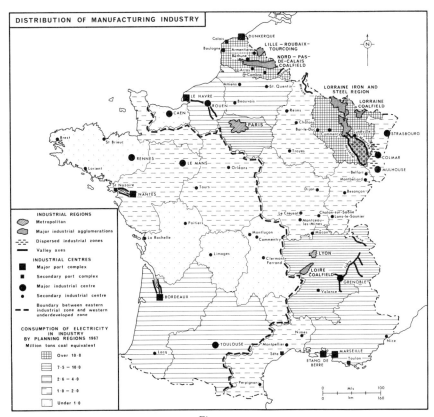

Figure 9.3

satellite towns. Characteristically, all but the very heaviest branches of industry are present, and the presence of an immediate very large market is a major location factor. Also important are direct contact with banking and commercial institutions, the availability of all types of labour and access to an elaborate transport network. The outstanding example is afforded by the Paris region, consisting of the inner and outer industrial suburbs, together with a surrounding matrix of smaller centres of more recent industrialization diffused from the capital. Although on a smaller scale, Lyon displays similar metropolitan characteristics in its industrial structure and has over 200,000 industrial workers within its urban complex.

MAJOR INDUSTRIAL AGGLOMERATIONS

As compared with the single dominant focal centre of the metropolitan case, industrial agglomerations are characterized by their polycentric structure. The clearest example is afforded by the northern coalfield, which has no single large urban nucleus, but rather a chain of medium-sized towns in the size range of 30,000 to 50,000 inhabitants together with an infill of approximately 100 small settlements of less than 10,000 inhabitants.[10] A similar situation occurs between Nancy and Metz, though the total population involved is much smaller and the degree of continuity in the built-up area less pronounced. A third example, with again a reduction in scale, is provided by the Loire coal basin. All three regions have in common a nineteenth-century origin based on the exploitation of minerals to support heavy industry. Finally, the Lille–Roubaix–Tourcoing industrial region may be placed in the same general category, though possessing certain individual features. In this instance, the motivating industry was textiles, and, in Lille, the region possesses a strong nucleus with a wide range of activities. The common characteristic of all the major industrial agglomerations is their experience of rapid growth in the nineteenth and early twentieth century and an apparent inability to achieve an equally dramatic participation in the modern technological revolution. Problems of urban renewal and industrial revitalization are here posed in their most acute forms.

INDUSTRIAL AXES

Axes of industrial development have been established along natural transport arteries. A distinction may be made between industry developed on the shores of estuaries and that located along valley routes. The phenomenon of the industrialization of estuaries is much less in evidence in France than in Britain, for obvious physical reasons. Only the Seine, Loire and Gironde possess broad estuaries with substantial penetration inland, and of these only the Seine affords deep water conditions. The Seine and Loire estuaries are the site of industrial axes but important contrasts exist between them. Although similar types of industry have developed (processing of metals, refining of petroleum and processing of food), the Seine estuary exceeds by far the volume of industry established on the Loire. In part this stems from superior navigational conditions, but more particularly results from a more advantageous situation and orientation with respect to the hinterland. Moreover, the axis of the Seine estuary is prolonged inland in the form of a linear distribution of industry extending to Paris, whereas manufacturing along the Loire axis is abruptly curtailed above Nantes.

Three major types of valley industrial axes may be proposed: expanding, contracting or stable, and embryonic. Examples of stable, and in some portions contracting, industrial axes are the Sambre and upper Moselle and Meuse valleys. On the other hand, the Rhône valley, below Lyon, may be considered an embryonic axis of industrial development which, by virtue of new hydroelectricity schemes and transport systems, is destined to play a major role in the future.[11] A changed evaluation of valley axes as sites for industrial development is apparent as compared with nineteenth-century conditions. The initial development was based on water-power sites and the movement of raw materials on canalized rivers, whereas contemporary factors favour those valleys which are the site of hydroeclectric schemes or which link major industrial regions with ports.

DIFFUSED INDUSTRIAL ZONES

These manufacturing regions are characterized by polycentric development in which the individual centres are small and scattered one from another. The best example is afforded by the broad zone extending from the flanks of the high Vosges to the plateau of southern Lorraine. The dominant activity of this zone is formed by the textiles industry, followed by light engineering and a miscellany of traditional industries such as glass and furniture making. Such locations are a carry-over from water-power sites and the utilization of scattered local raw materials. These activities are now very much exposed to modern trends of concentration and rationalization. Already similar dispersed zones of scattered small-scale industries have been virtually extinguished, as in Brittany and Haute-Normandie.

DISPERSED INDUSTRIAL CENTRES

It has been shown that France possesses few major industrial regions occupying a large extent, whether agglomerated or linear. The remaining industrial centres are of an isolated character, clearly separated from each other and from the concentrations described above.

COASTAL INDUSTRIAL CENTRES

For particular branches of industry a coastal location offers distinct advantages. The strength of these advantages is determined by the capacity of port facilities and the internal situation and external orientation of the port. On this basis a distinction may be made between major industrial port complexes with large port installations, an accessible and highly developed hinterland and a favourable orientation in relation to trading currents, and the secondary port centres, limited in handling capacity and with restricted hinterlands. In the former category may be placed Marseille, Le Havre, Dunkerque, Bordeaux and Nantes, while the inland ports of Rouen and Strasbourg share many of their characteristics. A certain change may be discerned in the basis of industrialization of these major complexes. The initial growth of industry was related to the refining and processing of raw materials in transit. In particular the trans-shipment point offered advantages for industries involving substantial reduction in bulk, facilitating redistribution to widespread markets, or re-export. Recent industrialization, however, has been tied to two main trends. The most substantial growth has resulted from the mass handling in very large volumes of specialized commodities, notably petroleum and iron ore, whereas industry based on general trade has had a more restrained growth. Secondly, the ports have attracted a considerable amount of new industry concomitant on their growth as large cities. In the latter case factors of labour supply, good inland communications, commercial organization and the strength of the local market may be more important than the utilization of the port facilities.

Two types of industrial structure thus result from present trends: the growth of major refinery complexes, frequently as separate annexes to the port nucleus, together with industrial estates, physically removed from the port on the periphery of the agglomerations, close to road communications and occupied by lighter branches of industry.

In the category of minor industrial ports may be placed a large number of small centres experiencing mixed fortunes. They are characterized by a narrow range of activities. In the simplest cases, industry consists merely of activities directly related to maritime functions, in the form of shipbuilding, ship repairing and marine engineering—for example St. Malo. More elaborate centres, as in the case of Calais, possess textile, chemical and engineering industries. Many of the smaller ports are in an exposed economic condition, since the decline of a single manufacturing firm may jeopardize not only industrial employment, but also the activity of the port itself.

MAJOR INDUSTRIAL CENTRES

The remaining inland centres of industry may be classified according to the scale, diversity and growth trends of manufacturing. A number of major industrial centres may be signalled, having a long history of commercial and industrial activity which has been reinforced by recent expansion. In this category may be placed Rouen, Strasbourg, Toulouse, Nancy and Grenoble. These centres have in common a wide range of industries, a focal position within inter-regional transport networks, and discharge regional functions in the spheres of commerce, administrstion and higher education.

SECONDARY INDUSTRIAL CENTRES

As opposed to the major centres of varied industrial activity indicated above, a further category of dispersed industrial centres may be proposed characterized by a smaller volume and narrower range of industrial employment. This encompasses a very wide variety of centres—for example Colmar, Mulhouse, Rennes, Le Mans, Amiens, Caen, Reims and Clermont-Ferrand—each marked by a certain degree of specialization of industrial functions. Many such centres have been the recipients of major industrial decentralizations, which have promoted a rapid expansion of employment, whereas others in this category urgently require new industry to confirm their importance as manufacturing centres. The most favoured centres have been those with important universities or rapid communications with Paris, giving a spontaneous basis for growth, but the less-favoured locations and centres, possessing declining traditional industries, have relied on the creation of incentives to attract new industry from outside.

MINOR CENTRES

The remaining industrial centres of France are extremely scattered and defy orderly classification. A distinction may be made between centres dependent on a single staple activity, often embodied in a single firm, and more diversified industrial centres. A distinction also may be made on the basis of the age of industry, as between towns with an industrial tradition extending over several centuries, and other towns which, as Lacq, are the site of recent implantations and which have a high growth potential. In the former instance the minor centres of industry grew up on the fringes of the old established industrial regions, benefiting from the general currents of industrial development but lacking specific local advantages by which to achieve substantial growth. This has applied in the case of a dense scattering of minor industrial centres in the départements of north-eastern France. In the second instance, new implantations have occurred in minor centres within the orbit of the largest cities of France, and form part of the growth of city regions. In such cases, industry is derived in a second-hand manner, spilling out from congested centres rather than attracted by virtue of positive growth factors in the minor centres themselves.

REFERENCES

[1] Clapham, J., *Economic Development of France and Germany*, 4th Edn., p. 53, 1963, Cambridge, Cambridge University Press.

[2] Pounds, N., 'The historical geography of the French iron and steel industry', *Ann. Ass. Am. Geogr.*, 1954, p. 3.

[3] Maillet, P., 'Quelques aspects de la concentration des entreprises en France', *Revue Econ. politique*, 1965, p. 496.

[4] 'La décentralisation industrielle et le Bassin Parisien jusqu'à 250 kilomètres de Paris', *Cah. Inst. Aménagement Urban. Rég. Paris.*, Vol. 6, 1966.

[5] Anon., 'Les opérations de décentralisation sont en baisse constante', *Patronat fr.*, No. 262, 1966, p. 10.

[6] Pierret, G., 'La décentralisation industrielle doit faire sa propre conversion', *Expans. rég.*, No. 41, 1966, p. 9.

[7] Chesnais, M. 'Les industries de la France Occidentale', *Norois*, 1968, p. 605.

[8] Durand, P., 'Dix ans de décentralisation industrielle', *Expans. rég.*, No. 38, 1965, p. 19.

[9] Houssaix, J., and Amoy, C., 'Quelques aspects de la concentration dans les industries françaises; l'exemple de l'industrie textile', *Revue Econ. politique*, 1965, p. 405.

[10] Thompson, I., 'A review of problems of economic and urban development in the northern coalfield of France', *Southampton Res. Ser. Geogr.*, No. 1, 1965, pp. 45–53.

[11] Rochette, R., 'Un exemple d'implantation industrielle dans la vallée du Rhône: l'agglomération de Roussillon', *Revue Géogr. alp.*, 1964, p. 173.

10

The Tertiary Sector

At the 1962 census, 7·3 million persons were employed in the activities of the tertiary sector, representing 39·4 per cent of the total labour force. The range of activities within the sector is extremely wide and an important distinction may be made between those which are strictly commercial—for example, wholesale and retail commerce, the hotel and catering trades—and those activities which are controlled by the public sector—such as public administration and much of the nation's education and transport systems.[1]

Tertiary activities are currently expanding at a high rate* and long-range estimates[2] point to a labour force of ten millions by 1985. However, some redeployment by types of activity may be anticipated as a result of rationalization processes already apparent and receiving government encouragement.[3] In particular, the machinery for the marketing of agricultural produce is in urgent need of reorganization. Inefficient methods of collection and distribution and the intervention of too many middlemen between producer and consumer contribute towards high food prices. The government, in creating a limited number of strong regional marketing centres, together with a reconstruction of the Paris wholesale market, is attempting to streamline marketing procedure. Similarly, in the retail trade France is characterized by a predominance of small units, especially in the case of food shops. The recent growth of supermarkets and self-service shops is an accelerating trend which will supplant many small shops and ultimately reduce the amount of employment consumed by wasteful duplication of services in small units†. In a nation often reproached for bureaucracy, the increased use of business machines and computers will permit increased efficiency in the administrative branches.

While the above are examples of activities in which employment

*Between 1954 and 1962 tertiary employment increased by approximately 900,000.

†Between 1960 and 1965, the number of supermarkets and self-service stores increased from 1,663 to 7,855.

growth may decelerate, the expansion of other activities will result from industrial growth, population increase and increased affluence and leisure time. Industrial expansion will make extra demands in the spheres of banking, finance, insurance and transport, while the increase in population will stimulate the demand for social services, public utilities and education. The growth in affluence will augment the demand for personal services and recreational amenities.

The detailed distribution of tertiary employment has been described at the level of the département by Coront-Ducluzeau[4] and on the basis of individual centres by Carrière and Pinchemel[5] and Le Guen.[6] In general terms, the importance of the tertiary sector varies in direct proportion to town size, but the composition of the employment is variable according to the dominant function of the individual towns. Thus, the administrative group assumes high proportions in département capitals, the transport group in the major ports and route centres, the hotel and catering sector in tourist resorts and the banking and financial group in the largest industrial cities and provincial capitals. The closest correlation with population size applies in the cases of retail commerce and personal and social services. The major exception to this tendency occurs in the case of a number of mono-industrial towns, chiefly mining centres, where the tertiary sector as a whole is weakly developed.[7]

Government plans for decentralization from Paris have involved tertiary activities as well as manufacturing industry. Restrictions on new office construction in central Paris have been in force since 1961, and in addition to the eight 'métropoles d'équilibre', eight smaller regional centres benefit from government assistance for the reception of tertiary employment.* Even certain government departments, the most centralized of all institutions, have been the subject of several recent decentralization operations†. Decentralization of tertiary functions is aimed at two particular situations: the creation of employment in areas lacking new industrial growth, and the reinforcement of the directional role of the 'métropoles d'équilibre'. In the latter case, the acquisition of head offices, administrative and financial institutions and advanced research centres is seen as essential to their intended function as poles of growth and animators of the economic life of their regions.[8]

A high degree of consistency exists in the regional significance of tertiary employment, the majority of regions having between 32 and 36 per cent of their labour force in the tertiary sector. A discrepancy exists between eastern and western France in the volume of tertiary employment

*These are Brest, Limoges, Poitiers, Clermont-Ferrand, Dijon, Besançon, Rennes and Montpellier.
†Examples are the establishment of a telecommunications research centre at Lannion, in Côtes-du-Nord, and the decentralization of the National Mint to Douai, Nord.

but there is no great divergence in the proportions employed by the sector. More emphatic is the divergence between the Paris region, with almost 30 per cent of the nation's tertiary workers, and the rest of the country. A detailed analysis of all branches of activity is not possible in the present context, and accordingly the tourist industry may be presented as a representative case study. This activity merits elaboration by virtue of its high growth rate, its role in regional economic development, and its interdependence with other branches of the tertiary sector, notably transport and retail trade.

THE TOURIST INDUSTRY

Natural and historical conditions have given France a vocation for tourism. The natural attraction of her coasts, rivers and mountains, allied to a rich cultural heritage and a renowned cuisine, determine France as a nation rich in tourist potential. Tourism has a fourfold function: a source of foreign revenue,[*] a generator of employment opportunities, a vital activity in underdeveloped areas lacking other resources, and a means of recreation for the increasingly urbanized population. The variations in the form and significance of tourism are discussed in the following regional chapters and emphasis is placed in the present context on the definition of broad trends that are transforming the character of the industry as a whole.

An essential distinction must be made between traditional commercial tourism, based on hotels and for the most part in established coastal resorts, spas and historic towns, and the more recent growth of popular tourism.[9] Traditional commercial tourism is a long-established feature, launched on the Riviera and Channel coasts, with fashionable outposts in Brittany, the Atlantic coast and at inland spas. Until 1936, the clientèle consisted predominantly of the wealthier classes, together with a cosmopolitan, though predominantly English, incursion of foreign tourists drawn from a similar social stratum. In 1936, the provision by law of 15 days of holiday stimulated hotel construction and substantially widened the social origin of holidaymakers. Since 1945, growing prosperity and the achievement of a month's paid holiday has produced an upsurge in popular tourism calling new forms of holidaymaking into being. In particular, the vast increase in car ownership has made the population more mobile and created forms of tourism related to car travel[†].

---

[*]This has shown some deterioration in recent years, from a net balance in the tourist account of 124 million dollars in 1963, 43 million dollars in 1964, 25 million dollars in 1966 to a loss of 56 million dollars in 1967.

[†]In 1964, 65 per cent of French holidaymakers utilized their own cars.

Although tourism represents a growth sector in the French economy, the full potential is far from being realized. An official inquiry reveals[10] that, in 1966, 21·5 million Frenchmen took a holiday away from home, rather less than 45 per cent of the total population. The number of people taking holidays increases annually by 600,000, but taking into account population growth it will not be until 1970 that over half of the population takes a holiday.

The greatest single factor which has promoted the growth of tourism was the introduction of a month's holiday with pay; this is invariably taken in full during July and August, rather than staggered over the summer season. In these conditions, the expense of a family holiday in a hotel becomes a heavy financial burden, and, for the lower income groups, prohibitively so. The acquisition of greater leisure time has thus produced a demand for cheaper forms of holiday. The most substantial growth has been in camping, benefiting from increased mobility and fulfilling the requirement for inexpensive accommodation. In 1966, 15 per cent of all French holidaymakers were campers, and the rate of growth is 15 per cent per annum. The growth of camping holidays has had the beneficial effect of spreading revenue from tourism, in the form of purchase of provisions and petrol, more widely. On the other hand, its growth threatens to compromise certain resorts highly dependent on hotel clientèle*

Since a month's holiday represents a substantial financial outlay, it has been a major factor attracting tourists to regions where climatic conditions offer the maximum advantage to be taken. In general, this element prejudices the resorts of the Channel coast and northern Brittany, where a rainy summer season. may produce a decline in clientèle during the subsequent holiday season. In addition to camping, the factor of cost has also encouraged the practice of renting apartments for the holiday period, often by family groups. This trend has stimulated much speculative development in the form of apartment blocks, converted cottages and individual villas, which has invaded many small settlements formerly unaffected by tourism.

The factor of expense also plays the dominant role in the growth of collective holidays available at cheap rates to members of various industrial, professional or social organizations. The most rudimentary form is the 'colonie de vacances'—a hostel for young children, possessing limited amenities, but invariably located in suitable countryside for outdoor recreation. Such institutions are commonly sponsored by industrial firms and religious bodies and make holidays for children possible for the

---

*A widespread reaction in such resorts is the conversion of former hotels into apartments for either seasonal or permanent occupation, the latter particularly for retired persons. The case may be cited of Dinard, where the majority of the prominent hotels on the seafront have suffered this fate.

Plate 9. New tourist developments. *Above*, the resort of La Grande motte under construction on the Lanquedoc coast. *Below*, the new winter sports resort of La Plagne (Savoie).

most modest income groups. At the other end of the scale, many professional organizations own fully-equipped holiday apartments and villas, available to members at rates far below those of their commercial equivalents

The most serious repercussions of the increased length of holiday and the failure to stagger the holiday period are the congestion of the more popular tourist areas during August and a tendency for prices to rise inordinately during this peak period. The situation implies that France must provide a tourist equipment, in terms of hotels, camp sites and other amenities, capable of serving the August peak but representing a considerable surplus capacity outside this month. The rise in prices is an inevitable result of the need on the part of the industry to secure the maximum revenue during a very short period of intense activity. This problem is particularly severe in the resorts of northern France and Brittany, where climatic conditions hinder any significant extension of tourism outside the summer months. The Mediterranean resorts benefit from a longer season, while the winter sports centres of the Alps and Pyrenees enjoy guaranteed income and employment during both the summer and winter seasons.*

The congestion and high prices of the established resorts, coupled with the growth of private transport, have led to a search for quieter and cheaper vacations in new areas as yet undisturbed by commercial tourism. Closely coupled with this trend is the growth in ownership of secondary homes. A high proportion of the French urban population lives in flats or small rented properties and, especially in the case of the professional groups, is able to devote income to the acquisition of a second residence, for weekend recreation, holidays, and often for ultimate retirement.[11] Since the rapid expansion of urban agglomerations is a modern feature, a majority of town dwellers are only a generation removed from the countryside and maintain close family connections with rural dwellers. Of the approximately 30 per cent of French holidaymakers who spend their annual vacation in the country, a majority are urban residents visiting relations in the region of birth or family origin†. The inheritance of family property may also lead to the maintenance of a second residence in the country for holiday and recreational purposes.

Many of the above trends may be exemplified by the case of Rothéneuf, illustrated in *Figure 10.1*.[12] Rothéneuf was formerly a small agricultural hamlet, situated some six kilometres east of St. Malo on the northern coast of Brittany. In the course of the last decade, Rothéneuf has become absorbed by a ribbon development, emanating from the growth of

*Over two million persons take winter sports holidays per annum in France.
†In 1964, 41 per cent of French holidaymakers stayed with relatives.

popular tourism, which has radically altered the character of the coastline east and west of the St. Malo-Dinard urban complex.[13] The original nucleus of the hamlet remains as the chief commercial zone of the settlement, but now forms only a small proportion of the built-up area. Natural conditions were particularly propitious for the growth of popular

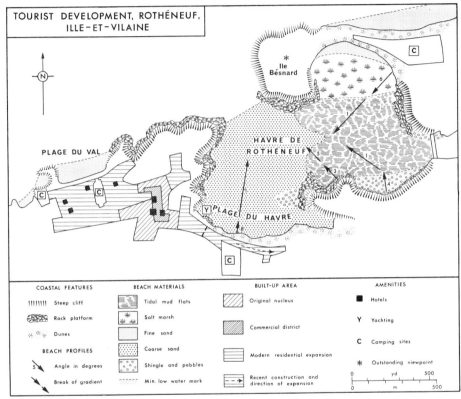

TOURIST DEVELOPMENT, ROTHÉNEUF,
ILLE-ET-VILAINE

COASTAL FEATURES		BEACH MATERIALS		BUILT-UP AREA		AMENITIES	
IIIIIIII	Steep cliff		Tidal mud flats		Original nucleus	■	Hotels
	Rock platform	✳	Salt marsh		Commercial district	Y	Yachting
	Dunes		Fine sand			C	Camping sites
BEACH PROFILES			Coarse sand		Modern residential expansion		
5	Angle in degrees	o o o	Shingle and pebbles			✳	Outstanding viewpoint
	Break of gradient		Min. low water mark		Recent construction and direction of expansion		

0   yd   500
0   m   500

(By courtesy of The Geographical Field Group)   *Figure 10.1*

tourism. To the east of the hamlet, the large bay of the Havre de Rothéneuf is practically enclosed by the tombolo joining the mainland to the Ile Bésnard. The silting of this bay has produced an almost level beach providing extremely safe bathing conditions and a large, sheltered expanse of water for yachting. The eastern half of the bay has extensive saltmarshes but the tombolo is the site of a major camp site sheltered by dunes and with an attractive beach on the northern side. The built-up area has expanded on the basis of individual villas and apartments and new construction is active along the coastal road. The clientèle consists of long-term visitors in rented villas or secondary homes, and shorter-term visitors staying in the number of small hotels or on camping sites. The population is thus swollen from a permanent figure of 500 inhabitants to a seasonal

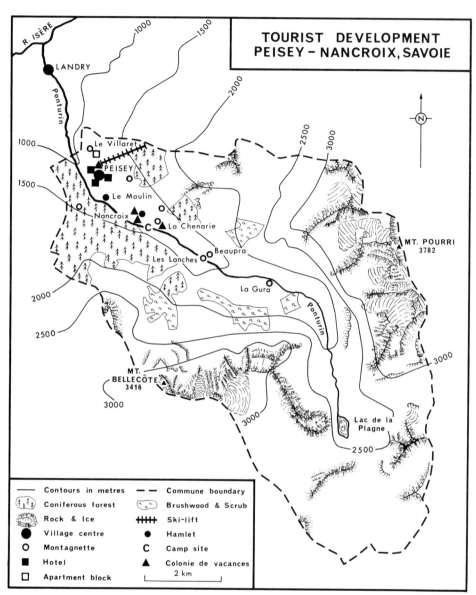

Figure 10.2

peak of approximately 3,000 in August. Rothéneuf owes its growth to natural conditions, ideal for family holidays and the safe recreation of young children, the availability of land for construction and camp sites, and a location within easy reach of the more sophisticated amenities of St. Malo and Dinard. The basic form of tourism is emphasized by the rapid transition to primeur cultivation within a hundred metres of shoreline.

While Rothéneuf represents a hamlet, formerly unimportant for tourism, which has flourished as a result of recent trends, the case of Peisey–Nancroix (*Figure 10.2*) offers an example of a mountain village in which a decadent tourism has been revitalized by the same general social trends. The commune of Peisey–Nancroix is formed by the valley of the river Ponturin, a hanging left bank tributary of the upper Isère, ten kilometres south of Bourg-St. Maurice. The scenic attraction of the valley was made the basis of a tourist industry between the wars at a time when moutain holidays were becoming increasingly fashionable. By 1924 the commune had seven hotels in the village centre and its tributary hamlet of Nancroix. This early eminence proved short-lived, as the valley was outgrown by other centres more favourably located and with a greater variety of amenities. The industry languished until after the Second World War but has subsequently made a strong revival. The starting point of this growth was the establishment of 'colonies de vacances'; although lacking in sophisticated amenities, the valley offers ideal conditions for youth activities. At the same time, the serious depopulation made available many cottages suitable for conversion and cheap building plots for the creation of secondary holiday residences. The valley was also patronized by campers and a well-equipped camp site has recently been built on the bank of the Ponturin. The commune centre, Peisey, has acquired commercial benefit from this development, but the greatest transformation has occurred in the tributary hamlets, which are now the sites of new chalets, apartments and 'colonies de vacances'. Only the higher 'montagnettes' have remained as yet unaffected by tourism. The factors promoting the recent growth of tourism have been the increase in car ownership, offsetting the factor of isolation, the growth of collective holidays for youth and the possibility of creating summer residences at lower cost than in the more fashionable centres. Although the commune operates a short ski-lift, winter sports are less exploited than at the nearby centres of Tignes, Val d'Isère and Pralognan. However, if present trends continue, a similar evolution may be anticipated in Peisey, leading to the ultimate decay of the present pastoral economic basis.[14]

Both the case studies presented above demonstrate the manner in which the changing character of tourism has produced a fundamental reassessment of tourist resources. New principles of the location of tourism are emerging[15] and are guiding the current heavy investment in the industry. The industry represents a major national asset and, as such, has received considerable government assistance.[16] Government action has been directed towards three general objectives. Loans and tax concessions are applied universally for the enlargement and modernization of existing hotel accommodation in order to increase the capacity of the industry and to improve its competitive position in international tourism.* Secondly, assistance has been given to finance major regional developments, as in Languedoc and Corsica, where the expansion of tourism is of vital importance to diversify employment. Thirdly, the government has assisted in the establishment of national and regional parks in order to preserve recreational areas for an increasingly urbanized society.

National parks were created in 1960 and characteristically consist of three zones†. A small central zone is preserved for scientific interest, with limited public access. This is surrounded by a much larger zone where public access is unlimited but regulations governing traffic and conserving wildlife are enforced, and the normal activities of forestry and grazing are carried out. A peripheral zone surrounds the park within which activities detrimental to the aesthetic and recreational function are controlled. National parks have been created in the Vanoise area of the Savoie Alps, the island of Port Cros off the Provence coast, and in the western Pyrenees. Further parks are proposed for Corsica, the Cévennes and the Maritime Alps. In 1967, a new concept in recreation was established with the designation of regional parks. These parks, with a minimum size of 10,000 acres, are primarily designed to provide recreational areas close to large urban concentrations. Examples have been established at St. Amand close to Lille and the agglomeration of the northern coalfield. Further regional parks are established or proposed for the Vercors area near Grenoble, the Chaîne des Puys near Clermont-Ferrand, the Grande Brière marshes accessible from Nantes–St. Nazaire, and at a site close to Toulouse.

REFERENCES

[1] Coquery, M., 'Secteur privé et secteur public des services', C.N.R.S. Mém: Docums, Tome X, Fasc. 2, 1965, p. 91.
[2] 'Réflexions pour 1985', Documn fr., 1964, p. 151.
[3] 'Projet de Loi de Finances pour 1967', Annexe 'Exécution du Plan en 1965 et 1966', Tome 2, Chapter 5, Le Commerce, p. 123.

*The targets established by the Fifth Plan are the creation of 32,500 new rooms and the modernization of 60,000 existing rooms.
†Nature reserves are a longer established feature. Reserves were created in the Pelvoux in 1914, and the Camargue in 1928, to which numerous other sites have been added. Their primary interest is scientific and public access is limited in most cases.

4 Coront-Ducluzeau, F., *La Formation de l'Espace Economique National*, 1964, Paris, Armand Colin.

5 Carrière, F., and Pinchemel, P., *Le Fait Urbain en France*, pp. 172–246, Paris, Armand Colin.

6 Le Guen, G., 'La structure de la population active des agglomérations de plus de 20,000 habitants', *Annls Géogr.*, 1960, p. 335.

7 Vakili, A., Pinchemel, P., and Gozzi, J., *Niveaux Optima des Villes. Essai de définition d'après l'analyse des structures urbaines du Nord et du Pas-de-Calais*, p. 47, Lille, CERES.

8 Rochefort, M., 'Une méthode de recherches des fonctions caractéristiques d'une métropole régionale', *C.N.R.S. Mém. Docums*, Tome X, Fasc. 2, 1965, p. 35.

9 'Le tourisme populaire en France des origines à 1961', *Notes Etud. docum.*, No. 2,902, 1962.

10 *Les vacances en 1966*, 1967, Paris, INSEE.

11 Barbier, B., 'Méthodes d'étude des résidences secondaires; l'exemple des Basses-Alpes', *Méditerranée*, 1965, p. 89.

12 Thompson, I., 'The St. Malo Region, Brittany', *Geogrl Field Group Stud.*, No. 12, 1968, pp. 42–44.

13 Delouche, G., 'L'activité touristique de la région malouine', *Norois*, 1956, p. 439.

14 Thompson, I., 'Economic transition in a high alpine valley', *Tijdschr. econ. soc. Geogr.*, 1962, p. 215.

15 Defert, P., *La localisation touristique. Problèmes théoriques et pratiques*, 1966, Berne, Gurten.

16 Defert, P., *L'Aménagement Touristique Régional*, Commissariat Général au Plan et à la Productivité, 1959.

11

Regional Disparities in Economic and Social Development

The broad patterns of economic activity which have formed the subject of this section have demonstrated a consistent tendency towards regional distortion. In turn, variations in economic levels promote discrepancies in the social sphere, resulting in regional contrasts in the quality of life. The existence of such regional socio-economic disparities creates fertile ground for extravagant imagery, and such phrases as 'the French desert' and 'the Far West', attached to the underdeveloped sections of the nation, are apt to confuse the issues through overdramatization. Nevertheless, the fact that opportunity and prosperity are not evenly distributed across the national space constitutes a central problem in French life. The mechanism of regional disparity is fundamentally economic in character and a brief discussion of the character and scale of the problem forms an appropriate summary to the present section and an introduction to the task of regional analysis.

Figure 11.1 is an attempt to establish in the simplest terms the dominant socio-economic cleavage in France. In the construction of this figure, the départements were ranked according to the proportions of the labour force employed in agriculture and industry respectively. The upper quartile of each ranked dispersion has been plotted and is superimposed on the distribution of major urban centres. In addition, départements which experienced a net decrease in population between 1962 and 1968 have been indicated. *Figure 11.1* illustrates that, in a general sense, a line drawn approximately from Le Havre to the Middle Loire and projected along the Rhône corridor divides the nation into two contrasted zones: an eastern zone of industrial dominance and a western zone of agricultural dependence. The eastern zone is animated by the Paris agglomeration, the nation's major industrial centres, and possesses a dense network of communications, the nation's major ports and the majority of the energy-producing capacity. Not surprisingly, this coincides with the greatest concentrations of urban population, tertiary employment and the largest regional markets. By contrast, in the western zone major industrial activity is restricted to a small number of individual centres and a high degree of dependence on agricultural employment persists. Moreover, the retarded structural characteristics of farming imply a progressive decline in employment opportunities as land reform and increased mechanization are achieved.

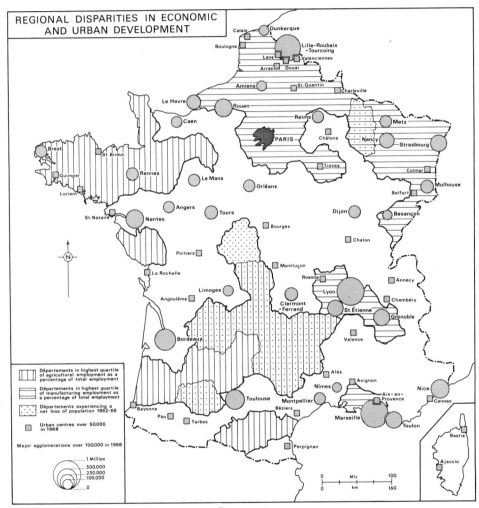

Figure 11.1

The opposition between eastern and western France expressed in *Figure 11.1* is a reality, but is also an oversimplification. In particular, the disparity in socio-economic level between the Paris region and the rest of the nation constitutes a further major cleavage, superimposed on the basic east–west contrasts.[1] This division of France into three socio-economic provinces forms a useful framework for the examination of the problem of disparity but conceals numerous exceptions to the general rule. Individual centres of positive growth exist in western France, particularly at Toulouse, Lacq, Rennes, Caen and Le Mans, while some of the older-established industrial centres of eastern France are now facing severe conversion problems. Similarly, Corsica, while located in the eastern zone, has economic, demographic and social problems more characteristic of western France. In the following discussion, use of data at the planning region level indicates the major variations within the broader socio-economic zones.

Table 11.1

REGIONAL VARIATIONS IN EMPLOYMENT STRUCTURE, 1962

	Percentage of labour force employed in		
	Industry	Agriculture	Services
1. PARIS REGION	44·4	1·6	54·0
2. EASTERN FRANCE			
Nord	54·0	10·2	35·8
Picardie	44·3	20·7	35·0
Haute-Normandie	41·2	17·1	41·7
Champagne	43·8	21·6	34·6
Lorraine	54·8	11·0	34·2
Bourgogne	35·7	28·2	36·4
Franche–Comté	49·6	21·6	28·8
Alsace	47·1	14·1	38·8
Rhône–Alpes	47·8	17·4	34·8
Provence–Côte d'Azur–Corse	35·6	14·7	49·7
3. WESTERN FRANCE			
Basse-Normandie	26·3	41·1	32·6
Bretagne	22·8	45·4	31·8
Pays-de-la-Loire	30·8	36·4	32·8
Centre	35·2	29·9	24·9
Poitou–Charentes	27·6	38·8	33·6
Limousin	27·5	43·9	28·6
Auvergne	32·9	35·0	32·1
Aquitaine	29·2	34·1	36·7
Midi–Pyrénées	29·4	39·1	31·5
Languedoc	28·2	31·8	40·0

Source: Recensement de 1962.

The most important single cause of the imbalance between eastern and western France is the under-industrialized character of the western zone. *Table 11.1* reveals that of the planning regions of eastern France, only Bourgogne and Provence–Côte d'Azur–Corse have less than 40 per cent of their labour force in industrial employment. By contrast, industry provides approximately 15 per cent less of the total employment opportunities in the regions of the west. Employment in tertiary occupations shows some consistency throughout the whole country at regional level and thus the under-industrialization of the west is reflected in the very high agricultural dependence. The proportion employed in agriculture in the western regions is between 30 and 40 per cent of the labour force, as compared with less than 20 per cent throughout much of eastern France. Since industrial and tertiary employment in the western zone is concentrated into relatively few manufacturing centres, administrative capitals and resort areas, it follows that the degree of agricultural dependence is effectively much higher than the generalized data present. The fact that the volume of agricultural employment in western France will inevitably continue to decline, and that the level of tertiary employment already approximates to the national average, casts great significance on the growth trend in industrial employment.

Important socio-economic disparities spring from the contrasts in employment structure summarized above. The high agricultural dependence and low proportion of industrial employment in the western regions imply a lower level of choice and opportunity than in Paris and the eastern zone. Industry is more concentrated into a limited number of centres, where it tends to consist of a small number of firms and a narrow range of activities. The opportunities for mobility and advancement are thus restricted as compared with the larger and more diversified industrial zones of the east. The problem of matching the decline in agricultural employment with a compensating increase in manufacturing has not yet been resolved. This problem is particularly severe in Brittany, where high rural densities and a high fertility level have coincided with a net reduction in industrial employment. Finally, the dependence on a retarded agriculture implies a lower average level of remuneration in western France. Even in industry, the degree of dependence on traditional staple industries and on small production units tends to depress salary levels below the level of the rest of the nation[2] (*Table 11.2*).

The basis of the economic disparity between the regions of the west and the remainder of France is thus not merely the degree of industrialization, but also the differential growth rate of new industrial jobs, the contrasts in the range of choice in type of manufacturing employment, differences in the possibility of mobility and advancement, and disparities in wage levels[3]

The contrasts in economic opportunity find their counterpart in social disparities of similar magnitude, but the level of the quality of life is less amenable to direct measurement. While certain material criteria may be recorded, the quality of life in a given region is based on many intangible

Table 11.2

REGIONAL VARIATIONS IN INCOME LEVEL, 1962

| | Income level per household[a] | | |
	Farmers	Farm workers	Industry[b]
1. PARIS REGION	701·0	189·2	130·7
2. EASTERN FRANCE			
Nord	143·6	98·9	95·1
Picardie	226·1	123·8	95·2
Haute-Normandie	140·4	65·5	103·2
Champagne	150·8	115·4	94·6
Lorraine	99·0	86·4	100·8
Bourgogne	114·3	70·7	87·3
Franche–Comté	101·3	138·1	92·2
Alsace	126·0	192·4	102·0
Rhône–Alpes	67·9	99·5	94·5
Provence–Côte d'Azur–Corse	94·6	98·9	90·4
3. WESTERN FRANCE			
Basse-Normandie	144·0	74·1	88·6
Bretagne	66·6	78·0	78·6
Pays-de-la-Loire	68·0	89·4	81·4
Centre	118·5	87·3	89·5
Poitou–Charentes	87·8	69·7	78·3
Limousin	70·6	87·3	83·2
Auvergne	59·5	74·4	89·1
Aquitaine	65·0	74·7	90·4
Midi-Pyrénées	64·0	70·3	89·5
Languedoc	100·0	86·0	77·8

[a]France = 100.
[b]Industrial wage earners.
Source: Etudes et Conjoncture 1966, 'Régionalisation des comptes de la nation 1962'.

factors that can only be assessed subjectively. The necessity for migration in search of employment can be expressed statistically but the degree of hardship inflicted by the separation of family members cannot be measured. Similarly, the long-term psychological effects of isolation, physical decay of outlying settlements and the loss of young people by migration are not revealed by impersonal statistics.

The opposition between the eastern and western zones is more subtle than in the case of economic disparities. Although on balance, the western regions have a material quality of life below that enjoyed in the national capital and much of eastern France, certain serious social problems have the reverse incidence. Thus urban housing shortages, atmospheric pollution, traffic congestion, overcrowded schools and limited access to recreational areas are more characteristic of the urbanized areas of eastern France. Of greater significance in the nation at large is the differential quality of life between urban and rural residence. Since western France has fewer large towns and a higher proportion of rural population it follows that important geographical disparities nevertheless remain. The intepretation of certain accepted indices is complicated by the differences in evaluation on the part of the population of the various regions. Thus the level of private car ownership shows little variation at the regional scale in spite of the greater prosperity of the urbanized eastern regions. Whereas in the urban agglomerations of the east, the existence of adequate public transport systems minimizes the need for private transport, car ownership is frequently the sole means of mobility in the large rural areas of the west deficient in public transport. Even in the most rural départements of western France car ownership is surprisingly high, at one car per six inhabitants. This reflects the needs of the farming community, the car often being a general-purpose vehicle, and also the need for private transport to permit journey-to-work movements by those not employed on the land. Similarly, the ownership of television sets shows few pronounced regional variations. The fact that television represents the sole form of entertainment for many millions of rural dwellers may account for this. The apparent consumption of durable consumer goods is therefore an unreliable indicator of variations in social levels, and the regional scale is too crude for meaningful differentiation.

Two indices which may be employed to infer important social distinctions are the regional distribution of highly qualified workers, and the variations in prosperity as expressed by average income levels.

Table 11.3 depicts the proportion of the employed population which has received a formal training in professional or technical aptitudes, and affords some indication of the distribution of the nations' most talented population. The dominance of the Paris region is emphatic and the explanation of this monopoly of the nation's skill and talent is readily apparent. The capital city has the largest number of institutes of higher learning, professional colleges and commercial schools, which attract talented individuals from the entire nation. Paris thus generates a high proportion of the nation's best qualified workers and at the same time provides an optimum cultural and economic environment for their retention. The high degree of centralization of government and head offices of industry and commerce, together with the concentration of advanced technology industries, stimulates an insatiable demand for highly-qualified labour and supports high levels of remuneration. This monopoly of talent is perhaps the most serious aspect of the socio-economic gap between Paris and the rest of the nation. The gravitation of the most skilled and able population towards what is undeniably one of the world's most important cultural centres appears irreversible. The second-ranking region of Rhône–Alpes, with a strong provincial capital and industrial

Table 11.3

INDICATORS OF REGIONAL SOCIAL DISPARITIES, 1962

	Employed population possessing professional or technical qualifications[a]	Average income[b]
1. PARIS REGION	211	16·4
2. EASTERN FRANCE		
Nord	70	10·2
Picardie	29	11·2
Haute-Normandie	29	10·8
Champagne	25	10·0
Lorraine	43	11·3
Bourgogne	30	8·3
Franche–Comté	20	10·7
Alsace	28	10·8
Rhône–Alpes	90	10·4
Provence–Côte d'Azur–Corse	61	11·0
3. WESTERN FRANCE		
Basse-Normandie	27	9·3
Bretagne	52	7·3
Pays-de-la-Loire	52	7·5
Centre	40	8·5
Poitou–Charentes	29	7·1
Limousin	17	7·4
Auvergne	27	8·3
Aquitaine	50	8·9
Midi-Pyrénées	44	8·5
Languedoc	28	9·5

[a]Per thousand employed workers.
[b]Average income per head of household (thousand francs).
Source: 'Exécution du Plan en 1965 et 1966', Tome III, 1966, p. 468.

centre at Lyon, has a proportion of highly-qualified workers less than half of the capital city.

The average income level per head of household shows an equally emphatic divergence between Paris and the rest of the country and a pronounced disparity between the eastern and western regions[3]. Although variations in the cost of living complicate the issue, the average income per head of household in Paris is double that of many of the western regions, while that of the eastern zone averages between 20 and 30 per cent more than western France. Since opportunities for highly-paid female employment are greater in the urbanized eastern zone, the true disparity in affluence is even wider.

In each of the preceding chapters of this section, attention has been drawn to the spatial distortion in specific aspects of the economic infra-structure and productive activity. It is logical to pose the question as to whether these distortions result from inherent and permanent factors of resource availability and geographical location, or whether from deficiencies in the economic organization of the national space. A distinction must be made therefore between certain immutable characteristics of western France which interpose barriers to development, and other problems which can be solved by institutional and functional reorganization. Certain physical constraints on economic activity must be regarded as permanent throughout the foreseeable future. The existence of extensive areas of uplands with mediocre soils and vegetation, the paucity of navigable waterways, the limited extent of indigenous power sources and the dearth of industrial raw materials are permanent facts inherent in the physical basis of western France. The location, peripheral in France and marginal in terms of the Common Market, is a permanent fact, although reorientation of agricultural production and improvements in transport may reduce the severity of this obstacle to progress.

Table 11.4

VALUE OF EXPORTS TO COMMON MARKET PARTNERS, 1965
(Million Francs)

1. PARIS REGION	6,064	3. WESTERN FRANCE	
2. EASTERN FRANCE		Basse-Normandie	171
Nord	2,706	Bretagne	290
Picardie	1,045	Pays-de-la-Loire	358
Haute-Normandie	510	Centre	354
Champagne	718	Poitou–Charentes	308
Lorraine	2,160	Limousin	105
Bourgogne	457	Auvergne	283
Franche–Comté	487	Aquitaine	630
Alsace	1,443	Midi-Pyrénées	526
Rhône–Alpes	1,755	Languedoc	285
Provence–Côte d'Azur–Corse	918	Total Western France	3,310
Total Eastern France	12,199		

Source: 'Exécution du Plan en 1965 et 1966', Tome 111, 1966, p. 375.

Table 11.4 demonstrates the weakness of western France in terms of its exporting performance to the Common Market partners; France's largest and most rapidly expanding market. The Paris region alone exports twice as much by value, and eastern France almost four times as much to the Common Market, as does western France. This is a measure of the low level of industrialization and the lack of structural adaptation of farming in the western regions to the demands of the Common Market.

While factors of resource base and geographical location are permanent factors, these disadvantages can be partially offset by improvements in economic organization. Improvements in the economic infrastructure—particularly in transport, education and marketing—are a prerequisite for new growth in the western regions. Agricultural reform in the fields of land consolidation, farm size, mechanization and use of fertilizers is capable of increasing output and raising farm income levels. Technological innovation is making industrial location less rigid, and in combination with state assistance is permitting decentralization, the growth of new industrial zones and the revival of areas of declining industries.

The scale of disparity between the three economic zones outlined at the beginning of this chapter is widely held to be excessive. On the other hand, there is no reason to believe that a regular pattern of distribution of activity and opportunity is possible or desirable. A policy aimed at a deliberate regional levelling of economic activity would conflict with potent location factors which confer advantages on particular regions for specific types of activity which must be fully exploited. The reduction of regional disparities must rather be based on a realistic appraisal of the particular vocation of each region, in the context of efficient production for highly competitive markets, and by the adaptation of the economic structure to fulfil this vocation to the maximum extent. This is the stated objective of French regional and prospective planning. The task of restructuring the economic geography of France so as to enable each region to fulfil a distinctive role with the maximum effectiveness forms the central theme of the concluding regional essays.

THE PROBLEM OF REGIONAL DEFINITION AND ANALYSIS

The task of defining regional systems appropriate to contemporary realities has been one of the most actively debated problems in France in recent years.[4-7] The objective of the regional essays which conclude this book is not to describe the geography of France within the conventional regional boundaries, but rather to restate the problems and trends described thus far largely in isolation from each other, in terms of their spatial inter-relationship. The regions adopted must therefore draw their integrity from the existence of consistent patterns of economic and social organization and the possession of distinctive development problems. They are thus viewed as functional regions, susceptible not only to spontaneous evolution but also to a planned exploitation of their specific vocations in the context of the national economy. The view that regions possess both an internal potential and an external relationship to the optimum organization of the national space and resources is a basic tenet of the recent development of applied geography in France.[8]

The spirit of the following regional essays is consonant with this enlarged perspective of regional study, which includes an applied, as opposed to a purely descriptive, approach. The delimitation of regions adopted is that utilized by the French government in the effort of regional planning. This adherence to the official planning regions implies both inconveniences and advantages. The obvious contention—that to accept a ready-made regional system for which detailed statistics are available is to adopt the line of least resistance—is difficult to refute. Equally, the use of planning regions involves the acceptance of boundaries that are frequently arbitrary and not necessarily permanent. Futher problems arise from the unfamiliarity of the nomenclature, although the presentation of a map of each region averts any possible amibiguity. In spite of these limitations, logic dictates that an approach designed to elucidate regional problems should be linked to a regional system which is being actively employed for their resolution. Further, the planning regions by definition afford a framework not only for the analysis of existing realities, but also to foreshadow future developments.

The organization of the regional chapters seeks to reflect the important areal disparities in economic and social levels described in the present chapter. A primary distinction is thus drawn between the three major provinces: the Paris region, eastern France and western France. Within this framework, chapters are devoted to each individual planning region, with the exception of Corsica, which is treated separately from Provence–Côte d'Azur. The term 'essay' is used deliberately since constraints of space preclude an exhaustive analysis of all the 22 regions thus arrived at. No attempt has been made to standardize the length of each essay, nor to standardize the approach to each region beyond a consistent emphasis on the exposition of regional problems in terms of their causation, consequences and remedial action. It is hoped that this flexible treatment permits the characterization of regional problems to better effect than would a rigidly formalized procedure.

REFERENCES

[1] 'Notes et Documents', *Population*, 1967, Fig. 1, p. 532.
[2] Madinier, P., 'Les disparités géographiques des salaires en France', *Etud. Mém. Centre Etud. Econ.*, 1960.
[3] Maurau, M., 'Le revenu des ménages français par catégories socio-professionelles et par région', *Expans. rég.*, 1967, No. 2, p. 9.
[4] McDonald, J., 'Current controversy in French geography', *Prof. Geogr.*, 1964, p. 20.
[5] Sister Mary Annette, 'The changing French region', *Prof. Geogr.*, 1965, p. 1.
[6] Juillard, E., 'La région, essai de définition', *Annls Géogr.*, 1962, p. 483.
[7] Claval, P., and Juillard, E., 'Région et régionalisation dans la géographie et dans d'autres sciences sociales. Bibliographie analytique', *Cah. Inst. Etud. politiques Univ. Strasbourg*, 1967.
[8] Labasse, J., *L'Organisation de l'Espace*, 1966, Paris, Hermann.

Part Three
REGIONAL ESSAYS

KEY TO REGIONAL MAPS

NICE Over 200,000

TOULON ● 100,000 – 200,000

AIX ■ 50,000 – 100,000

━━━ Motorway

□ □ □ □ Motorway under construction

＋ ＋ ＋ Railway

Hydro electric station

Grasse ■ 25,000 – 50,000

BERRE ● 10,000 – 25,000

Bollène ● Under 10,000

═══ Main road

＝ ＝ ＝ ＝ Proposed motorway

┴┴┴┴┴┴ Canal

▮ Nuclear power station

12

The Paris Region

As the fourth largest city in the world, Paris must be regarded as exceptional not only in France but in the world as a whole. The city of Paris had a population of 2·6 million inhabitants in 1968, but the addition of the suburban extension swells this figure to 8·2 millions in the whole of the agglomeration. The entire Paris region had a total of 9·2 million inhabitants in 1968, or over 18 per cent of the national population. To encompass a description of this world city within a brief chapter is clearly impossible, and the present discussion is limited to an introduction of the central problems relevant to the planning of the city region. Even this task can only be attempted selectively, and emphasis is placed on two related themes: the problems of concentration and congestion. The term 'concentration' is applied to the extraordinary degree to which Paris monopolizes the economic, political, social and cultural substance of France. By corollary, the term 'congestion' refers to the whole spectrum of planning problems resulting from the excessive degree of concentration of activity in the Paris agglomeration.

The most obvious expression of concentration is demographic; with only 2·2 per cent of the national land area, the Paris region had 18 per cent of the national population in 1968, and almost 30 per cent of the total urban population. The Paris agglomeration is over seven times more populous than the nation's second largest agglomeration, that of Lyon. This demographic concentration is essentially a modern feature. In 1861, the Paris region accounted for only 7·5 per cent of the national total, and by the close of the nineteenth century had risen to only 11 per cent. Between 1901 and 1946, while the national population decreased slightly, that of the Paris region increased by over 40 per cent, and the proportion of the national total increased to 16 per cent. The demographic processes which produced this transformation have been described by Chevalier[1] and by Pourcher,[2] but are less important in the present context than the economic and social consequences. With over four million workers, the

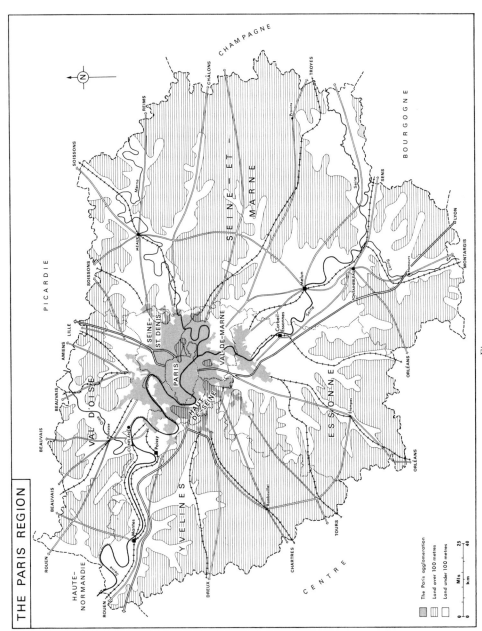

THE PARIS REGION

The Paris agglomeration
Land over 100 metres
Land under 100 metres

Mls   25
       40
km

0

Figure 12.1

Paris region employs 21 per cent of the total French labour force. Even more serious is the extent to which the region monopolizes qualified labour, with 21 per cent of the nation's skilled industrial workers, 39 per cent of the professional and managerial grades, 48 per cent of the nation's qualified engineers and 72 per cent of the total research workers.[3] The concentration of qualified, and therefore highly-paid,* workers is a consequence of the extent to which Paris has accumulated advanced technology industry. The region accounts for 56 per cent of the output of the aircraft industry, 80 per cent of the private vehicles, 68 per cent of the precision engineered products and 75 per cent of radio and television sets. A measure of this industrial dominance is the fact that the region contributes 35 per cent by value of the nation's exports.

An equally emphatic concentration occurs in the tertiary sector. The capital has a quasi-monopoly of banking and insurance and 64 per cent of the nation's registered companies have their head offices in Paris. Approximately half of the nation's tourist capacity is located in Paris. The centralization of government is reflected in the fact that 25 per cent of all civil servants work in Paris. This combination of business and government centralization implies an overwhelming concentration of the power of decision in the national capital in both the public and private sectors of the economy. This economic supremacy is matched by an equally strong concentration of the nation's cultural life, as expressed in the possession of renowned institutions of higher education, a high level of literary and artistic activity and monopoly of the mass media of communications. In short, Paris enjoys a concentration of activity, power, wealth and cultural activity out of proportion to its population size, and exercises a degree of primacy in the national life unequalled in any other industrialized west European nation. This primacy is, however, obtained at a cost, not only to the provinces, but also to the region itself. This cost is congestion, the inevitable reverse face of the accumulation of the nation's substance in a single agglomeration.

The problem of congestion has many facets in addition to the literal sense of an overcrowding of people and traffic. Congestion is a direct consequence of the rapid growth of Paris in the last 100 years and the relative anarchy which has attended the evolution of the urban fabric.[4] In 1850 the Paris agglomeration was contained within the lines of the 1840 fortifications, although ribbon development was already apparent along the 'routes nationales' converging on the city. At this time, the morphology of Paris was essentially concentric, conforming with the successive enlargements of the fortified perimeter, within which an overall grid-iron street

---

*The region employs 20 per cent of the nation's paid workers but expends 38 per cent of the national wage bill.

pattern was inscribed. With the construction of railways after 1850, the morphology of the agglomeration took on a new form, that of tentacles of built-up land along the railway lines radiating from central Paris. This star-shaped morphology was accentuated between the two World Wars during a speculative era free from planning restrictions. The basis of this explosive suburban growth was a myriad of individual building plots,[5] developed speculatively and with little regard to harmony of building style or rational provision of services. Bastié[6] has described, in the case of one of the southern 'tentacles' of growth, the influence of the speculative development of 'lotissements' in creating a sea of houses on diminutive plots, in incoherent suburbs served by the railway lines. Between the fingers of development extending along the transport axes open country was preserved and agricultural activity sustained.[7]

The process of tentacular development, most pronounced south of the Seine where relief exercises a more marked influence on the lines of communication, proceeded unchecked until the Second World War, absorbing many pre-existing small urban centres as industrial or residential satellites. The hesitant application of physical planning measures had little impact since little could be done to direct the growth of the metropolis without some measure of control of the economic forces generating this growth.

Since the war, more positive planning measures have been adopted in response to a renewed surge in the expansion of the agglomeration. The immediate problem was that of housing a population which between 1946 and 1954 increased by 620,000 and between 1954 and 1962 by approximately one million. The inevitable result was pressure on the interstices between the tentacular growth of past decades. In the context of a housing shortage and soaring land values, a high proportion of the new construction was of high-density apartment blocks, and especially H.L.M. complexes.* The logical conclusion of this trend was the proliferation, since 1950, of huge 'grands ensembles'.[8, 9] These complexes, of which Sarcelles with 40,000 residents was the prototype, have contributed further to the blocking of the remaining open spaces close to Paris, while discharging large volumes of daily commuters to the centre of the agglomeration.

While the interstices between the tentacles are now being completely built up, reducing the star-shaped morphology once more to a concentric form, the next stage of radial development is already apparent. The construction of motorways and high-capacity roads, coupled with the great increase in private vehicle ownership, has created new axes of movement from ever more distant centres now in the process of incorporation into the agglomeration. The exits from motorways now fulfil the role of the

---

*'Habitations à loyer modéré', see Chapter 4, p. 63.

suburban railway stations in the nineteenth and early twentieth century extension, with the difference that the mode of transport has a lower efficiency and the problems of congestion are proportionately greater.

The growth pattern outlined above has led to serious problems of physical congestion in terms of movement, the stock of building and the allocation of land to competing uses. The process of physical expansion was unaccompanied by any significant nodular development of industrial and commercial activity. Consequently the expansion of the agglomeration has implied an increasing separation of residence from place of work and the necessity for daily journey-to-work movements. Lucchi[11] has demonstrated that the number of commuters in the Paris region increased from 100,000 in 1901 to 1·2 million in 1962* The central core of the city is the principal pole of attraction, surrounded by an industrialized inner suburban ring where the number of outward commuters is balanced by a reciprocal movement from central Paris and from the outer suburbs. The outer suburban zone constitutes a virtual reservoir of labour for central Paris. The significance of this vast daily displacement of labour is twofold: the movement is of itself unproductive, consuming a large amount of time and human energy, while the periodicity of the movement creates severe strains on the transport system at peak hours. Lucchi[12] has estimated that the average time lost through journey to work is 1 hour 24 minutes, or approximately 16 per cent of the daily working time. Since a high proportion of commuters make one or more changes in the course of the journey, and a majority of rush hour commuters must travel standing†, the element of fatigue is inevitably high. The strain imposed on the transport system[13] is a function of the manifest tendency for the growth of commuting to outrun the pace of investment in additional capacity. Approximately 72 per cent of the total labour force employed some form of transport to reach work in a survey in 1960, including 51 per cent who utilized the public transport system. The 'métropolitain' underground network totals 206 kilometres, but has the disadvantage of serving only the centre and inner suburbs. As a result, the capacity of the system is saturated at rush hours by the tens of thousands of commuters needing to transfer from the underground to the suburban train service and vice versa. Moreover, the network has been only slightly extended since 1939. The suburban railway service totals 970 kilometres but has several deficiencies. The initial suburban extension of the agglomeration, itself stimulated by railway construction, is well served, but the intervening

---

*Commuting is defined as a change of commune between residence and workplace.
†The capacity of rush-hour suburban trains is calculated on the basis that over 78 per cent of the travellers are standing.

lacunae, now densely built-up, frequently have only a rudimentary network.[14] Inter-suburban movement by rail is particularly difficult. The omnibus service suffers the inconveniences of slow travel,* the risk of traffic jams at rush hour and, again, the weak development of connections between suburbs, even though in the latter case this often represents the sole form of public transport.

Slightly more than 21 per cent of commuters in 1960 used private transport, including 11 per cent using private cars. The level of car ownership in Paris attained 1·2 million units in 1965 or one car for every 4·8 inhabitants. Moreover, a 31 per cent increase in circulation on the 'routes nationales' of the agglomeration occurred between 1955 and 1960. The intra-urban road network is incapable of handling this volume efficiently, in spite of the completion of expressways along the banks of the Seine. The existing motorways are not as yet fully interconnected through the agglomeration and their function is essentially that of long-distance inter-urban connections rather than acting as freeways linking suburban and central Paris. Hall[15] has noted the vocation of the Haussman boulevards as one way systems but notes the bottlenecks caused by their tendency to converge on complex 'rond-points'. Similarly the low absorptive capacity of central Paris in terms of parking space is an unsolved problem.

To the phenomenon of commuting with its specific strains, must be added the general high level of circulation essential to the functioning of any large city. The resultant situation is not yet one of asphyxia, and the work now in progress on the 'boulevard périphérique' express road may bring some much needed relief to central Paris. Rather the problems are associated with the lack of efficiency of the present transport system, imposing delays, fatigue, a high level of atmospheric pollution and inconvenience at the local level of inter-suburban travel.

Infringement of the freedom of circulation is but one aspect of physical congestion. Equally serious is the congestion of buildings, whether for residential, industrial or commercial usage. Paris has the highest ratio of built-up to open land of any French city, resulting in extraordinarily high population densities. This problem is intensified by the very high average building height in central Paris, in turn frequently the result of the development of small and irrationally shaped building plots. As a consequence large and densely-populated areas of the city are in need of redevelopment with a view to the elimination of old and substandard housing, the achievement of lower housing densities, the recuperation of land for recreational purposes and the implantation of community and social services. Several comprehensive rehabilitation schemes are in

*The average journey speed by omnibus in central Paris is 12 kilometres per hour, and in the suburbs 20 kilometres per hour.

operation in central Paris,* but the pace of achievement is slow. More commonly, redevelopment is spontaneous and piecemeal, involving the demolition of old housing and its replacement by apartments giving even higher densities of occupation and unaccompanied by improvements in amenities.

The problems confronting industry are no less serious. A high proportion of the industries of Paris are located on sites occupied during the nineteenth century and subsequently hemmed in by housing and transport developments, while others, often of artisan origin, have only expanded by recourse to the occupation of several separate sites. Many firms thus occupy constricted sites with difficult access and no room for expansion. The same problem confronts many services and public institutions. As a result, spontaneous decentralizations have occurred to the periphery of the agglomeration, to more expansive sites with lower land values and, in many instances, access to motorways. Examples in industry are the Renault works at Flins, the SNECMA aircraft engine works at Evry and Simca at Poissy. In the case of service activities, the decentralization of Les Halles food market to Rungis, the 'Grandes Ecoles' and science faculties to Orsay and the television centre to Champigny may be cited. Many more industrial, commercial and institutional activities have been decentralized away entirely from the agglomeration in response to government restrictions on new building and financial incentives to relocate in the provinces.

A final aspect of physical congestion is the intensification of the competition between differing types of land use. At the margins of the agglomeration this competition is phrased in fundamental terms between the use of land, much of it of high quality, for agricultural purposes, and its sterilization by building.[16] Within the perimeter of the agglomeration intense competition for sites exists between industry, housing, commerce and public utilities. This intense competition is a measure of the pressures exerted by the city on land resources, and, except where planning intervenes effectively, is a battle fought on financial terms, the market value of a given terrain ultimately determining its usage. Reference to the financial implications of land use competition serves to introduce the second connotation of congestion. In addition to being a physical phenomenon, urban congestion also imposes an economic burden and remedial action can only be implemented at a high financial cost.

The economic consequences of congestion are felt alike by the public and private sectors. Public expenditure on essential services is the victim of a vicious circle in which expensive programmes of investment tend to be immediately offset by population growth, calling for yet further

*As, for example, Maine–Montparnasse, La Défense, Ménilmontant and Les Halles.

investment at a higher cost. This situation applies with particular force to the transport system, which is operated at a substantial financial loss, subsidized by the government exchequer, and at the same time requires a massive input of capital to finance new construction and equipment. The same applies in the case of schools, hospitals and low-cost housing, where the pressure of additional population is added to the cost of trying to improve inadequate standards in the existing services. The cost of providing social services is made doubly expensive by two further consequences of congestion: the high wage and salary levels as compared with the provinces and the inflated prices of land. High wages result from the high cost of living in Paris, especially the cost of housing and rents, and the expenses incurred in journey-to-work movement. Inflated land values are also a result of the pressure on unbuilt land in the agglomeration coupled with an acute housing shortage. In spite of government measures to restrict speculation on designated land, the inflated cost of land purchase, coupled with high labour costs in construction and high wage levels for employees, limits the pace at which local authorities can expand and improve social services. Industry also suffers the same economic consequences of congestion in terms of inflated wage bills and the high cost of building land. The decentralization movement is thus not only an attempt to escape from the physical confinement of congested sites but also to secure an economic environment of reduced direct operating costs.

Concentration and congestion thus epitomize the planning problems of Paris. An undue concentration of the nation's economic activity in the agglomeration, and an even more excessive concentration into the centre of the built-up area, readily explain the multitude of problems summarized as congestion. It follows that only the stringent application of physical planning measures, within the context of a long-term development plan, in turn balanced against the needs of the provincial regions, can restore the Paris region, both in terms of its efficient operation and the quality of the urban environment.

POST-WAR PLANNING IN THE PARIS REGION

The keynote of the expansion of the Paris agglomeration has been a liberal, laissez-faire attitude on the part of the authorities, interspersed with periodic attempts to correct the faults inherited from past anarchic growth and less frequent attempts to introduce comprehensive physical planning. It was not until 1960 that Paris received its first comprehensive and coordinated development plan, the 'Plan d'Aménagement et d'Organisation Générale' (PADOG). This plan was short-term in perspective, dealing with the period from 1960 to 1970. PADOG was not only restricted to the circumference of the existing agglomeration, but was based on the assumption that the anticipated growth by one million inhabitants during the decade could be accommodated within the existing agglomeration, and new construction outside the perimeter was restricted. Rejecting the idea of new towns, the PADOG attempted to base the decongestion of Paris on the creation of stronger suburban nodes, the encouragement of industrial decentralization and major improvements in transport. The plan received widespread comment[17-19] and no small amount of criticism,[20, 21] principally on the grounds of the lack of a precise programme, the lack of realism in the assumption that Paris could or should be restrained, and the failure to involve the wider city region in terms of specific proposals.

The publication of the PADOG was immediately followed in 1961 by the creation of the District of Paris,[22] which marked a decisive step in the direction of planning within the context of the city region. The District embraces the entire planning region, including the former départements of Seine, Seine-et-Oise and Seine-et-Marne, and has the status of a public body constituted by representatives of the local authorities. The function of the District is to coordinate the development plans of the constituent local authorities and to prepare and execute integrated planning over a much longer time perspective than that of the PADOG. To accomplish this task, the District administers a regional budget* under the control of an executive council and guided by a permanent planning research institute. The immediate task of the District was to prepare a revision of the PADOG plan and to compile a long-term master plan for the entire region. The first revision of the principles of the PADOG appeared in 1963 as the 'Livre Blanc',[23] applying to the period 1963–75. This report also attempted to extrapolate the growth of the Paris region to the year 2000 in an effort to define the magnitude of the problems being studied in the preparation of the master plan. The assessment published in the 'Livre Blanc' differed widely from the appreciation presented in the PADOG, estimating a rate of growth at double that assumed in the latter study, leading to a population in the region of at least 12 millions and possibly 16 millions by the year 2000. Far from being able to contain this growth —a process leading to high land values and land speculation—the 'Livre Blanc' proposed the acquisition of additional terrain as a prerequisite for successful development, involving the planned extension of the agglomeration.

The master plan was thus prepared against a background of an

*In the case of large-scale developments, such as road construction, additional government grants are involved and the degree of state control proportionately higher.

'expansionist' interpretation of the future growth of the agglomeration. Publication of the plan was preceded by an administrative reform in 1964, by which the département of Seine was subdivided into four new départements and that of Seine-et-Oise into three new départements. This reform, completed in 1966, was an indispensable adjustment of the administrative structure to new demographic and economic conditions, which had overburdened the existing machinery. The Préfet de Région of the Paris region also serves as the executive head of the District of Paris.

The master plan, the 'Schéma Directeur d'Aménagement et d'Urbanisme de la Région de Paris'[24] was published in 1965 and has created world wide attention. It fulfilled the role of a revision of the PADOG report, by including indications for priority infrastructure developments for the period up to 1975,* but also outlined an overall plan for the entire Paris region up until the year 2000†. It is not proposed to describe here the details of the Schéma Directeur, which has formed the subject of several articles,[25, 26] since the passage of time will undoubtedly bring modifications, but rather to discuss the underlying strategy and principles. The plan has attracted so much interest, in the form of both criticism and approbation, that it is important to establish what the Schéma Directeur seeks to fulfil.[27] The Schéma Directeur is neither a detailed physical plan nor a precise programme of investment in specific developments, but rather an attempt to provide a framework of the major options and orientations of future development. Thus the basic blueprint is a map, at a scale of 1 : 100,000, indicating the extent of the future built-up area and a general zoning of urban land uses, on which is superimposed the major anticipated developments in the road, rail and air transport systems.[28]

The strategy of the plan rests on three basic premises: the creation of new urban centres both within the existing agglomeration and as extensions to it, the adoption of preferential axes of growth for the siting of new towns, and the employment of the city region as a functional planning unit. The decision to build new urban centres is a response to the double problem of the excessive congestion of central Paris and the inability of the suburbs at present to supply an adequate service provision for their populations. Not all of these urban centres will be new towns, but rather will result from the strengthening of existing suburban centres in the agglomeration, as at Créteil and Bobigny, or from comprehensive renewal projects, as at La Défense (*Figure 12.2*). The latter centre is already well advanced, having been initiated in 1958 and confirmed in the PADOG proposals as a new tertiary node. In addition to housing and commercial

---

*Intended as a guide to investment in the Paris regional budget of the Fifth and Sixth National Plans.

†The year 2000 is a purely nominal date, approximating to the time when the Paris agglomeration will attain 14 million inhabitants.

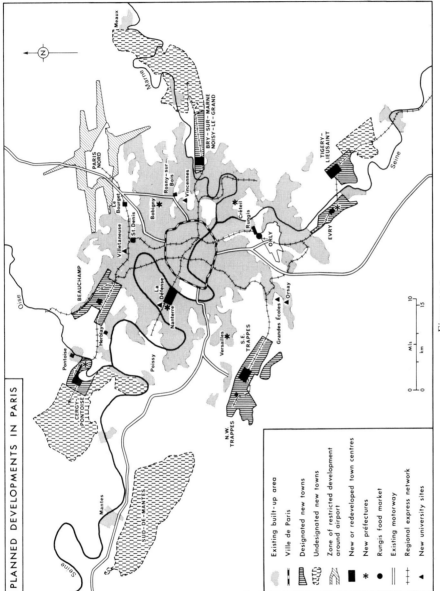

PLANNED DEVELOPMENTS IN PARIS

Seine

Mantes

SUD-DE-MANTES

Oise

Pontoise

CERGY-
PONTOISE

Herblay

BEAUCHAMP

Poissy

Nanterre

La
Défense

Villetaneuse

St. Denis

Bourget

Bobigny

PARIS
NORD

Meaux

Marne

BRY - SUR - MARNE
NOISY - LE - GRAND

Rosny-sur-
Bois

Vincennes

N.W.
TRAPPES

S.E.
TRAPPES

Versailles

Grandes Écoles

Orsay

ORLY

Rungis

Créteil

EVRY

TIGERY-
LIEUSAINT

Seine

Mls

km

0   10
       15

Existing built-up area

Ville de Paris

Designated new towns

Undesignated new towns

Zone of restricted development
around airport

New or redeveloped town centres

New préfectures

Rungis food market

Existing motorway

Regional express network

New university sites

Figure 12.2

development,* the new centre includes the 'Centre National des Industries et des Techniques'† and is adjacent to the new préfecture and university of Nanterre. However, eight of the proposed urban centres will be located in entirely new towns, distributed along two preferential axes located tangentially to the existing agglomeration. The essence of these axes is their basis in strong lines of movement, to be facilitated by new motorways and by a new railway system, the 'Réseau Express Régional', partly underground but principally built on the surface.

The size of the proposed new towns varies from 100,000 to 600,000, and the form of urbanization is also variable. In the case of the northern axis, new towns are proposed at Cergy–Pontoise, Beauchamp and at Bry-sur-Marne. The plateau west of Pontoise is proposed as the site of a completely new town housing 300,000 inhabitants, whereas the new town of Beauchamp is seen as an extension to the valley of Montmorency.[29] St. Denis and Le Bourget suburban area, already in the process of renewal, the entire area being scheduled to accommodate 600,000 additional inhabitants. To the east of the agglomeration, the preferential axis follows the line of the Marne Valley and a chain of new towns centred on Bry-sur-Marne is proposed, with a total population of between 300,000 and 500,000. Five new towns have been proposed on the southern preferential axis extending from Mantes to Melun. A new town is proposed to the south of Mantes, although the precise form and population are not designated in the Schéma Directeur. Two adjacent new towns are proposed south-west of Versailles between the Bièvre and Chevreuse valleys at Trappes, to accommodate 400,000 inhabitants. Finally, twin new towns are proposed on either side of the Seine south-east of the agglomeration. On the left bank, Evry, the administrative centre of the new département of Essonne, could accommodate 120,000 inhabitants, while on the right bank a new town of 400,000 inhabitants is proposed at Tigery–Lieusaint.

Although diverse in form and population size, the proposed new towns would share certain common features. It is intended that they should be self-sufficient in employment through the location of new factories and tertiary activities, and not residential suburbs of central Paris. They would be interconnected by motorway and regional express train services without the necessity of changing in central Paris. In addition to the motorway and railway construction, the Schéma Directeur proposes a new airport, 'Paris Nord', at Roissy-en-France, capable of handling supersonic aircraft. This airport, scheduled for opening in 1972, will also be the site of an industrial and commercial complex employing 50,000 people, and by 1975 the existing airport at Le Bourget will be closed.

*Including the entire administration of the Esso petroleum company.
†The largest exhibition hall in France.

The proposals indicated thus far concern only the agglomeration and its future extension, an area in total accounting for only 20 per cent of the Paris region. A further 20 per cent of the region consists of forests, and the remaining 60 per cent of agricultural land with a scattered distribution of small and medium-sized towns currently expanding at a high rate. The Schéma Directeur indicates few specific proposals for the region outside the agglomeration, but rather enunciates a number of principles designed primarily to protect the recreational value of the environment and especially the forests. The principle of a green belt around the agglomeration is not proposed but rather the provision of wedges of open land between the two preferential axes is indicated. The siting of the new towns corresponds with plateau surfaces with the intention that the valleys of the Seine and Marne and their tributaries should be preserved and developed as recreational amenities. The plan anticipates that the outlying towns of the region will double their populations by the year 2000. In summary, the Schéma Directeur foresees that by the year 2000 the central agglomeration will have a slightly decreased population of 2·5 millions, the population of the existing suburbs will increase from 4·7 to 7 millions, the new towns will approximately double the size of the agglomeration and house 3 million inhabitants, while the remainder of the region will double its population to 1·5 million, giving a grand total of 14 million inhabitants.

Inevitably such a radical plan has aroused controversy within France, much of it emotional rather than related to the very real problems with which the planners had to deal. The plan is still at the stage of consultation; amendments are likely, and indeed, if past precedents are followed, the chances that the entire plan will be completed are slim. Accordingly the plan may only be assessed in terms of its strategy in relation to the problems involved and the implications for regional development elsewhere. In this context certain ambiguities must be mentioned and several apparent advantages alluded to.

Chief of the criticisms levelled against the plan is the element of cost. In fact the report is not costed, on the grounds that to forecast costs thirty years ahead is impossible and that it will be cheaper in the long term to adopt the plan rather than to accept the increased costs of congestion resulting from the absence of physical planning. Perhaps more insidious is the cost in terms of human resources and talent, in that the implementation of the plan will absorb the best-qualified planners, architects and engineers for a considerable period of time. Concern too has been expressed on the likely infringement of public freedom by the necessary measures of expropriation, compulsory purchase and freezing of land values, about which the plan is singularly reticent.

Perhaps the most bitter attacks have been made by those who fear that the implementation of the plan will have unfavourable repercussions on the development of other regions, and who see in the plan yet further evidence of preferential treatment of the capital at the expense of the provinces. Specifically, publication of the plan has been held responsible for the slowing down of the decentralization movement.[30] This argument may be countered by the fact that the growth of Paris markedly decelerated between 1962 and 1968, and the rate of growth, 7·9 per cent, was substantially exceeded by practically every agglomeration of over 50,000 inhabitants in the nation, with the exception of certain mining agglomerations. This deceleration is in large measure attributed to the success of decentralization policies and the restriction of industrial and office development in central Paris. The forecast of 14 million inhabitants, moreover, assumes that the decentralization policy will be strengthened and that the urban centres of France will continue to expand at a high rate, with a consequent reduction in migration to Paris.

The author of the plan, Delouvrier, has countered these and other criticisms by stressing the reality of the central problem of congestion,[31] and certain advantages in the strategy adopted may be cited. The choice of axial development would seem to offer to the agglomeration an opportunity to break free from the past concentric growth which has contributed so much to the congestion of the centre.* Moreover, the lines of the preferential axes may be considered as 'elastic', in that as demand occurs they can be extended east and west. The plan too may be regarded as being courageous, in that unlike the PADOG it attempts to come to terms with a megalopolis situation. The assessment of demographic projections is realistic and is seen within the context of the city region. Two aspects of the plan are, however, crucial in relation to the problem of congestion. The proposal to double the size of the agglomeration must be accompanied by a full implementation of the transport proposals. In the final analysis, the size of the agglomeration is of less consequence than the ability to circulate freely, both within the built-up area and, increasingly, in search of recreation. Secondly, the new towns must, as far as possible, be self-contained in terms of employment and services, and not become giant dormitory suburbs disgorging a new generation of commuters.

The selection of a single theme—the planning problems resulting from concentration and congestion—does scant justice to the geography of this world city. Few inhabitants of Paris would deny, nevertheless, that this is

*Alternative locations for the new towns in rings around the agglomeration were considered, but were rejected on the grounds that in the long term this too would produce concentric growth and a loss of open space close to Paris. In this respect the evidence of Greater London was considered conclusive.[32]

the essential leitmotif of their daily life, and that the future of the agglomeration depends on a rational solution to this problem.[33]

REFERENCES

[1] Chevalier, L., *La Formation de la Population Parisienne au XIX*ᵉ *Siecle*, 1950, Paris, Presses Universitaires de France.

[2] Pourcher, G., *Le Peuplement de Paris*, 1964, Paris, Presses Universitaires de France.

[3] D'hotel, A., 'Paris et sa région face à l'avenir', *Suppl. Econ.*, No. 1,061, 1968, p. 10.

[4] Bastié, J., 'La Région Parisienne. Croissance et organisation', contribution to *L'Urbanisation Française*, p. 97, 1964, Paris, Centre de Recherche d'Urbanisme.

[5] Chombart de Lauwe, P., *Paris et L'Agglomération Parisienne*, Figure IX, p. 18, 1952, Paris, Presses Universitaires de France.

[6] Bastié, J., *La Croissance de la Banlieue Parisienne*, pp. 229–277, 1964, Paris, Presses Universitaires de France.

[7] Phlipponneau, M., *La Vie Rurale de la Banlieue Parisienne*, 1956, Paris, Imprimerie Nationale.

[8] George, P., 'Paris; présentation d'une capitale', Vol. 1, *Notes Etud. docum.*, No. 3,463, 1968, pp. 16–19.

[9] Clerc, P., 'Grands Ensembles, banlieues nouvelles', *Population*, 1967, p. 297.

[10] Bastié, J., *op. cit.*[4], p. 121.

[11] Lucchi, A., 'Les migrations alternantes dans la région Parisienne', *Annls Géogr.*, 1966, p. 39.

[12] Lucchi, A., *op. cit.*[11], p. 55.

[13] Merlin, P., *Les Transports Parisiens. Etude de géographie économique*, 1966, Paris, Masson.

[14] Caralp, R., 'L'évolution des transports de banlieue dans la région parisienne', *Inf. géogr.*, 1965, p. 111.

[15] Hall, P., *The World Cities*, p. 72, 1966, London, Weidenfeld and Nicolson.

[16] 'L'agriculture dans la région parisienne', *Notes Etud. docum.*, No. 3,438, 1967.

[17] Hall, P., *op. cit.*[15], pp. 85–94.

[18] *Urbanisme*, No. 68, 1960.

[19] Bastié, J., *Paris en l'An 2000*, p. 136, 1964, Paris, SEDIMO.

[20] Pilliet, G., *L'Avenir de Paris*, 1961, Paris, Hachette.

[21] Short, G., 'The Parisian Agglomeration', *Tn Ctry Plann.*, 1961, p. 266.

[22] Piquard, M., 'Le District de la Région de Paris. Rôle et Méthodes', *Expans. rég.*, No. 41, 1966, p. 31.

[23] Delouvrier, P., *Avant-projet de programme duodécennal pour la région de Paris*, 1963.

[24] 'Schéma Directeur d'Aménagement et d'Urbanisme de la Région de Paris', *Documn fr. illustr. (no. spécial)*, No. 216, 1966.

[25] Sibert, E., 'Regional plan for Greater Paris', *Tn Ctry Plann.*, 1966, p. 23.

[26] Abraham, J., 'Changing face of Paris', *Geogrl Mag.*, Vol. XLI, No. 2, 1968, p. 129.

[27] Reference 24, pp. 28–32.

[28] Beaujeu-Garnier, J., and Bastié, J., *Atlas de Paris et de la Région Parisienne*, Plate X, 1967, Paris, Berger-Levraut.

[29] Josse, R., 'Problèmes d'expansion et d'aménagement dans la vallée de Montmorency', *Annls Géogr.*, 1966, p. 569.

[30] Janrot, P., 'Les conséquences du schéma', *Expans. rég.*, No. 41, 1966, p. 27.

[31] Delouvrier, P., 'L'aménagement de la Région de Paris', *Confs Ambassadeurs*, No. 21, 1966.

[32] Reference 24, p. 82.

[33] Beaujeu-Garnier, J., 'L'avenir de la région parisienne', *Inf. géogr.*, 1966, p. 47.

13

Nord

'Le Nord est une région difficile à comprendre parce que, au sens fort du terme, il est incomparable; c'est une région unique en son genre, dont on ne trouve pas l'équivalent en France'.[1] The singularity of the Nord* is at once both specific and subjective. Specifically, the region is situated at a point where the national frontier is most indecisive in a strategic sense, and arbitrary in terms of economic patterns. Historically, this region alone in France experienced the undiluted force of the industrial revolution and has experienced the destruction of total war three times in the last century. The region is bisected by the nation's largest coalfield and, in spite of the absence of estuaries, possesses three of the nation's largest ports within a coastal arc of 70 kilometres. Lille–Roubaix–Tourcoing is the only clearly-developed large nineteenth-century industrial conurbation of France, and the coalfield agglomeration, of over one million inhabitants, is the most extensive urbanized area in the nation after Paris. Equally distinctive is the subjective image of the Nord in the minds of Frenchmen outside the region. The features popularly ascribed to the region are a frigid climate, monotonous relief, a grim and disfigured urban environment and a staid, traditionalist population. This distorted external image is of more than academic interest; it vitally affects the efforts of renewal and expansion which form the theme of this chapter.

LOCATION AND ENVIRONMENT

Factors of history and geography have combined to place the Nord at a major crossroads in western Europe. Roughly central in the Paris–London–Ruhr triangle, the region is situated at the intersection of the Paris–London route with routes diverging to the ports and cities of Benelux. It cannot be

*Nord is constituted by the départements of Nord and Pas-de-Calais. To avoid confusion, the planning region will be referred to as 'the Nord', while 'Nord' without the article refers to the département.

218

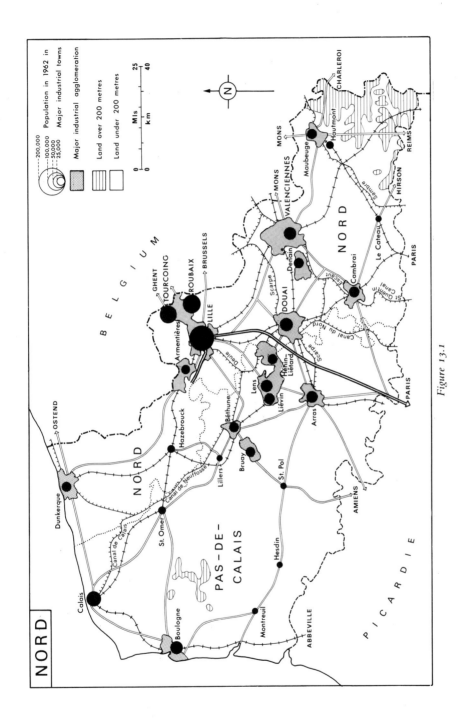

Figure 13.1

said that this crossroads location has been fully exploited. Antwerp has pre-empted the role of entrepôt for the Lys, Scheldt and Meuse basins, while Antwerp and Rotterdam, served by motorway connections and European-gauge canals, monopolize the transit trade of the Ruhr. The economic development of the Nord has been more closely tied to its location relative to Paris rather than to neighbouring regions or international connections. Separated by only 200 kilometres from the capital, the Nord was linked early by canal and rail to Paris, supplying power, raw materials and semi-finished goods for the expansion of the capital's industries. Lille is now linked by electrified rail to Paris, bringing the capital within two hours' travelling time. As yet few material advantages have accrued from this improved connection. However, the enlargement of the port of Dunkerque, the achievement of connections between the Paris–Lille motorway and the Belgian network and the possible construction of the Channel Tunnel promise to enhance the crossroads location of the Nord in the future. In the past, the location close to the foyers of the agricultural and industrial revolutions was of great benefit to the region. Location is not, however, a static factor, and a major renewal of the infrastructure and urban fabric is called for if the region is to gain the maximum advantage from the present transport and technological revolutions.

Striking variations in relief are absent in the Nord, but the planning region is far from being a featureless plain. Minor variations in terrain are of the utmost importance to economic activity and give rise to abrupt contrasts in the cultural landscape. *Figure 13.2* suggests that the Nord is almost equally divided between two physical provinces, both of which extend beyond the limits of the planning region. The southern half of the region is formed by the tilted outer rim of the Paris Basin, differentiated at its western extremity by the denuded anticline of the Boulonnais and in the east by the contact with the Hercynian massif of the Ardennes. The northern half is formed of the Flanders Plain, consisting predominantly of Tertiary rocks and projected without differentiation into Belgium. At the contact of these two provinces is a discontinuous depression formed by portions of the Scheldt, Sensée, Scarpe, Lys and Aa valleys, characterized by alluvial accumulations and an indeterminate drainage pattern.

The axis of the southern upland province is the chalk anticline of Artois (IVA), rising gradually from the plain of Picardie but plunging abruptly at its north-eastern rim beneath the clays and sands of the Flanders Plain. Artois preserves the classic features of the chalk landscape of the northern Paris Basin. The thick 'limon' cover is exploited in an advanced arable system of cereals, sugarbeet and fodder crops. Settlement is nucleated in the valleys and the farms are among the largest and most highly

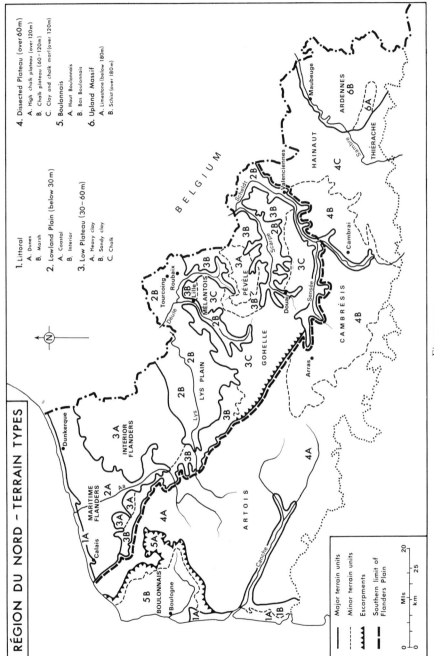

RÉGION DU NORD – TERRAIN TYPES

1. Littoral
   A. Dunes
   B. Marsh
2. Lowland Plain (below 30 m)
   A. Coastal
   B. Interior
3. Low Plateau (30–60 m)
   A. Heavy clay
   B. Sandy clay
   C. Chalk
4. Dissected Plateau (over 60 m)
   A. High chalk plateau (over 120 m)
   B. Chalk plateau (60–120 m)
   C. Clay and chalk marl (over 120 m)
5. Boulonnais
   A. Haut Boulonnais
   B. Bas Boulonnais
6. Upland Massif
   A. Limestone (below 180 m)
   B. Schist (over 180 m)

Major terrain units
Minor terrain units
Escarpments
Southern limit of Flanders Plain

Mls   20
km   25

Figure 13.2

mechanized in France. The rolling open-field landscape is diversified by woodland on the deposits of clay-with-flints and patches of Tertiary sands. The western portion of the Artois anticline has been denuded, revealing the underlying Jurassic and Primary rocks of the Boulonnais. A contrast exists between the Haut-Boulonnais (VA), the chalk rim of the lower Cretaceous, where cereals remain important, and Bas-Boulonnais (VB), the underlying impermeable Jurassic clays supporting pasture for dairy farming and horse-rearing. In contrast with the elevated plateau of Artois, Cambresis (IVB), to the east is a depressed zone and a natural route for the canals and railways linking the Flanders Plain to the central Paris Basin. Agriculture is highly evolved here and yields are unsurpassed elsewhere in the Paris Basin. Cereals and sugarbeet support brewing and refining industries in Cambrai and are rotated with artificial grasses, fodder roots and vegetables. To the east of Cambresis, the middle Cretaceous is constituted by a chalky marl giving impermeable conditions in Thiérache (IVC). A bocage landscape of small, family-owned farms provides dairy produce for the urban market of the Nord. The upland rim is completed by the intrusion of a segment of the Ardennes massif into the Nord. An elevated and wooded plateau, the Ardennes is sparsely settled except in the valley of the Sambre, which forms the perimeter.

The lowland province of the Flanders Plain offers a total contrast to the terrains of the upland rim. The plateau gives way to a level plain, the network of dry valleys to abundant surface drainage and the large farms to a mosaic of small farms and dispersed buildings. Variations in the landscape of the Flanders Plain occur chiefly in response to the level of the water table and the constituents of the bedrock. The coastal margin of the plain, Maritime Flanders (IIA)—seldom more than five metres above sea level—has a totally artificial landscape. The Quaternary silts have been exploited only by virtue of centuries of unremitting effort by empoldering and fertilizing to achieve the present high yields of flax, barley, oats and sugarbeet. The more elevated plain of interior Flanders (IIIA) supports a very wide range of crops, including many localized specializations such as tobacco, chicory and hops. The Lys Plain (IIB) produces potatoes, vegetables, flax and wheat, but as Lille is approached the proportion of market garden and dairy farming increases. A narrow band of chalk, formed by a shallow structural dome in Gohelle and Mélantois, separates Maritime and Interior Flanders from a second, more complex lowland of clays and sands traversed by the Scheldt, Scarpe and Sensée valleys. The core of this zone is the synclinal Eocene plateau of Pévèle (IIIA). The intensity of industrial crops diminishes, being replaced by pasture on the clays and woodland tracts on the sands.

The physical endowment, combined with centuries of improvement, provides the Nord with an extremely productive and diversified agricultural resource base. The nineteenth-century industrial revolution stimulated agriculture by providing an immediate demand both for cereal, vegetable and livestock produce, and for specialized industrial crops. In few regions of France do the agricultural and industrial economies more completely merge. Moreover, the daily exodus of rural dwellers to urban employment, particularly in the département of Nord, add to the rural–urban continuum.

THE NINETEENTH CENTURY LEGACY

Substantial though the land resources of the Nord are, it is the existence of power resources which has most conditioned the economic development of the region. In this respect, the events of the nineteenth century and the legacy of the industrial revolution are crucial to a comprehension of the present problems.

The region did not lack industry before the discovery of coal; wool and linen textile industries had a widespread distribution both as rural artisan industries and in small family-owned factories in Lille, Roubaix, Tourcoing and Armentières. The exploitation of coal in Nord at the beginning of the nineteenth century, largely capitalized by the textile firms, revolutionized the volume of the textile industry and concentrated activity in the Lille conurbation. By the middle of the nineteenth century the exploitation of coal had attained Douai, at the border of Nord and Pas-de-Calais. The extraction of coal stimulated canal building, linking Valenciennes to Lille and the coast and inland to Paris. In 1837 the first blast furnaces were built at Denain and after 1880 a steel industry developed at Denain and Valenciennes. After 1850 the extension of the coalfield into the Pas-de-Calais was discovered and frantic exploitation was triggered off. By this time railway construction was in full expansion and mineral lines rather than canals linked the mushrooming towns of the western coalfield. By 1860 cotton was replacing linen in the textile industry and this further increased the concentration in the Lille area, while at the turn of the century steel production expanded rapidly but remained rooted in the eastern basin,* leaving the western basin entirely dependent on mining. In 1900 the northern coalfield was established as the largest producer in the nation and by 1914 was producing 27 million tons out of a national output of 45 million tons.

Thus by the close of the nineteenth century the classic triumvirate of the industrial revolution had been established; coal extraction and processing into power and heavy chemicals, iron and steel with heavy

*The only exception is Isbergues, built in 1881 to the north of the western coal basin.

engineering, and the textile industry. Associated with this industrial expansion was an equally characteristic pattern of urban development. On the coalfield the initial 'corons'—terraced rows of miner's cottages—had mushroomed into vast 'cités-minières'—urban aggregates devoid of amenities—juxtaposed with industry and lacking in true urban character. In the Lille conurbation, the textile workers were housed in overcrowded, insanitary 'courées'. In the inter-war years, little evolution occurred in the basic industrial structure inherited from the nineteenth century. By 1929 the coalfield established a record output of 35 million tons, but the following depression years halted investment, especially in the textile sector. At the outbreak of the Second World War, little progress had still been made either in rationalizing the staple activities or in introducing lighter branches of engineering and consumer goods industries.

The legacy of the industrial revolution and its aftermath at the beginning of the twentieth century thus contained several sinister implications which have since been translated into severe development problems. Prime among these is the dependence on staple activities in varying degrees of desuetude. In the case of the textile industry, too many small family firms were ill-equipped technically and structurally to meet competition. Similarly, the coal basin was exploited by 34 private companies operating over 100 mines, precluding rational production, investment and marketing. The combination of obsolescent installations and the progressive exhaustion of the seams of the western basin made the post-war reorganization of the coal industry inevitable.

A second legacy of the nineteenth century, stemming from the dependence on a limited number of staple activities, is the existence of a certain rigidity in both the labour force and manufacturing installations. The labour force is characterized by a predominance of unskilled and semi-skilled workers, especially on the coalfield, and by one of the lowest female participation rates to be found in France. Equally inflexible, in terms of the conversion to new activities, are the industrial plants no longer required to fulfil their original functions. Disused mining installations, or small factories located in high-density aging residential districts of the Lille conurbation, do not lend themselves to an easy conversion to modern light industry.

To the rigidity of the fabric and labour force of industry must be added the repellent effect of an urban environment which grew too rapidly and with little regard to principles of planning other than securing the closest physical proximity of workplace and place of residence. Specifically, the urban environment attains its most unsatisfactory character in the western coal basin, precisely where the need for conversion and the attraction of new industry is most critical. Finally, the heritage of the industrial revolution is an infrastructure of communications geared to the demands and dimensions of nineteenth-century circulation. The improvements made by the construction of the Paris–Lille motorway and electrified railway have benefited external links, but intra-urban communications and the canal network are grossly inadequate. The failure to achieve the transition from a nineteenth-century basic industrial region to a modern, diversified, technology-based manufacturing region has produced the image of the Nord as the 'milch cow' of France, producing power, fuel agglomerates, heavy chemicals, textile yarn and cloth, steel sheet and other base products, exported for further elaboration and finishing outside the region. In too many instances the mundane stages of primary transformation are the province of the Nord, while the stage of greatest added value, carrying higher wage levels and greater employment growth rates, takes place outside the region.

THE ECONOMIC STATUS OF THE NORD

In spite of the contraction of certain basic activities, the contribution made by the Nord to the national economy is out of proportion to the population and surface area of the region. Statistics appropriate for regional accounting are sparse and their interpretation difficult, but *Table 13.1* attempts to assess the economic output of the Nord in 1960, at a time when the effort of renewal was gaining momentum.

Table 13.1

THE ECONOMIC STATUS OF THE NORD, 1960
(Proportion of national totals, per cent)

Population (1962)	12·5	Agricultural product	5·0
Land area	2·2	Industrial product	13·6
Labour force	6·3	Commercial product	6·9
Agricultural labour force	3·4	Gross national product	9·4
Manufacturing labour force	10·8	National budget receipts	8·0
Tertiary labour force	6·3		

Source: R. Monier[2]

Some measure of the external economic importance of the region may be gained from the fact that in 1965 the Nord contributed 10 per cent by value of the nation's exports, a proportion exceeded only by the Paris region. When individual commodities are considered, the leading position of the Nord in the national production can be more fully appreciated.

Table 13.2

THE ECONOMIC OUTPUT OF THE NORD, 1960
(As percentage of national production)

Coal	53	Window glass	77
Thermal energy	33	Paper and cartons	17
Pig iron	14	Fish	26
Crude steel	23	Beet sugar	20
Finished steel	23	Beer	30
Cotton yarn	32	Milled wheat	10
Cotton cloth	28	Sulphuric acid	46
Wool yarn	89	Nitrate fertilizer	65
Woollen cloth	32	Cement	18
Bricks	53		

Source: R. Monier.[2]

Table 13.2 emphasizes the dominant role of base production and it may be suggested that the lack of equilibrium between staple activities and modern industries with high growth rates is symptomatic of much wider distortions affecting the entire socio-economic structure of the Nord.

THE DEMOGRAPHIC STRUCTURE

The Nord has traditionally provided population to other regions, this migration being offset by extremely high rates of natural increase, but for the first time since the beginning of the nineteenth century the Nord failed to increase its proportion of the total national population at the census of 1962. Since 1962, the Nord has shown further signs that it is beginning to lose its demographic dynamism.

Table 13.3

POPULATION CHANGE IN THE REGION DU NORD, 1962–1968

	Population 1968 (thousands)	Rate of population change, 1962–68 (per cent)		
		Natural increase	Net migration	Total
Nord	2,418	+5·4	0·0	+5·4
Pas-de-Calais	1,397	+5·8	−3·5	+2·3
Région du Nord	3,815	+5·6	−1·3	+4·3

Source: Recensement de 1968, Premiers Résultats.

Table 13.3 reveals that the region increased its population at a much slower rate than that of the nation as a whole between 1962 and 1968. On balance, the persistence of high fertility was heavily eroded by migration. The region lost 48,000 persons by migration during the period, exclusively from the département of Pas-de-Calais. The fundamental distortion is thus a propensity towards high natural increase in combination with a tendency towards stability in economic growth. The total employed labour force has remained practically constant in the last decade, but in certain activities such as textiles and coal mining, with highly specific locations, severe reductions have taken place. Thus the département of Nord, having the more diversified industrial structure and a greater volume of tertiary employment and containing the more active portion of the coalfield and the two major ports, has proved more resistant to migrational loss than has the Pas-de-Calais, which has a greater agricultural dependence and contains the declining portion of the coalfield. The problem of the imbalance between, on the one hand, the increasing number of school-leavers, displaced workers from declining industries and from agriculture, and underemployment of females, and, on the other hand, the inability of the region to expand employment opportunities, results from a second socio-economic distortion: the structure of industry.

THE INDUSTRIAL STRUCTURE

The burden of the nineteenth-century inheritance is manifest in that out of a total industrial labour force of 607,000 workers in 1962, 335,000 were employed in textiles, coal, steel and metallurgy. While these staple activities are at best stable, or more commonly declining in the employment offered, the region has acquired only modest amounts of new industry. Between 1954 and 1967, less than 1,000 extra jobs were created yearly in industries involving the transformation and finishing of base products. The decline of staple activities is not per se an unfavourable trend; it results from far-reaching re-equipment and rationalization which have placed these branches in a more competitive position. The essence of the problem is the highly specific distribution of the declining activities, constituting localized areas of hardship, and the great difficulty of achieving conversion of labour within a regional economy that has expanded at a rate below the national average.

The staple activity which initiated the trend of contraction was the textiles branch. The persistence of machinery installed between the two wars, increased foreign competition in export markets and the loss of internal markets to synthetic fibres enforced a process of rationalization on the industry between 1952 and 1957 which was rapidly translated into a massive reduction in employment.[4] From a total employment level of

168,000 in textiles in 1954, the figure had fallen to 129,000 by 1962 and 102,000 by 1967. The closure of many small firms, the regrouping of others and the installation of machinery giving higher productivity has had two specific effects. The reduction in labour has particularly affected the female labour force while the trend towards technically-advanced production methods has increased the male participation rate. Secondly, although the textile industry is overwhelmingly located in the département of Nord, a high proportion of the labour force is drawn from the Pas-de-Calais section of the northern coalfield, where alternative female employment opportunities are deficient. The decline in output and employment has affected all types of natural fibre production[5] but has been greater in the wool industry, where a weaker structural organization was present, than in cotton, which forms a smaller proportion of the total industry and has larger firms.

Unlike the crisis atmosphere of the rationalization of the textile industry, the decline of coal mining was a planned and predictable operation financed by the government.[6] Moreover, the decline was subject to trends of timing and location that were not solely governed by market forces, but also by the progressive extinction of a fixed resource. Although the coalfield has a potential life span of 60 years,[7]★ the extinction of the western groups is imminent and poses an immediate problem of conversion. By 1970 it is estimated that the number of active mines will have been reduced to approximately 25 and that 27,000 jobs will have been lost, overwhelmingly in the western and central groups. It must be stressed that the nationalized industry involves more than the extraction of coal; it is an extremely powerful combine producing fuel agglomerates, domestic and industrial gas and electricity and is intimately linked with the chemical and steel industries (*Figure 13.3*). The coalfield thus presents short-term and long-term problems of great complexity. In the immediate present, the task of conversion in the mono-industrial mining settlements of the western groups is the most critical problem facing the entire planning region. In longer-term perspective, the extinction of the coal reserves will complete a major chapter in the economic history of France. The arrival of natural gas from Holland and the construction of a second oil refinery in the region, located at Valenciennes, may well hasten the dénouement.

Production and employment trends in the third staple activity, the iron and steel industry, are superficially more encouraging. Production of pig iron rose to 3·7 million tons in 1967 as compared with 3·5 million tons in 1966, while steel production increased from 5·0 to 5·2 million tons.

★Assuming a gradual run-down in production of 2 per cent per annum. However, the decrease in output between 1966 and 1967 was closer to 8 per cent.

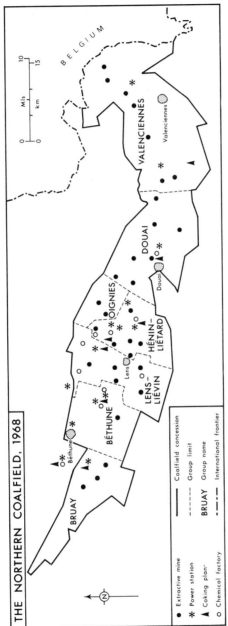

Figure 13.3

Against this must be set a loss of 10,000 jobs in metallurgy in the single year of 1967, and the fact that markedly varying rates of growth are occurring in the three major steel districts. The growth in output was entirely due to the expansion of the new USINOR plant at Dunkerque.* The minor production centre of the Sambre valley is turning increasingly towards rolling and finishing, while the merger of USINOR with Lorraine-Escaut[8] may foreshadow important reorganizations in the Valenciennes–Denain district. The coastal steelworks of Dunkerque, opened in 1962 and employing over 5,000 workers, now has 80 per cent of the region's steel-making capacity.

Three basic industries thus dominate the Nord, and together with their ancillary activities—chemicals, heavy engineering, glass-making, ceramics and brick manufacture—account for a disproportionate amount of the total labour force. This distortion is not merely a matter of dependence on activities characterized by contraction, but also of numerous concomitant structural deficiencies; for example, the low level of formal and technical qualification of the industrial labour force, the excessively low female activity rate, the low wage rates prevalent in many unskilled jobs and the burden of long-distance commuting in search of work. Above all, the considerable rejuvenation of the physical plant of the staple industries, enforced by the inexorable pressures of competition, has as yet not formed a springboard for general growth in the region's economy. Implicit in this trend is the danger, condemned by Deligny,[9] of a perpetuation into the twentieth century of the feudal role played by the Nord in the nineteenth century, as the provider of the sinews of industry rather than the creator of the final and more remunerative stages of accomplished products. Inevitably, the distortions of the industrial structure are mirrored in parallel distortions of the urban structure.

THE URBAN STRUCTURE

The Nord is the most highly urbanized planning region of France after the Paris region; 80.2 per cent of the population resided in urban communes in 1962 and 91.3 per cent in 'Zones de Peuplement Industriel ou Urbain'. More remarkable than the intensity of urbanization is the originality and complexity of the urban structure and its strict relationship to specific economic activities. The distinction between urban and rural forms of settlement assumes a degree of ambiguity unequalled elsewhere in France.[10] Elaborate research has revealed the complexity of the urban

*This dominance has increased with the creation of a third blast furnace in 1968.

environment and the magnitude of the fundamental research which remains to be accomplished.[11] The most distinctive feature of urbanization in the Nord is its basis of agglomerations, the urban nuclei of which are commonly very small in relation to the total complexes. In the case of the northern coalfield it is often very difficult to detect true towns at all, but rather does the urban fabric consist of sprawling urban 'aggregates' with little internal differentiation.

Three distinctive types of urban structure are found in the Nord, although the degree of further subdivision possible is limitless: discrete urban centres, the industrial agglomerations of the northern coalfield, and the conurbation of Lille–Roubaix–Tourcoing. Although discrete urban centres not immersed within huge agglomerations are not absent from the Nord, they form a small proportion of the total urban population of the region. A network of small and medium-sized towns characterizes the southern and western portions of the Nord. Many are historic towns, most are marketing centres, but the extent of their modern growth is variable. Whereas Le Cateau, St. Pol, Hesdin, Montreuil, Bapaume and Desvres have remained virtually stationary since 1936, while experiencing a depopulation of their hinterlands, other centres such as Arras, Cambrai, St. Omer and Calais have expanded, although the scale of their industrialization has been insufficient to give birth to large agglomerations. Boulogne, and more particularly Dunkerque, on the other hand, can no longer be considered as discrete urban centres but have developed into substantial agglomerations.

It is on the northern coalfield that the process of agglomeration has progressed furthest and with the greatest degree of anarchy. In a detailed study of the urban structure of the coalfield, the author[12] has described the relationship between urban forms and mining activity. The core of the structure is a chain of towns extending in an arc from Valenciennes through Denain, Douai, Hénin-Liétard and Lens to Béthune. The interstices between these centres, none of which exceeds 51,000 inhabitants, are occupied by over 100 small settlements and 'cités-minières'. *Figure 13.4* illustrates that the dominant urban terrain is constituted by a small service centre with appended 'cités-minières', the latter usually containing the greater proportion of the population but often being physically isolated from the service centre. The service centres are commonly no more than enlarged villages, whereas the 'cités' frequently have populations of several thousands, devoid of amenities and service facilities and dependent on a single source of employment. The problems inherent in this distorted urban structure are too numerous to treat in detail. It suffices to mention the high population totals and densities dependent on a single declining activity, the indiscriminate intermingling of residential and industrial land

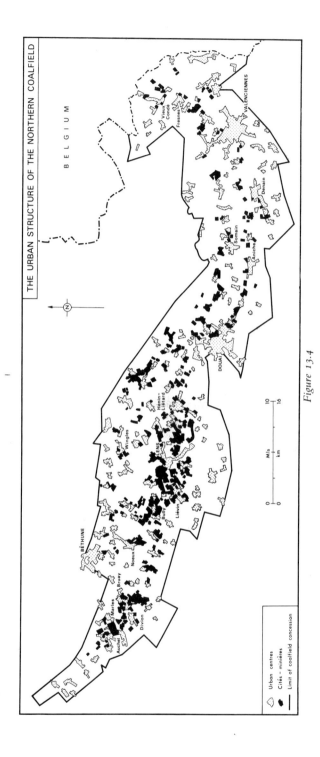

THE URBAN STRUCTURE OF THE NORTHERN COALFIELD

BELGIUM

VIEUX Condé
Fresnes
VALENCIENNES
Denain
Somain
Aniche
DOUAI
Hénin-Liétard
Wingles
LENS
Bully
Liévin
BÉTHUNE
Noeux
Bruay
Marles
Auchel
Divion

N

Mls 0   10
km 0   16

Urban centres
Cités – minières
Limit of coalfield concession

Figure 13.4

uses, the absence of amenities in the 'cités' and the incapacity of the small service centres to fulfil the needs of the mining population, and the low female participation rate resulting from the mono-industrial function and weak development of the tertiary sector. Added to these structural problems are the social problems resulting from inadequate housing, the lack of social mobility and the general unsightliness of an urban environment disfigured by industry and monotonous in terms of architecture and the landscape setting. The degree of distortion is not uniform throughout the coalfield. A more balanced structure prevails in the département of Nord, but unfortunately it is in the western groups of the Pas-de-Calais where the greatest hardships from the run-down of mining are present and where the worst distortions of the urban structure occur. *Figure 13.4* indicates the distorted settlement pattern of the western groups, coincident with a large number of mine closures, and the consequent net loss of over 20,000 inhabitants between 1954 and 1962 resulting from the difficulty for such an area to attract new industries.

As compared with the uncoordinated agglomerations of the coalfield, a greater degree of cohesion is present in Lille–Roubaix–Tourcoing, and the term 'conurbation' may be loosely applied. Lille is not a conurbation in the sense of a fully-integrated structure revolving around a single commercial and industrial pole. Roubaix and Tourcoing do possess particular industrial and commercial functions, and the daily displacement of labour is on the basis of an interchange between the three centres. It is the growth of ribbon development between the three towns, and particularly the expansion of an outer ring of industrial suburbs around Lille, which has created the fusion of the built-up area. The dominance of Lille within this urban constellation is less a function of its population size, in which the advantage is only marginal, than the undoubted commercial, administrative, cultural and institutional superiority. The function as administrative capital of the département of Nord and seat of the regional prefect, the possession of two universities and numerous technical institutions, a stock market, museum and opera house, a regional newspaper, a modern airport, a major surgical hospital and a trade fair, indicate not only the dominance of Lille within the conurbation but its unrivalled position as the regional capital of the Nord.[13] The detailed urban structure of the conurbation has been described by Bruyelle[14] and many of the problems encountered on the coalfield are again present. In particular the drastic reduction of the staple activity, the lack of attractiveness for new firms and the need for massive renewal of housing[15] are priority problems.

The evidence presented thus far can lead to only one conclusion: that the Nord is an old industrial region, suffering from the blight of rapid nineteenth-century expansion, which has bequeathed socio-economic distortions affecting all aspects of life in the region. In these circumstances the task of renewal is not a slogan or an ideal, it is a necessity for survival.

THE EFFORT OF RENEWAL

The task of renewal has a double aspect in the Nord; it is a physical task in the sense of renewing housing and replanning decayed urban environments and it is a structural task, involving a fundamental rejuvenation of the regional economy. The urgency of physical renewal results from the large amount of nineteenth-century building which still survives, especially in the Lille conurbation and on the coalfield. It may be argued that wholesale renewal cannot be extended to the entire coalfield environment, and that as their original raison d'être disappears so many of the small coalfield settlements are destined to disappear. It would seem logical to concentrate investment in the renewal of the infrastructure and the housing stock in a selected number of growth points capable of attracting industry and also of discharging service functions on behalf of the surrounding smaller settlements. Such an approach would involve an attempt to provide a rational structure of urbanization, lacking in the present pattern, which conforms to no orderly size-ranking[16] or hierarchy system.[17, 18]

The scale of the problem of structural renewal may be judged from the fact that if present trends continue the size of the labour force will not have increased between 1954 and 1970. Between 1968 and 1975, it is anticipated that 35,000 jobs will be lost in mining at an average rate of 7,000 per annum. Similarly, employment in textiles is expected to diminish at a rate of 2,000 per annum. Between 1954 and 1962, the region lost over 40,000 agricultural jobs, chiefly of paid labourers. At the present time, unemployment is calculated at 50,000 workers or approximately 4 per cent of the labour force, of which 40 per cent is constituted by persons under 25 years old. In addition, the region suffers a particularly low activity rate, especially in the case of females, without which unemployment levels would undoubtedly be higher.[19]★

The achievement of a better balance in the industrial structure is dependent on the attraction of specific types of manufacturing. Particularly desirable is employment offering high growth rates, high wage levels and using qualified labour, if the monolithic structure of basic industry is to be broken. The region also requires a number of large-scale firms in order to provide employment in sufficient quantity and to act as growth

★In 1962, the employed proportion of the male population was 54 per cent and of the female population 21·4 per cent. This compares with proportions of 61·6 and 36·4 per cent in the Paris region and national figures of 58 and 28 per cent respectively.

leaders through the attraction of component and ancillary industries. As yet the Nord has failed to attract sufficient new industries in these categories, for a wide number of reasons ranging from deficiencies of the infrastructure, the problem of labour retraining, the repellent effect of the urban environment and the counter-attraction of alternative locations outside the region. This is not to deny that a considerable effort has gone into the task of facilitating structural renewal. Government assistance has been afforded to the Pas-de-Calais section of the coalfield, designated successively as a 'zone critique', a 'zone de conversion', and now a 'zone d'adaptation industrielle', with a view to the establishment of firms on new industrial estates. In the course of the Fifth Plan, the Paris–Lille motorway has been completed, work has started on additional sections of motorway and other roads will be improved, while the Dunkerque–Lille–Valenciennes canal has been enlarged to receive pushed convoys of 3,000 tons. The Fifth Plan also envisages additional new industrial estates, concentrated especially on the western part of the coalfield (*Figure 13.5*). A major effort of renewal has been made in the last 15 years, financed by government, regional, local and even international funds* The results obtained thus far, although by no means negligible, are insufficient to solve the problem of structural conversion. In the western coal basin, a major tyre factory has located at Béthune and a large number of clothing firms have been established. The latter are attracted to large pools of female labour and the new industrial estates have permitted movement from the congested Lille conurbation. The creation of female employment does little, however, to resolve the more serious problem of redeploying displaced mineworkers†. The Simca car firm has announced its intention to build an assembly plant on the La Bassée industrial estate, but further large-scale implantations are necessary if workers are to be successfully redeployed from basic industry and the new generation of well-educated young workers retained in the region.

PERSPECTIVES

Whether or not the efforts of renewal thus far engaged are commensurate with the magnitude of the problems involved is a matter for debate. What is certain is that the Nord has reached a critical turning point in its evolution and that the pattern of the future will be determined by the actions under-

*The large new industrial estate at La Bassée was financed by the European Coal and Steel Authority. The nationalized coal industry has also encouraged the effort of renewal by making available disused industrial land in areas of mine closures for the creation of new estates.
†Between 1954 and 1962, 21,000 male jobs were lost while 3,000 female jobs were created in the conversion zone.

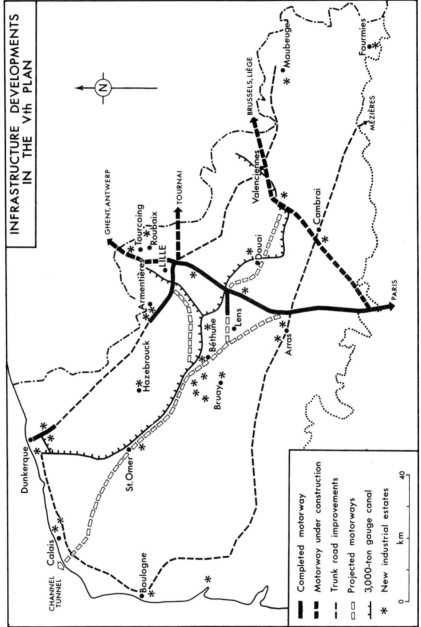

INFRASTRUCTURE DEVELOPMENTS
IN THE Vth PLAN

N

GHENT, ANTWERP

Tourcoing
Roubaix
Armentières
LILLE

TOURNAI

BRUSSELS, LIÈGE

Maubeuge

Valenciennes

Fourmies

Cambrai

MÉZIÈRES

Douai

Hazebrouck

Béthune

Lens

Bruay

Arras

PARIS

Dunkerque

St.Omer

Calais

CHANNEL
TUNNEL

Boulogne

	Completed motorway
	Motorway under construction
	Trunk road improvements
	Projected motorways
	3,000-ton gauge canal
*	New industrial estates

km
0   40

Figure 13.5

taken during the remainder of the Fifth Plan and in the course of the Sixth Plan. In assessing the future perspective it is important to differentiate between official aspirations and the evidence already provided by spontaneous trends. The latter often more realistically reflect the true nature of a region's vocation.

The general strategy for planned development has been revealed by the publication of the white paper of the 'Organisme d'Etudes d'Aménagement de'Aire Métropolitaine du Nord'.[20] This report, which covers the vast majority of the planning region, divides the area into three zones for prospective planning purposes. The 'littoral' zone, west of a line from Bergues to St. Omer and Hesdin, has a present population of 560,000 which is expected to double by the end of the century. The report proposes as priority developments the creation of a major industrial and urban complex at Calais and the elevation of the tourist industry to a level competitive with the major areas of western Europe. Of these two objectives, the latter would seem to be the less realistic in view of the limited natural amenities for tourism. Moreover, the choice of Calais as the natural growth pole of the littoral seems speculative in view of the present dynamic growth of Dunkerque, the sole industrial centre in the Nord currently expanding at a rate which could ultimately qualify it for a European role. The second, 'central urban', zone, is accorded three priority developments: the strengthening of the role of Lille as a regional metropolis, the completion of the industrial conversion of Roubaix–Tourcoing, and Lens–Hénin–Liétard, and the revival of the subregional capitals of Béthune, Douai, St. Omer and Arras. In the whole of the central urban zone it is estimated that agriculture and mining will employ only 20,000 by the close of the century, as compared with 145,000 in 1962. Finally, the 'south-eastern' zone has a present population of 800,000, of which 60 per cent is resident in the Scheldt and Sambre valleys. The report envisages the creation of a major economic axis linking Cambrai, Valenciennes and Mons along the line of the Scheldt, and improvements in communications to offset the isolation of the Sambre valley industrial district.

Lacking clairvoyance extending to the year 2000, it is fruitless in the present context to comment on the proposals of the Nord Metropolitan Area Study. It is, however, extremely relevant to enquire whether the present planned and spontaneous trends appear to be leading in the same direction, or whether alternative space structures may be proposed. It is possible to foresee the development of two economic axes in the Nord. A 'heavy' axis already exists, linking Dunkerque—an industrial port with steel manufacture, petroleum refining and shipbuilding—with the Lille conurbation—the centre of textiles, chemical and heavy engineering industries—and the eastern coalfield—where Douai is the focus of mining activity and Valenciennes the centre of the steel industry. This axis is now linked by a European-gauge canal and partially by motorway. It has external links by motorway to Paris and motorway connections with Belgium are under construction. Electrified rail-links exist between the axis and Paris and also Lorraine. The future strengthening of this axis seems assured, with the expansion of port and industrial activity of Dunkerque, the establishment of Lille as a 'métropole d'équilibre', the location of the majority of the remaining coal reserves in the eastern basin, and the likely reorganization of the Valenciennes steel industry. The regional park of St. Amand will be developed as a primary recreational resource for the majority of the population in this axis.

It is also possible to suggest that a second 'light' axis, as yet embryonic, may develop to the south. The nuclei of this axis are Arras and Cambrai, to be linked to Paris by motorway and via trunk road to the coast and the Channel Tunnel, and orientated along the Scheldt valley towards Valenciennes and Belgium. The term 'light' attaches to this axis by virtue of the dominant role to be played by light industry in its future expansion. The western arm of this axis offers two alternative possibilities. The official proposal is to connect Arras to the Channel Tunnel by motorway through the western coalbasin and St. Omer (see *Figure 13.5*). It could be argued that, in view of the difficulty already experienced in attracting new industry to the western coalbasin, a good case exists for concentrating investment along the trunk route from Cambrai and Arras to Boulogne and Calais via Hesdin and St.Pol. Arras and Cambrai are mature towns with established urban functions and institutions. They are set in an agreeable environment with access to recreational areas. Arras is already the site of positive growth and the conditions for the attraction of new firms would seem to be better fulfilled here and in the small towns of Artois than in the mono-industrial aggregates of the western coalfield. The task of renewal does not, of necessity, involve in situ conversion; a displacement southwards of economic activity to an urban system constructed to the needs of the twentieth century rather than the attempted conversion of an urban fabric and industrial structure built specifically to the needs and standards of the nineteenth century should at least be considered. The keynote of prospective regional planning must be to anticipate the location factors of the next stages of the transport and technological revolutions, together with an awareness of rising social aspirations in matters of urban living conditions and diversity of employment opportunities. The effort of planning and investment in the Nord must be concentrated into locations where these conditions can be fulfilled.

REFERENCES

[1] Pinchemel, P., 'Clés pour le Nord', *Perspect. Nord–Pas-de-Calais*, No. 2, 1967, p. 5.

[2] Monier, R., 'L'Economie de la Région du Nord et du Pas-de-Calais', *Notes Etud. docum.*, No. 2,837, 1961.

[3] CERES, *Nord 1954–1962. Bilan de l'évolution entre les deux recensements*, Lille, 1966.

[4] CERES, *Les industries textiles dans le Nord et le Pas-de-Calais*, Lille, 1958, pp. 85–90.

[5] Falise, M., and Boca, M., 'Les fluctuations d'activité dans l'industrie textile régionale', *CERES Docums Etud.*, No. 1, 1966, pp. 11–22.

[6] Thompson, I., 'A geographical appraisal of recent trends in the coal basin of northern France', *Geography*, 1965, p. 252.

[7] Gardent, P., 'L'avenir des houillères du bassin du Nord et du Pas-de-Calais', *Energies*, Nos. 13 and 20, March 1964.

[8] Bruyelle, P., 'Un événement majeur dans l'industrie régionale: la fusion d'Usinor et de Lorraine-Escaut', *Hommes Terres Nord*, 1966, p. 98.

[9] Deligny, H., *Le Nord Demain*, p. 16, 1964, Paris, Gamma Presse.

[10] Pinchemel, P., 'Le peuplement urbain et industriel de la région Nord–Pas-de-Calais', *C. r. Colloque 'Le peuplement et les mouvements migratoires de la région Nord–Pas-de-Calais'*, Lille, 1961.

[11] Vakili, A., Pinchemel, P., and Gozzi, J., *Niveaux Optima des Villes*, 1959, Lille, CERES.

[12] Thompson, I., 'A review of problems of economic and urban development in the northern coalfield of France', *Southampton Res. Ser. Geogr.*, Vol. 1, 1965, p. 45.

[13] Beaujeu-Garnier, J., 'Lille—une grande ville', *Hommes Terres Nord*, 1963, No. 2, p. 118.

[14] Bruyelle, P., 'Lille–Roubaix–Tourcoing', *Notes Etud. docum.*, No. 3,206, 1965, pp. 28–59.

[15] Bruyelle, P., 'La rénovation du quartier Saint-Sauveur', *Hommes Terres Nord*, 1967, p. 58.

[16] Adam, H., and Loos, A., 'Une application de la règle de la taille suivant le rang à l'étude des villes de la région du Nord', *Hommes Terres Nord*, No. 2, 1964, p. 77.

[17] Monimart, J., 'Armature urbaine et région Nord–Pas-de-Calais', *Hommes Terres Nord*, No. 2, 1965, p. 2.

[18] Delsaut, P., 'Hiérarchie des villes de la région du Nord d'après leur fonction de place centrale', *Hommes Terres Nord*, No. 1, 1966, p. 7.

[19] CERES, 'La régionalisation du Ve Plan', *Perspect. Nord–Pas-de-Calais*, No. 2, 1967, p. 27.

[20] *Pour une politique d'aménagement régional*, 1969, Lille, OREAM.

14

Lorraine

Permeating the economic geography of Lorraine is the paradox of a region rich in natural resources, well situated in terms of the Common Market and having one of the highest rates of urbanization in France, and yet at the present time confronted with severe economic problems reflected in the net loss by migration of 70,000 inhabitants between 1962 and 1968. The fact that 40,000 of this migrational loss was sustained by the two industrialized départements of Meurthe-et-Moselle and Moselle differentiates this movement from the normal inter-regional migration associated with declining agricultural employment, and points rather to severe structural problems affecting the entire regional economy.

Although firmly associated in the popular mind with the steel industry, the mining and metallurgical districts of Lorraine occupy but a small proportion of the planning region. In general terms four geographical units may be indicated. The western half of Lorraine, being a structural continuation of the eastern Paris Basin, has a scarpland topography developed on alternating limestone plateaux and clay vales. The eastern front of this unit is the escarpment of the Oolite limestone, the Côte-de-Moselle, overlooking the second geographical element, the depression etched out in the Liassic marls, drained by the Moselle, which forms the economic spine of the region. Continuing eastwards, Triassic marls, sandstones and limestones constitute the Lorraine plateau, merging topographically into the fourth unit, the Vosges mountains, of which the crestline gives a definite eastern boundary to Lorraine. This diversity of rock types and land-forms invests Lorraine with a wide variety of land resources. For centuries the region was devoted to cereal production, the open fields of the dip slopes and plains alternating with forests on the scarp fronts, vineyards* and orchards at the base of the escarpments and pasture on the poorer soils of the limestone summits and badly drained

---

*The combination of phylloxera and competition from the Midi ruined the viticultural economy and the vine has only local importance, mainly near Toul.

portions of the clay vales. While this general correspondence between land use and relief remains in evidence, Lorraine agriculture has assumed a more mixed character in response to economic changes.

The basis of agricultural production is of small farms of 10 to 50 hectares, and although remembrement began early★ the present rate of achievement is less than optimum.[1] The constant drift of population from

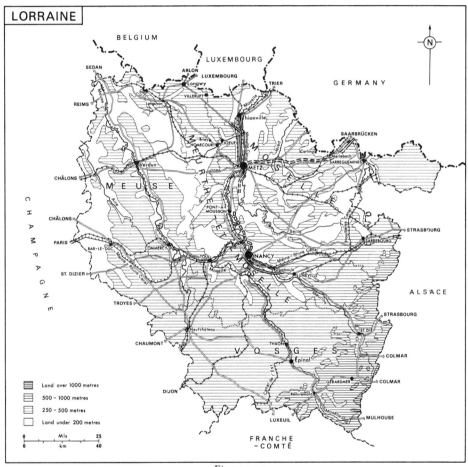

Figure 14.1

the land to the industrial towns has been accompanied by increased mechanization and a steady evolution in farm size,[2] while the growth of the regional demand for meat and whole milk finds its response in the adoption of mixed farming in which milk provides a substantial proportion of farm revenue. Cereals still occupy about half the arable acreage and yields equate with the national average, but grain farming is

★Under a government provision to restore the economy after the destruction of the First World War.

increasingly associated with permanent and temporary grass. This trend is particularly the case when remembrement is achieved, especially on the fertile lowlands of the Woëvre, the Moselle depression and the Lorraine plateau. The adoption of a grassland system, rather than intensive root and leguminous fodder production, appears to be an effort to reduce labour requirements in an area which has witnessed rural–urban migration for more than a century. The process of rural exodus is also reflected in the areas of poorer soils by an extension of the area in woodland or social fallow* In the scarpland zone, some effort to reclaim fallow is being made by a regional development company.[3] However, in the Vosges, the haphazard reafforestation of small marginal farms has sterilized land which could otherwise have been incorporated into the agricultural land area by remembrement and the intervention of the SAFER organization.

In common with the rest of the nation, the agricultural population has diminished rapidly recently. Between 1954 and 1962 the agricultural labour force diminished by 25 per cent. This reduction has been notably age-selective and in 1963 52 per cent of Lorraine farmers were over 56 years of age. Disturbing though the trends towards under-use of land resources and increasing elderliness in the farm population may be in terms of their implications for the future, less than nine per cent of the total population depends on agriculture and the wealth of Lorraine lies less in her soil than in the rock structures beneath it.

MINERAL RESOURCES AND INDUSTRIAL ACTIVITY

The industrial geography of Lorraine is inextricably tied to the exploitation of minerals both as a source of energy and as raw materials. Vast deposits of rock-salt are located in the Saulnois, east of Nancy. The 14 saltworks produce 300,000 tons of refined salt per annum together with 1·7 million tons of brine used in the chemical industry. Chemical works at Dombasle, Château-Salins, Dieuze and Sarralbe produce large quantities of base chemicals, sodium carbonate, caustic soda and hydrochloric acid.

Lorraine possesses the nation's largest reserves of coal†, situated in a concealed field which is a structural continuation of the Saar basin. Conditions of extraction are more favourable than in the northern coalfield and productivity is more than twice as high.[4] The field has experienced a complicated political history which continues to affect production[5]

*A term applied to land in varying stages of abandonment because of social rather than physical reasons, such as shortage of hired labour, uneconomic farm size and fragmentation, unsuitability for mechanization or the lack of a successor.

†Over half the national reserves.

After ceding the right to exploit the German Saar deposits in the Warndt, the nationalized mining industry is now in the process of completing the reorientation of output on to the French portion of the basin, necessitating considerable investment and the sinking of new mines.[6] The large size of the reserves, the growth of the chemicals sector and progress in the conversion of the coal into metallurgical coke have encouraged heavy investment in modernization. However, the consequent gains of productivity have resulted in a decline in labour needs and the number of miners fell from 26,000 in 1958 to 17,000 in 1967. A continuation of this decline at a rate of 1,200 per annum is anticipated. Total production has remained stable at 15 million tons per annum in recent years, approximately 28 per cent of the national total in 1967. The coal is put to three principal uses, the generation of power, coke production and chemical processing. Several power stations are situated on the field while a new station has been completed at Pont-à-Mousson capable of absorbing 14 per cent of the total coal output. A further major plant is projected at La Maxe, on the Moselle. The coalfield is a major producer of gas for the region and also pipes gas to Paris. Approximately 2·4 million tons of coke are produced per annum and sales to the steel industry have benefited from advances in the technology of coking and also from changes in the pricing system.[7] Production of gas and coke is also linked to an expanding chemicals output located at Carling, Merlebach and Marienau. Carling is the principal complex and in addition to chemicals derived from coal also participates in petrochemicals, the raw materials deriving by pipeline from a refinery in the Saar. The latter trend marks an effort by the nationalized industry to diversify its activities in face of increasing difficulties in marketing coal. To the competition of the Strasbourg refineries will be added that of the projected new refinery near Metz, while the improvement of the Moselle canal gives advantage to Ruhr coke.

Important although the coal and chemical resources are, it is the deposits of iron ore at the base of the Oolitic limestone that have most influenced the industrial development of Lorraine. One of the largest fields in the world, the ore nevertheless suffers the multiple disadvantages of a lean iron content,* a high phosphorus content, and being difficult to enrich on an economic basis. On the other hand, extraction conditions are favourable and many of the ores are self-fluxing. The ore fields fulfil virtually the entire needs of the Lorraine iron and steel industry but export is proving increasingly difficult in competition with high-grade foreign ores. Falling transport rates have enabled Swedish and African ore to price Lorraine ore out of traditional markets in the Nord and Belgium.[8] The Ruhr no longer uses Lorraine ore and export outlets are now very

*An average of 35 per cent iron content.

largely to immediately neighbouring regions, as Luxembourg and the Saar. The position of Lorraine ore in the local industry remains unchallenged by virtue of minimal transport costs and the fact that the steel companies exploit their own concessions. Improvements in extraction methods, concentration of output on mines with high productivity and the fall in exports have had serious repercussions on employment in ore mining.[9] In 1962 the number employed was 26,000 but by 1967 the total had fallen below 15,000.

It is useful to precede discussion of the Lorraine iron and steel industry by some reference to wider national trends in this vital base industry. In recent years, France has ranked as the sixth producing nation in the world of pig iron and crude steel; occupying an intermediate position within the Common Market, substantially behind the output of West Germany, but producing over twice as much iron and steel as any of the remaining numbers.[10, 11]

The present distribution of production[12] is the end-product of a very complex evolution in which access to raw materials and technological advances in production methods have been the determining factors of location.[13] *Figure 14.2* attempts to illustrate the position of the Lorraine industry within the national pattern of distribution.* The figure differentiates between plants producing both iron and steel, with varying degrees of integration, and those producing pig iron only. Outside Lorraine, a distinction is also made between steelmaking plants and plants which are engaged in finishing but which do not produce crude steel. *Figure 14.2* indicates that it is the primary stage—the smelting of iron ore—which has the most concentrated distribution, approximately 85 per cent of the nation's pig iron being produced in Lorraine. With the closure of Le Boucau, in 1965 and Chasse in 1967, the small plants of Fumel and Decazeville are the only blast furnaces located south of a line from Caen to Neuves-Maisons.

The manufacture of steel has a wider distribution since the transfer of refined iron represents a considerable reduction in bulk and weight over the original raw materials. Nevertheless, the dominance of the north-east remains emphatic since Lorraine produces approximately 64 per cent and the Nord-Pas-de-Calais group 25 per cent of the nation's crude steel. The remaining plants consist of small units related to the use of hydroelectric power, as in the Alps and Pyrénées, or represent the surviving capacity of a once important iron and steel industry, this survival being based on the production of special steels, as in the case of the Loire coalfield group. The principal exception is the Caen iron and steel works, where the use of

Figure 14.2 is intended to illustrate only the location pattern and does not represent the scale of production.

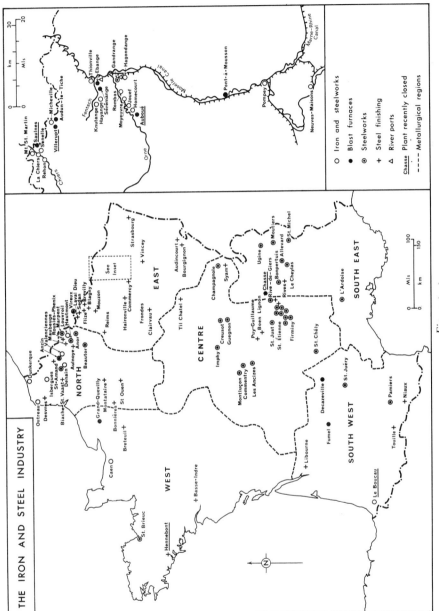

THE IRON AND STEEL INDUSTRY

Inset (upper right):

km 30
Mls 20

Mt.-St. Martin
La Chiers
Rehon
Saulnes
Senelle
Villerupt
Micheville
Audun-le-Tiche
Fontoy
Knutange
Hayange
Sérémange
Rombas
Moyeuvre
Homecourt
Jœuf
Auboué
Thionville
Ebange
Gandrange
Hagondange

Moselle Canal
Orne

Pont-à-Mousson
Pompey
Neuves-Maisons

Marne-Rhine Canal

○ Iron and steelworks
● Blast furnaces
◉ Steelworks
+ Steel finishing
△ River ports
Chasse Plant recently closed
– – – Metallurgical regions

Main map:

WEST
NORTH
CENTRE
EAST
SOUTH EAST
SOUTH WEST

St. Brieuc
Hennebont
Basse-Indre
Caen
Outreau
Desvres
Dunkerque
Isbergues
St-Amand
Blache
St. Vaast
Denain
Grand-Quevilly
Montataire
Bonnières
Breteuil
St. Ouen
Anzin
Valenciennes
Maubeuge
Rousies
Phénix
Louvroil
Hautmont
Marpent
Aulnoye
Anor
Beautor
Vireux
Liaval Dieu
Eliza
Sedan
Blagny
Breuilly
Mouzon
Reims
Hairionville
Commercy
Frondes
Clairvau
Til Chatel
Mouzon
Strasbourg
Vincey
Audincourt
Bourgignon
Champagnole
Syam
Imphy
Creusot
Guegnon
Montluçon
Commentry
Les Ancizes
Puy-Guillaume
Boen Lignon
Chasse
Ugine
Moutiers
Bonpertuis
Allevard
St. Michel
Rive-de-Giers
Le Cheylas
St. Just
St. Étienne
Firminy
Rives
L'Ardoise
St. Chély
St. Juéry
Libourne
Decazeville
Fumel
Le Boucau
Touille
Pamiers
Niaux

Mls 100
km 150

N

Figure 14.2

Normandy ore and imported coal supports a large integrated works.

The final stage of production—the rolling and pressing of finished steel—is again concentrated in Lorraine and Nord. Elsewhere, this branch frequently represents the last stage of activity after the extinction of blast furnaces and steelmaking capacity. This applies notably in the Ardennes, where only Vireux produces steel, and in the Meuse valley, where no steelmaking capacity exists. In other instances the mills are highly specialized and are part of local linkages, as for example exists between the Basse-Indre tin-plate works and the food conserving industry of Nantes.

The iron and steel industry is more inert than most branches of manufacturing by virtue of the close tie to raw material supply and the high level of fixed investment in plant. The major changes in the location pattern emanate from the post-war trend towards financial concentration within the industry. The industry has a long history of gradual financial concentration, most of the existing large firms having been formed by fusions and amalgamations. This trend has been stimulated since 1945 by the increased competition in export markets, the stimulus of the Coal and Steel Community, the difficulties encountered by smaller firms and the active encouragement of rationalization by the government. Although approximately 80 companies existed in 1965, only eight had an annual output in excess of one million tons per annum, and five companies★ produced over 60 per cent of the nation's crude steel. The process of massive financial concentration began in 1948 with the creation of USINOR, grouping Denain-Anzin and Nord-Est, and the formation of the holding company of SOLLAC, in which de Wendel, SIDELOR and a number of smaller shareholders are associated. Since 1965, this type of association has been superseded by a number of full-scale mergers which have resulted in two giant companies dominating French production; USINOR-Lorraine-Escaut, merged in 1966, and de Wendel, SIDELOR and Mosellane de Sidérurgie (SACILOR), merged in 1967.

This reorganization of financial control in the steel industry has had serious repurcussions on the location pattern which have affected Lorraine directly and indirectly. The drive towards rationalization has resulted in the elimination of many of the outlying small plants, such as Hennebont and Le Boucau, rendered uneconomic by virtue of their small scale and need for expensive re-equipment. Conversely, the formation of powerful combines has permitted the creation of new plant, the outstanding example being the integrated steelworks built by USINOR at Dunkerque. This may mark the onset of a new trend, already apparent in other Common Market countries,[14, 15] in favour of coastal location, where to the advantage

★These were USINOR, 4·0 million tons; SOLLAC, 2·3; Lorraine–Escaut, 2·2; de Wendel, 1·8; and Mosellane de Sidérurgie, 1·7 million tons.

of cheap assembly of raw materials is added that of a favourable location for export.* The possibility of a second coastal plant at Fos, near Marseille, implies growing competition for Lorraine. Within Lorraine, the trend towards financial concentration has been accompanied by a programme of rationalization resulting in both new construction and closures. The creation of the SOLLAC group in 1948 permitted the construction of steel works and hot-strip mills at Séremange, and cold-strip mills at adjacent Ebange in the Fentsch valley. The steelworks are nourished by the de Wendel blast furnaces at Hayange but also finish steel produced by the other companies associated in SOLLAC. On the other hand, several of the smaller blast furnaces have fallen victim of the rationalization movement and those of Saulnes, Villerupt and Auboué have recently been closed.

This brief digression into general considerations affecting iron and steel production illustrates the national importance of the Lorraine industry and some of the forces at work within the region. The monumental researches of Prêcheur,[16] the studies by Pounds[17] and the detailed analysis of recent trends by Martin[18,20] require that little need be presented in the way of factual information on the Lorraine industry. Control of production is now dominated by two groups, each with a marked geographical concentration. USINOR-Lorraine-Escaut has works in the Longwy area together with an outlying plant at Thionville. The works are linked to the northern coalfield by the Valenciennes–Longwy–Thionville electrified railway. The new SACILOR group is concentrated in the Orne and Fentsch valleys, with outlying plants in the Moselle valley at Hagondange and Pont-à-Mousson.

The reorganization of financial control has thus permitted a restructuring of the industry and one of its major handicaps, the fragmentation of plant owned by individual companies and the limited development of large-scale fully integrated works, is being overcome. The development of greater integration has been accompanied by a major effort to modernize plant, especially in the introduction of the Kaldo pure oxygen process and the expansion of steel strip plant. Since 1966, the task of modernization has been aided by a convention giving government-guaranteed loans. This same convention has allowed the threatened works of Neuves-Maisons to be maintained on social grounds; when completed, the southern extension of the Moselle canal may offer improved prospects for this plant.

A particular feature of recent rationalization and new investment is the 'sliding' of the industry towards the Moselle valley. This is a function

*In recent years France has exported approximately a quarter of her steel, chiefly in the form of plate and wire.

partly of the improvement of the Moselle canal to European gauge, stimulating the transfer of both coke imports and steel exports from rail to water transport. Partly too, it reflects the increased importance of Lorraine coke and also the existence of extensive sites as opposed to the congestion of the tributary valleys. These factors encouraged the choice of the lower Fentsch valley close to the confluence with the Moselle, and served by the de Wendel river port, for the siting of the SOLLAC strip mills. Similarly, the new steel plant at Gandrange being built by SACILOR★ occupies a comparable site in the lower Orne valley, close to the SIDELOR river port.

Stimulated in turn by the Monnet Plan, the development of the Coal and Steel Community, a buoyant home demand and, since 1950, by the expansion of finished steel production, the Lorraine steel industry experienced a period of sustained activity necessitating recourse to imported labour†. The situation has changed very rapidly in recent years and is now less favourable. Increased production in the world at large has reduced export outlets overseas, while increased capacity in the Common Market has led to stiffer competition in neighbouring markets. This coincides with the process of plant modernization, leading to reduced labour demands, and rationalization of structure causing redundancies in closed plants. Coupled with the crises in employment in ore mining, the present situation gives cause for alarm, especially in view of the appearance on the labour market of young workers born during the post-war upsurge in the birth rate, which in Lorraine was both emphatic and sustained. This difficulty underlines the extent to which the industrial economy of Lorraine has failed to achieve maturity, and the reliance on heavy industry is the most critical aspect of the regional economy.

THE PROBLEM OF DIVERSIFICATION

A measure of the dependence on the steel industry is offered by the fact that in 1962, 83,000 persons were employed in the primary stages of iron and steel production‡. This accounted for half of all male employment in manufacturing in the département of Meurthe-et-Moselle, and 63 per cent in the département of Moselle.[23] In these same départements, extractive industry and iron and steel accounted for almost 150,000 male jobs, whereas all other branches of manufacturing provided less than

★The plant is scheduled for opening in 1969 with an initial output of 1·6 million tons per annum, to be expanded to 2·5 million tons by 1971.
†Recourse to foreign labour was also made by the coal mining industry[21] in spite of high natural increase.[22]
‡Excluding ore extraction.

70,000 male jobs in 1962. Like Nord, Lorraine failed to gain sufficient advantage from its ouput of basic materials in the form of the latter stages of elaboration into finished goods. In part this stems from the reluctance of companies in the past to invest in an area that was strategically sensitive, but also results from the lack of investment 'downstream' by the steel companies in the engineering branches. Consequently, a high proportion of the steel produced leaves the region in crude form or semi-processed as plates, bars, tubes and wires, and only recently has sheet steel been produced in large quantity. In spite of the region's overwhelming dominance of national steel output, the engineering industry employed fewer workers than textiles and clothing in 1962, and even fewer than the combined total of such traditional activities as woodworking, glass and ceramics, and leather working.

The crucial need for a more diversified industrial structure is rendered more urgent by the decline in the region's second staple activity: textiles. This industry is concentrated in the Vosges, with primary centres at Epinal, St. Dié, Gérardmer and Thaon, but virtually every valley has some connection with the spinning, weaving or dyeing of cotton. The decline of employment is a function of increased competition, especially from artificial fibres, the structure of small firms★ and factory units, and the increase in highly automated machinery. Compensating for this decline is some increase in the clothing branch, but whereas some firms have remained active through cooperative arrangements, many of the smaller firms have closed and some premises have been converted to light engineering.

Faced with the prospect of rising unemployment, the government has reacted by strengthening the amount of state assistance afforded to new industry. The iron ore and coalmining districts, together with the textiles district of the Vosges, benefit from industrial reconversion grants. Northern Meuse and the Lorraine plateau are eligible for fiscal exonerations on new factories. Government assistance has been instrumental in the creation of new industrial estates throughout the region and, in the case of the ore and coal fields, has been complemented by finance provided by the Authority of the Coal and Steel Community. New estates have been established on the coalfield, and on the ore field near Longwy. They have also been built at isolated points of employment difficulty, as Neuves-Maisons, and on the airbase near Toul, vacated by the American forces. Two new estates have been built on the Moselle canal, at La Maxe, where a new power station is under construction, and at Hauconcourt, near Metz, the site of a new refinery to be nourished with crude oil by pipeline from Strasbourg.

★The main exception is the nationally important firm of Boussac.

The combination of financial assistance, prepared reception areas and government pressure, has resulted in the establishment of several important new firms in Lorraine. These include the Lucas group, which has built a factory manufacturing disc brakes at Bouzonville, to the north of the coalfield; Kléber-Colombes, which has installed a tyre factory on the former Toul air base; Renault are building a forging plant at Gandrange; and Citroën are locating a gearbox and component plant near Metz. The latter case is an indication of government pressure on behalf of Lorraine, as the new plant, which is being assisted from state funds, was a condition of Citroën being permitted to redevelop their assembly works in Paris. The factory is to be opened in 1970, employing 1,200 workers initially with a possible expansion to over 4,000 workers.

URBAN DEVELOPMENT

Approximately 90 per cent of the population of Lorraine is resident in urban-industrial zones. The region is not, however, heavily urbanized in the sense of possessing a number of large urban centres. Nancy and Metz have over 100,000 inhabitants, but the only other large towns are Epinal, Thionville and Longwy, each with less than 40,000 inhabitants. Rather is Lorraine characterized by urbanized districts and weakly coordinated agglomerations. Four main forms of urbanization may be distinguished. The coal industry has virtually created towns in the forest in an area where urban development was previously absent. Most of the mining communities scarcely merit the status of a town, since they consist of cités-minières with little elaboration of urban functions. Forbach is the centre of an agglomeration of 85,000 inhabitants, and the relationship to mining is reflected in the drop of population by 8,000 between 1962 and 1968.

Whereas the coalmining industry fostered the development of virtual new towns, the ore-mining and steel industries merely grafted population in a haphazard manner on to pre-existing settlements. Thus Briey, at the centre of a productive ore field, expanded from village proportions to over 5,000 inhabitants; Homecourt and Jouef to over 10,000; and Villerupt to 14,000 inhabitants. The character of relief and the disposition of mines promoted urban development of the valleys leading to linear patterns of almost unbroken urbanization but within which few towns of magnitude developed. Thus the Orne valley from Hagondange to Briey houses a linear agglomeration of approximately 120,000 inhabitants, the agglomeration of Thionville and the Fentsch valley has 130,000 inhabitants, the Chiers valley has an agglomeration of 50,000 inhabitants, and Villerupt is the largest town of an agglomeration of almost 30,000 projected along the Alzette valley into Luxembourg. In common with the coalfield, these agglomerations no longer maintain a high rate of increase. The Longwy agglomeration expanded by only two per cent between 1962 and 1968 and suffered a net loss of 3,500 inhabitants by net migration. The agglomeration of Thionville expanded by eight per cent during the same period, entirely as a result of high natural increase, but a net loss of over 1,000 migrants was sustained.

The third category of towns, that of old urban centres which have acquired modest amounts of industry in the lighter branches, has escaped both the past rapid growth and the present incipient decline of the above categories. Such towns as Verdun, Bar-le-Duc, Toul, St. Die and Epinal have between 20,000 and 35,000 inhabitants, and their status as historic centres with established commercial tributary areas has not been submerged by modern industrial growth.

Finally, at the head of the regional hierarchy of urban places are the twin centres of Metz and Nancy. Although the two cities are of equivalent size—107,000 and 123,000 inhabitants respectively—Nancy has by far the larger agglomeration with 258,000 inhabitants in 1968. While Nancy is the undisputed regional capital of Lorraine, the two centres tend to complement each other in the organization of the regional economy. Metz has little industry but is the financial and commercial nucleus of the iron and steel district, a major rail junction and, unlike Nancy, has direct air links with Paris. Nancy, on the other hand, is highly industrialized, with engineering, chemicals, textiles and food processing especially prominent. It is the largest banking and commercial city of Lorraine, has a major university, and its historic role as a provincial capital is maintained in its present function as a regional capital. The complementary character of the two centres, combined with the small distance between them, led to the decision to designate Nancy–Metz as an arterial 'métropole d'équilibre'.[24,25] Already linked by electrified rail, the construction of the Nancy–Metz motorway and the extension of the Moselle canal to Nancy were included in the Fifth Plan.

PERSPECTIVES

Lorraine may be characterized as a region that, in spite of an impressive scale of industrial activity, has failed to achieve maturity. A forceful comparison may be made with the Saar, where in spite of lesser resources an elaborate and diversified industrial base has been established. At the heart of Lorraine's lack of economic maturity is the weak internal integration between the coal, steel, chemicals and enginnering sectors, in part attributable to poor east-west transport facilities for the exchange of bulky and heavy materials, but also to the past fragmentation and compartmentalization of industrial interests.[26] Secondly, the region has been weakly linked to neighbouring regions of France and adjacent countries. East–west canal links are of small gauge, southern Lorraine is practically a cul-de-sac and the Moselle canal has been raised to European gauge only since 1964. As a consequence the Lorraine economy has been operating in physical, commercial, structural and economic conditions inimical to the optimum use of her resources and inhibiting its European vocation. The aquisition of new industries is thus not a matter merely of combating declining employment in staples, but of locating in Lorraine industries which should logically be already well-represented. In this category an expansion of engineering, chemicals and a wide variety of consumer goods industries is clearly appropriate. In the longer term, a closer integration with the Common Market neighbours, and specifically with the evolution of the Rhône–Rhine axis, of which the Moselle artery is a branch, must be secured. The minutiae of regional planning, such as the water shortage in the steel industry, the introduction of new energy sources, the problems of urban renewal and the development of tourism in the Vosges, may thus only be resolved in so far as Lorraine continues to advance in terms of wider strategic objectives and supra-regional planning.

REFERENCES

[1] Comité Régional du Bassin Lorrain, *Perspectives du Ve Plan en Lorraine*, p. 7, 1967, Nancy.
[2] Peltre, J., 'Chronique Lorraine', *Revue Géogr. Est*, 1965, p. 208.
[3] Cointat, M., 'Le problème des terres abandonnées dans l'Est de la France', *Grands Aménagements rég.*, 1963, No. 2, p. 54.
[4] Charbonnages de France, *Rapp. Gestion 1967*, p. 42.
[5] Haby, R., *Les Houillères Lorraines et leur Région*, Vol. 1, 1965, Paris, SABRI.
[6] Gruninger, P., 'L'évolution de l'exploitation du fond dans les Houillères du Bassin de Lorraine', *Arts Mfres*, No. 105, 1961, Fig. 1, p. 9.
[7] Martin, J., 'New trends in the Lorraine iron region', *Geography*, 1968, p. 376.
[8] Martin, J., *op. cit.*[7] pp. 377–379.
[9] Biard, R., *Une richesse nationale en péril, les mines de fer de Lorraine*, 1966, Paris, Editions Sociales.
[10] *Notes Etud. docum.*, 'La Sidérurgie Française', No. 3,144, 1964.
[11] Beaujeu-Garnier, J., 'La Sidérurgie Française', *Inf. géogr.*, 1962, p. 93.
[12] Prêcheur, C., *La Sidérurgie Française*, pp. 70–134, 1963, Paris, Armand Colin.
[13] Pounds, N., 'The historical geography of the French iron and steel industry', *Ann. Ass. Am. Geogr.*, 1957, p. 3.
[14] Fleming, D., 'Coastal steelworks in the Common Market countries', *Geogrl Rev.*, 1967, p. 48.
[15] Warren, K., 'The changing steel industry of the European Common Market', *Econ. Geogr.*, 1967, p. 314.
[16] Prêcheur, C., *La Lorraine Sidérurgique*, 1959, Paris, SABRI.
[17] Pounds, N., 'Lorraine and the Ruhr', *Econ. Geogr.*, 1957, p. 149.
[18] Martin, J., 'Location factors in the Lorraine iron and steel industry', *Trans. Inst. Br. Geogr.*, 1957, p. 191.
[19] Martin, J., 'Recent trends in the Lorraine iron and steel industry', *Geography*, 1958, p. 191.
[20] Martin, J., *op. cit.*[7]
[21] Rochefort, R., 'Sardes et Siciliens dans les grands ensembles des charbonnages de Lorraine', *Annls Géogr.*, 1963, p. 272.

22 Doumergue, Y., 'La vitalité démographique du bassin houiller lorrain d'après le recensement de 1962', *Inf. géogr.*, 1963.

23 INSEE, *Tableaux de l'Economie Lorraine*, Table 3, p. 86, 1966, Nancy.

24 Anon., 'L'aménagement de la métropole Lorraine', *Expans. rég.*, No. 37, 1965, p. 22.

25 George, P., *La France*, pp. 182–183, 1967, Paris, Presses Universitaires de France.

26 Nistri, R., and Prêcheur, C., *La Région du Nord, Nord-Est*, p. 133, 1959, Paris, Presses Universitaires de France.

15

Picardie

Situated between the industrial Nord and the Paris region, the planning region of Picardie appears as a lacuna in the urban-industrial pattern of Northern France. In several particulars Picardie is anomalous as compared with the more highly developed neighbouring regions. The average population density of 77 per square kilometre is low in comparison with 705 in the Paris region, 296 in Nord and 114 in Haute-Normandie. In turn this is accounted for by the low level of urbanization; only two towns, Amiens and St. Quentin, exceed 50,000 inhabitants. Superficially Picardie has greater affinity with its neighbour to the east, Champagne, which also has a relatively low urban proportion and a history of rural depopulation, but superior land resources enable Picardie to support rural population densities double those of Champagne, while the intrusion of the Paris complex into the southern margin introduces a further original feature.

In general outline, the planning region consists of three natural units. The reclaimed coastal marshes together with the lower valleys of the Somme and the Authie constitute a zone of alluvial accumulation devoted to pasture and feed crops. The core of the planning region is formed by the broad chalk plain of Picardie, delimited north and south by the anticlines of Artois and Bray.[1] A thick cover of 'limon' and loess provides excellent soil exploited in a rational arable farming system. The proportion of arable to pasture is extremely high and cereals, sugar-beet and potatoes are the principal elements. A blending of tenancy and owner-operation prevails on holdings averaging 25 to 50 hectares, highly mechanized as a result of the advanced state of remembrement. East of the Oise, the south-eastern third of Picardie is formed by the Tertiary limestone plateau of the Ile-de-France. As compared with the undulating surface of the Plain of Picardie, the heavy dissection of the calcaire grossier and the calcaire de St. Ouen results in a broken relief. The frequent alternation of plateau surface, escarpment slopes and alluvial valleys made this a classic area for the development of distinctive 'pays' units. The 'limon' cover is almost continuous and an advanced arable farming has developed similar to that of the Picardie Plain. In total, the planning region is characterized by the munificence of natural conditions for agriculture and by the general ease of circulation over the open plain and along the Oise and Aisne valleys in the Ile-de-France. The only physical constraint on movement is the limited number of crossing points on the Somme.★

Against this background, the persistent depopulation of the region over the last century appears paradoxical. Pinchemel[2] has demonstrated that

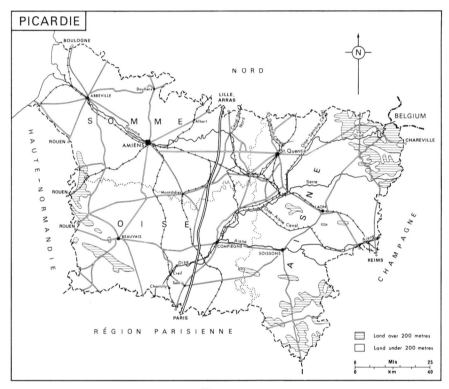

Figure 15.1

rural depopulation was an entirely rational adjustment to the events of the industrial revolution. In the mid-nineteenth century, Picardie was, in a certain sense, overpopulated. The combination of farming with village artisan industries supported artificially high rural population densities. The concentration of manufacturing activity after the introduction of steam-powered machinery impelled a redistribution of artisan workers from dispersed rural centres to the burgeoning industries of Nord, Paris and the Basse-Seine. This redistribution of rural artisans towards more effective

★The Somme valley, deeply entrenched in the chalk and often marshy, has been described as a natural 'fosse anti-char', a grim allusion to its role in the First World War.

industrial locations was accompanied by a depopulation of the agricultural sector through the elimination of small farm units.*

The release of artisans and labourers from the countryside was of little benefit to the towns of the region. The majority of the urban centres, located at crossing points of rivers and at the intersection of valley routes, were essentially small market centres. St. Quentin and Amiens, located on rail and canal routes, had access to the coal of the northern field and experienced some expansion of industry in the textiles branch, but this in no sense counterbalanced the scale of rural depopulation. The migration from the countryside was in very large measure a movement out of the region altogether, and the present population of Picardie is substantially below the total in 1861. The trend of declining rural population and virtually stable urban centres persisted until the outbreak of the Second World War. Increased mechanization concomitant with land consolidation stimulated renewed rural emigration between the wars. The major towns, while possessing in total a very wide range of manufacturing in the textile, clothing, food processing and engineering branches, were characterized by small factory units and a stable level of employment.

Since 1945, Picardie has experienced a certain reversal of these trends as a result of important changes in industrial location factors. The difficulties encountered by firms in the Paris agglomeration in seeking to expand their factories, the improvement in internal communications by the electrification of railways and the construction of the Nord Motorway, and the high growth rate of manufacturing industries not tied to accessibility of high-bulk raw materials, have transformed the evaluation of Picardie as a situation for industrial activity.

Two types of location in particular have benefited from these fundamental changes in location factors. An outer ring of large centres, situated some 120 to 150 kilometres from Paris, involving Amiens and St. Quentin in Picardie and continued through Reims and Châlons in Champagne, has attracted important decentralizations from Paris. The particular attractions involved were the existence of good road communications, skilled labour pools released by the run-down in textiles, substantial base populations† replenished by high natural increase and supplemented by daily influxes of rural commuters, and the initiative of local authorities in creating and equipping new industrial estates. In this manner, Amiens has attracted several major firms, including the manufacture of tyres and chemicals, while St. Quentin has established engineering and electronics industries. Secondly, a much larger number of smaller towns with populations of

*This involved particularly the 'ménagers'; small landowners who possessed no equipment or work animals but who hired out their services as labourers and borrowed equipment periodically to work their own land.[3]
†Amiens 136,000 and St. Quentin 71,000 in their agglomerations in 1968.

approximately 20,000 inhabitants, located on the periphery of the Paris agglomeration and on the valley routes running northwards from the metropolis, form a virtual overspill zone of new industries. The critical factor here was the short distance and travelling time from the Paris market and head offices, which in most cases is less than one hour. The Oise and Aisne valleys in particular have proved ideal reception areas for decentralization operations, even though lacking the incentive of government grants. Such towns as Creil, Beauvais, Chantilly, Senlis, Noyon and Soissons have experienced rapid growth of metallurgical, engineering, chemical and food processing industries.

These economic trends have inevitably influenced the demographic evolution of Picardie. Between 1954 and 1962, the population increased by 6·4 per cent, followed by a further growth by 6·5 per cent between 1962 and 1968. Population growth has been most rapid in Oise, the département situated closest to Paris. The scale of rural depopulation has also been much reduced as a consequence of the function of the expanding towns as 'anchor points' employing rural workers on a commuting basis, as demonstrated by Andrian-Benoit.[4]

Table 15.1

EMPLOYMENT GROUPS OF THE RURAL LABOUR FORCE OF PICARDIE, 1962

| | Proportion of the rural labour force (per cent) | | |
	Primary	Secondary	Tertiary
Aisne	37·0	36·4	26·6
Oise	28·2	45·0	26·8
Somme	41·9	34·7	27·4

Source: Andrian-Benoit, *op. cit.*[4], p. 48.

The blurring of the distinction between rural and urban population in a functional sense is amply demonstrated by *Table 15.1*. Agriculture is a minority occupation of the rural labour force in all the départements of Picardie, while tertiary activities account for approximately a quarter of employment, and industry one third or more. These figures represent a revival of the traditional interest of the rural population in industrial activity but on a changed basis; through daily commuting to the towns rather than in dispersed rural industries. The pattern of rural depopulation is thus undergoing a mutation. The sectorial depopulation of agriculture continues but, rather than leaving the region, the rural workers are finding employment in the towns within the region.

Picardie has entered a new stage in its development, related less to its past function as a region of transit than to its relationship to the evolution of the Paris city region. Although the option of developing a ring of new towns around Paris was specifically rejected in the Schéma Directeur for the Paris region,[5] a spontaneous expansion of the 'couronne' of existing centres within a radius of 100 to 150 kilometres from Paris has already occurred, and is represented in Picardie by Amiens and St. Quentin. Secondly, the smaller towns of the Oise and Aisne valleys, linked to the capital by good communications, form an axis tangential to the Paris agglomeration which has a rational basis for growth.[6] Uninhibited by the nineteenth-century structures of Nord and free from the congestion of central Paris, these two types of location have expanded in the context of the decongestion of Paris through decentralizations. In the future, the structural links with Paris are likely to strengthen but the threshold is being crossed from dependence on Paris to self-sustaining growth as new industrial linkages develop. The creation of new industries and a new university at Amiens suggest that the town can evolve in its own right rather than as a satellite of Paris.[7] This new evolution is not, however, shared by all parts of the planning region. A contrast is emerging between eastern Somme, Oise and Aisne—where remembrement[8] is far-advanced, cereal farming has prospered under the Common Market arrangements, and industrial decentralizations have located—and the western half of Picardie. To the west of Amiens in Vimeu, Ponthieu and the coastal 'bas champs', remembrement is less advanced, rural depopulation still occurring and rural life less evolved.

Picardie made little response to the events of the nineteenth century which transformed Nord and reinforced the dominance of Paris, but is much more receptive to the conditions of modern economic and urban development. In this respect, good communications, prolific natural increase and juxtaposition with the national metropolis are the factors of new growth.

REFERENCES

[1] Pinchemel, P., *Les Plaines de Craie*, 1954, Paris, Armand Colin.
[2] Pinchemel, P., *Structures Sociales et Dépopulation Rurale dans les Campagnes Picardes de 1836 à 1936*, 1957, Paris, Armand Colin.
[3] Pinchemel, P., *Le Bassin Parisien*, p. 90, 1960, Lille, AGEL.
[4] Andrian-Benoit, J., 'Population rurale Nord-Picardie', *Hommes Terres Nord*, 1967, p. 32.
[5] 'Schéma Directeur d'Aménagement et d'Urbanisme de la Région de Paris', *Documn fr.*, 1965, pp. 80–82.
[6] Carillon, R., 'Le développement de la région parisienne doit s'intégrer dans une croissance harmonisée du Bassin Parisien', *Expans. rég.*, No. 38, 1965, p. 25.
[7] Josse, R., 'L'expansion d'Amiens, réalisations et perspectives', *Inf. géogr.*, 1967, p. 63.
[8] Rieucau, L., 'Le remembrement dans le départment de la Somme', *Hommes Terres Nord*, 1966, p. 87.

16

Champagne

The outlines of the ancient province of Champagne are preserved in the present planning region bearing this name. With an eye to securing a variety of complementary resources, the counts of Champagne established control over a sequence of contrasted environments and this same internal diversity characterizes the landscape of the modern planning region. Champagne intervenes between more highly developed neighbours, Lorraine and the Paris region, but it is the latter which has exerted the stronger influence throughout history and which now inspires many of the economic changes taking place in Champagne. In 1968, Champagne had a population of only 1·3 million inhabitants, giving the lowest overall population density of eastern France.

The distinctiveness of the planning region is based on history rather than on physical geography, for the region is composed of a number of totally dissimilar environments. The only element of coherence is that imposed by the rhythmic alternation of scarp and vale, and by the consistency in the orientation of the drainage network. The core of the region is formed by the parallel elliptical landscapes of Dry Champagne and Champagne Humide and the remainder of the land area consists of the intrusion into Champagne of physical units more extensively developed outside the region. Notorious in the past for its sterility and poverty, the history of Dry Champagne is one of changing resource evaluation with related transformations of the cultural landscape. The thin decomposed chalk soils lack a 'limon' cover, and until the nineteenth century carried a mediocre and discontinuous vegetation. The eminences were devoted to sheep grazing, the natural manuring permitting poor cereal crops to alternate with long periods of fallow. The valley floors supported better pasture and cropland, but the resultant economy was unable to support a high population density and by the middle of the nineteenth century rural exodus was firmly established.

In the latter half of the nineteenth century, a complete transformation

259

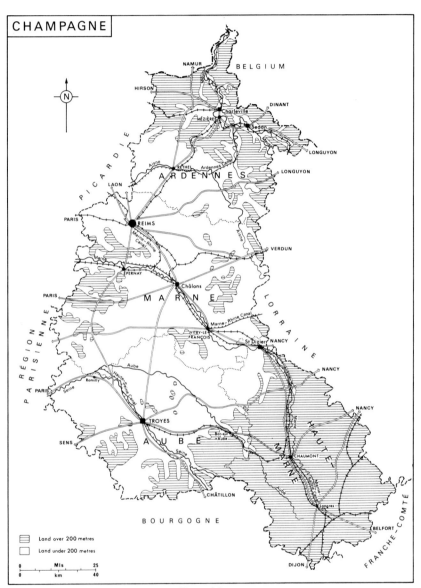

CHAMPAGNE

BELGIUM

NAMUR

HIRSON

DINANT

Charleville
MÉZIÈRES
Sedan

LONGUYON

P
I
C
A
R
D
I
E

LONGUYON

BETHEL   Ardennes Canal

A R D E N N E S

LAON

Aisne

PARIS

REIMS

Aisne

VERDUN

Marne

Marne-Rhine
Canal

EPERNAY

Châlons

M A R N E

L
O
R
R
A
I
N
E

PARIS

Marne-Rhine Canal

VITRY-LE-
FRANÇOIS

St Dizier   NANCY

P A   R É G I O N E
P A R I S I E N N E

Aube

NANCY

PARIS   Seine   Romilly

Haute-Seine Canal

Seine

TROYES

A U B E

Bar-sur-
Aube

H
A
U
T
E

NANCY

SENS

Seine

CHÂTILLON

CHAUMONT

M
A
R
N
E

Marne

B O U R G O G N E

Langres

F
R
A
N
C
H
E
-
C
O
M
T
É

BELFORT

DIJON

Land over 200 metres

Land under 200 metres

Mls
0   25
0   40
km

Figure 16.1

of the landscape occurred through the planting of pine forests to stabilize and fertilize the soils. The interfluves, except where devoted to military purposes, were covered in woodland, patches occasionally being cleared to plant crops, benefiting from the accumulated humus. The present landscape, however, belongs essentially to the twentieth century.[1] The history of depopulation, together with the war losses of the First World War, created large reserves of land available at cheap prices. This triggered off a reclamation movement between the wars, aided by advances in farming technology, which has accelerated since the Second World War. The woodland cover has now almost entirely disappeared and has been replaced by a modern mixed farming economy. Widespread remembrement has permitted the creation of large compact farms, apt for mechanization, while the heavy use of artificial fertilizers has permitted the implantation of commercial farming sufficiently profitable to offset reclamation costs and amortize investment in machinery. The basis of the rotation is cereals, sugar beet, potatoes, fodder root crops and lucerne, giving valuable cash crops and supporting dairy farming for the Paris market. This revolution in farming has not produced a marked increase in population density. The comparatively large farm size and the reliance on machinery has perpetuated the traditional deserted appearance of the plain.

At the contact with the sands and clays of the Lower Cretaceous, a total change in landscape and economy takes place in Champagne Humide. Woodland alternates with pasture and orchard in a land-use system devoted to dairy farming. The bocage landscape, abundant surface drainage and dispersed hamlets contrast abruptly with the open monotonous plain and concealed valley settlements of Dry Champagne.

Surrounding the core of the planning region are fragments of contrasted environments. In the west, the limon-covered plateaux of Brie and Tardenois support intensive mixed farming, while their escarped front is swathed in the vineyards of the champagne wine district. In the south-west, the Pays d'Othe is elevated above the level of Dry Champagne, and its clay-with-flints cover gives rise to a woodland and pastoral landscape. In the département of Haute-Marne, the south-east projection of Champagne is composed of Jurassic rocks forming the bleak plateaux of Barrois and Langres. Finally, in the extreme north of the region a triangular penetration of the Ardennes massif donates three individual landscapes: the thickly wooded plateau zone in which clearings support grazing, the Meuse valley metallurgical district, and the depressed foreland zone devoted to dairy farming.

Clearly, the land resources of Champagne are inherently of first quality only in a limited number of areas, as in Brie Champenoise, and elsewhere the environment is only modestly endowed for agriculture or has been made productive by unremitting effort. The industrial resource position is equally unpromising. The region lacks coal, and power resources—other than the atomic plant at Chooz in the Ardennes—are derived from outside. The scattered mineral resources have been exhausted, the forested area has been much reduced, and the vast sheep flocks which formerly nourished the textile industry are a thing of the past. Not surprisingly, the history of Champagne has been marked by rural exodus and, more recently, by a concentration of population into the urban centres.

The population of Champagne in 1962 was slightly lower than the total in 1861, whereas in the same period the population of Lorraine increased by 30 per cent and that of the Paris region by 300 per cent. The region has not suffered catastrophic depopulation but rather a general stagnation due to the erosion of natural increase by emigration and periods of decline during the World Wars. Underlying this century of demographic stagnation was the influence of Paris, attracting rural migrants leaving an unrewarding agriculture and unable to find employment in the region's towns, in turn languishing in face of the concentration of economic activity in the national capital. Since the Second World War, and particularly since 1950, some modification of this trend has taken place. The rate of rural depopulation has moderated and the rise in the birth rate, coupled with a revival of industrial activity, has enabled the towns to expand at very high rates. It is particularly noticeable that the

Table 16.1

CHANGE IN THE EMPLOYMENT STRUCTURE OF CHAMPAGNE, 1954–1962
(per cent)

	Primary	Secondary	Tertiary
Ardennes	− 20·7	+ 2·1	+ 5·3
Aube	− 24·5	+12·5	+ 4·9
Marne	− 16·9	+13·4	+10·0
Haute-Marne	− 20·3	+ 8·7	+ 3·2
Champagne	− 20·1	+ 9·2	+ 6·8
France	− 25·0	+ 8·8	+11·7

Source: *Notes et Etud. Doc.*, No. 3436–3437, 1967, p. 20.

smaller towns of 10,000 to 50,000 inhabitants have expanded more rapidly than the larger agglomerations of Reims, Troyes, and Charleville-Mézières. This is explained by the fact that many of the smaller towns have experienced growth by industrial decentralization, whereas in the larger towns the benefits of new industrial growth have been partially offset by a decline in traditional activities. Implicit in the recent demographic revival is a redistribution of population and a changing balance of the occupational structure.

The regional agricultural labour force declined by 20 per cent between 1954 and 1962, but this is shown by *Table 16.1* to be rather below the national average decline. By contrast, the increase in industrial employment occurred at a greater rate than in the nation as a whole, but with varying performances in the constituent départements. The rate of growth was lowest in Ardennes, where the metallurgical industry is experiencing difficulties, and in Haute-Marne, where the urban population is small. On the other hand, the départements closest to Paris clearly show the effects of the arrival of new firms. *Table 16.1* also reveals the very slow rate of growth achieved in the tertiary sector; only in Marne did the rate even approach the national average.

The redistribution of population is thus specifically related to recent industrial trends.[2] The modernization of agriculture compels labour shedding in the rural sector, while in addition to retaining their natural increase most of the towns are able to attract rural migrants by virtue of the employment opportunities created by new industrial growth. The relative success of individual urban centres varies in this respect in accordance with their balance between traditional and growth industries. Over the past 15 years, heavy metallurgy, textiles and wood industries have suffered contractions, the food processing industries have remained relatively stable, while hosiery and garment making, engineering and chemicals have advanced in importance. The pattern of industrial location is dispersed, the major centres being Reims, Troyes, Châlons-sur-Marne and St. Dizier, and only in the Ardennes does a polycentric industrial zone appear.

The reorganization of the iron and steel industry has reduced the Ardennes district to the finishing of steel and the production of tubes, forgings, heating equipment and hardware goods. Pig iron is no longer produced but is imported, as is steel, from Lorraine. The metallurgical industry still employs over 30,000 workers but the continued existence of the smaller firms is menaced.

The industrial structure of Reims is far more diversified, the traditional branches being matched by advanced technology industries. The three major components are the engineering, textile and food industries. A wide range of engineering products is manufactured, involving locomotive and vehicle components and domestic consumer goods; aircraft are assembled from imported components. In addition to the processing of foodstuffs, the town also has ancillary industries such as the manufacture of bottles, corks and packaging. The textiles sector is less active but balances the male dominated engineering industries by absorbing female labour. Situated at a major crossroads of the Calais–Basle and Paris–Strasbourg routes, only one and a half hours distant from Paris, and possessing new industrial estates on the periphery of the agglomeration,[3] Reims is ideally placed for the attraction of further decentralized industry.[4]

The industrialization of Troyes was initially based on textiles supported by the locally produced wool. Despite the reorganization of the industry, the hosiery and knitted garment branch has remained very active, relying on imported wool and on synthetic fibres. As at Reims, a range of new industries has been attracted since 1950, especially in the light engineering category, alleviating the dependence on textiles and providing much needed male employment.

Outside the above three principal concentrations, manufacturing is widely dispersed among the smaller towns, many of which have experienced rapid growth of late. St. Dizier has strengthened its traditional metal-using industries by the acquisition of new engineering firms and Châlons-sur-Marne has new precision and electrical engineering works. Vitry-le-François, Epernay and Romilly-sur-Seine have also benefited from decentralizations, attracted by good communications with Paris, the availability of industrial sites and reserves of labour.

REGIONAL PLANNING PROBLEMS

Champagne may claim considerable success in the field of regional economic development. In the last 15 years the production of cereals has tripled and the area devoted to sugar beet has doubled. Between 1950 and 1965 milk production has increased by 60 per cent and meat production has doubled. Since 1950, industrial activity has increased dramatically, diversifying the traditional structure, bringing advanced technology to the region and revitalizing the smaller towns.

This success may be attributed to three outstanding circumstances. Firstly, in the case of agriculture, the progress achieved is due to the effectiveness with which structural and technical reforms have been executed. In 1965, Champagne ranked third among the regions of France in relation to the completion of remembrement and the achievement of large consolidated farms has been accompanied by the installation of younger progressive operators, trained in the application of modern techniques. The provision of agricultural training institutes, experimental stations and improved processing and marketing facilities has given a favourable infrastructure for the support of a competitive commercial agriculture. Secondly, the situation of the region in relation to the Nord,

Paris and Lorraine, at an intersection of routes leading to these markets, endows Champagne with particularly favourable conditions for the attraction of decentralized industries. Finally, the region is notable for the strength of initiative, both private and collective, which has characterized economic affairs since the last war.[*]

As a result of these three circumstances, Champagne has made a successful beginning to the process of adjusting her economy to the changed conditions of the post-war era. The central planning problem is thus to assure the continuance of the progress achieved and to extend the process to the relatively few areas and sectors where new growth is lacking. Three problems are specifically posed with urgency. The Ardennes metallurgical district has not as yet shared in the general trend of new industrial implantation, although it is the area with the greatest need in view of its dependence on staple declining activities. An infusion of new firms is urgently required to balance the reduced opportunities in heavy industry and to create female employment. Secondly, the transport network, although dense, has, with the exception of the railways, certain deficiencies. The canal network has retained its nineteenth-century Freycinet gauge, while the region is devoid of motorway connections and has little high-capacity trunk road construction. The major transport projects—the motorways from Calais to Basle and from Paris to Strasbourg—and the improvement of the canal link from Paris to Lorraine cannot be realized in the immediate future, but urgent improvement is necessary in the road connections with Paris and in the north–south roads linking Troyes, Châlons and Reims. Thirdly, the recent growth in urban population has been unaccompanied by a commensurate expansion in tertiary employment. The only important centre of tertiary activity is Reims, stemming from its importance as a route and tourist centre, the possession of regional branches of the major national banks, the commercial activity generated by the wine trade, and the existence of a number of wholesale companies of national importance. To this must be added the recent creation of a university and the selection of Reims as the site of the regional administration. Too close to Paris to serve as an effective regional capital for the whole of Champagne, the direct sphere of influence of Reims is largely confined to the département of Marne. The best prospect of expanding tertiary employment would seem to be in the field of tourism. At present tourism is primarily of a transient nature, the region being situated on recognized tourist routes, both national and international. Possibilities for the establishment of holiday centres exist in the Ardennes, well placed to serve the Nord industrial

[*]Even before the close of the war, France's first economic expansion committee was constituted at Reims, in 1944.

region, in the forest of the Argonne, and at the reservoirs built in Champagne Humide to regulate the flow of the Seine.[5]

The abiding impression of Champagne remains that of emptiness, resulting from the low population density, and ironically this may be an important asset in the future. Champagne is ideally constituted to serve as a reception area for the decongestion of the Paris agglomeration and its future seems inexorably bound up with that of the capital. The axial development of Paris foreshadowed in the Schéma Directeur suggests that an eventual integration of much of Champagne in the Le Havre–Seine valley–Paris urbanized axis is likely, in the form of a diffused eastern extension.

REFERENCES

[1] Chabot, G., Géographie Régionale de la France, pp. 304–305, 1966, Paris, Masson.
[2] Dellon, P., 'L'Economie de la région Champagne-Ardenne', Notes Etud. docum., No. 3,436–3,437, 1967, p. 70.
[3] Anon., 'L'Agglomération de Reims', Expans. rég., No. 38, 1965, p. 34.
[4] Krist, M., 'Une forme de décentralisation industrielle. La réanimation des grandes villes situées entre 100 et 200 kilomètres de Paris; le cas de Reims', Bull. Sect. Géogr. Com. Trav. hist. scient., 1961, pp. 55–71.
[5] Gravier, F., L'Aménagement du Territoire et l'Avenir des Régions Françaises, p. 208, 1964, Paris, Flammarion.

17

Haute-Normandie

The outlines of the historical province of Normandie are preserved in the present planning regions of Haute and Basse-Normandie. The historical integration of the area rested on bonds of allegiance rather than on any physical and economic uniformity,[1] and the present division of the province into two planning regions conforms with contrasts in economic orientation, level of development and differing planning problems. The line separating the two regions is the northern limit of the economic divide between eastern and western France. West of a line from the mouth of the Seine to the hills of Perche, a gradual attenuation of economic forces comes into play and it is appropriate to place the chapter devoted to Basse-Normandie in Part Three of the regional analysis: the regions of the west.

Physical definition of Haute-Normandie is provided by the coastline, by the denuded anticline of Bray in the north-east and by the Pays d'Auche in the south-west. The southern boundary, formed by the contact with the Tertiary rocks of the Ile-de-France, is less determinate in a physical sense. The region is divided administratively in almost equal proportions between the départements of Seine-Maritime and Eure, but in economic terms the dominant division is between the axis of the Basse-Seine and the predominantly rural areas to the north and south.

To the north of the Basse-Seine, the dominant landscape is the limon-covered chalk plateau. At its northern limit, an original element is introduced by the denuded anticline of Bray, termed by Chabot 'une sorte de Champagne humide qui serait au milieu d'une Champagne sèche'[2]; an allusion to the exposure of Jurassic marls, clays and sandstones, propitious to pasture supporting whole milk and dairy production for the Paris market. The Pays-de-Caux is constituted by the triangular western portion of Seine-Maritime, a level chalk surface thickly coated with limon. Cereal farming predominates on medium-sized, well-managed farms, but the demands of Le Havre and Rouen are favouring an extension

of animal farming. Over the centuries, a high proportion of the land has
been acquired by citizens and business interests of Le Havre and Rouen.[3]
In the east of Seine-Maritime, the dissected plateau of Vexin is differentiated
by the larger farm size, attributed to investment emanating from Paris,
and the greater emphasis on industrial crops.

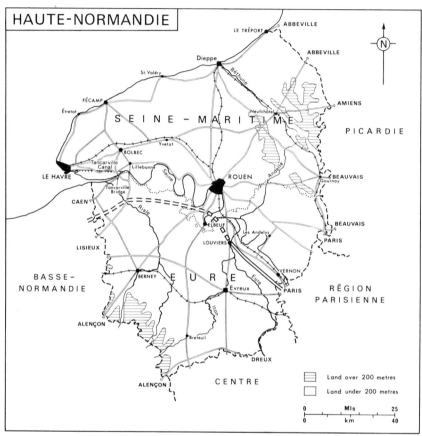

Figure 17.1

Urban development north of the Seine axis is limited to two main types.
Yvetot, Neufchâtel and Gournay are agricultural marketing and processing centres for the Pays-de-Caux, Bray and Vexin respectively, but
none has a population exceeding 10,000 inhabitants. Secondly, a chain of
coastal towns extends from Etretat to Le Tréport. The littoral is bordered
by an impressive façade of cliffs and an absence of sites suitable for large-
scale port development. Only Dieppe, with a population of 30,000, has
important commercial port activity. The combination of cross-Channel
traffic, fishing and the importing of tropical fruit animates the port, which

in turn supports small-scale marine engineering. Some diversification of the industrial base has resulted from the recent creation of factories manufacturing synthetic textiles and in the mechanical and electrical engineering branches. Fécamp, with 20,000 inhabitants, is specifically a fishing port, the landings of cod and herring being conserved locally. The miniature conurbation of Eu–Le Tréport–Mers, with a combined population of 17,000, is primarily a tourist centre, as on a smaller scale are St. Valéry and Etretat. The coastal tourist industry has experienced a relative decline, and in terms of total hotel capacity, number of visitors and the number of secondary holiday homes is far outranked by the coast of Basse-Normandie.[4]

South of the Basse-Seine axis, the alternating plateaux and vales of the département of Eure are subject to a greater intrusion of the influence of Paris than is the case north of the Seine valley. The construction of the Normandy motorway has now reached Eure and has been a major factor in the wave of decentralizations which has revived the small towns of the département.[5] The location of new firms in Evreux, Bernay, Breteuil and Vernay has attracted population from surrounding rural areas and from the metropolis.[6] The influence of Paris also extends to the establishment of many secondary residences in the Eure valley, scarely more than an hour removed from central Paris. The vocation of the network of small towns as an overspill zone for industry and population from Paris, suggested by Gravier,[7] has been confirmed by the events of recent years. The combination of proximity to the industrialized zone of western Paris, fast road connections with the capital, Rouen, and, via the Tancarville bridge, with the port of Le Havre, and the existence of small towns suitable for expansion and set in an agreeable environment, outweigh the disadvantage of ineligibility for industrial development grants.

The economic core of the region is the Basse-Seine axis, itself susceptible to various definitions. In the strict physical sense it is formed by the Seine valley, which meanders in nine major loops within the region, enclosed by steep bluffs, before reaching its broad estuary. In the sphere of economic and urban organization, it is more realistic to accept as boundaries the routes nationales 14 and 13 linking Paris, Rouen and Le Havre to the north of the river, and the parallel left-bank routes linking Paris via Elbeuf and the Tancarville bridge to Le Havre as the southern limit, with the navigable Seine as the spine of the axis thus defined. In longer-term planning perspective, the metropolitan area of the Basse-Seine has been defined as a broad corridor extending some 25 to 30 kilometres on either bank of the river. In the present context, the Basse-Seine is defined in terms of the axes of transport, since this adequately confines the existing urban and industrial complexes.

The essence of the Basse-Seine is its function as a corridor of movement, punctuated at intervals by two major and several minor urban-industrial agglomerations. Le Havre ranks as the second largest port of France by tonnage handled, and Rouen the fourth largest, while the Seine carries a third of the cargo of the nation's inland waterways as expressed in ton-kilometres. Le Havre and Rouen are linked to Paris by electrified rail and by a complex network of oil pipelines and high-tension electricity lines. Work is advanced on the Normandy motorway, to be paralleled later by a second motorway on the right bank. The term 'axis' must be interpreted purely in terms of movement as an integrating force, for in detail the Basse-Seine is constituted by several individual complexes rather than a continuous chain of towns lining the banks of the river. Moreover, the two major complexes—Le Havre and Rouen—account for the vast majority of commercial and industrial activity, and the strengthening of the axis at intermediate points is as yet in an incipient stage.

THE LE HAVRE URBAN-INDUSTRIAL COMPLEX

Le Havre is the centre of an agglomeration of approximately 250,000 inhabitants, combining the functions of a major port and a centre of industrial activity. For a port of such stature, the size of the industrial labour force is comparatively small, in 1965 amounting to only 25,000 workers. Two major branches dominate manufacturing activity: metallurgy and associated engineering industry employing approximately 17,000 workers, and petroleum refining and petrochemicals employing 4,000 workers. The completion of the Renault vehicle assembly plant at Sandouville, near Le Havre, has recently added a further 4,000 jobs.

A distinct pattern of location exists in the distribution of industry, which in the main is peripheral to the mass of the built-up area.[8] Two separate industrial zones may be distinguished, differing in types of industry represented, their relationship to the port, the age of their creation and their present growth trends. In the immediate vicinity of the port and west of the Tancarville canal are grouped the older industries, including many, as textiles and metallurgy, directly related to the arrival of raw materials. Also present are many large firms only indirectly related to the port function but benefiting from the concentration of transport facilities serving the port. By contrast, a second industrial concentration has developed on the reclaimed lowland east of the port, bordered inland by the Tancarville canal. This dates from the creation of a planned industrial estate, developed since 1957, designed to receive industries demanding large amounts of space. As compared with the staple character of the industries of the port zone, the branches represented on the Tancarville zone are essentially in the advanced technology category, involving a high level of automation, high capitalization and, in spite of rising levels of output, a comparatively small work force. The prime force behind the rapid expansion of this new zone is the petroleum refinery of Gonfreville l'Orcher, which nourishes petrochemical industries which in turn have attracted ancillary activities. Compared with the rather fragmented organization of the portside industries, the Tancarville zone is characterized by a high degree of complex linkages. The refinery-petrochemicals complex has recently been joined by a second group of activities resulting from conversion and decentralization operations, involving chiefly aeronautical engineering (SNECMA) and vehicle assembly (Renault).

The imposing new industrial plants and the continuous improvements to the port facilities conceal an underlying trend of stability in the industrial labour force, which scarcely expanded between 1954 and 1965. The decline in employment in textiles and ship repairing and the stability in the metallurgical sector have been offset by new industries which by nature are capital intensive and create only modest amounts of new employment. At present, the improvement of the port and industrial zones, the construction of a new power station and the development of major residential complexes occupies approximately 10,000 workers, while the port employs a further 4,000 workers. A major proportion of the labour force is thus engaged in public works, which, once completed, will create a demand for alternative employment. A certain doubt surrounds future industrial trends since Le Havre has an undue concentration of manual and unskilled workers and an extremely low female employment rate. Further problems stem from the increasing isolation of the location of new industries from the areas of residence as the Tancarville estate expands eastwards away from the agglomeration. The problem is exacerbated by the atmospheric pollution emanating from the refinery complex, which acts as a major constraint on the integrated planning of industrial and residential areas near the Tancarville estate.[9] A certain paradox thus exists between the growing status of Le Havre as a port and the moderate growth rate in industrial employment. Various arguments may be advanced to explain this apparent contradiction. The lack of export-orientated industries, the low level of local investment in industry,* the absence of a steel-producing industry and the decline of certain staples are in large measure responsible for the fact that manufacturing industry employs little more than 25 per cent of the total labour force. It seems inevitable that this situation will change in the future in view of the

*The large industries are almost all subsidiaries of national industries and international consortia or are controlled by the public sector.

undeniable advantages enjoyed by Le Havre as an industrial location. The ability to receive and discharge rapidly the largest vessels, the existence of vast land reserves adjacent to deep water and the projected improvements in communications with the hinterland must, in the long term, prove irresistible forces.

A second paradox consists of the contrast between the size of the agglomeration and national importance of the port, but the modest status of Le Havre as a regional centre. Totally rebuilt after the war-time devastation,[10] Le Havre nevertheless has an extremely limited sphere of direct influence. This is explained partly by the physical situation of the town: at the extremity of a peninsula and surrounded by an exclusively rural hinterland. Before the construction of the Tancarville bridge, the sphere of influence of Le Havre was abruptly curtailed to the south, allowing Caen full dominance of Basse-Normandie. More important is the proximity of Rouen, a historical capital, cathedral and university city, capital of a département and the seat of the regional administration, and possessing a greater range of high-order retail and professional services. In terms of hierarchy, the status as a sous-préfecture, the limited powers of control and decision in industry, and the under-equipment of Le Havre in the sphere of tertiary activities, relegate the town to a lowly position in relation to its population size. An opposition therefore exists between world-wide external contacts and a comparatively limited local sphere of influence.[11]

THE ROUEN URBAN-INDUSTRIAL COMPLEX

The situation of Le Havre as a major industrial port at the mouth of an estuary is unique in France. Rouen, by contrast, forms part of a coherent structure: the 'couronne' of provincial towns around Paris, situated at a distance of between 100 and 120 kilometres distant from the capital. Within this broader structure, Rouen possesses two distinctive features: it is by far the largest town of the 'couronne'—its nearest rival, Reims, has an agglomeration only one third as populous—and its function as the outport of Paris. Rouen far outclasses Le Havre in population size; the agglomeration has a population of 370,000 inhabitants, but the built-up area extends via Orival and Oissel to Elbeuf, forming a conurbation of over 400,000 inhabitants. Moreover, Rouen is expanding rapidly in size. The rate of increase of 17·3 per cent between 1954 and 1962 was exceeded only by Grenoble and Metz among the major urban centres of France.[12] Between 1962 and 1968 the agglomeration increased by 12·7 per cent.

The industrial structure of Rouen is both larger and more diversified than that of Le Havre, and has shown a more impressive growth rate in recent years.[13] The internal location pattern, although closely allied to the port zone, is more complex than that of Le Havre.[14] The oldest branches of industry, notably the textiles and engineering activities, are located on the left bank and in the valley of the Cailly on the right bank. The modern growth of manufacturing has occurred in linear fashion downstream between the port and Grande-Couronne, and upstream, in a less contiguous fashion, as far as Elbeuf. The total industrial labour force is double that of Le Havre.

Table 17.1

MAJOR INDUSTRIAL EMPLOYMENT GROUPS IN THE ROUEN AGGLOMERATION (1964)

Metallurgy and steel production	17,100
Electrical engineering	6,000
Energy, chemicals, petroleum refining, petrochemicals	12,800
Textiles, clothing, tanning	13,000
Food industries	4,800

Source: Gay, *op. cit.*[13]

In 1964 the total industrial labour force was 59,000, representing 37 per cent of the total employed labour force (*Table 17.1*). The female participation rate of 30 per cent compares favourably with the abnormally low rate of 22 per cent at Le Havre. The staple activities of textiles and ship-building have suffered similar contractions to those experienced at Le Havre and a large number of fusions and conversions have been undertaken. Employment in the metallurgical branches, formerly centred on the blast furnaces of Quevilly, has been increased by the creation of major steel-using industries in the agglomeration, but two factors in particular underlie the recent surge of industrialization: the growth of the petro-chemicals sector and the success in attracting decentralized industries. The former development is related to the expanded output of the refinery of Petit-Couronne, which now nourishes a range of petrochemical in-dustries. The success of decentralization involves the arrival of such major firms as Renault, at Cléon, near Elbeuf, in 1958, and other national firms such as Sidélor and Carnaud in the heavy engineering branch and Péchiney-St. Gobain in the chemicals branch, as well as the smaller-scale conversion of textile firms to clothing manufacture. The attraction of decentralized industry has occurred throughout the greater Rouen area, including electrical engineering and electronics in the Cailly valley. Starting from an already diversified base, Rouen has added to the variety of its industrial activities, compensating for the decline in textiles and contrasting sharply with the limited achievements of Le Havre in this field.★

Rouen discharges the function of regional capital throughout Seine-Maritime and much of Eure. Its full development as a regional centre has always been restricted by the proximity of Paris and denies the agglomeration the role of a métropole d'équilibre. The internal structure of the agglomeration also poses delicate planning problems. The agglomeration is divided between 23 communes of varying size and stage of development, and only three bridges, all in central Rouen, cross the river. Various options are under consideration to encompass the inevitable expansion of the agglomeration. The choice falls largely between an eastern axial expansion and the construction of an outer ring of satellite towns, the latter situation being already present at Elbeuf.[15]

The urban-industrial complexes of Le Havre and Rouen dominate the economic life of the Basse-Seine, but it is possible to delimit two further industrial zones related to the Seine axis of movement. Immediately east of the Tancarville bridge, a small valley cut into the Pays-de-Caux is the site of the Bolbec–Lillebonne industrial area. Ten kilometres north of the Seine, on the main Rouen–Le Havre road, Bolbec was established at the turn of the century as a textile centre. This industry is now in sharp decline, employing little more than 1,000 employees. Some conversion to electrical engineering has taken place but the centre of gravity of industry has moved downstream to Lillebonne, close to the confluence with the Seine. The motivators of industry here are the refineries of Port-Jérôme and Notre-Dame de Gravenchon, established under the terms of the 1928 refinery act, but now greatly expanded under the control of American companies.[16] A number of chemical, plastics and synthetic rubber plants are dependent on the refineries, which can be reached by tankers of up to 20,000 tons. Small engineering firms complete this expanding site, which, with Bolbec, employed approximately 9,000 workers in 1965. Secondly, upstream from Elbeuf a more diffuse zone of new industrial activity is centred on the towns of Louviers, Les Andelys and Vernon†. Once again, textiles created the basis of an industrial tradition and the formation of · labour pools. The conversion of the textile industry has been achieved by the attraction of decentralized firms, especially in the electronics branch, capitalizing on sources of female labour and a location escaping the congestion of the Paris agglomeration.

★Gay estimates that three quarters of the industrial building permits granted between 1954 and 1964 in the département of Seine-Maritime were located in the Rouen agglomeration.

†Vernon has been chosen as the site of a new refinery currently under construction.

THE FUTURE DEVELOPMENT OF THE BASSE-SEINE

The Basse-Seine is clearly a sensitive zone in terms of economic and physical planning. Internally, the agglomerations of Rouen and Le Havre are experiencing problems associated with rapid physical expansion; the capacity of the two ports has increased and the infrastructure of land communications is being progressively improved. Already the area has fulfilled a spontaneous role in the decongestion of Paris, not only through the reception of industries but also through the ability of the towns to absorb rural migrants. Gosselin[17] has demonstrated that only 4 per cent of rural migrants leave the region for Paris. The combination of internal and external pressures necessitates that the Basse-Seine should be treated as an integrated planning unit, as envisaged in the White Paper of the Metropolitan Area Study.[18] The latter accepts as inevitable the continuation of axial development but points to several serious dangers. The expansion of industry and the growth of satellite towns around Rouen threatens valuable recreational areas, while the problem of river and atmospheric pollution must be brought under control. The present motorway plans for dual axes north and south of the river will result in feeble interconnection unless transverse links are created. There is also the risk that an undue development along new transport arteries may distort the balance of the existing hierarchy of centres, to the detriment of the outlying towns. The White Paper also draws attention to the threat of the Basse-Seine becoming a Paris suburb. This refers not only to the residential sense, since by the year 2000 the development of rapid transport will place the whole of the Basse-Seine within immediate reach of Paris, but also to the fact that the vast majority of industry is controlled by Paris head offices and parent firms. The notion of the Basse-Seine as a boulevard in the Paris city region is not in the realms of fantasy. The completion of the Normandy motorway to Caen, and the existing link via the Tancarville bridge, lead Lacaze[19] to speculate that the triangle Le Havre–Caen–Rouen could form the urban framework of the future, underlain by a secondary network of smaller centres and new towns as yet unbuilt, as a counterweight to Paris.

Whatever the future holds in terms of organization, the vocation of the Basse-Seine is clear. The valley below Rouen offers large deep-water sites for industry and, above Rouen, ample locations within immediate reach of the Paris agglomeration. In other words, the axis offers locations where industry can operate efficiently and competitively at a European scale. The exploitation of this situation must be balanced against the achievement of a planned process of urban development and against the competing investment needs of the less fortunate parts of the country.

REFERENCES

[1] Musset, R., *La Normandie*, pp. 8–32, 1960, Paris, Armand Colin.

[2] Chabot, G., *Géographie Régionale de la France*, p. 352, 1966, Paris, Masson.

[3] Elhai, H., 'Recherches sur la propriété foncière des citadins en Haute-Normandie', *Mém. Docums Centre Documn*, 1965.

[4] *Atlas de Normandie*, Plates G6 and G7, 1966, Caen, Association Pour l'Atlas de Normandie.

[5] Parry, C., 'Un exemple de décentralisation industrielle; la dispersion des usines de "La Radio Technique" à l'ouest de Paris', *Annls Géogr.*, 1963, p. 148.

[6] Burgel, G., 'La main d'oeuvre des établissements industriels décentralisés, l'exemple de l'Eure', *Annls Géogr.*, 1965, p. 416.

[7] Gravier, J., *L'Aménagement du Territoire et l'Avenir des Régions Françaises*, p. 197, 1964, Paris, Flammarion.

[8] *Atlas de Normandie*, Plate E11, 1966, Caen, Association Pour l'Atlas de Normandie.

[9] Gay, F., and Damois, J., 'Le Havre, aspects géographiques et sociologiques de la croissance urbaine', *Urbanisme*, No. 93, 1966, p. 37.

[10] Damais, J., *La nouvelle ville du Havre. Reconstruction et repopulation*, 1963, Paris, C.N.R.S.

[11] *Atlas de Normandie*, Plate G11, 1966, Caen, Association Pour l'Atlas de Normandie.

[12] Gay, F., 'Note sur la croissance de l'agglomération rouennaise', *Norois*, 1962, p. 449.

[13] Gay, F., 'La croissance de la région de Rouen et ses problèmes', *Etud. normandes*, No. 171, 1964, p. 4.

[14] *Atlas de Normandie*, Plate E10, 1966, Caen, Association Pour l'Atlas de Normandie.

[15] Anon., 'Rouen et son agglomération', *Expans. rég.*, No. 38, 1965, p. 29.

[16] Musset, R., 'Le pétrole dans la Basse-Seine', *Annls Géogr.*, 1959, p. 409.

[17] Gosselin, R., *Eléments sur les migrations récentes*, Comité Regional d'Expansion Economique de Haute-Normandie, 1966,

[18] *L'Avenir de la Basse-Seine*, Organisme d'Etudes d'Aire Métropolitaine de la Basse-Seine, Rouen, 1967.

[19] Lacaze, J., 'Les incidences du rôle futur de l'ensemble portuaire Rouen–Le Havre sur le Schéma d'Aménagement de la Basse-Seine', Rapport No. 7, *Colloque International 'Les Grands Ports et Trafics de l'Atlantique-Nord'*, Rouen and Le Havre, 1968.

18

Alsace

Alsace is by far the smallest of the planning regions of France. Composed of the départements of Bas-Rhin and Haut-Rhin, Alsace has a total land area of only 8,309 square kilometres and a population of 1·4 million inhabitants. At a time when economic and social organization is being increasingly orientated on to large units, it is arguable that Alsace is too small a unit to exist as a viable planning region. Against this it may be stated that factors of history, physical geography and the external relationship to western Europe give Alsace an individual personality without replica elsewhere in France. Sharing boundaries with West Germany and Switzerland, and linked by the Rhine waterway to Rotterdam, Alsace is the most international in character of the planning regions, and enjoys a privileged position with respect to trade with France's European partners.

Alsace is generally considered as a marchland in a climatic sense. The Vosges mountains act as an obstacle to the penetration of Atlantic air masses and the regime is markedly continental in character. The severe winters give way to summer conditions of great heat, luminosity and a maximum of convectional rainfall. The effect is to endow Alsace with favourable conditions for agriculture and especially for viticulture and grains. In structural terms, Alsace forms but half of the major structural unit of the Rhine trough system. An eventful structural history has produced a series of linear north–south aligned terrains, contrasted in physical characteristics and resource value. The most basic division is east–west, between the mountain province of the Vosges and the diverse landscapes of the Alsatian Plain.

The boundary with Lorraine follows the crestline of the Vosges, interposing a substantial barrier to movement between the two regions. The elevation of the crestline increases southwards from 400 metres in the low sandstone Vosges to over 1,400 metres on the summits of the high crystalline Vosges. A distinction between the two zones has more than geological significance for the sandstone Vosges are formed by a dissected

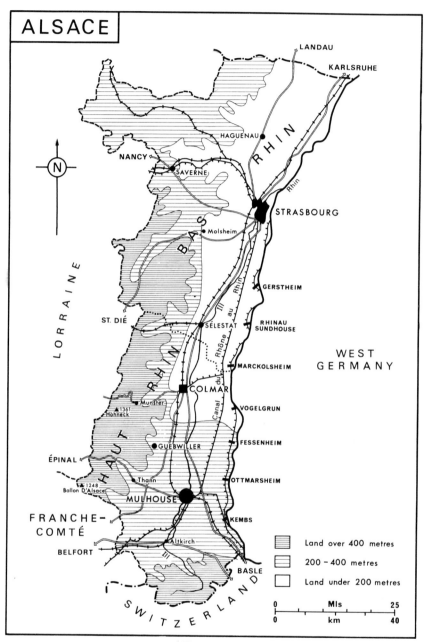

ALSACE

LANDAU
KARLSRUHE
HAGUENAU
RHIN
NANCY
SAVERNE
STRASBOURG
Rhin
Molsheim
LORRAINE
BAS
RHIN
GERSTHEIM
ST. DIÉ
Ill
au
Rhin
SÉLESTAT
RHINAU
SUNDHOUSE
WEST
GERMANY
Rhône
MARCKOLSHEIM
COLMAR
Munster
1361
Hohneck
VOGELGRUN
HAUT
RHIN
Canal
du
GUEBWILLER
FESSENHEIM
ÉPINAL
1248
Thann
OTTMARSHEIM
Ballon D'Alsace
MULHOUSE
FRANCHE-
COMTÉ
KEMBS
BELFORT
Altkirch
Ill
BASLE

Land over 400 metres
200 - 400 metres
Land under 200 metres

SWITZERLAND

Mls
0   25
0   40
km

Figure 18.1

tableland, thickly wooded to the summits, whereas the crystalline Vosges are deeply penetrated by glacially overdeepened valleys and are sufficiently high to carry summer pasture above the tree line. As a consequence, the high Vosges have historically had the greater resource value and the valleys support high population densities. The downfaulted eastern front of the Vosges constitutes a clearly defined foothill zone 300 to 400 metres in altitude and from three to five kilometres in width. The surface has a superficial cover of solifluction material but the favourable aspect of the eastern and southern facing slopes results in a concentration on viticulture, yielding high-quality white wines.

In total, the Vosges province occupies roughly half of the planning region; the remainder, with the exception of the Jura foothills abutting the Swiss frontier, may be considered as the Plain of Alsace. This is by no means a uniform environment, but rather a composite of landscapes related to the variable character of the superficial cover. The Rhine trough is infilled with a variety of deposits of differing age, mode of origin and physical constitution. The successive glacial maxima discharged material subsequently eroded during the intervening interglacials, forming a series of terraces of which that related to the Wurmian is well preserved. The rivers flowing from the Vosges have built detrital fans on the floor of the plain, while during the Quaternary large expanses of löess were deposited and reworked and still cover extensive areas of the plain. Finally, recent alluvium lines the courses of the Ill and the Rhine.

Analysing the effects of these deposits on the pattern of resource use, Juillard[1] insists on the trilogy of landscapes found on the plain. 'Limon' is preserved on the detrital hills of the Sundgau and as intermittent sheets on the terraces of the floor of the plain. The effect has been to support intensive arable farming and high population densities on areas which would otherwise have little agricultural merit. This landscape of rich farming and compact villages is termed the 'land'. The second landscape type is developed on the gravel terraces and on the detrital fans, where thin, free-draining podsols support a dry woodland landscape, to which the generic term 'hardt' is applied. The major development of this terrain is on the low interfluve between the Rhine and Ill courses. Finally, a depressed zone of alluvium corresponds with the former flood plains of the Rhine and Ill. The resultant 'reid' landscape is characterized by marshland, peat accumulations, water meadows and occasional woods of poplar and willow. The disposition of these three landscapes—the 'land', 'hardt' and 'reid'—being conditioned largely by the orientation of past and present drainage lines, tends to design a pattern of elongated north–south running zones, and in conjunction with the Vosges affords Alsace a wide range of land resources yielding complementary products.

The Vosges province is essentially devoted to a pastoral form of agriculture, but within which some evolution is currently taking place. The summer pasture zone of the summits is now of less significance than in the past. The impact of industrialization in the towns of the foothills and the plain has been to bring supplementary income to the farming community and has permitted an intensification of agriculture on the valley floors, and a change in enterprise from cheese-making and cattle rearing to dairy and veal production. Many of the higher farms have been abandoned and converted to tourist use or improved as secondary residences by urban dwellers. To an increasing extent the valleys of the high Vosges form a functional annexe of the Alsatian Plain. As compared with the livestock basis of the mountains and valleys, the traditional agriculture of the plain is an intensive polyculture in which cereals occupy almost half of the arable acreage. The background to this system is a high rural population density consisting of small owner-operated farms with a high element of self-sufficiency. The end-product of this pattern of a land-owning peasantry is a very high degree of morcellement and a fragmentation of holdings, especially on the open fields of the limon zones. The introduction of cash crops during the last hundred years has only slightly modified the system of polyculture. Potatoes, sugar-beet, hops, soft fruit, barley for brewing, tobacco, and vegetables for the conserving industry have entered the rotation, but largely as a cash ingredient within polyculture rather than as a specialization. Two other trends are of major importance for the future evolution of Alsatian agriculture. The development of hybrid strains of maize has enabled the crop to gain in importance as a fodder and cash grain,[2] and mechanization has made considerable progress in spite of the problem of fragmentation. Much remains to be achieved in the sphere of land consolidation. In 1965, remembrement had been completed in 175 communes and was in course in a further 79 communes, but only one third of the 350,000 hectares requiring remembrement had been consolidated. The extension of mechanization is dependent on further remembrement and the reduction of polyculture in favour of more specialized production.[3] In the meantime, the cooperative use of machinery enables the smaller farms to avoid the problem of overcapitalization.

Although the rural population density is the highest in France, agriculture occupied only 14 per cent of the labour force in 1962 and farm employment is decreasing rapidly in total. Between 1954 and 1962, the agricultural labour force declined from 116,500 to 74,300 workers. This reduction in employment is related to the progress in mechanization, a sharp decline in employment of female labour and the retirement of elderly farmers. The fall in the agricultural work force also corresponds with the increasing interpenetration of urban and rural life resulting from the greater mobility of the rural population and the growth of industrial employment in the towns of the plain.

Poorly endowed in industrial resources—the potash deposits north of Mulhouse being the major exception—Alsace has nevertheless played an important part in the evolution of French manufacturing industry. This industrialization has occurred in clearly defined stages accompanied by related shifts in the location pattern. As elsewhere in eastern France, the origins of industry were rooted in artisan activities—woodworking, tanning and glass-making—carried out in the context of a predominantly rural society. The launching of the industrial revolution began in the eighteenth century with the development of the textile industry, initiated by the protestant bourgeoisie and aided by Swiss capital. The industry was located in the towns bordering the Vosges foothills and was later diffused to water-power sites in the mountain valleys. The scale of industrialization remained small until improvements in transport were effected in the first half of the nineteenth century. The construction of the Rhine–Rhône and Rhine–Marne canals was followed by a wave of railway building, especially on the plain. These improvements triggered off a new phase of industrial expansion and initiated an eastward shift in location which has persisted to the present day. Strasbourg, Colmar and Mulhouse were the sites of brewing, tanning and engineering while the cotton textile industry became concentrated on Mulhouse, Colmar, Guebwiller and Thann. During the course of the present century, the movement of industry eastwards towards the Rhine has become more emphatic, to the detriment of the small towns of the Vosges. This has been in response to three main circumstances: the greater ease of circulation and construction on the plain as compared with the foothill and mountain zone, the importance of the Rhine as a waterway, and the construction of hydroelectric schemes on the Grand Canal d'Alsace.

The comprehensive improvement of the Rhine has been a lengthy process and as yet is incomplete.[4] The double objective has been to improve navigation by the construction of lateral and loop canals accessible to barges of 1,500 tons, and to generate hydroelectricity at a number of power stations, taking advantage of the natural gradient of the river and the large head of water available. The improvement dates from 1924 with the construction of the Grand Canal d'Alsace between Huningue, at the Swiss frontier, and Neuf-Brisach, a distance of 52 kilometres. The power station of Kembs was built in 1932 but the remaining power stations on the canal were not completed until after the close of hostilities; Ottmarsheim in 1952, Fessenheim and Vogelgrun in 1959. North of Neuf-Brisach, the improvement takes the form of a series of loop canals, each with a power station; a form agreed by treaty with West Germany so as to return the water immediately to the river and prevent interference with the water table in the adjacent productive farming area of Baden. The canals of Marckolsheim, Rhinau and Gerstheim have been completed and a fourth is projected to the south of Strasbourg. When finally completed the Rhine power stations will have installed capacity of eight million kilowatts. As a result of the Grand Canal d'Alsace, the old Rhine–Rhône canal has fallen into disuse, the Rhône–Rhine traffic being diverted at Mulhouse via the Huningue Canal to join the Rhine waterway system.

The progressive movement of industry eastwards during the present century has also been accompanied by changes in the character of manufacturing. The position of textiles has been much reduced since the Second World War and metallurgy and engineering have now assumed a dominant position. The textile industry has submitted to a series of mergers, resulting in the closure of many of the small family-owned firms and a halving of the labour force, with serious repercussions in the valleys of the Vosges.[5] Heavy and mechanical engineering, on the other hand, has gained strength. From an initial basis of textile engineering and the construction of rolling stock, a wide range of products are now manufactured, including heavy electrical and diesel motors, vehicles and domestic consumer goods. The distribution of engineering is widespread on the plain with the greatest concentration occurring in Strasbourg, Mulhouse, Colmar, Hagenau, Saverne and Selestat. The development of hydroelectricity has attracted many new firms in the aluminium, plastics and chemicals branches and new industrial estates have been established close to the power sites, as at Neuf-Brisach and Ottmarsheim. Such sites have an optimum location abutting the national frontier, possessing power supplies, access to the Rhine waterway and, ultimately, to the future Strasbourg–Basle motorway. The attractiveness of this new location may be judged from the heavy participation of foreign investment in the industrialization of the Rhine axis. A final element confirming the potential of the Rhine axis is the recent construction of two refineries at Strasbourg, linked to Lavéra by the south European pipeline, and with a refining capacity of eight million tons.

The effect of a dense rural population, served by a network of small service centres and the varied experience of industrialization, has been to implant a coherent pattern of urban development. Juillard[6] has drawn attention to the contrast between the towns of the Vosges foothills and those of the plain, differing in age, function and present rate of growth. A chain of small towns lines the contact of the foothills and the plain, the more important centres being those commanding access to the major valleys, such as Selestat, Munster and Thann. This chain of towns, extending from Neiderbron to Altkirch, gained its initial wealth from viticulture and expanded further with the introduction of textiles. With the reorientation of communications and industry on to the plain, these towns have tended to stagnate with few exceptions. The exceptions are such centres as Guebwiller, Thann and Saverne, which have managed to retain their industrial functions, and other small towns which have become residential satellites of major towns on the plain, such as Obernai for Strasbourg and Rouffach for Colmar. By contrast, there are fewer towns on the plain, they are of later foundation, but their economic and demographic expansion is generally more impressive. Owing their original importance to locations in areas of prosperous agriculture, towns as Hagenau, Bischwiller, Neuf-Brisach and Altkirch rose to greater prominence in the latter half of the nineteenth century as a result of their location on new transport lines, facilitating the acquisition of industries. Superimposed on this double pattern of small towns, the three major centres of Colmar, Mulhouse and Strasbourg dominate the urban hierarchy.

Colmar is located at the edge of the Vosges foothills and grew in response to its function as the centre of the wine trade in Haut-Rhin, as an important nucleus of the textiles industry and ultimately as the capital of the département. Colmar is now the centre of an agglomeration of 75,000 inhabitants but has been overtaken by Mulhouse in terms of population size, industrial importance and the extent of the direct sphere of influence. Overshadowed by Strasbourg and Mulhouse, the creation of a port industrial zone in 1958 on the Vogelgrun canal represented an attempt to remain in contact with new location factors drawing activity towards the Rhine.

Mulhouse, the centre of an agglomeration of 200,000 inhabitants, has experienced a chequered career. Due almost entirely to the activities of the textiles industry, the town grew from a mere 6,000 inhabitants to almost 100,000 in the course of the nineteenth century, to be followed by an equally pronounced period of stagnation. This was as a result of the decline in textiles following the German annexation and perpetuated by the post-war contraction of the industry. The last decade has produced a resurgence related to the rationalization of textiles and the diversification of the industrial structure through the expansion of engineering. Like Colmar, Mulhouse has established an outport and industrial estate on the Rhine, near Ottmarsheim. A plastics factory, timber mill and a branch of the Peugeot vehicle company were the first industries to locate there. Reflecting this new phase of increased growth, Mulhouse has undergone considerable urban renewal, has established institutions of higher eduction, and has pre-empted the role of the effective capital of Haut-Rhin, a position hitherto enjoyed by Colmar. The potash industry is located to the north of Mulhouse and has been completely modernized since the heavy war-time destruction. After a sharp increase since the war, the output has now levelled off as a result of the difficulties of disposing of chemical waste and the threat of overproduction. Approximately 10,000 workers are employed in the mines and related chemical plants.

The city of Strasbourg[7] occupies a special position in the urban geography of France by virtue of its location on an international frontier, on an international routeway and its acquisition of certain economic and cultural functions of European importance. As compared with Lille, the only other large French city with a frontier location, the recent economic and demographic growth has been more substantial and, in the context of western Europe, more significant. The industrialization of Strasbourg occurred relatively late in the city's history and the raison d'être of the city has always been its strategic location at a major crossroads in the transport network of Europe.[8] Located at a convenient crossing point of the Rhine, Strasbourg is situated at the intersection of routes from Paris, via the Saverne gap, and the Rhône corridor, via the Belfort gap, with the international highway of the Rhine valley leading downstream to Mannheim, Frankfurt, Cologne, the Ruhr and Rotterdam, and upstream to Basle. In large measure the fortunes of the city have followed the fluctuations in the frequentations of the road, rail and inland waterway networks focusing on it. The impediments to interchange brought about by warfare, an unstable national frontier and restrictions on navigation are mirrored by periods of stagnation in the city's growth. Conversely, periods of international stability and improvements in the infrastructure of transport coincide with phases of demographic expansion.

In addition to the natural advantages of a strategic location, Strasbourg gained specific impetus from its function as a break of bulk point for Rhine barges prior to the construction of the Grand Canal d'Alsace. Strasbourg thrived as an entrepôt for Switzerland and as a collecting and distributing point for the agricultural products of the Plain of Alsace. The importance of the port was also enhanced by the interchange of German coal and Lorraine iron ore, via the Rhine–Marne canal. After 1918, with the re-establishment of free navigation on the Rhine, Strasbourg attained its apogee as an entrepôt. The site of dock construction moved from the Ill to the more spacious site on the Rhine and in 1924 Strasbourg was nominated as a 'port autonome'. Since that date, certain changes have occurred which have tended to weaken the port function. The lack of modernization of the Rhine–Marne canal enabled the railways to monopolize the traffic in ore and coal between Germany and Lorraine, taking advantage of a more direct route. In any case, the volume of German imports of Lorraine ore was rapidly dwindling in the period between the wars. Secondly, the construction of the Grand Canal d'Alsace brought Basle within the direct reach of 1,500-ton barges and deprived Strasbourg of its function as an entrepôt for Switzerland. More recently, the completion of the Moselle canal has afforded a direct outlet for Lorraine ore and steel products, rival new ports have appeared on the Rhine at Colmar–Neuf-Brisach and Mulhouse–Ottmarsheim, and the construction of the south European pipeline has assured direct delivery of crude petroleum. These adverse trends have not undermined port activity at Strasbourg but have been responsible for a change in emphasis. Denied the exclusive advantages of an entrepôt, Strasbourg has advanced as an industrial port.[9] This has been achieved by the modernization of the port facilities and by the construction of large port industrial zones, including a refinery and petrochemicals complex. This has enabled Strasbourg to retain its position as the second largest river port of France, after Paris, and the sixth largest port of France by tonnage handled, which now exceeds 12 million tons per annum. Exports consist of cereals, potash, refined petroleum products and engineering goods, while the much lower total of imports includes coal and timber.

Its function as an entrepôt and route centre enabled Strasbourg to develop as an important commercial and business city, and ultimately as a university and cultural centre. In spite of the accumulation of capital and commercial experience on the part of the bourgoisie, initiative in the field of industrial activity was late in developing. Throughout the nineteenth century industry tended to reflect the character of the rich agricultural hinterland of the limon-covered Ackerland Plain. Strasbourg became established as the processing centre of Bas-Rhin, engaging in brewing, tanning, flour milling, food conserving, timber milling and paper-making. Since the turn of the century a second group of industries has grown up, more particularly related to the passage of raw materials through the port and the excellence of Strasbourg as a distributing centre. Thus engineering, chemicals, metallurgy and more recently oil refining, petrochemicals and electronic industries have been added. From mundane industrial origins, Strasbourg is steadily emerging as a centre of advanced technology industries with a high capacity for growth. All the requirements of modern industry are fulfilled in the agglomeration, which possesses a repository of commercial experience and institutions, a modern airport, a well-known science faculty, a strong cultural life and access to hydroelectric power in addition to the transport advantages already cited.* The industrial growth has, however, brought attendant problems. Population expansion has created problems of housing, and the city, noted for the low density of past suburban development, is resorting to the construction of 'grands

---

*A specific advantage of the port is the modernized barge fleet. The French pioneered the technique of pushed convoys on the Rhine and convoys of six 1,500 ton barges now use the port.

ensembles' and the large-scale renewal of the older areas.[10] Secondly, the physical expansion of the city is hindered by the airport and rich agricultural land to the west, by the river and frontier to the east, and, to a lesser extent, by the new port and refinery complexes to the north. As a result, development is now being channelled largely to the south, following the natural line of economic expansion, the Rhine axis.

Between 1954 and 1962, the agglomeration of Strasbourg increased from 260,000 to 307,000 inhabitants, and in 1968 attained 335,000 inhabitants. The city is the seat of the Council of Europe, is an established intellectual and cultural centre, the site of the regional préfecture of Alsace and has been elevated to the status of 'métropole d'équilibre'. This international and regional status is fitting to the situation, history and cultural importance of the city, but in reality Strasbourg does not yet fully achieve the role of regional metropolis for which it has been designated. Situated eccentrically within Alsace, the direct sphere of influence is limited to the département of Bas-Rhin and adjacent portions of Lorraine. Within Bas-Rhin, the control of Strasbourg is absolute in terms of commerce, marketing, banking and the provision of high-order retail and professional facilities. By contrast, the direct influence of Strasbourg within Haut-Rhin is more tenuous, and for most purposes Haut-Rhin falls within the sphere of influence of either Mulhouse or Colmar.[11] The failure of Strasbourg to serve as the undisputed regional capital is partly a result of its location in the north of the region, allowing Mulhouse to fulfil a reciprocal role in the south.

REGIONAL PLANNING PROBLEMS

Alsace is a small region, which has emerged from a troubled past to face new opportunities to exploit the inherent advantages of its location. This task has been aided by considerable state investment in the Rhine improvement and by the added incentive of the birth of the Common Market. The textile industry, for long the staple manufacturing industry, has now achieved a measure of stability after a difficult period of reorganization, and the employment lost in this branch has been offset by the introduction of new activities. The problems now confronting the region may be summarized as the need to consolidate the new internal balance called into being by demographic revival, changes in location factors and the evolution of European integration.[12]

The most crucial balance to attain is between population growth and employment opportunities, especially for the bulge in the young element now entering the labour market. The combination of increased birth rates in the post-war period, mounting rural–urban migration and the increase in commuting to urban centres, implies a need for expanding industrial employment if the region is to retain an increasingly youthful and well-qualified labour force. Already several thousand Alsatians commute across the West German frontier and to Basle in search of industrial employment and higher levels of remuneration. Secondly, a new balance must be found in agriculture in terms of structural organization and market orientation. The present high agricultural population densities, the product of generations of intensive polyculture, cannot easily be adjusted to the present trends in market demands. The need is for further land consolidation, increased mechanization and an abandonment of irrational polyculture in favour of more specialized production in commodities where Alsace can be competitive and for which the domestic and export potential demand is high. Thirdly, the problem of the spatial balance of activity within Alsace is becoming ever more apparent. The Vosges province is experiencing a contraction of its agricultural land area,[13] has been hard hit by the reorganization of the textiles industry and possesses a number of small towns in danger of becoming decadent. Inherent in present trends is thus the risk of a widening economic disparity between the western sections of Alsace and the towns of the plain and the Rhine axis.

A more likely development, however, is the exploitation of the Vosges as a natural recreational and tourist area. Easily accessible from two of the most densely populated areas of north-eastern France, industrial Lorraine and the Alsatian Plain, and situated close to international tourist routes, the scenic attraction of the mountains and picturesque settlements of the Vosges stamps the area as a natural recreational zone for the juxtaposed urban concentrations and a tourist attraction for summer holidays. The combination of tourism with commuting for employment in the towns of the foothill zone may offer a viable future for the valleys of the Vosges, but with the probability of reduced population densities.

The adjustment of the economy of Alsace to the emergent patterns of the Common Market demands that the transport infrastructure should be improved and more fully integrated into the networks of the neighbouring states. Two developments are critical in this respect: the Rhine–Rhône waterway and the Strasbourg–Basle motorway. The principle of improving the existing canal link to the Rhône was adopted in the Fourth Plan and work began during the Fifth Plan on enlarging the section south of Mulhouse to accept barges of over 1,000 tons.[14] The completion of the canal, providing a continuous waterway from Rotterdam to Marseille, may be expected to contribute to the advantages of Alsace. Enjoying a position midway along the axis, Alsace will have an excellent location for the assembly of raw materials and for the distribution of manufactured goods within the Common Market and to Switzerland and for export overseas via Rotterdam and Marseille. The Strasbourg–Basle motorway is an equally urgent need; passing via Mulhouse and with a spur to the Belfort–Montbéliard industrial area, the new motorway will be a major factor strengthening the Rhine axis and promoting integration of the two départements of Alsace. As yet the motorway is only at the projection stage and priority has been given to the Mulhouse–Basle section and the southern exit of Strasbourg. Moreover, even when completed, the motorway will be isolated from the remainder of the French motorway network for some considerable time. The fruition of both the above schemes is as yet some time distant and in the meantime other, less spectacular improvements are necessary, such as the modernization of the Rhine–Marne canal and the establishment of Strasbourg as an international airport.

In spite of its small extent, it seems clear that Alsace is poised to capitalize on its position in relation to the economic integration of Europe. This will result in a reversal of the past experience of Alsace and a mutation from a peripheral position in France to a central location on the spine of the Common Market. To achieve this end, regional planning must be firmly set within a broader international spectrum.[15]

'Tiraillée pendant des générations entre deux mondes hostiles, l'Alsace peut maintenant remplir son rôle de carrefour et de lien, elle peut jouer ses atouts, qui sont nombreux, au coeur d'une Europe devenue sa chance et son espoir.'[16]

REFERENCES

[1] Juillard, E., *L'Alsace. le Sol, les Hommes et la Vie Régionale*, p. 21, 1963, Strasbourg, Dernières Nouvelles.
[2] Godard, A., 'La culture du maïs-grain en Alsace et en Bade du Sud', *Revue Géogr. Est*, 1967, p. 3.
[3] Nonn, H., 'L'Alsace. Une région en pleine mutation', *Tendances*, No. 37, 1965, p. 406.
[4] Huguet, H., 'L'Economie Alsacienne', *Notes Etud. docum.*, No. 3,050, 1963, pp. 17–20.
[5] Huguet, H., *op. cit.*[4], pp. 37–38.
[6] Juillard, E., *op. cit.*[1], p. 61.
[7] Juillard, E., Nonn, H., and Rochefort, M., 'Les Grandes Villes Françaises, Strasbourg', *Notes Etud. docum.*, No. 2,993, 1963.
[8] Nonn, H., 'Le carrefour strasbourgeois', *Revue Géogr. Est*, 1966, p. 354.
[9] Nonn, H., 'Les efforts de conversion du port autonome de Strasbourg devant les réalisations récentes de l'aménagement du territoire', *Revue Géogr. Est*, 1966, p. 351.
[10] Pflimlin, P., 'Une métropole régionale, Strasbourg', *Expans. rég.*, No. 35, 1964, pp. 33–37.
[11] Juillard, E., *et al.*, 'La 45 e Excursion géographique interuniversitaire, l'Alsace', *Annls Géogr.*, 1964, p. 537.
[12] Nonn, H., 'L'Economie Alsacienne à la veille du Ve Plan', *Revue Géogr. Est*, 1965, p. 551.
[13] Nonn, H., 'Les résultats d'une enquête agricole dans le Haut-Rhin', *Revue Géogr. Est*, 1966, p. 350.
[14] Pilkington, R., 'Joining the Rhine and Rhône', *Geogrl Mag.*, XXXIX, 1966, p. 214.
[15] George, P., *La France*, pp. 186–187, 1967, Paris, Presses Universitaires de France.
[16] Huguet, H., *op. cit.*[4], p. 47.

19

Bourgogne

Bourgogne stands with Alsace and Aquitaine as a region on which the importance of routeways has stamped an individual character. While Alsace is essentially an international threshold and Aquitaine a region of passage within underdeveloped France, Bourgogne is a focus of inter-regional routes connecting the most highly developed regions of eastern France. The strategic location between the agglomerations of Paris and Lyon, together with the excellent connections via the Belfort Gap to Alsace, to Lorraine, Champagne and the northern Massif Central, has provided the region with a stimulus for growth in the last decade and enabled Bourgogne to reverse its history of depopulation.

The physical components emphasize the convergent nature of Bourgogne for it contains portions of the Massif Central, the Paris Basin and the Saône corridor. The region is bisected diagonally by an upland zone, extending north-east to south-west and forming the divide between the Saône system and the Seine and Loire basins. This upland axis, constituted in the south-west by the crystalline Morvan and in the north-east by the limestone 'montagne', interposes a negative area separating more productive areas. The Morvan attains a height of 900 metres and is an isolated area, lacking in towns, having lost half of its population in the last hundred years. Mediocre pasture supports cattle rearing on small farms, alternating with an extensive woodland cover.[1] The 'montagne' is a limestone plateau, between 500 and 600 metres in elevation, with very low population densities and a high proportion of woodland. This central divide separates areas of markedly superior land resources. To the east of the 'montagne', the limestones are downfaulted, forming a lower plateau at 200 metres, fronted by the escarpment of the Côte d'Or. The dip slope grows vines yielding wines of ordinary quality, but the well-exposed light soils of the Côte d'Or support the famous Burgundy vineyards, extending from Dijon to Chagny, with Beaune as the capital of the wine trade.

At the foot of the Côte d'Or is the Saône plain—a composite area

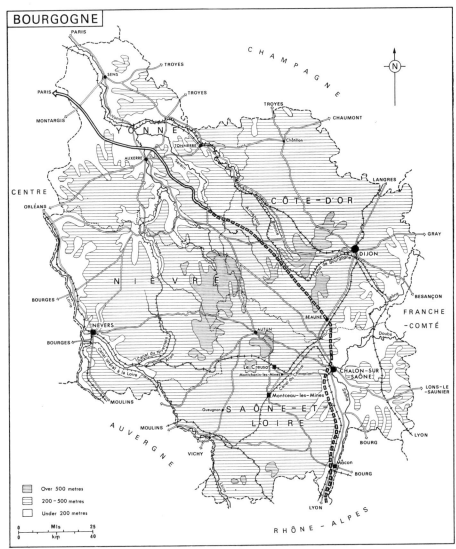

Figure 19.1

consisting of a high plain of clays and sands, a low plain with lighter soils and, south of Châlon-sur-Saône, the basin of Bresse. The heavy soils of the high plain have a cover of woodland and pasture while on the lower plain cereals, sugar-beet, market garden and fruit crops are dominant. The basin of Bresse is devoted to dairy farming, producing butter and quality cheese. To the west of the 'montagne', the scarplands of Basse-Bourgogne are drained in fan fashion by the Loire, the Seine, the Yonne and its numerous tributaries. Settlement is concentrated on the narrow clay vales while the limestone plateaux support grain farming. The river breaches in the escarpments are the sites of numerous towns but the rural population has been greatly reduced by emigration. In the south of the region, Morvan is bordered on three sides by limestone depressions devoted to cattle farming, but to the south is abruptly delimited by the coalfield furrow of the Blanzy basin. The coalfield was the scene of nineteenth-century industrialization which has survived in modified form centred on Le Creusot and Montceau-les-Mines. Finally, in the extreme south, the clay marls of Charolais support cattle farming 'par excellence'.

The resources of Bourgogne have clearly favoured an agricultural dominance in the region's output, and farming still employed 27 per cent of the labour force in 1962. The quality of the land resources is extremely uneven and accordingly farming systems vary from mechanized arable farming in Yonne and intensive cattle rearing in Charolais, to marginal hill farming in the Morvan, with proportionate variations in farm income. At the regional level, one third of the land area is devoted to arable crops and rotational grasses, one third to woodland and fallow, and the remaining third predominantly to permanent pasture; the balance is made up of intensive specialized crops such as vines, orchards and market gardens. In total, the farming economy must be considered productive and progressive, yielding 3·4 per cent by value of the nation's agricultural product in 1966. Outside the areas involved in specilized production there has been a marked tendency for farm size to increase since the last war. The SAFER and FASASA organizations are very active and remembrement is well advanced. However, the benefits of land reform and structural improvement have been concentrated in the areas where farming is most productive. By contrast, the demand for farms in the poorer upland, even when enlarged by the intervention of the government agencies, is less apparent, and there is a danger that the area of abandoned land, already high, will be further enlarged.

Although agriculture dominates the region's production its contribution to employment has shrunk drastically. *Table 19.1* reveals a drop in the total labour force by 27 per cent between 1901 and 1962, entirely due to a two thirds reduction in the size of the agricultural work force. Extractive

Table 19.1

TRENDS IN THE EMPLOYMENT STRUCTURE OF BOURGOGNE, 1901–1962
(Numbers employed, thousands)

	1901	1936	1954	1962
Agriculture, forestry	411·6	316·4	214·1	155·7
Industry[a]	198·0	166·4	176·4	197·0
Tertiary activities	153·1	166·2	188·2	198·0
Total labour force	762·7	649·0	578·6	555·5

[a]Including building and public works.
Source: Recensement de 1962.

and manufacturing industry employed just over 35 per cent of the labour force in 1962, but industrial activity does not intrude unduly in the landscape of Bourgogne. This results from the tendency for manufacturing to be widely dispersed, for industrial plants to be small in size and for individual industries to lack concentration in terms of location. The only multi-urban industrial zone is that of the Blanzy coal basin, where Montceau-les-Mines, Montchanin, Blanzy and Le Creusot constitute an industrial zone of 150,000 inhabitants based on mining, steel production and engineering. Elsewhere, only Dijon and Châlon-sur-Saône can be considered leading industrial towns by virtue of the scale and diversity of their manufacturing, and the recent arrival of many decentralized firms has strengthened the basic diffused pattern of location. The great diversity

Table 19.2

THE MAJOR BRANCHES OF MANUFACTURING INDUSTRY IN BOURGOGNE, 1962

	Numbers employed	Total	Number of factories 200–1,000 workers	Over 1,000 workers
Building materials[a]	10,967	771	6	1
Steel	17,785	9	2	3
Metallurgy	7,459	230	7	1
Mechanical engineering	23,213	3,287	23	3
Electrical engineering[b]	7,668	209	17	–
Chemicals	6,777	151	5	1
Food products	13,300	3,237	10	–
Textiles	5,755	375	6	–
Clothing	6,393	1,883	4	–
Wood and furniture	6,412	1,864	–	–

[a]Principally cement, bricks, ceramics and constructional glass.
[b]Including electronics.
Source: Notes et Etud. Doc., No. 3,350, 1966, p. 47.

of manufacturing has been a factor resisting decline, since the recession of certain branches has been offset by increased activity in others. However, the very large number of small firms, especially in engineering, is a source of structural weakness and closures have been numerous. *Table 19.2* indicates the major branches of activity and highlights the small number of large firms.

Bourgogne no longer has any active blast-furnaces, but steel is produced at three locations: Le Creusot, Guegnon and Imphy. All produce high-quality steels using electrical processes. By far the largest plant is the Schneider works at Le Creusot, based until 1957 on the coal of the Blanzy basin brought to the plant's own port on the Canal du Centre. The survival of the plant is due to its complete modernization, its ability to nourish a wide variety of engineering industries in the vicinity with special steels—used for items as large as locomotives and as small as machine components—its success in export markets, and the integration of the steel-works with company-owned engineering factories at Le Creusot and Châlon-sur-Saône? The plant employed approximately 9,000 workers in steel production in 1966. South-west of Montceau-les-Mines, the Guegnon plant employs 5,000 workers in the production of stainless steels, while Imphy, near Nevers, employs 2,500 workers and produces alloy steels.

Based initially on local ores and the coal of Blanzy and Decize,* the Bourgogne steel industry has had to adjust technically and structurally to changing external circumstances. By specialization and the adoption of advanced production methods, the industry has performed well in recent years, but reorganization has reduced employment from 18,000 in 1962 to less than 15,000 at present. The metallurgical industry is represented chiefly by foundries producing forgings and castings for use in the engineering and building industries, but large plants are located at Montbard, producing steel tubes, Ste. Colombe-sur-Seine, manufacturing steel cables, and at Dijon, producing aluminium foil.

The largest single manufacturing category is mechanical and electrical engineering, the products ranging from heavy lifting gear and agricultural machinery to miniature electronic components. The chemicals sector on the other hand is not heavily represented in the region, but the Kodak plant at Châlon-sur-Saône has been extended to employ 1,000 workers. By contrast, the textiles and clothing branch is of growing importance. Textile production is dominated by hosiery while the clothing branch has been reinforced by the arrival of 30 decentralized firms between 1954 and 1967. The region of Bourgogne is synonymous with gastronomy, and the food industry ranges from base activities such as brewing, flour milling and sugar refining, to the making of quality wines and delicatessen foods.

*In the case of Imphy.

The industrial structure of Bourgogne has undergone a substantial mutation in the course of the last decade. Employment in coal mining and steel has declined while that in metallurgy, chemicals, heavy engineering, food processing and wood working has remained relatively stable. The largest gains have been made in light engineering and electronics, as a result of the installation of decentralized firms. Decentralization has been the principal growth factor in Bourgogne's industry since the war; between 1950 and 1966, 130 new firms were established, adding 25,500 new jobs. This success must be attributed to the factors of geographical location and external communications, rather than to state assistance, which has been minimal with the exception of the conversion zone of Blanzy. Thus the attraction of new firms must be held to reflect intrinsic rather than artificial qualities.

PLANNING PROBLEMS

Bourgogne suffered throughout the nineteenth century and the first part of the present century from its juxtaposition with the Paris and Lyon agglomerations, both attracting labour from Bourgogne. The maximum population was attained in 1861 and the present total of 1·5 million is still more than 150,000 below the 1861 level. Since 1954 Bourgogne has staged a demographic recovery through the expansion of its towns. Two priority problems arise from the revival of urban growth and industrial activity. Since the attraction of industry has been achieved by factors of geographical location, it follows that the maximum effort should be made to improve transport further in order to gain the greatest benefit from the region's chief advantage. Secondly, the progress achieved in industrialization must be consolidated, for in 1962 the region was still predominantly rural and agriculture will inevitably continue to shed labour.

The task of improving communications is already advanced with the completion of the Paris–Lyon motorway between Auxerre, Beaune and Mâcon. However, this central motorway spine lacks high-capacity connecting roads to Dijon and onwards to Lorraine, and via Besançon to Alsace. An equally urgent need is to modernize the Loire valley road system. The canal network is not equipped for modern traffic, the canals of Bourgogne, Midi and Nivernais all being small in gauge and circuitous in alignment. Their improvement is unjustified by their present level of traffic but the completion of the Rhône–Rhine waterway would present a new opportunity to revitalize certain segments. An improvement of the Canal du Centre between Montceau-les-Mines and Châlon-sur-Saône, and the Bourgogne Canal between Dijon and the Saône, would place the region's two major industrial centres in direct contact with the new waterway. The region occupies a privileged position on the nation's three greatest inter-regional arteries of the future: the Lille–Paris–Lyon–Marseille motorway, the Paris–Lyon–Marseille rail route and the Rhône–Rhine waterway. It is vital that the entire region should benefit from this by the provision of adequate internal access to these arteries.

The reanimation of industrial activity by decentralizations must be used as a springboard for further industrial development. Two difficulties in particular must be resolved: the conversion of the Blanzy basin and the absorption of surplus agricultural labour. In 1947, the Blanzy coalbasin employed 12,000 workers and produced 2·3 million tons of coal. Production is still over two million tons but employment has fallen to 4,700 workers and in 1980 will total less than 2,000.[4] A new power station will absorb 500,000 tons per annum by 1972, but combined with reduced employment in steel production, the Montceau-les-Mines–Le Creusot district has a vital need for diversification. A vigorous effort has already been made through the creation of industrial estates—financed in part by Charbonnages de France and the Coal and Steel Community—and new firms qualify for conversion grants.

The redeployment of agricultural workers is a more diffused problem, affecting not only the areas of marginal farming but also the more prosperous areas as rationalization of farm structures proceeds. The central upland core poses the specific problem of the use of land at present abandoned or underused. Likely developments are afforestation and an increase in tourism. Already Yonne has the largest number of secondary homes owned by Parisians in the Paris Basin[5] and the Morvan offers excellent terrain for weekend and vacation recreation.

REFERENCES

[1] Bonnamour, J., *Le Morvan. La Terre et les Hommes. Essai de géographie agricole*, 1966, Paris, Presses Universitaires de France.
[2] Labasse, J., and Laferrère, M., *La Région Lyonnaise*, pp. 91–94, 1960, Paris, Presses Universitaires de France.
[3] Grandperrin, C., and Voirin, Y., 'L'Economie de la Bourgogne', *Notes Etud. docum.*, No. 3,350, 1966, p. 45.
[4] Labasse, J., and Laferrère, M., *op. cit.*, pp. 94–99.
[5] Bonnamour, J., 'L'arrondissement de Sens en 1964', *Revue Géogr. Est*, 1965, p. 420.

20

Franche-Comté

Located at the convergence of routes bringing cultural influences from northern, central and southern Europe, Franche-Comté bears the imprint of a long civilization. In the north-west of the region, the plateaux of the Haute-Saône merge imperceptibly into the landscape of southern Lorraine and northern Burgundy, displaying the same open features and low intensity of settlement. By comparison, the Jura province in the east and south of the region is a separate world, compartmentalized but not isolated, and in spite of definite environmental restrictions, having a diversified and evolved economy. The miniature region of the Porte de Bourgogne between the Jura and the Vosges has its own distinctive landscape, dominated by the urban-industrial complexes of Belfort and Montbéliard.

The integration of these three dissimilar zones is achieved by a central artery of communications extending from Belfort to Besancon along the axis of the Doubs valley. West of Besançon the artery bifurcates, one route following the edge of the Jura via Lons-le-Saunier to Lyon, while another, including the Rhône–Rhine canal, branches westwards via Dole to Dijon and the Saône valley. The three zones of Franche-Comté are so contrasted in terms of landscape, economic evolution and development problems that a separate discussion is a necessary prelude to a review of problems affecting the entire region.

THE PLATEAUX OF THE HAUTE-SAONE

The dissected limestone plateaux of the Haute-Saône is an undistinguished area, a territorial no man's land, and, in terms of movement, a cul-de-sac. No major inter-regional routes follow the upper Saône valley, and the canal link via the Canal de l'Est to Lorraine is limited to barges of 280 tons and made difficult by frequent locks. The plateau surface, averaging

296

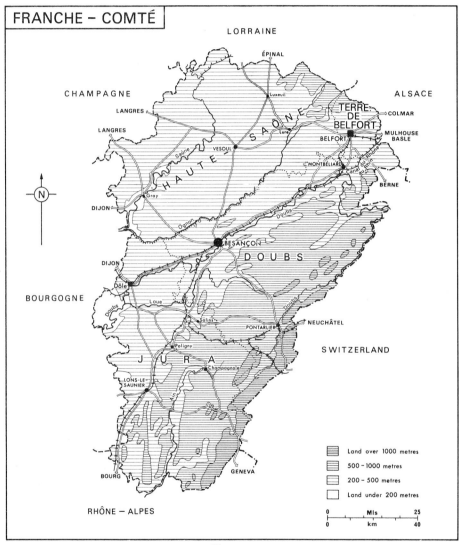

FRANCHE – COMTÉ

LORRAINE

ÉPINAL

CHAMPAGNE

ALSACE

LANGRES

TERRE
DE
BELFORT

COLMAR

LANGRES

Luxeuil

MULHOUSE
BASLE

Lure

BELFORT

VESOUL

Saône

MONTBÉLIARD

HAUTE - SAÔNE

Canal du Rhône au Rhin

DIJON

Gray

BERNE

Ognon

Doubs

DIJON

BESANÇON

D O U B S

Dôle

Loue

BOURGOGNE

Doubs

Salins

Doubs

Loue

PONTARLIER

NEUCHÂTEL

Poligny

SWITZERLAND

J U R A

Champagnole

LONS-LE-
SAUNIER

	Land over 1000 metres
	500 – 1000 metres
	200 – 500 metres
	Land under 200 metres

BOURG

GENEVA

RHÔNE – ALPES

| 0 | Mls | 25 |
| 0 | km | 40 |

N

Figure 20.1

between 400 and 500 metres in elevation, was formerly devoted to cereal farming but is now turning increasingly to dairy farming. Heavy rural depopulation has reduced population density to less than half that of the national average.* The plateaux are occupied by a 70 per cent rural population and only four towns are of significance. Vesoul is an administrative centre, Gray has engineering works and Luxeuil-les-Bains, formerly a spa town, has attracted a number of light industries.[1] The largest town is Dole, with 25,000 inhabitants. Situated midway between Besançon and Dijon, Dole is a focus of road, rail and canal routes, and may anticipate some benefit from the expansion of the Doubs valley concomitant on the improvement of the Rhône–Rhine canal link.

THE PORTE DE BOURGOGNE

The small lowland corridor between the Vosges and the Jura is one of the most active manufacturing regions of eastern France. Industry is concentrated on two locations separated by a distance of ten kilometres: the agglomeration of Belfort, with 72,000 inhabitants, and the urban complex of Montbéliard, with 115,000 inhabitants. Belfort conforms with the industrial pattern of Alsace, the basis of early growth being the textile industry, the position of which has now been seriously eroded. The industrial structure of the town is now dominated by the Alsthom electrical engineering works—producing electric motors, locomotives and turbines—and to a lesser extent by the electronics industry.

The form of industrial and urban development at Montbéliard is entirely different, being a nebula of towns clustered around the Peugeot automobile works at Sochaux. The towns of Montbéliard, Sochaux, Audincourt and Valentigny employ 50,000 industrial workers drawn from these towns and from rural areas within a 50 kilometre radius. In addition to vehicle manufacture, the engineering industry includes the making of cycles, typewriters, hardware and watches, but the Peugeot works employs half of the total industrial labour force†. The rapid growth of the automobile industry has engendered urban extension and only one quarter of the total population of the urban complex resides in the town of Montbéliard. The growth of satellite towns around the Peugeot works has resulted in a fragmentation of residential and commercial structures leading to a polynuclear urban pattern.[2] The expansion of industry has

*The plateaux are approximately coincident with the département of Haute-Saône, which has lost one third of its population in the last hundred years.
†In 1966 the Peugeot factory at Sochaux employed 25,000 workers.

also attracted large numbers of foreign workers,[3] principally Italian, Spanish, North African and Portuguese, posing problems of assimilation*

THE JURA

The Jura is not only a component of Franche-Comté but is also one of the major mountain systems of France, 250 kilometres in length, up to 65 kilometres in width and reaching a maximum elevation of 1,723 metres. An essential distinction must be made between the plateau foreland, between 500 and 1,000 metres in height, and the fold chains of the eastern Jura, reaching greater elevations and more obstuctive to communications. The valleys contain a mantle of alluvial deposits and glacial detritus, which in combination with a high precipitation contrives a generally verdant appearance in spite of the predominance of limestone bedrock. Woodland occupies between 30 and 50 per cent of the land area and the majority of the remaining land is under pasture. Obstacles to through-communications are considerable but international roads cross from Dole via the Col de la Faucille to Geneva and from Besançon via Pontarlier to Vallorbe. Similarly, international rail routes cross via Pontarlier to Neufchâtel and Berne and via the Mont d'Or tunnel to the Simplon route. Thus the Jura is not an entirely isolated region but the orientation of economic activity on to the valleys has inevitably produced a high degree of internal separation of population into scattered pockets.

In spite of the restrictive environment the Jura was early settled and a polyculture agrarian system established. Farming was supplemented by craft industries and by seasonal migration to outside employment. Manufacturing was concerned with the use of forest resources and with the skilled use of small amounts of imported raw materials, as in the watch industry. By the nineteenth century the Jura had become a virtual workshop, the pattern of location being like a scattering of specks of dust.

Improved communications since the end of the nineteenth century have wrought profound changes. The arable acreage fell rapidly, being replaced by dairy farming specializing in cheese production. The area of cropland is continuing to decline but the western edge of the Jura plateau has retained its specialization in high-grade viticulture. Pastoralism is supreme in the high Jura where the use of summer mountain pasture is integrated with winter stall feeding for the production of gruyère, processed and marketed on a collective basis.

Industry has also experienced modifications in structure and location, the dominant trend being the decline of artisan industry and the con-

*In 1965 approximately 5,000 foreigners worked in the Montbéliard area and over 3,200 in Belfort.

centration of manpower into factory units. Hydroelectricity has replaced mechanical water power but the basic characteristic of industry—the application of skill to produce high-value goods—remains. The most obvious continuation of past industrial traditions is the importance of watchmaking,* but the wide range of activities includes optical goods, toys, jewellery, plastics, food processing and special steels. Steelmaking is located at Champagnole in the Ain valley, where electrical processes are used in the production of special steels for the machine tool industry. From its hearth in the high Jura, the process of concentration is tending to displace industry towards the western edge of the plateau—an important communications line—towards the Swiss frontier at Pontarlier, where Swiss investment is concentrated, and towards the south, where at Bellegarde power is available from the Génissiat and Seyssel schemes in the region of Rhône-Alpes. In the high Jura, the reduction of artisan industry is compensated by the expansion of forestry and the growth of tourism.

REGIONAL PROBLEMS

Thus far, Franche-Comté has escaped extreme problems, managing to maintain equilibrium by adjusting its economy to changing circumstances. There are nevertheless certain fundamental incipient problems which could become serious distortions if left uncorrected. The most obvious lack of balance is in the demographic structure; the combined départements of Doubs and the Territoire de Belfort having a population density three times higher than the national average while those of Haute-Saône and Jura have only half the national average. Recent trends have served to widen this discrepancy, for whereas growth has been rapid in Belfort, Montbéliard and Besançon, the départements of Jura and Haute-Saône are lacking in strong urban centres to focus industrial expansion and stem the flow of rural exodus.

A more specific distortion afflicts the Montbéliard agglomeration as a result of its narrow dependence on the automobile industry†. The expansion by 16 per cent in the population of the agglomeration between 1962 and 1968 was sustained by the expansion of existing industry, and especially the Peugeot vehicle plant, rather than by the introduction of new industry.[5] This excessive dependence affects not only the agglomeration but also the commuting population attracted from as far distant as the Sundgau and the Haute-Saône plateau.

*The Jura produces 70 per cent of French output of watches and clocks.
†Gravier has estimated that half of the families in the Montbéliard district depend on the Sochaux car plant for their livelihood.[4]

The completion of the Rhône–Rhine waterway will clearly introduce a new element into the region, tending to strengthen the axis of Belfort–Montbéliard–Besançon–Dole but holding little advantage for the Haute-Saône or Jura. It must be anticipated that any stimulus to industry deriving from the canal will tend to concentrate population still further in the Doubs Valley and the Porte de Bourgogne. It is difficult to suppose that in the short term the depopulation of the Haute-Saône plateau can be reversed but conditions are more propitious on the Jura plateau. In particular it may be proposed that the axis of the plateau edge, followed by road and rail links from Lyon to Besançon, by the south European Pipeline and provided with hydroelectricity from the Ain valley, could be strengthened to counterbalance the attraction of the Rhône–Rhine axis. In this respect, the contrast with the chain of industrial towns lining the margin of the Swiss Jura serves to indicate the degree of present underdevelopment.

REFERENCES

[1] Chapuis, R., 'Luxeuil-les-Bains', *Revue Géogr. Est*, 1967, p. 223.
[2] Claval, P., 'La croissance de l'agglomération Montbéliardaise et l'évolution des équipements commerciaux', *Revue Géogr. Est*, 1965, p. 441.
[3] Dézert, B., 'Les migrants étrangers de la Porte de Bourgogne', *Revue Géogr. Est*, 1966, p. 268.
[4] Gravier, J., *L'Aménagement du Territoire et l'Avenir des Régions Françaises*, p. 240, 1964, Paris, Flammarion.
[5] Claval, P., *op. cit*?, p. 450.

21

Rhône-Alpes

By most criteria of social, economic and demographic development, Rhône-Alpes must be judged the most highly-evolved region of France after the Paris region.[1] The region possesses in Lyon the only agglomeration other than Paris exceeding one million inhabitants and the only 'métropole d'équilibre' which at present approaches the fulfilment of its allotted role. Rhône-Alpes is a composite of landscapes spanning many eras. The commercial strength of Lyon dates from the Middle Ages, the landscape of the Loire coalbasin bears the imprint of the nineteenth century, while the hydraulic schemes of the Rhône and of the Alps are products of the present century. Running through the patterns of economic geography is the consistent integrating force of the Rhône axis and the strength of the regional capital, Lyon. In terms of the character of economic activity and the nature of development problems, however, the three major components of the region—the eastern Massif Central, the Alpine province and the Rhône–Saône corridor—preserve separate identities and merit separate analysis in the first instance.

THE EASTERN MASSIF CENTRAL

Approximately one quarter of Rhône-Alpes is situated within the Massif Central. The faulted basins of Roanne and Forez introduce expanses of lowland into an otherwise upland domaine comprising the plateaux of Beaujolais, Lyonnais and Vivarais and the more rugged terrain of the northern Cevennes. Rainfall exceeds 800 millimetres throughout the area, with the exception of the faulted basins, and woodland or scrub covers a high proportion of the plateaux summits. Animal rearing for meat is the dominant agricultural enterprise, ranging from intensive beef production in the basins of Roanne and Forez, to more extensive cattle and sheep grazing in the Cévennes. The eastern slopes of Beaujolais,

Lyonnais and Vivarais produce quality wine, and fruit is grown in the Eyrieux and Ardèche valleys.

Manufacturing activity is limited outside the Loire coalfield industrial zone. Roanne, with textiles, clothing and engineering industries is the centre of an agglomeration with 73,000 inhabitants (in 1968) and

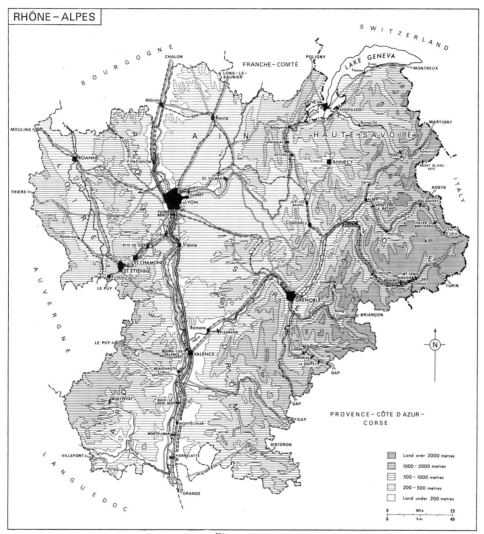

Figure 21.1

Montbrison is a smaller replica in the Forez basin. By far the largest concentration of industry, not only in this area but in the whole of the Massif Central, is located on the Loire coal basin[2] in a continuous chain of towns extending from Firminy and St. Etienne to St. Chamond, Rive-de-Gier and Givors, totalling over 400,000 inhabitants in 1968. This was the cradle of the industrial revolution in France, and, until the close of the nineteenth century, was the leading area of coal production and an important centre of the steel industry.

During the present century, both coal and steel production have suffered a serious decline. Difficulties of working and the high cost of transport,* together with the competition from hydroelectricity and, latterly, natural gas, have enforced a reduction in output. Production in 1967 totalled two million tons, offering employment to 4,400 miners. The coal and coke is consumed in large part on the coalfield, chiefly in the power stations near St. Etienne and Givors. The iron and steel industry has contracted by stages in the face of competition from Lorraine. The blast furnaces are no longer active and steel production is predominantly by electric processes, concentrating on special steels used in local metallurgical industry. The organization has now been rationalized into two firms, the 'Ateliers et Forges de la Loire' employing 12,000 workers in six plants located at St. Etienne and Firminy, and the 'Société Marrel', employing 1,500 workers at Rive-de-Gier. In total, the metallurgical industry, including steel-using industries, employs approximately 50,000 workers. The manufacture of armaments, cycles and heavy machinery are long-established but recent growth has consisted of lighter precision engineering.

The towns of St. Chamond, with 74,000 inhabitants in its agglomeration, Firminy and Rive-de-Gier, are essentially industrial concentrations, but St. Etienne, the largest city of the Massif Central and the ninth largest city of France in 1968, has more diversified functions. In spite of the proximity of Lyon, St. Etienne discharges regional functions within the eastern Massif Central, but lacks the more dynamic growth as a regional pole present at Clermont-Ferrand. St. Etienne is linked to the 'métropole d'équilibre' of Lyon, which will be less than an hour distant when the motorway connection is completed. An expansion of tertiary functions complementing those of Lyon is a necessary development in view of the decline of the coal industry and the concentration of steel production. Benefiting from conversion grants and subventions from the coal industry, a number of decentralized firms manufacturing clothing, plastics and precision engineering goods have been attracted, but population growth has been modest in recent years†.

---

*The coalbasin has only a short section of canal, from Rive-de-Gier to the Rhône.
†Between 1962 and 1968 the agglomeration expanded by 5·2 per cent as compared with 18·9 per cent at Clermont-Ferrand and 14·8 per cent at Lyon.

THE ALPINE PROVINCE

Within the Alpine province may be included the southern portion of the Jura, which intrudes into Rhône-Alpes between the Ain and Rhône valleys. The high limestone chains give way abruptly eastwards to the depression of Gex, drained by the upper Rhône, producing quality cheese and also dairy and vegetable produce for Geneva. The hydroelectric schemes of Genissiat and Seyssel supply energy to the industries of the southern Jura, especially at Oyonnax and Bellegarde. The whole of the northern Alps are included in the planning region and variations in economic activity and settlement are closely correlated with the four structural divisions of the mountain range.

The pre-Alpine zone of folded and dislocated limestones, attaining crests of 2,000 metres, is breached by tributaries of the Rhône into distinctive massifs. Economic and urban development is concentrated in these transverse valleys, the 'cluses' of the Arve, Annecy, Chambéry and Grenoble, which are the gateways of the Alpine province and extensions of the second structural zone, the sub-Alpine furrow. This lowland trench extends 125 kilometres from north to south and is up to 10 kilometres wide. The climate is gentler and drier than in the pre-Alps and conditions are favourable for dairy farming, fruit, vegetables, tobacco and grains. The importance of the furrow as a routeway, intersecting the east–west 'cluses', was also propitious for urban development and over 75 per cent of the population of the northern Alps is located here.[3] The largest centres are Annecy, Chambéry and Grenoble, commanding exits to the Rhône corridor.

Annecy[4] has important clothing and metal industries which combine with its summer tourist function to support an agglomeration of 81,000. Chambéry, with 75,000 inhabitants in its agglomeration, is an administrative and resort centre and the key communications centre of the northern Alps. Both agglomerations are currently expanding at very high rates.* These towns are overshadowed in importance by the Grenoble agglomeration of 332,000 inhabitants in 1968.[5,6]

The phenomenal post-war growth of Grenoble[7] is due to the success of its industrial development. Based initially on such staples as glove-making, textiles, paper manufacturing and food processing, the development of hydroelectricity ushered in a new industrial era based on new technology. Grenoble played a major part in the equipping of the alpine hydro-electricity schemes, leading to the creation of firms manufacturing turbines and tubing and important civil engineering companies. In turn,

*Between 1962 and 1968, the agglomeration of Annecy expanded by 28 per cent and that of Chambéry by 19 per cent. In the same period Grenoble expanded by 27 per cent.

the availability of electricity fostered the growth of chemical industries, plastics and a wide range of engineering activities. The latest stage of industrial expansion has been associated with the growing importance of the city as a research centre, focused on the university, the hydrological research institute, the centre of nuclear studies, and the large number of industrial laboratories. This 'quaternary' sector of the economy has enabled the city to attract new industries dependent on advanced technology and skilled labour, as the electronics industry and the construction of nuclear plant. Grenoble has also played an important part in the expansion of alpine tourism, as a staging centre and by the manufacture of machinery for ski-lifts and cable cars used throughout the Alps. The success of industry has sustained an enormous population increase and the core of the city is now submerged in a sea of concrete construction and mush-rooming satellite and industrial suburbs. Population has been drawn from the mountain hinterland, but by virtue of the demand for highly-qualified labour and the attraction of the recreational facilities, also from throughout the nation.

Urban development in the sub-Alpine furrow consists of a chain of small towns,[8] each related to metallurgical or chemical industries utilizing hydroelectric power. The range of products is extremey wide and includes the manufacture of comparatively rare metallic alloys and chemical goods. The largest individual plant, at Ugine, produces 60 per cent of the special steel manufactured in the Alps, and steel is also produced at Allevard and ferro-alloys at Albertville. The most wide-spread metallurgical industry is aluminium refining, with important centres at Praz and Chedde. Finished goods are primarily light items, as watches and clocks, or components, as the manufacture of steel screws and bolts in the Arve valley. An entirely different activity is carried out in the southern extension of the furrow, where the anthracite deposits of La Mure yielded an output of 750,000 tons in 1967, employing 1,300 miners.

The core of the Alps is constituted by high, crystalline massifs, extending 150 kilometres from Mt. Blanc to the Pelvoux Massif. The traditional pastoral economy is now of secondary importance in an area which has suffered heavy rural depopulation. Tourism is the principal commercial activity,[9] including established valley resorts such as Chamonix and Megève and entirely new stations built since 1950 such as Chamrousse and l'Alpe d'Huez, created as winter sports complexes at high altitudes in the 'alpage' zone. The rivers are festooned with hydroelectricity barrages and some of the largest stations are located in this zone. Finally, east of the crystalline massifs, the intra-Alpine zone enjoys a rain shadow effect and has warmer summers and earlier springs than elsewhere in the northern Alps. Traditional pastoralism involving transhumance survives and is orientated towards the rearing of store cattle and cheese production. Tourism is now highly developed, especially in new stations such as Pralognan, Courchevel and La Plagne, but has also revived some of the valley settlements such as Bourg St. Maurice and Val d'Isère. Industrial activity is centred on the three major corridors—the Isère, Arc and Romanche valleys—and is identical in character to that of the sub-Alpine furrow. The hydroelectric schemes are nourished by complex diversions of numerous streams to power very large stations. On this basis, the Arc valley has a number of important electro-metallurgical centres between Modane and St. Jean-de-Maurienne.

THE RHONE-SAONE CORRIDOR

The third major unit, the axis of the lower Saône and middle Rhône valleys, has a double significance as an economic spine integrating the region of Rhône-Alpes and as a major transport artery permitting inter-regional and international movement. The lower Saône drains a broad depression between the Jura and the Massif Central, occupied by the contrasted landscapes of Bresse and the Dombes. The lacustrine clay plain of Bresse constitutes the boundary zone with Bourgogne. A bocage landscape is present in which small family dairy farms produce cheese, butter, pigs and poultry. The morainic cover of the Dombes plateau supports a myriad of étangs, reclaimed to create large estates for the bourgeoisie of Lyon. More recently, beef fattening has gained ground and the large estates have been joined by a proliferation of secondary homes owned by inhabitants of Lyon.

South of Lyon, a clear distinction exists between the Rhône Valley, which here takes the form of a succession of basins separated by narrow defiles, and the broad piedmont zone of Bas-Dauphiné to the east. The debris-covered piedmont has undergone severe rural depopulation and there are few urban centres. Within the Rhône corridor, economic activity attains its greatest intensity in two situations: the agglomeration based on Lyon, a city with over 2,000 years of history, and in the vicinity of the integrated hydraulic schemes on the Rhône, products of the last 20 years.

With a population of one million in its agglomeration, Lyon is the second city of France and the unchallenged capital of the region. Under-lying this eminence is the crossroads location of the city, commanding the principal route from Paris to the Mediterranean world at the point of intersection with routes leading via the Ain to Switzerland, via the Isère corridor to Italy, and westwards to the heart of the Massif Central.

Served by motorway connections, electrified rail and by inland waterway, Lyons is the hub of the transport network of south-eastern France. To the inherent advantages of this situation must be added the factor of initiative in technological and commercial skills which has enabled Lyon to become one of the largest centres of manufacturing in the nation.[10,11] At the base of industrial expansion was the silk industry, present in the city for over four centuries. Based on small dispersed units organized by Lyon merchants, the silk industry was a major factor in the accumulation of capital, a skilled work force and the acquisition of linked industrial activities. In the course of the nineteenth century, industry burgeoned from its textiles base, financed by local capital, and by outside interests attracted by the growing market, a favourable commercial environment and by functional linkage with textiles. Chief of the new activities were the chemicals industry and metallurgy. The latter was concerned initially with the production of rails, rolling stock and barges, but ultimately with machinery.

The present century has witnessed a great diversification of activity, largely within the chemicals and metal-using industries. The chemicals industry is located principally along the banks of the Saône and includes the nation's largest companies. The range of products is enormous, from heavy chemicals and fertilizers to artificial fibres, plastics, and pharmaceutical products. Lyon is the leading producer of rayon in France and artificial fibres have now almost completely replaced natural fibre in the silk industry. The wide range of products has led to the development of complex linkages within the chemicals sector and between chemicals, textiles and engineering. The most active branch of the metal-using industry is vehicle construction, represented by the Berliet heavy vehicle plant which employs 15,000 workers. Mechanical and electrical engineering are also well represented and in total the metallurgical and engineering activities employ approximately 40 per cent of the industrial labour force of the agglomeration.

The high rate of manufacturing development has led to the growth of industrial suburbs centred on industrial complexes or estates, as at Villeurbanne and Venissieux to the east and Saint-Fons and Pierre-Bénite to the south.[12] This process is continuing with the establishment of a new industrial estate at Feyzin, served by the new refinery and the Pierre-Bénite power scheme. Industrial expansion is no longer related merely to classic location factors but to the momentum created by the existence of large successful firms, at the forefront of technological progress by virtue of large research facilities, which guarantees new firms access to base materials, machinery, semi-finished goods and components. The existing advantages of communications have been enhanced by the improvements in internal and regional circulation by road, the expansion of the airport, improvements in inland navigation and progress on the Paris–Lyon–Marseille motorway. Industrialization has also been favoured by the growing importance of the Rhône-Alpes region as a market, with 4·4 million inhabitants in 1968, and the capacity of Lyon to serve as the principal distributing point and leading commercial centre within the market.

Lyon has been an important commercial centre since the Middle Ages, the crossroads location favouring the interchange of products between regions. The complex financial transactions necessitated by the fragmented silk industry stimulated the growth of banking during the nineteenth century. In 1863, the Crédit Lyonnais was created, becoming one of the most important banks in the nation.* Although most of the large firms in the region are national or international in character, with investment controlled by head offices in Paris, local capital[13] still plays an important role in industrial and building investment, through the banks of Lyon and the 'Société de Développement Régional du Sud-Est'. After Paris, Lyon is also the most important trade exhibition centre in France, with a large annual fair. In spite of its impressive industries and commercial importance, the second city of France has only one eighth of the population of the Paris agglomeration and a much smaller significance in terms of power of command in economic and social organization.[14] The city is at the threshold of metropolitan status but as yet there are few signs that a decisive independence from the national capital will be quickly attained†. Nevertheless, Lyon has greater credibility as a 'métropole d'équilibre' than any of the other cities so nominated.

The improvement of the Rhône is an excellent example of the interplay of physical, economic and political forces.[15] The dominant physical factor is that of the enormous physical force of the flow, reinforced by the Saône, Isère and Ardèche, resulting in a liability to flood and shifting channels, thus rendering the river unsuited in its natural state for navigation by large barges. In economic terms the Rhône possesses great potential for the integrated development of hydroelectricity, irrigated farming and improved navigation. Political factors intrude in the relative priority accorded to these three objectives in relation to the vested interests of the participating members of the development company. The Rhône improvement is being executed by the 'Compagnie Nationale du Rhône', constituted as a mixed economy company in 1931, uniting the interests of local authorities, the Paris–Lyon–Méditerranée railway company and electricity companies in Paris and Lyon, under overall government

*The Crédit Lyonnais is now nationalized.
†The airport, for example, has few direct international flights and all long-distance connections are via Paris.

supervision. With the subsequent nationalization of the railways and electricity production, the government is the dominant partner but the mixed economy basis has been retained. The overall plan envisages 20 major developments between the Swiss frontier and the delta, but work has thus far been concentrated in the middle course, between Lyon and Orange, where the energy potential is high, the impediments to navigation are severe and the greatest benefits are to be obtained from irrigation. Political motives dictated that priority investment should be concentrated in power production, where national interests were best served and economic profitability would be more rapidly obtained. Initial work was executed in the upper Rhône valley, where the site of Genissiat was completed in 1948, followed by the compensating barrage of Seyssel.

Since 1950 attention has been transferred to the middle Rhône, where the sites at Donzère, Montélimar, Baix and Beauchastel have been completed and work on Bourg-les-Valence commenced. Each scheme consists of a barrage and power station by-passed by navigation canals. In 1967, the Pierre-Bénite scheme south of Lyon was inaugurated, which, although uneconomic purely in terms of energy production, was justified by its juxtaposition with the Feyzin refinery and industrial estate and by the possibility of continuous navigation from the Rhône to the Saône without trans-shipment. The completion of the Rhône improvement may take a further 20 years but the works completed thus far have already transformed the valley. By 1968 output of electricity had attained over 8,000 million kilowatt hours, and improved navigation established on more than 100 kilometres of waterway. The 'Compagnie Nationale du Rhône' has assisted in the creation of industrial estates at Donzère, Montélimar, Feyzin and Valence where the combination of energy, port facilities and water supplies offer a powerful attraction. Over 4,000 hectares of land have been irrigated,[16] but sufficient water reserves exist to multiply this amount tenfold once the necessary remembrement has been carried out.

PROBLEMS OF REGIONAL ECONOMIC DEVELOPMENT

Symptomatic of the success, in economic terms, of Rhône-Alpes is that in recent years the region has achieved mobility of labour from agriculture to the industrial and tertiary sector without recourse to external migration. The region has generated sufficient new growth, in industry and tourism particularly, to redeploy workers from farming and from declining industries, and to absorb a high rate of population growth. The region nevertheless is not lacking in development problems, partly as a result of the uneven distribution of growth. Specifically, the Rhône axis forms a dividing line between an eastern portion of high economic growth rates, and a western section, within the Massif Central, which has experienced little net gain, reproducing in smaller scale the dichotomy in economic levels between the eastern and western halves of the nation. The département of Ardèche remains predominantly rural and has enjoyed few of the benefits of recent developments.[17] The population declined steadily between 1861 and 1962 and has remained virtually stagnant since. Similarly, the département of Loire faces severe problems of urban renewal and industrial diversification, and, in spite of the high urban proportion, experienced only modest population growth between 1962 and 1968. The increase in population during this latter period of under four per cent in Ardèche and Loire compares with rates of eight per cent in Ain and Savoie, and over 12 per cent in Isère, Drôme, Rhône and Haute-Savoie.

The function of Lyon as a 'métropole d'équilibre' is as yet unattained[18] and the basis of its linking with St. Etienne in this function is ambiguous. It is desirable, for this to become a reality, that St. Etienne should complement Lyon in a spatial sense, by extending the influence of the metropolis into the Massif Central, and in a functional sense, by providing certain facilities such as industrial retraining not developed at Lyon. In the long term, an aggrandizement of the status of Lyon, and greater independence from the control of Paris, may best be achieved in an international context. Lyon occupies a strategic location on the future Rhône–Rhine axis and planned motorways may strengthen connections with Switzerland and Northern Italy. At present the Rhône–Saône waterway is a cul-de-sac and the volume of traffic relatively modest.* The competition from the south European Pipeline, the Lyon–Marseille motorway and electrified railway seem to preclude any spectacular increase in traffic until the link to the Rhine is completed and further industrialization of the entire axis occurs.[19] Similarly, the extension of irrigated agriculture will encounter competition from developments in the Durance, Bas-Languedoc and the Garonne Valley in the sphere of fruit farming, but the accelerating growth of the region's urban population could provide a sufficiently large market for vegetable and dairy produce.

Finally, the long-term consequences of axial growth must be recognized,[20,21] and especially the impetus towards internal disparities involved in the maximum exploitation of the Rhône transport artery and power belt. Although tourism brings seasonal prosperity to the high Alps and the present wave of construction offers employment, this development favours a limited number of sites and has left unaffected large areas of less accessible

*In 1966 the port of Lyon handled 2·1 million tons of cargo.

terrain which continues to lose population. Similarly there is a tendency for new industrial activity to 'slide' downstream from the alpine corridors towards Grenoble and Annecy. Grenoble,[22,23] and to a lesser extent Annecy, are strong growth poles, capable of offsetting the attraction of Lyon and new sites on the Rhône. The future equilibrium of the region may depend on the promotion of further strong centres of self-sustaining growth away from the central axis—for example at Roanne and Bourg—reinforced by decentralizations from Lyon rather than Paris.*

REFERENCES

[1] Documentation Française, 'L'Economie de la Région Rhône-Alpes', *Notes Etud. docum.*, Nos. 3,491–3,492, 1968.

[2] Schnetzler, J., 'Le bassin houiller de la Loire', *Inf. géogr.*, 1966, p. 110.

[3] Veyret, P., et al., 'L'organisation de l'espace urbain dans les Alpes du Nord: contribution à l'étude des problèmes de régionalisation', *Revue Géogr. alp.*, 1967, p. 5.

[4] Blanchard, R., *Annecy: essai de géographie urbaine*, 1957, Annecy, Société des Amis du Veil Annecy.

[5] Veyret, P., 'Grenoble et son cadre', *Revue Géogr. alp.*, 1958, p. 5.

[6] Arnaud, G., and Marie, C., 'Les grandes villes françaises, Grenoble', *Notes Etud. docum.*, No. 3,288.

[7] George, P., 'Le développement de quelques villes de province; Grenoble', in *L'Urbanisation Française*, p. 85, 1964, Paris, Centre de Recherche d'Urbanisme.

[8] Veyret, P., and Veyret, G., 'Petites et moyennes villes des Alpes', *Revue Géogr. alp.*, 1964, p. 85.

[9] Billet, J., 'Le tourisme dans les principales stations des Alpes du Nord', *Revue Géogr. alp.*, 1966, p. 621.

[10] Avocat, C., 'Les industries rhodaniennes', *Revue Géogr. Lyon*, 1965, p. 277.

[11] Lafettère, M., *Lyon Ville Industrielle*, 1960, Paris, Presses Universitaires de France.

[12] Labasse, J., and Laferrère, M., *La Région Lyonnaise*, Fig. 12, p. 117, 1960, Paris, Presses Universitaires de France.

[13] Labasse, J., *Les Capitaux et la Région*, 1955, Paris, Armand Colin.

[14] Boudeville, J., *Problems of Regional Economic Planning*, pp. 59–60, 1966, Edinburgh, Edinburgh University Press.

[15] Tournier, G., 'La vallée du Rhône et son aménagement', *Tendances*, No. 34, 1965, p. 185.

[16] Bethemont, J., 'Progrès technique et réactions paysannes; l'irrigation dans la plaine de Montélimar', *Revue Géogr. Lyon*, 1961, p. 347.

[17] Schnetzler, J., 'A l'intérieur de la région Rhône-Alpes un département en crise; l'Ardèche', *Revue Géogr. alp.*, 1964, p. 463.

[18] Labasse, J., and Laferrère, M., *op. cit.*,[1,2] pp. 132–154.

[19] Laferrère, M., 'Le projet de liason fluviale Rhin-Rhône et la géographie industrielle de la région Lyonnaise', *Revue Géogr. Lyon*, 1962, p. 113.

[20] Laferrère, M., 'Introduction au plan d'aménagement de la région du Rhône et des Alpes', *Revue Géogr. Lyon*, 1961, p. 243.

[21] Labasse, J., 'L'aménagement de la région Centre-Est', *Revue Géogr. Lyon*, 1962, p. 131.

[22] Brush, J., 'The function of Grenoble as a central place', *Geogrl Rev.*, 1960, p. 586.

[23] Vivian, H., 'La zone d'influence régionale de Grenoble', *Revue Géogr. alp.*, 1959, p. 539.

*This process has in fact already begun, with the creation of a Berliet vehicle plant at Bourg.

22

Provence-Côte d'Azur

Provence-Côte d'Azur* has become firmly established as the most rapidly expanding region of France as far as population growth is concerned. Between 1962 and 1968, the increase in population by 17·0 per cent was almost double the rate experienced by the Paris region and substantially greater than the rate of 10·3 per cent achieved by Rhône-Alpes, the nearest rival. Moreover, all the constituent départements, with the exception of Hautes-Alpes, participated in this explosive growth. If this rate is maintained, the 1968 population of 3·3 million will have almost doubled by the end of the century. This growth is all the more remarkable when considered against the uncompromising physical background of the region.

Provence-Côte d'Azur must be regarded as a region of difficulty and extremes, and the present level of development has only been achieved by an unrelenting effort to remove the restrictions imposed by a rigorous environment.[1] The problem of summer drought is the essential backcloth of agricultural land use. In their natural state, the rivers are capricious, alternating between dry water courses and disastrous flooding. The 'mistral' can inflict freezing temperatures on the lower Rhône valley in winter and intensify the drought by provoking excessive plant transpiration in summer. The natural vegetation has low economic merit and pasture is of poor nutritive value in the unmodified Mediterranean climate. The highly accidented relief limits extensive accumulations of deep soil to the lower Rhône valley and to a number of interior basins in Provence. Coal is present in only one small basin at Gardanne, and the only other important mineral resource is the rich bauxite deposit at Brignoles. The compartmentalization of the region into micro-units, separated by upland barriers, has obstructed the development of communications and the Rhône, after giving life to the inland regions, terminates in a delta which until recently was a largely negative area. The coastline, for the most part

*Although part of the same planning region, the island of Corsica is the subject of a separate chapter.

313

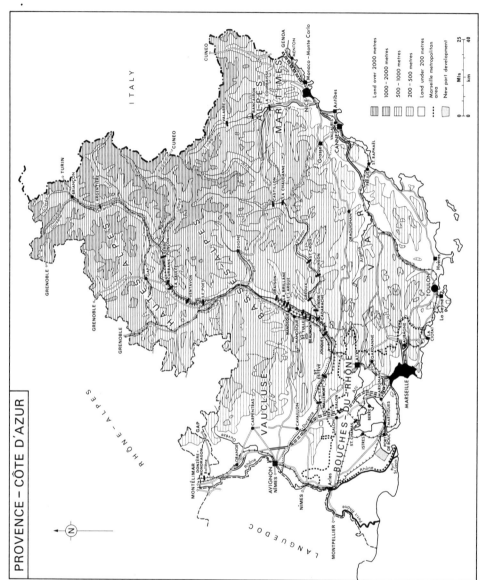

PROVENCE – CÔTE D'AZUR

Land over 2000 metres
1000 – 2000 metres
500 – 1000 metres
200 – 500 metres
Land under 200 metres
Marseille metropolitan area
New port development

Mls 0 25
km 0 40

Figure 22.1

rocky and irregular, offers few commodious sheltered sites for port development. The temperature conditions permit the widest crop range and longest growing season in France, but without irrigation these advantages cannot be fully exploited. Similarly, the climate endows the region with a natural vocation for tourism, but problems of accessibility and lack of investment limited its growth to the narrow strip of the Côte d'Azur until relatively recently. It follows that the achievements of the region are largely the fruits of man's efforts, rather than the gift of a benign Nature.

The detailed complexity, especially of the rural economy, cannot be encompassed in the space of a brief survey, but three crucial considerations may be presented which serve to characterize the region and the manner in which it is evolving. The present demographic expansion is in certain measure an artificial phenomenon and does not entirely result from commensurate economic development. Secondly, the diversity of the environment is such as to impose important sub-regional and even local variations in the level of economic activity and prosperity within the region. Thirdly, implicit in the struggle against environmental restrictions is massive investment in infrastructure works of a long-term character, which has led to the popular designation of the region as a 'chantier', an almost permanent construction site.[2]

THE DEMOGRAPHIC EXPLOSION

Table 22.1 indicates that the region's outstanding growth is almost entirely due to its capacity to attract migrants, and that on the basis of natural growth the region is revealed as possessing a degree of vitality markedly below the national growth rate of 4·1 per cent between 1962 and 1968.

Table 22.1

THE COMPONENTS OF POPULATION CHANGE, PROVENCE-COTE D'AZUR, 1962–1968

| | Population 1968 | Rate of change (per cent)[a] | | |
		Total change	Natural increase	Net migration
Basses-Alpes	104,813	14·1	3·1	10·9
Hautes-Alpes	91,790	5·0	3·5	1·4
Alpes-Maritimes	722,070	16·8	0·1	16·7
Bouches-du-Rhône	1,470,271	17·8	4·2	13·4
Var	555,926	18·4	3·5	15·6
Vaucluse	353,966	16·6	4·5	12·1
Region	3,298,836	17·0	3·1	14·0

[a]All values positive.
Source: Recensement de 1968, Premiers Résultats.

Out of a total population growth of 480,000 between 1962 and 1968, 390,000 was accounted for by net migration. This influx is accounted for by several separate streams of varying magnitude. The figure includes a small and declining number of Italian immigrants,[3] employed primarily in agriculture and especially in the intensive systems of Provence and the Rhône valley. A much larger number consists of industrial workers and their families, attracted particularly to the Marseille agglomeration. In a similar category are construction workers employed in major civil engineering works in the Rhône and Durance valleys and in the building industry of Marseille, Toulon and the Côte d'Azur. However, the largest individual category consists of retired persons, and concerns essentially the Riviera and its immediate hinterland. Above all the influx is an urban phenomenon and a feature of the largest agglomerations.[4]

Table 22.2

POPULATION GROWTH IN THE AGGLOMERATIONS OF PROVENCE–COTE D'AZUR, 1962–1968

	Total increase	Net migration		Natural increase	
		Total	Rate per cent	Total	Rate per cent
Marseille	122,022	92,789	11·1	29,233	3·5
Nice	44,798	44,601	12·9	84	0·0
Cannes	43,230	40,616	23·9	2,546	1·5
Avignon	23,464	17,125	28·0	6,122	5·4
Aix-en-Provence[a]	21,629	18,469	28·0	3,504	5·3
Menton-Monaco[b]	9,500	10,643	22·7	−1,183	−2·5

[a]Figure for town.
[b]French sector only of the agglomeration.
Source: Recensement de 1968, Premiers Résultats.

Over 50 per cent of the region's total growth and almost 60 per cent of the migrational gain were accounted for by the six agglomerations listed in *Table 22.2*. Some differentiation is apparent between Marseille, where the migration included a majority of active population,* and the predominantly tourist centres, where the migration rate is higher and the proportion of retired persons extremely high. The resultant effect on natural increase is shown by Nice, where a net gain by natural change of only 84 was recorded, and by Menton–Monaco, where a net loss of over 1,000 was experienced on the balance of births and deaths. A specific, and temporary, stream of migration affecting the region has been the influx of French North Africans, especially in the category of retired or semi-retired.

The appearance of demographic buoyancy is thus in large measure

*Including a large number of migrants originating within the region.

illusory, and when exception is made of the non-active and largely non-productive sector of the migrant population in search of retirement, a situation much closer to the national average is discernible. Far from being an unqualified source of human resources, the acquisition of migrants imposes certain inconveniences on the region stemming from an age-structure which is artificially top heavy*

By most measures of output, Provence-Côte d'Azur has enjoyed an economic growth rate in excess of the national average, but certain qualifications must be made. In both industry and agriculture, the increase in output has been achieved by greater productivity rather than by a large increase of employment. Thus the conversion of dry farming in the Rhône and Durance valleys to intensive irrigated farming with increased mechanization in large measure accounts for the increase in volume and value of agricultural production. The Provence coal basin at Gardanne increased its output from 1·4 million tons in 1964 to 1·7 million tons in 1967 while reducing the number of miners by 15 per cent to the present total of approximately 1,500. Similarly, in petroleum refining and petro-chemicals increased output has been obtained by extensions to plant with a high degree of automation.

On the other hand, certain activities that were formerly large employers of labour have tended to lose ground. This applies particularly to ship-building and repairing at Marseille, La Ciotat and La Seyne. The port activity of Marseille supports a declining number of workers in the docks as a result of the decline in general traffic since Algerian independence and the closure of the Suez canal. The expansion of the port traffic is accounted for entirely by the growth of petroleum traffic and the average number of dockers employed per day in 1968 was only slightly over 2,000. Mention also must be made of the high proportion of the labour force† employed in building and public works, subject to fluctuations in activity according to budgetary allocations. The tourist industry, for long a guaranteed source of income and employment on the Côte d'Azur, has in recent years suffered from the growth of cheaper forms of holidaymaking, especially camping, creating less employment, and also from the competition from rival centres in Languedoc, Corsica, Spain and Italy.

The dramatic increase in population and the high growth rate of the regional economy can not be taken as indicative of an absence of economic problems. On the contrary, the region is still in a process of rapid change as new economic and geographical orientations are developing.[5] More-

*In the region as a whole 20 per cent of the population was over 60 years of age in 1962. In Alpes-Maritimes this proportion increases to 25 per cent.

†Approximately 140,000 workers, or 13 per cent of the employed labour force in 1962.

over, the post-war growth has not been shared by all parts of the region and all branches of activity in equal proportion.

INTERNAL CONTRASTS

The region may be divided into five generalized zones with varying levels of development and recent progress: the lower Rhône Valley, the Rhône delta, coastal Provence, interior Provence and the southern Alps.

Only the eastern bank of the lower Rhône valley is located within the region. It has the form of a triangular lowland plain, the Comtat, described on Orange, Tarascon and Cavaillon, and traversed by the lower Durance. Formerly a hostile environment of alternating marshland and dry terraces, liable to flooding by the Rhône and Durance, the Comtat has been transformed into one of the most productive agricultural regions of the Midi. The combination of irrigation from the Durance,[6] permitting the substitution of intensive market, gardening for the former dry farming, and the arrival of rail communications, facilitating rapid transport to distant urban markets, has stimulated the growth of commercial farming. A bewildering variety of production is achieved on small holdings in a 'huerta' landscape. Early vegetables, apricots, peaches, small fruit and melons are the dominant crops and are marketed through large railway markets at Avignon, Châteaurenard, Cavaillon[7] and Carpentras. The processing and conserving industry is expanding rapidly and is necessitated by the saturation of the regional market for fresh produce. Avignon, with 86,000 inhabitants, is the commercial and route focus of the Comtat and the principal processing centre.

The Rhône delta complex is contrasted east and west of the main outflow. To the east, the Crau is a dejection cone of gravels on the former course of the Durance. Originally fit only for the winter grazing of sheep,[8] which were moved to the Alps during the summer drought, the Crau has been transformed by irrigation into an area of fruit farming, market gardening and dairy farming. Irrigated pasture provides hay sold for livestock feeding elsewhere in Provence. By contrast, to the west of the Rhône, the Camargue suffers from excessive humidity, liability to flooding from both branches of the Rhône and high salinity. A traditional landscape and economy persists in the south of the Camargue; bulls and horses are reared and salt is produced on the margins of the étangs. Further north, the Camargue is reclaimed and large farms of 200 hectares grow vines, fruit and rice. Rice cultivation[9] expanded rapidly after 1945, based on highly mechanized production and employing seasonal Spanish labour. Production meets national requirements but the area has declined recently due to the problem of weed infestation, and labour demands are falling with the suppression of hand transplanting and the total mechanization of production.[10] Arles is the capital of the delta, the lowest bridging point of the Rhône and the marketing and service centre for the new forms of agriculture. Port St. Louis is a river port dealing with bulk trade in timber and cement and with a chemical industry based on salt.

Maritime Provence is distinctive as being the most densely settled and highly urbanized section of the French littoral. This high degree of urbanization is the more emphatic by virtue of its juxtaposition with the low densities of interior Provence. A break in the continuity of urbanization occurs in the crystalline massif of Maures. To the west, urbanization is centred on the agglomerations of Marseille and Toulon. Marseilles had an agglomeration of almost a million inhabitants in 1968 and is the nucleus of an urbanized region extending westwards to the Rhône and northwards to the Gardanne basin and Aix-en-Provence. The problems of Marseille cannot be disassociated from the wider context of this urban region, which is the subject of a later discussion. In 1968, Toulon, with its industrial annexe of La Seyne, formed an agglomeration of 340,000 inhabitants. Its expansion was stimulated by the military arsenal, the naval installations and the shipbuilding and repairing activities of La Seyne, all functions of reduced importance at present. Tourism has taken on an added significance but the conversion of the shipyards through the attraction of new industries is an urgent problem. Between these two agglomerations, La Ciotat is a major shipbuilding centre, extensively modernized since the Second World War, but also facing employment difficulties.

East of the massif of Maures, the pattern of urbanization takes a different form. At first intermittently, between St. Tropez and Fréjus, and then more emphatically, east of Cannes, an unbroken façade of urban development lines the coast as far as the national frontier. The linear agglomeration of the Côte d'Azur has a population of over 700,000, distributed within a few kilometres of the sea. Founded in fashionable tourism at a limited number of resorts such as Nice, Monte Carlo, Cannes and Antibes, the Côte d'Azur has become the greatest zone of popular tourism in France,[11] attracting over two million visitors each summer from all over western Europe. Former villages have mushroomed into tourist centres, pushing further inland the cultivation of flowers for sale and perfume manufacture.[12] To the influx of commercial tourists must be added the rapid increase in the construction of secondary residences and in the number of retired persons, affecting also the villages and small towns of the hinterland.

The success of tourism manifest in this rapid urban extension is not without associated problems.[13,14] The influx of visitors places an unsupportable strain on the coastal roads and resort centres, which the completion of the Esterel motorway will only partially relieve. Soaring land values[15] are a deterrent to industrial development, badly needed to relieve seasonal unemployment. Many of the older resorts[16] are ill-equipped to meet new demands in tourism, which are for cheaper accommodation, elaborate camping sites, additional sailing facilities and a more informal mode of holiday making. More seriously, the volume of tourist revenue has shown a decline in recent years, less as a result of a reduction in the number of visitors than in the amount of time spent on the Riviera.* This results from such factors as congestion, high prices during the peak season and the competition offered by Italian and Spanish resorts. The largest centre, Nice,[17] with an agglomeration of almost 400,000 inhabitants, has offset the vicissitudes of tourism by the attraction of a major firm, I.B.M., by its elevation to university status with 9,000 students in 1968, and by the expansion of its transport functions. Nice has electrified rail, a rapidly growing international airport and an increasing maritime traffic with Corsica and Italian ports.[18]

By contrast, interior Provence lacks the vitalizing influence of the sea and suffers the full effects of summer drought. The most characteristic feature is the patchwork landscape imposed by the alternation of dry garrigue uplands with fertile basins. In dry farmed areas the traditional cereals, vines and olives pattern of land use persists and land abandonment and rural depopulation are rife. Irrigated basins appear as oases devoted to vegetables and fruit.[19] Future hopes for an intensification of agriculture rest on the projected diversion of water from the Verdon by the canal de Provence, permitting irrigation and also the supply of water to Marseille and Toulon. Interior Provence is not without mineral resources; France's largest deposits of bauxite are worked at Brignoles and the basin of Gardanne produced 1·7 million tons of coal in 1967. Over one third of the coal is consumed on the field by a major power station and the coalfield is also the site of one of the largest alumina plants in France. The most striking development in interior Provence is the integrated improvement of the Durance valley, which is considered below.

North of the line of the lower Durance and the Verdon extends the alpine province of Provence-Côte d'Azur. As compared with the northern Alps, the southern extension is a deterioration in environmental terms, and economic and urban development is but a pale reflection of its northern counterpart. The majority of the province is constituted by the pre-Alpine zone, of dry limestone massifs deeply scarred by tortuous gorges and canyons. The summer aridity restricts land use to sheep grazing, the impenetrable relief has precluded urban development, and

*Whereas at the height of the fashionable era a wealthy clientèle passed six months on the Riviera, the average length of stay in 1967 was four and a half days.

rural depopulation began early and has persisted to the present day. Paradoxically, it is the higher mountains of the intra-Alpine zone of Briançonnais, Ubaye and the Alpes-Maritimes which offer the greater resource base and which are currently experiencing some revival of activity. The greater rainfall provides pasture for cattle grazing and milk is produced for processing* Heavy snowfall combined with high in-solation has stimulated the recent expansion of winter sports resorts near Briançon[20] and in the Alpes-Maritimes.[21] The essential corridor of movement is the upper Durance Valley and hydroelectric energy is used in electrochemical works at l'Argentière and St. Auban. The depopulation of the alpine province has been checked but internal redistribution is still active,[22] with rural exodus prevalent in the pre-Alps and a greater con-centration of population into the main towns, tourist centres[23] and secondary service centres.[24]

MAJOR DEVELOPMENT SCHEMES

The description of Provence-Côte d'Azur as a 'chantier' is an apt allusion to the vast amount of construction work in progress in the region. In part this is a spontaneous adjustment to the region's growing population and economy in the form of new residential districts, hotel and tourist com-plexes, new industrial estates and the construction of motorways. On the other hand, two developments are distinctive by virtue of their scale, their long-term nature and an importance which extends beyond their im-mediate locality and even the region. These are the development of the Durance valley and the extension of the port-industrial complex of Marseille in the Gulf of Fos.

The problems of the Durance valley epitomized those of interior Provence as a whole. Agriculture was subjected alternately to dessication and flood, while the energy of the Durance, potentially the largest fluvial source after the Rhône and Rhine, was tapped only by small water-level stations, dating in some instances from the turn of the century. In the post-war decade intensive research into a multi-purpose project of flood control, irrigation, hydroelectricity generation and urban water supply was executed, culminating in 1955 in a long-term programme to be implemented by Electricité de France.[25, 26] The key element in flood control is the Serre-Ponçon dam, built at the confluence of the Durance and the Ubaye and completed in 1959. This immense earthen dam retains a vast artificial lake, regulating the flow of the Durance and nourishing a power station generating 700 million kilowatt-hours per annum. Below

*Especially at the Nestlé factory at Gap.

Serre-Ponçon, the development is divided into two stages. Between Serre Ponçon and the confluence with the Verdon at Cadarache, a new canal has been built parallel to the middle Durance on which seven new stations are to be built, supplementing the five existing small stations. New power stations have been completed at Curbans, Oraison and Manosque, are under construction at Beaumont and St. Tulle II and are projected at Sisteron and Aubignosc. South of Cadarache, a new canal has been built on the south bank of the Durance feeding two new power stations at Jouques and St. Estève, and a third is under construction at Mallemort. At Mallemort the canal swings southwards, diverting the Durance through the Alpille range along its former course to the Etang de Berre, powering stations at St. Chamas and Salon. The flow of the Verdon is regulated by a major dam at Castillon, completed in 1950, and a number of smaller stations generate power between Castillon and Cadarache.

In the space of little more than a decade, the Durance has been tamed and when completed will contribute approximately 6,000 million kilowatt-hours to the nation's electricity supply. Its waters no longer reach the Rhône although provision is made to release water when necessary to the irrigation canals of the Comtat should ground water supplies be inadequate. The major benefit to the valley, other than the elimination of disastrous floods, has been the extension of irrigated farming. The creation of a new power belt has not as yet resulted in any significant industrialization. A nuclear research centre is located at Cadarache, but most of the hydroelectricity is fed into the grid system.

The extension of the Marseille industrial-port complex must be seen in the wider context of the problems of the port of Marseille and the development of the Marseille metropolitan area. Outward appearances give Marseille the aspect of a successful port of European dimensions and a thriving agglomeration of almost a million inhabitants. In fact, the département of Bouches-du-Rhône has one of the highest unemployment rates in France, new industrial growth has been hesitant in recent years and, in the short term at least, the Marseille urban complex faces severe problems. That Marseille should have become the largest port of France is in certain respects a contradiction of the physical conditions of its site and immediate hinterland. Hemmed in by mountains and removed from direct access to the Rhône Corridor, for centuries Marseille turned its back on domestic trade in favour of participation in the currents of Mediterranean trade. Modern economic conditions have, however, operated in favour of a greater national rôle. The major factor in its modern growth was the optimum location with respect to colonial trade, especially with the North African territories. Work began on an artificial expansion west of the 'vieux port' in the middle of the nineteenth century, coinciding with the arrival of the railway, the introduction of steam navigation, the exploitation of Algerian resources and the opening of the Suez canal. Port development began independently on the Etang de Berre in 1855, linked to the Rhône by the Arles to Bouc canal. In 1919, the Etang de Berre was incorporated into the port of Marseille and by 1929 was linked to the main port by canal via the Rove tunnel. The increase in petroleum imports from the Middle East and the advent of large tankers necessitated the construction of a specialized port at Lavéra in 1948, supplying the refineries of Lavéra, La Mède and Berre. The Etang de Berre rapidly became an industrial growth point as petrochemical industries were established at the refineries.[27,28]

The situation 20 years after the war thus appeared favourable for continued expansion, but in recent years it has become apparent that Marseille has entered a difficult period in its evolution. The port handled over 61 million tons of cargo in 1967, but of this traffic 53·4 million tons were of petroleum handled by the Etang de Berre annexe. The level of general cargo handled has fallen since Algerian independence,[*] as has the volume of passenger traffic. Moreover, since the completion of the south European Pipeline much of the crude petroleum discharged is transported directly to inland refineries. Although possessing a number of processing and engineering firms, the agglomeration does not have a level of industrial development proportionate to its population or to the volume of raw materials handled by the port. In many respects the port fulfils a transit function, which, unlike Rotterdam and Antwerp, is not balanced by a high level of industrial activity. Again, unlike Rotterdam, Marseille does not as yet enjoy access to a densely populated, industrialized and international hinterland by high-capacity waterway.

The solution to these problems is seen in twofold action: the creation of a new port and industrial complex at Fos, to the west of the existing Etang de Berre annexe, and the expansion of the function of Marseille as a 'métropole d'équilibre'. The details of the Fos project have been amply described[29,31] and need only be stated in outline. The Gulf of Fos is located 50 kilometres from Marseille between Lavéra and the mouth of the Rhône, and possesses certain features which render it ideal for port and industrial construction. Deep water exists inshore, unperturbed by tides and currents, over a frontage of ten kilometres. The Crau plain offers a vast expanse of undeveloped terrain with sound foundations and abundant water supplies. In 1964, the government[†] instituted a development programme of which the first stages are already realized.[32] A 20-

[*]The situation has been exacerbated since 1967 by the closure of the Suez canal.

[†]The government is bearing the majority of the infrastructure cost; 80 per cent in the case of dredging costs and 60 per cent in the case of dock construction.

metre deep water channel has been dredged leading to an oil terminal capable of receiving tankers of 250,000 tons, serving the new refinery of Fos completed in 1965. Three huge basins are to be excavated, two of which will have specialized terminals and container berths. A mineral terminal is completed, handling bauxite for the Gardanne alumina plant, and earmarked to serve a projected waterfront iron and steel plant.

The third basin, nearest Port-St. Louis, is intended as a reserve plan in the event of the saturation of the port of Marseille. This basin alone would be quivalent to the existing capacity of Marseille. Behind the port installations 5,500 hectares have been reserved for industrial development, and plans exist to expand the Istres air base into an international airport.

The significance of the Fos scheme lies in its relationship to the planned expansion of the entire Marseille metropolitan area.[33] The latter is a rectangular area with the corners at Arles, Aix-en-Provence, la Ciotat and Port-St. Louis, enclosing a population of approximately 1·3 million inhabitants in 1968. At the heart of this metropolitan area, Marseille is linked as a 'métropole d'équilibre' with Aix-en-Provence, the latter town discharging administrative and university functions complementary to the port, commercial and industrial activities of Marseille.

The dominance of Marseille as the regional capital of Provence-Côte-d'Azur is far from complete and the agglomeration is currently experiencing some decline in its economic base[34,35] as a result of the difficulties of the port, shipbuilding and repairing and the lack of new industrial growth. Marseille is challenged in the east by Nice;[36] while to the north the Durance valley development is controlled by the central government, as is the Fos development to the west. The ability to direct the regional economy—the intended function of the 'métropoles d'équilibre'—is thus impaired by the fragmentation of authority within the region. Similarly, the impact of the Fos scheme on the activity of Marseille is ambiguous. When the scheme becomes fully operative, provisionally by 1985, the basic activities will employ 32,000* while the attraction of further industries could triple this figure, possibility necessitating the construction of a new town. The successful completion of the Fos scheme would thus create a second urban-industrial complex within the metropolitan area, linked to Marseille by motorway but inevitably militating against that city exercising an unequivocal role as a regional metropolis. In the long-term, the significance of Fos, the most ambitious port expansion scheme in western Europe, will be supra-regional. It is not yet clear that the specific advantages of the site are matched by an equally favourable situation. The planned capacity of the port clearly exceeds the demands of

*On the assumption that the steelworks is built.

the regional hinterland and the success of the port depends on the establishment of the Rhône–Rhine axis as a functioning reality.

REFERENCES

[1] Wolkowitsch, M., 'Provence et Côte d'Azur', *Inf. géogr.*, No. 31, 1967, p. 8.

[2] Guichard, O., 'La région du Sud-Est, Chantier de l'Europe', *Urbanisme*, No. 95, 1966, p. 2.

[3] Faidutti-Rudolph, A., *L'Immigration Italienne dans le Sud-Est de la France*, 1964, Gap, Ophrys.

[4] Barbier, B., 'La croissance démographique du Sud-Est méditerrannéen', *Bull. Soc. Géogr. Marseille*, 1962, p. 5.

[5] Reboul, C., *La Provence de Mistral à l'Atome*, 1964, Paris, Gamma Presse.

[6] Carrère, P., and Dugrand, R., *La Région Méditérranéenne*, Fig. 19, p. 118, 1960, Paris, Presses Universitaires de France.

[7] Pelissier, R., 'La production maraîchère et fruitière et le marché de Cavaillon', *Méditerranée*, 1964, p. 279.

[8] Livet, R., 'Les élevages provençaux' *Méditerranée*, 1965, pp. 186–190.

[9] Bethemont, J., 'Le riz et la mise en valeur de la Camargue', *Revue Géogr. Lyon*, 1962, p. 153.

[10] La Cognata, G., 'Vers une suppression du repiquage en Camargue', *Méditerranée*, 1967, p. 239.

[11] Comité de Tourisme Provence-Côte d'Azur-Corse, *La Région du Soleil*, 1963, pp. 90–109.

[12] Racine, J., 'L'utilisation, les revenus, et les caractères généraux de l'appropriation du sol dans le département des Alpes-Maritimes', *Méditerranée*, 1968, p. 60.

[13] Hermitte, J., 'Problèmes et perspectives de développement sur la Côte d'Azur et dans son arrière-pays', *Mém. Docums CRDCG*, Tome X, Fasc. 2, 1965, p. 103.

[14] Reyne, G., 'Dynamisme de la Côte d'Azur', réalisations et projets', *Méditerranée*, 1963, p. 55.

[15] Kayser, B., *Campagnes et Villes de la Côte d'Azur*, pp. 448–467, 1958, Monaco, Editions du Rocher.

[16] Guéron, L., 'Le tourisme à Menton', *Méditerranée*, 1966, p. 51.

[17] Blanchard, R., *Le Comté de Nice*, 1961, Paris, Arthème Fayard.

[18] La Documentation Française, 'Les grandes villes françaises: Nice', *Notes Etud. docum.*, No. 3,106, 1964.

[19] Livet, R., *Habitat rural et structure agraire en Basse-Provence*, 1964, Gap, Ophrys.

[20] Dupré, J., 'Le tourisme et son influence économique dans le Dévoluy et les vallées des deux Buech', *Méditerranée*, 1965, p. 67.

[21] Lecomte, C., 'Le tourisme de la neige dans trois vallées des Alpes du Sud', *Méditerranée*, 1965, p. 9.

[22] Bravard, Y., 'Le dépeuplement des hautes vallées des Alpes-Maritimes: ses caractères et ses conséquences démographiques économiques et sociales', *Revue Géogr. alp.*, 1961, p. 5.

[23] Barbier, B., 'Méthodes d'études des résidences secondaires. L'exemple des Basses-Alpes', *Méditerranée*, 1965, p. 89.

[24] Barbier, B., 'Les centres élémentaires à fonctions urbaines des Alpes du Sud', *Méditerranée*, 1964, p. 299.

[25] Hoyle, B., 'Changes in the Durance valley', *Geography*, 1960, p. 110.

[26] La Documentation Française, 'L'aménagement hydraulique et agricole Durance-Verdon et le canal de Provence', *Notes Etud. docum.*, No. 3,034, 1963.

[27] Verlaque, C., 'Le transport et le raffinage du pétrole dans le bassin Méditerrannéen', *Méditerranée*, 1966, pp. 121–126.

[28] Hoyle, B., 'The Etang de Berre—Recent port expansion and associated industrial development at Marseilles', *Tijdschr. econ. soc. Geogr.*, 1960, p. 57.

[29] Barrilon, C., 'Le port de Marseille et le delta rhôdanien', *Urbanisme*, No. 95, 1966, p. 26.

[30] Saigat, J., 'Les lignes directrices de l'opération de Fos', *Urbanisme*, No. 95, 1966, p. 10.

[31] Pasqualini, F., 'Giant harbour complex in South France', *Dock Harb. Auth.*, No. 574, 1968, p. 142.

[32] Clout, H., 'Expansion projects for French seaports', *Tijdschr. econ. soc. Geogr.*, 1968, pp. 273–275.

[33] Livre Blanc, *Organisation pour les études d'aménagement de l'aire métropolitaine Marseillaise*, 1968, Marseille.

[34] Carrère, P., 'Le contexte démographique et économique de la région Marseillaise', *Urbanisme*, No. 95, 1966, p. 16.

[35] Lacroix, G., 'La ville de Marseille devant son avenir', *Urbanisme*, No. 95, 1966, p. 42.

[36] Barbier, B., et al., *Les zones d'attraction commerciale de la région Provence-Côte d'Azur-Corse*, 1966, Paris, Gauthier-Villars.

23

Centre

The region of Centre forms a hexagon at the core of the hexagonal outline of the nation as a whole. Situated astride the boundary between the eastern and western provinces of the nation, the region shares characteristics of both zones and may be taken almost as an average of the social and economic geography of France: Centre is not highly urbanized, but the towns are strong centres of growth whereas the countryside is shedding population. The region contains the most modern farm structures in France but also areas where traditional farming patterns persist. Economic growth is most rapid where the direct impact of the Paris city region is present, and more attenuated with distance away from the capital. The title of the region might thus allude not only to its approximate location at the centre of the national space, but also the general position of the region close to the centre of the spectrum of the nation's social and economic characteristics. There is no single dominant economic focus within the region; the three largest towns, Tours, Orléans and Bourges, recall that Centre is an amalgamation of the provinces of Touraine, Orléanais and Berry, rather than a single physical or economic unit.[1]

The modern evolution of Centre has been one of sustained decline, during which the region lost ground in terms of its share of the nation's population and economic growth, followed, more recently, by a recovery which is as yet incomplete. The period of demographic decline extended throughout the latter half of the nineteenth century and the early twentieth century, and was coincident with the gradual modernization of agriculture and the migration of rural population to Paris. The post-war revival of Centre is in large measure a reciprocal movement, the re-animation being sustained by industrial growth emanating from Paris through decentralization. This general growth pattern is closely reflected in demographic trends, which also indicate significant variations within the region.

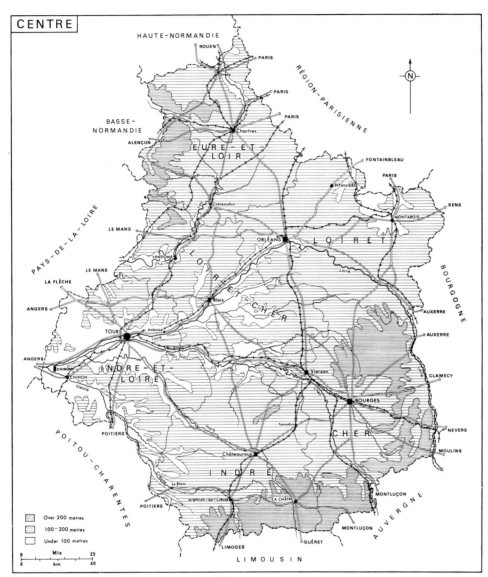

Figure 23.1

Table 23.1

DEMOGRAPHIC TRENDS IN THE CENTRE REGION

	Date of minimum	Date of maximum	Change (per cent) 1954–62	Change (per cent) 1962–68
Eure-et-Loire	1921	1968	+7·4	+ 8·9
Indre-et-Loire	1872	1968	+8·2	+10·8
Loiret	1921	1968	+8·8	+10·5
Cher	1954	1891	+3·3	+ 3·8
Loire-et-Cher	1936	1891	+3·7	+ 6·8
Indre	1936	1891	+1·3	− 1·7

Source: Recensements de 1962 and 1968.

Table 23.1 indicates a contrast between the départements of Eure-et-Loire, Indre-et-Loire and Loiret, where depopulation was checked early and demographic recovery has been rapid, and the remaining three départements, where depopulation was more prolonged, recovery has been more hesitant and the maximum populations of the nineteenth century have not yet been regained. Clearly important differentials exist within the planning region, coinciding approximately with a division north and south of the Loire valley. This differential growth and attendant planning problems may be analysed further by reference to the specific sub-regions involved.

The most extensive sub-region north of the Loire is the limestone plateau of Beauce. Covered by a thick layer of 'limon' and with the driest conditions in the Paris basin, the plain of Beauce is the foremost wheat-growing area of France. Favoured by almost unbroken relief, mechanization has been systematically applied to the plain of Beauce in conjunction with remembrement. Approximately 75 per cent of the farms are tenant-operated, creating a favourable environment for modernization and the reduction of labour input. In an effort to reduce labour needs, the acreage devoted to sugar-beet has declined in recent years in favour of the more easily mechanized maize and colza. Cereals occupy 75 per cent of the arable area, being favoured by the high price levels under the Common Market arrangements. Cooperative production and marketing and joint use of machinery and silos give the large farms of over 100 hectares an optimum economic structure. By contrast, the small owner-operated farms, of less than 40 hectares, do not enjoy such economies of scale and retain a more diversified farming, including fodder crops, cattle and pigs. The towns of Beauce, and the neighbouring margins of Perche and Thimerais, developed as marketing centres with processing industries.

Recent growth, however, owes more to the arrival of new industries by the decentralization process. Thus Chartres has added radio components and aluminium working to its staple manufacture of agricultural equipment; Montargis manufactures rubber; Dreux has acquired electronics; and Vendôme printing and light engineering. Proximity to Paris is also reflected in the large number of second homes owned by Parisians, especially in the environs of Beauce in the Eure and Loire valleys.

North of the Loire, the region of Centre has thus enjoyed a period of economic progress in recent years. The agricultural reform movement is of long standing and has given Beauce a sound farming structure in which mechanization has led to high productivity, congenial working conditions and a high level of remuneration. The acquisition of new industry has transformed the towns into minor growth poles, capable of absorbing both their own natural increase and a certain influx of rural migrants.*

The valley of the Loire has an entirely different character, being an arterial sub-region animated by two major and several secondary urban centres.[2] As compared with the open landscape, large farms and monocultural aspect of Beauce, the Loire valley is characterized by a heterogeneity of terrain facets dependent on the variable character of the alluvial deposits, the height of the water table and variations in aspect. The title 'garden of France' alludes to the intensity of farming, the variety of land uses and the small field and farm size. On the deep alluvial loams high-grade horticulture is present, including vegetables, fruit and nurseries, and the importance of dairy farming is increasing. On the dry soils of the limestone flanks enclosing the valley in Touraine vineyards yield quality wine. To the harmony of the agricultural landscape must be added the specific attraction of the châteaux, the basis of an important tourist traffic.

The Loire valley does not impose itself as a corridor of movement to the same extent as the Seine; describing an arc with its peak at Orléans, the Loire is not a single artery, but rather two separate axes†, converging across the region towards Paris. The extreme variations in flow make the Loire unsuitable for modern inland navigation, the width of the bed, with its complex bifurcations, has acted as an obstacle to crossings, and the natural focus of tributary drainage is westwards whereas the major economic currents are orientated north-eastwards towards Paris. In any case, the relief features of Centre are subdued, offering little resistance to movement by direct lines irrespective of the drainage pattern. If not of primordial importance as a routeway, the Loire valley has, nevertheless, exerted considerable influence on urban development.

*The agglomeration of Chartres, for example, grew by 10,000 inhabitants between 1962 and 1968 —at a rate of 21 per cent—including a net gain by over 7,000 migrants.

†The Paris–Bordeaux route via Orléans and Tours, and the Paris–St. Etienne and Clermont-Ferrand route via the Loing, Loire and Allier valleys.

Orléans is the centre of an agglomeration of 167,000 inhabitants, which expanded by almost 20 per cent between 1962 and 1968. Orléans owes this very rapid growth to its excellent situation, 120 kilometres from Paris, at the junction of routes from Bordeaux and Toulouse to the capital and at the virtual crossroads of the middle Loire valley. This situation has given Orléans a vocation for the decentralization, not only of industry, but also of tertiary and intellectual activity. Before the Second World War, the industrial base was established almost entirely on food industries and the manufacture of agricultural machinery. During the war, certain strategic defence industries were relocated at Orléans and have since been converted to civil production, but the essence of recent industrial expansion is the arrival of new firms with no relationship to the earlier industrial history of the town. Chief of the new industries are the manufacture of vehicle components and tyres,* heating equipment, synthetic textiles, chemicals and pharmaceuticals. To these new industries may be added tertiary decentralizations† and new research and university establishments. Orléans shares with Tours the new university of 'Val de Loire', possessing the Science Faculty, while the latter town houses the Arts and Medical Faculties. Also decentralized to Orléans are branches of government research institutions and several industrial laboratories. In response to this growth in employment, the agglomeration has undergone a major extension and a new satellite town, 'La Source', housing the university, is in course of construction to the south of the existing agglomeration.

Tours, with 201,000 inhabitants in the agglomeration in 1968, is the largest urban centre in the region. Sited between the Loire and Cher close to their confluence, the agglomeration has recently expanded on to the limestone plateaus, overlooking the Loire corridor, to north and south‡[3]. At the intersection of the Paris–Bordeaux and Nantes–Lyon rail routes, Tours has benefited from excellent communications to consolidate its function as a commercial centre, a cultural and tourist centre, and a collection and distribution point with important marshalling yards. The sustained post-war growth of the agglomeration is related to a general expansion of these functions, together with further industrial growth, rather than to any individual new development. In addition to the traditional industries such as printing, newer activities include the manufacture of rolling stock, ball-bearings, rubber and chemicals. In spite of its impressive post-war growth in population, the sphere of influence of Tours remains comparatively small, being confined to Indre-et-Loire and

*Decentralized branches of Renault and Michelin respectively.
†Including an administrative centre of I.B.M. employing 2,000 workers.

‡Between 1962 and 1968 the agglomeration increased in population by 22·5 per cent.

the northern portion of Indre.[4]

The urban organization of the middle Loire valley is dominated by Tours and Orléans, but the valley is punctuated by a number of smaller centres. Blois, with over 40,000 inhabitants in its agglomeration, is the largest of the secondary centres. The tourist function is being elaborated by the construction of a barrage on the Loire, creating a lake as the centre piece of a new tourist complex.[5] The tourist activity is now balanced by new industrial activities, including aeronautical and electrical engineering. Upstream from Orléans, the small towns have received decentralized firms, including the Simca vehicle component factory at Sully and electrical engineering and metallurgy at Gien. The construction of nuclear power stations on the Loire at Avoine, near Chinon, and St.-Laurent-des-Eaux, near Blois, has stimulated the expansion of adjacent communes,[6] but has not as yet led to any significant urbanization.

Practically the whole of the northern half of Centre thus shows a positive evolution, in both the agricultural and industrial centres, matched by a parallel strengthening of the urban centres. The situation is very different south of the Loire in the province of Berry. Three types of landscape and economy are present: the poorly drained forests of Sologne and Brenne, the open plateaux of Champagne Berrichonne and the bocage landscape of the clays of the Boischaut. The Sologne is constituted by Miocene deposits of sands and clays, thickly wooded and with abundant surface water. The former unrewarding agriculture was abandoned between the wars as large recreational domains were created with valuable hunting and fishing. In recent years some revival has taken place, land relamation leading to maize cultivation and cattle rearing.[7]

In the south of Indre, the Brenne represents, in smaller scale, a similar terrain. Reclamation is limited to the periphery, and in the centre of Brenne 130,000 hectares of wood, heath and swamp is practically un-exploited. By contrast, Champagne Berrichonne is a dry open plain developed on the Cretaceous and Jurassic limestones, recalling Beauce topographically but lacking the 'limon' cover. It is an area in which agricultural progress is related to a distinctive background social pattern.[8] Historically land ownership was dominated by the acquisition of very large estates controlled on behalf of the proprietors by managers, who in turn engaged métayers to work the land. With the decay of métayage during this century, tenant farming has been introduced and a favourable organization created for modernization. Machinery and fertilizers are heavily employed in a system of mixed farming in which cereals alternate with sugar-beet and leguminous fodder crops, associated with the feeding of dairy cattle and sheep. By contrast, the smaller farms persist with polyculture, combined with paid work as stockmen and tractor drivers on the large farms. Inevitably, as mechanization proceeds the demand for hired labour is diminishing and rural depopulation gathers force. In the extreme south of the region, the Lias clay vale of Boischaut marks the transition to the Massif Central, reflected in a dense bocage landscape, an emphasis on animal farming and a very high dependence on agricultural employment. The basic economy is polyculture in which the rearing of Charolais cattle is the main commercial element. Approximately 52 per cent of the population of Boischaut depends on agriculture for a livelihood but conditions are far from optimum. Past emigration has created a situation in which over 30 per cent of the farmers are over 60 years of age and many have no natural successors. The agricultural population of the département of Indre declined from 53,000 to 36,000 between 1954 and 1962, and, lacking strong urban centres, in areas like Boischaut this implies emigration leading to heavy rural depopulation.

In the whole of Centre south of the Loire only three large urban centres have developed: Bourges, Vierzon and Châteauroux. Bourges has the distinction of being close to the geometric centre of the nation. The town has long been an important cultural centre but its recent rapid growth, to a size of 76,000, is a result of the arrival of major industries. Chief of these are the aircraft and missile works of Nord-Aviation, employing 2,200 workers, and the Michelin tyre factory, employing 2,500 workers. Situated at a strategic focus of the national road network, the former military importance, manifest in the arsenal, is perpetuated in the location of scientific military education centres.

Situated 20 kilometres from Bourges, the town of Vierzon has the advantage of being located on the Paris–Toulouse railway, and has a population of 32,000. The staple porcelain industry has been rationalized and a number of new metallurgical, textile and chemical firms have been established recently.[9]

Châteauroux, with 55,000 inhabitants in its agglomeration, is the capital of the département of Indre. Its post-war growth owed much to the creation of an American air base in 1951, which represented the largest single source of employment in Indre with 4,100 civilian jobs.* The decision to close the base in 1967 has thus compromised the economy of Châteauroux and exceptional government measures have been applied to reduce unemployment.[10] A number of decentralized firms, ranging from shoe manufacture to plastics, have been established, but the rate of population growth, 5 per cent between 1962 and 1968, is by far the lowest of all the major towns of the planning region.

*The civilian wage bill of the base in 1965 was 36 million francs.

REGIONAL PLANNING PROBLEMS

From this brief description of trends in the separate sub-regions of Centre, it is apparent that problems of economic development are contrasted as between the northern and southern halves of the planning region. Indeed, the region is not a particularly well integrated unit, in turn a function of its very large size and the lack of a decisive urban focus. Orléans is the regional administrative centre, but its sphere of influence is limited and its orientation is towards Paris. Of all the cities of the 'couronne' approximately 100 kilometres from Paris, Orléans may well have the greatest difficulty in exerting a separate identity as a regional capital as opposed to an outlier of the Paris city region.* Gravier[11] sees the strengthening of the university, research and tertiary activities of the city as being essential to maintain independence from Paris. Lacking an undisputed regional capital, Tours and Orléans maintain a rivalry within a state of equilibrium based on contrasted specializations, as epitomized by the splitting of the new university between the two centres. Orléans is an administrative capital and the chief growth point of advanced technology industry. Tours has greater commercial importance, is the capital of the tourist industry and is a leading provincial cultural centre.

The planning problems affecting the northern half of the region are thus not posed in a critical form. Agricultural modernization is well-established in the heartland of Beauce and is extending to Perche and Touraine. The shedding of agricultural labour is taking place, however, against a background network of primary and secondary urban poles capable of offering employment opportunities.

South of the Loire planning problems are more acute, both in terms of specific critical areas, as Châteauroux and Boischaut, and in terms of the general problem of the run-down of agricultural employment without compensating growth in industrial activity. Various proposals have been made, ranging from the suitability of the railway triangle Bourges–Vierzon–Châteauroux as a national centre for collection and distribution of freight traffic,[12] to the obvious suitability of the Brenne as a tourist district. However, in the short term the most serious need is for increased industrial employment at the level of the small country town, especially in Indre, as a means of rationalizing the redeployment of labour from agriculture. At present the degree of disparity between the northern and southern halves of the region is increasing. The contrast is between demographic advance north of the Loire, both by high natural increase and migrational gain, and demographic stagnation south of the Loire, where natural increase is only half as high. The population of Indre declined by

*It is significant that journalists already refer to the spectre of Orléans as 'Paris-sur-Loire'.

almost 2 per cent between 1962 and 1968, bringing the demographic characteristics of the Massif Central into the Paris Basin. This may be offered as evidence that the wave of decentralizations around Paris has as yet succeeded in pushing back the margins of the 'désert français' only as far as the Loire in the south-western Paris Basin.

REFERENCES

[1] Verrière, J., 'Réflexions sur la région dite "du Centre" ', Norois, 1968, p. 503.

[2] Babonaux, Y., Villes et régions de la Loire moyenne—Touraine, Blessois, Orléanais, fondements et perspectives géographiques, 1966, Paris, SABRI.

[3] Babonaux, Y., 'Tours' in L'Urbanisation Française, p. 49, 1964, Paris, Centre de Recherche d'Urbanisme.

[4] Estienne, P., and Joly, R., La Région du Centre, p. 145, 1961, Paris, Presses Universitaires de France.

[5] Babonaux, Y., 'Chronique Ligérienne', Norois, 1967, p. 329.

[6] Babonaux, Y., op. cit.[5], p. 331.

[7] Chabot, G., Géographie Régionale de la France, p. 328, 1966, Paris, Masson.

[8] Wolkowitsch, M., 'Essai sur les catégories sociales à la campagne, en Berry', Norois, 1954, p. 429.

[9] Dubois, R., 'L'expansion de Vierzon', Annls Géogr., 1966, p. 675.

[10] Babonaux, Y., op. cit.[5], p. 339.

[11] Gravier, J., L'Aménagement du Territoire et l'Avenir des Régions Françaises, pp. 219–220, 1964, Paris, Flammarion.

[12] Gravier, J., La Vie Française—Economies Régionales, Spring 1965, 'Le Berry', p. 35.

24

Basse-Normandie

In almost every geographical sense Basse-Normandie is a region of transition between the eastern and western provinces of France. Within the confines of the region occur the changes in physical landscape, dominant land use, agricultural economy and urban and economic organization which differentiate the developed regions of the east from the less developed regions of the west and centre.

A basic distinction exists between the western two thirds of the region, comprised by the western margin of the Armorican Massif, and the eastern third where the crystalline rocks disappear beneath the limestones and clays of the Jurassic and the chalk plateau of the Cretaceous. Structural and hydrographic differences permit a further division of the Armorican section into the northward-jutting Cotentin peninsula and the east–west orientated and more elevated Bocage Normand. Throughout the Armorican section, livestock farming is supreme. This reaches its highest intensity in the Cotentin peninsula, largely coincident with the département of Manche. Manche has by far the largest cattle population of any département; the total of 666,000 greatly exceeds the human population. Production of milk is largely for butter, the skimmed milk being used for pig fattening. Cooperative processing and marketing is highly developed and the production of butter, cheese and milk powder is the only industrial activity widespread in the Cotentin. The relief of the Bocage Normand is more tormented and carries a higher proportion of woodland, but the emphasis on dairy farming is equally profound. The success of the dairy industry is in part related to a propitious climate, which permits outdoor grazing all year in Cotentin, in part to cooperative organization, but in part also to the qualities of the 'Normande' breed of dairy cattle.[1]

Urban development in the Armorican section is extremely limited. The most characteristic settlements are small market centres, such as Coutances, St. Lô, Avranches and Vire, which have lost their former importance as local industrial centres making textiles and hardware. Separate from this pattern, and in fact little related to the general regional economy, are the towns of Granville and Cherbourg. Cherbourg, the centre of an agglomeration of 72,000 inhabitants in 1968, owed its growth to factors which are no longer of great importance. Built as a military port, furnished with an arsenal, and later equipped as a transatlantic port of call, the port has no sub-

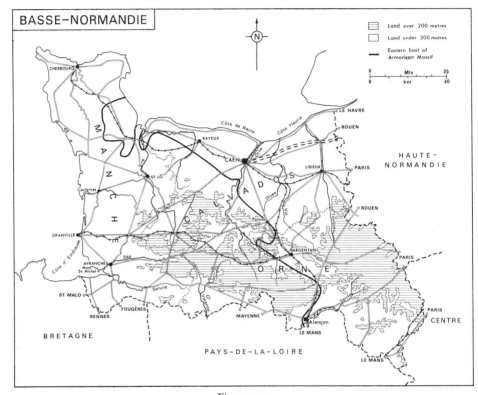

Figure 24.1

stantial hinterland and has gradually lost its raison d'être. Reduced activity in the arsenal, the retirement of large vessels which habitually used the port and the superior location and facilities of Le Havre have combined to diminish the maritime functions on which the port was based. The expansion of the trawling fleet and the creation of car ferry links with Southampton have brought some relief, while the attraction of new industries has broken the rigid dependence on the port. The needs of the agricultural hinterland are reflected in the growth of the manufacture of farming machinery and the release of skilled labour from the arsenal has been absorbed in a general growth of engineering.[2] At the other extremity of the peninsula, Granville has food processing industries, a small fishing fleet and boat connections with the Channel Islands, but its recent growth is more closely connected with the rise of tourism.

The resources of Armorican Basse-Normandie dictate an agricultural economy but industrial resources are not entirely lacking; iron ore deposits occur within the Bocage Normand. In recent years these deposits have provided approximately five per cent of the total national production, and have an iron content of between 37 and 45 per cent. In 1965 six mines were active, of which those of Soumont, Halouze and La Ferrière were the most productive. The mines of Soumont are linked directly to the steelworks at Caen, 25 kilometres distant, which own the concession. The output of the Normandy fields exceeds the absorptive capacity of the Caen steelworks and overseas exports have always been important. It is the decline of overseas sales in competition with cheaper foreign ores which explains the general reduction in output. Less than one third of the ore is now exported and almost one half is consumed by the Caen steelworks. The number employed in mining has declined steadily and now totals approximately 1,500.[3]

The eastern third of Basse-Normandie may also be divided into two sub-units. At the contact with the Armorican Massif, the Jurassic limestones and clays give rise to a discontinuous depression formed successively by the plains of Caen, Argentan and Alençon. To the east, a cuesta in the Cretaceous produces the Pays d'Auge, a chalk plateau bordering Haute-Normandie. The plain of Caen is distinguished by its fertile 'limon' soils and an intensive mixed farming economy prevails with a higher arable proportion than elsewhere in the region. The Plain of Caen is prolonged in the upper reaches of the Orne by the Plain of Argentan. At a nexus of road and rail communications, the town of Argentan has gained new impetus from the arrival of a number of small decentralized firms.[4] Alençon occupies a similar position in the Sarthe valley and developed as a centre of marketing and exchange with the Armorican section of the region. To the east of the Dives, the arable farming of the Jurassic plains gives way to the pastoral economy of the Pays d'Auge. The landscape is characterized by a dense bocage in which the average farm size is large as a result of the acquisition of land by dairy processing industries, horse breeders and meat wholesaling companies. The dairy industry is orientated towards cheese production, especially Camembert and Pont-l'Evêque. The resemblance with the Armorican bocage is superficial, for the greater farm size, the direct participation of processing firms in agriculture and the orientation towards the Paris market elevate the quality of farming.

THE REGIONAL ECONOMY

The modest declines in the total rural population of 3·8 per cent between

1954 and 1962 conceal a much higher rate of contraction in the employment level in the agricultural sector. The proportionate resistance of the rural population as a whole to decline is accounted for principally by the practice of commuting to urban centres and to the employment offered by building activity, formerly in war-devastated towns and currently in connection with the tourist industry. Faced with a continuing decline in the primary sector as a whole, the regional economy must increasingly hinge on two growth sectors: new industrial development and the expansion of tourism.

Thus far the growth of industry has been centred on the extraordinary rise of Caen since its heavy war-time destruction. Before the war the economy of Caen rested on the steelworks at Mondeville, the activities of a small port, and a collection of small-scale processing industries and tertiary services supporting a population of slightly more than 60,000 inhabitants in 1936. At the present time Caen is the centre of an agglomeration of 152,000 inhabitants and an urban-industrial region of over 200,000 inhabitants.[5] Between 1962 and 1968 the agglomeration grew by 25·8 per cent and experienced a 16·6 per cent gain by migration. This spectacular growth, without parallel in north-western France, results from the rapid evolution of Caen from being a sub-regional centre with a heavy dependence on the steel industry to a status as a minor-regional capital and the centre of a complex of modern growth industries. The steelworks at Mondeville, to the east of Caen, are still very active and give employment to approximately 5,000 workers. Owned by the Société Métallurgique de Normandie, the works produce over 600,000 tons of steel per annum and support by-product activities as chemical and cement works. Improvements in the Ouistreham Canal allow coal carriers of 15,000 tons to discharge at the works, and exports of iron ore and steel goods maintain a reasonable balance between import and export tonnages. Moreover, the industrial expansion of Caen is more particularly related to the arrival of major decentralized firms such as SAVIEM, manufacturing car components, Radiotechnique, making semi-conductors, and other firms in the spheres of electronics and engineering. The success of Caen in this respect may be attributed to a wide range of factors seldom found in a single location. The rebuilding of the town with new residential areas, industrial zones and public amenities, the improvement of the port, the creation of a new university, good road and rail connections and access to pleasant beaches, were all factors in the attraction of major firms. Caen, which began life as a collection of villages,[6] still has a fragmented urban organization in which a number of satellite settlements line the Ouistreham canal and the coastal resorts are increasingly serving as dormitory settlements.[7] The eventual construction of the Normandy motorway to Caen will

strengthen the attraction of the town and tie its development still closer
to the urban-industrial complex of the Basse-Seine and the Paris Basin.

Commensurate with this industrial expansion, the commercial functions
of Caen have grown and it now dominates the urban hierarchy of Basse-
Normandie.[8] The second largest town, Cherbourg, has too peripheral a
location to serve as an effective intermediary. There is thus the possibility
of a distorted pattern of regional development in which Caen could become
increasingly congested while the smaller towns of the hierarchy undergo
a diminution of their importance. Gravier[9] has drawn attention to the
tendency of the towns of Basse-Normandie to be grouped in pairs with
short intervening distances; for example, Alençon–Argentan, Avranches–
Granville, Saint Lô–Coutances. By appropriate implantation of industries,
these could be promoted as secondary axes of development, capable of
absorbing rural migrants and with an improved service provision.

The tourist industry of Basse-Normandie is of long standing, being the
subject of a deliberate launching in the latter half of the nineteenth century.
Conceived initially as watering places for a wealthy and cosmopolitan
clientèle, the resorts of Deauville and Trouville, situated closest to Paris,
were the first to develop. Since the Second World War, tourism has
developed intensively along the littoral between Honfleur and Courseulles,
but the character of the industry has changed. Villas, rented apartments,
camp sites and secondary homes have replaced the fashionable industry
based on high-quality hotels. A distinction may be made between the
'Côte Fleurie', containing the original centres and backed by a pleasant
hinterland in the Pays d'Auge, and the 'Côte de Nacre', west of the mouth
of the Orne, of more recent expansion. Here camping and nautical sports
are the principal attractions together with the historical and architectural
interest of Bayeux. The Armorican coastline may also be divided into two
contrasted sections. The northern portion of Cotentin, from St. Vaast-le-
Hague to Carteret, has a cliff coastline with few extensive beaches. South
of Carteret to Granville, dune belts fringe the coast giving rise to camping
and holiday villages, and at the extreme limit of the region Mt. St. Michel
is one of the most visited tourist sites in France.

The tourist industry has been intensively studied in terms of its growth[10]
and the character of its infrastructure.[11] As a lever for economic growth
the region possesses both assets and disadvantages. The proximity to Paris,
the existence of underdeveloped coastal sites and the popularity of the
region for the construction of secondary homes by residents of both Paris
and Caen are important assets. Similarly, the car ferry connection with
Southampton via Cherbourg has strengthened the attraction of the western
coast of Cotentin for British tourists, principally on a transient basis en
route to destinations in Brittany or further south. The main disadvantage

is the short duration of the holiday season and the problem of equating expensive infrastructure developments against low utilization rates outside the months of July and August.

The region of Basse-Normandie remains a marchland between eastern and western France. This condition is by no means of necessity a permanent one. The expansion of Caen, the success of the smaller centres in attracting light industry, the projected Paris–Caen motorway, the functions as a provider of livestock produce to Paris and as a tourist and recreational zone for the urban population of Paris and the Basse-Seine are all factors pointing to a closer integration with the regions located to the east. The possibility of a future amalgamation of Haute and Basse-Normandie as a single planning unit has thus a certain logical geographical basis.

REFERENCES

[1] Musset, R., *La Normandie*, p. 184, 1960, Paris, Armand Colin.

[2] Seronde, A., 'L'agglomération Cherbourgeoise', *Norois*, 1967, p. 158.

[3] Brunet, P., 'Déclin des mines de fer normandes', *Norois*, 1963, p. 461.

[4] Frémont, A., Ambrois, M., and Chesnais, M., 'Argentan rénovée par la décentralisation industrielle', *Norois*, 1964, p. 419.

[5] Escourrou, G., 'La ville de Caen', *Inf. géogr.*, 1966, p. 150.

[6] Musset, R., *op. cit.*, p. 161.

[7] Brier, M., 'Un canton en crise, le canton de Douvres-la-Déliverande, Calvados', *Norois*, 1967, p. 290.

[8] *Atlas de Normandie*, Plate G11, 1966, Caen, Association Pour l'Atlas de Normandie.

[9] Gravier, J., *L'Aménagement du Territoire et l'Avenir des Régions Françaises*, p. 319, 1964, Paris, Flammarion.

[10] Clary, D., 'La fréquentation touristique sur la côte normande (1963, 1964, 1965) par la méthode de la variation de consommation de farine', *Norois*, 1967, p. 473.

[11] *Atlas de Normandie*, Plate G6, 1966, Caen, Association Pour l'Atlas de Normandie.

25

Bretagne

At once both a peripheral and a terminal region* Brittany has remained apart from the mainstream of economic trends, preserving a specific cultural and social identity. Eccentric location, internal isolation, the absence of indigenous energy resources and remoteness from the hearths of both the industrial and agricultural revolutions, combined to retard the economic evolution of Brittany, promoting a large-scale exodus of population. The retarded economic structure and loss of population are the central problems of the region's life and have been symbolized in the evocative phrase 'le mal Breton'.[1] The theme of this essay is thus a diagnosis of the 'mal Breton' in terms of its manifestations and the efforts made to effect a cure.

The problems of Brittany must be set against a basic duality in the region's internal structure, between the littoral and the interior. The high population densities (commonly over 100 per square kilometre) of the littoral, reflect a favourable combination of resources not present in the interior. Temperate climatic conditions combined with light 'limon' soils have permitted the development of 'primeur' cultivation on the northern littoral. Fishing has since antiquity afforded a supplement to agriculture, while more recently tourism has provided both a source of revenue and seasonal employment. The combination of land and marine resources has endowed the littoral with a privileged position vis-à-vis the interior expressed in the term 'ceinture dorée'. In particular, the more intense activity of the littoral has fostered urban development; a double chain of towns corresponding with locations at the mouths and heads of the rias. *Figure 25.2*, illustrating the functional zones of the St. Malo agglomeration, demonstrates the diversified economic base of the coastal zone, producing a mixture of port, tourist, commercial and industrial land uses.[2]

The economy of interior Brittany rests more exclusively on agricultural foundations and on a polyculture basis. A distinction must be made

*A characteristic intensified with the advent of the Common Market.

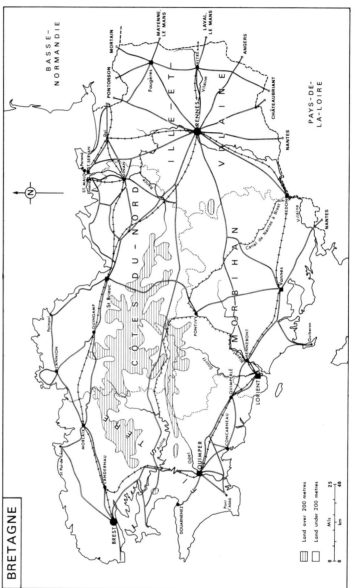

Figure 25.1

between the western and central basins, where isolation is more pronounced and technical evolution less advanced, and the eastern basin, that of Rennes. Less isolated from external influences, favoured by deep soils and possessing a strong urban focus, the basin of Rennes is a progressive farming region, in which cereal and fodder crops support veal, pig and dairy farming.

To the fundamental contrast between the coastal zone and the interior

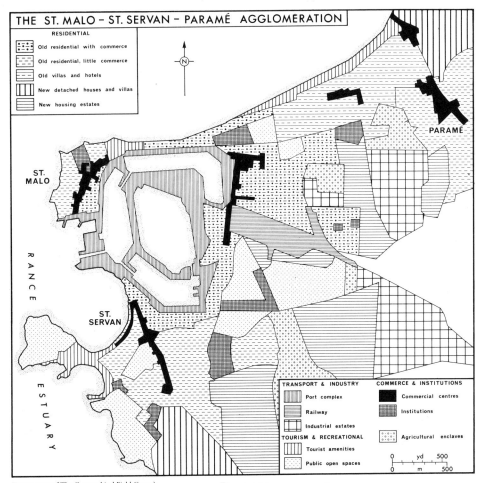

(By courtesy of The Geographical Field Group) *Figure 25.2*

must be added the further contrast between eastern Brittany, 'Haute-Bretagne' and western Brittany, 'Basse-Bretagne'. Haute-Bretagne benefits from contact with adjacent regions, relative ease of communications and possesses in Rennes an agglomeration of over 190,000 inhabitants (in 1968). By contrast, Basse-Bretagne is physically more remote, contains a higher proportion of broken relief, is weakly integrated by communications and is an area of endemic depopulation. The diagnosis of the 'mal Breton' must take into account these important variations in conditions within the region.

THE ELEMENTS OF THE 'MAL BRETON'

The overriding symptom of the 'mal Breton' is the exodus of population which has been likened to a haemorrhage of its human resources. No single reason underlies this exodus, but rather a number of elements which collectively depress the quality of living and opportunity in the region. The most obvious manifestation of underdevelopment is the high agricultural dependence and the retarded structure of farming. In 1962, the proportion of the total population dependent on agriculture was 34·3 per cent, compared with a national figure of 16·1 per cent. The overwhelming characteristic of Breton farming is its basis in polyculture, the small size of average holding, the high degree of fragmentation and the generally low level of technical evolution. The average farm size, of 11·8 hectares, is characteristically a family-operated tenanted farm, producing cereals, fodder crops and vegetables, and supporting a small number of cattle and pigs. This insistence on a variety of production stems from inherited traditions of self-sufficiency but accords ill with efficient modern commercial production. With the exception of the 'limons', the soils of Brittany are not of first quality, but given the addition of lime and artificial fertilizers high yields are obtainable, and climatic conditions give Brittany a natural vocation for animal farming. The fundamental problem of farming is not lack of production* but a low level of remuneration. The need is to replace polyculture with more specialized production attuned to marketing conditions, and the adoption of modern methods to reduce production costs. In turn, increased specialization is dependent on an increase in farm size and consolidation to permit rational investment. The technical backwardness of much of Breton farming stems from the lateness and incompleteness of the agricultural revolution,[4] the existence of abundant manual labour, the stultifying effect of fragmented and small holdings, and the lack of capital formation to finance greater recourse to machinery and fertilizers. The practical consequence is that Breton farming is overmanned, and returns per capita in a system poorly related to commercial realities are commensurately low. Rural exodus has resulted from the inability of the polyculture system to create sufficient employment to absorb the product of high fertility levels, and, above all,

*Phlipponneau estimates that Brittany contributes approximately 8 per cent of the gross agricultural product, with only 6·4 per cent of the national land area.[3]

to guarantee an adequate level of remuneration.

The problem of an inert agricultural system coupled with a dynamic demographic background implies the necessity for compensating industrial activity to absorb excess rural population. Herein lies the second element of the 'mal Breton', for just as only the echoes of the agricultural revolution reached Brittany, so the industrial revolution virtually by-passed the region. Brittany by no means lacked nineteenth-century industrial activity—a plethora of small-scale artisan and craft industries, now in the process of extinction, animated the countryside—but conditions were not propitious for the establishment of large industries. The high cost of imported fuels, the weak infrastructure of communications, the lack of internal capital, the absence of raw materials and the absence of strong industrial traditions minimized the impact of the processes which transformed the economy of Paris and north-eastern France. In these conditions heavy industry could not develop, beyond token representation in the naval arsenals of Brest and Lorient and the small steelworks of Hennebont★ and St. Brieuc.[5] Industry remained dispersed, small-scale and concerned chiefly textiles, clothing and the processing of agricultural, fish and forestry products. In a region with 2·4 million inhabitants in 1962, manufacturing industry employed only 130,770 workers, and as a result of the decline of small firms, the number of manufacturing jobs decreased between 1954 and 1962 by 2,000, while the total population increased by approximately 50,000. In 1962, of a total of 23,300 industrial firms only approximately 350 employed more than 50 workers, and by 1966 the average firm size was only 5·4 employees.[6]

The failure of Brittany to industrialize has suppressed urban development; in 1962 the population was almost 60 per cent rural by residence, and only Finistère, dominated by Brest, had a majority of urban population, while Côtes-du-Nord was 75 per cent rural. Le Guen[7] has demonstrated that interior Brittany is virtually devoid of industrial towns, the north coast lacks towns of predominantly industrial character, and only the southern coastal towns possess some degree of industrial dependence. Given the lack of an industrial impetus to urban growth[8] the towns of Brittany have proved incapable of absorbing the surplus population of the countryside and have been but stepping stones on the route to emigration out of the region for the majority of rural migrants.

To the combination of an overpopulated farming sector, an under-developed industrial sector and restrained urban growth, must be added the prevalence of an unsatisfactory level of living as an expulsive factor.[9] The question of inadequate living standards is not merely a material matter, although in the farming community the level of remuneration is clearly

★Now closed.

below the average for the remainder of provincial France, but rather the poverty of opportunity in rural Brittany, the necessity to break family ties through migration, and the general atmosphere of isolation prevalent in a dispersed rural settlement pattern. In these conditions, it is the well-qualified, and especially the young, who most feel the necessity to migrate to better opportunities outside the region.

THE EXODUS FROM BRITTANY

Brittany has been traditionally a region of high fertility and the first half of the nineteenth century was marked by substantial population growth. In the course of the second half of the nineteenth century, as the scale of exodus increased so the rate of population growth decelerated, and, throughout rural Brittany, was reversed. The rate of emigration reached severe levels in the first half of the present century, over 700,000 Bretons leaving the region, but the persistence of high fertility enabled the overall total to increase at a moderate rate. However, between 1945 and 1954, when the French population as a whole increased at a very high rate, that of Brittany remained virtually stable. Since 1954, natural increase has been maintained at a level close to the national average but migration has remained unabated.[10,11] While natural increase yielded a net gain of approximately 120,000 in the regional population between 1954 and 1962, a migrational deficit of over 85,000 was recorded. Le Guen[12] has demonstrated that this under-represents the true scale of depopulation in Brittany. The net loss of 85,000 migrants resulted from 200,000 emigrants and approximately 110,000 immigrants. In the former category must be placed a very high proportion of young persons, while the return current of migration consists largely of older and retired persons, many of them being Breton by birth. In terms of productive forces, the migrational loss experienced by Brittany thus exceeds the arithmetical difference between

Table 25.1

MIGRATION BETWEEN BRITTANY AND THE PARIS REGION, 1954–1962

Direction	Under 35 years		Over 55 years	
	Number	Per cent	Number	Per cent
Brittany–Paris	80,680	84	4,420	4·6
Paris–Brittany	18,820	52	9,580	26·0
Balance to Brittany	−61,860	–	+5,160	–

Source: Le Guen, G., op. cit.[12]

arrivals and departures. This unfavourable interchange is particularly the case of the dominant flow of migration, between Brittany and Paris★ (*Table 25.1*).

Secondly, the total migration loss of 85,000 gives an inadequate impression of the scale of rural depopulation. Taking into account rural–urban migration within Brittany, the loss of rural population between 1954 and 1962 amounted to over 200,000. The drift to the towns is very unevenly distributed, only Rennes, Brest and Lorient having absorbed large numbers of rural migrants.

During the course of a century of emigration, the demographic structure of Brittany has been profoundly modified. No longer can rural Brittany be portrayed as the most fertile and youthful population in the nation. Age-selective migration, reduced fertility, a distorted sex ratio and high mortality rates have combined to reduce the level of natural increase.[13] The regional value of 5·3 per cent for the period 1954–1962 compares with a national average of 5·6 per cent, while the département of Côtes-du-Nord, worst affected by depopulation, experienced a natural growth of only 4·0 per cent.

The 'mal Breton' has thus been diagnosed as a complex ailment, combining retarded farm structures and unprofitable forms of agricultural production with stagnation in industrial growth, in which the creation of new development has been exceeded by the closure of existing firms. As a consequence Brittany exports her youth, emptying her rural areas, and receives in return principally retired persons, thus heightening the desolation of interior Brittany and markedly reducing the level of the activity rate. It must not be assumed that the Bretons have passively accepted this situation, but rather has increasing awareness of the underdeveloped state of the region stimulated an effort to revive the economy.

THE REVIVAL OF BRITTANY

Brittany has been a pioneer in the field of regional planning, largely due to the spontaneous development within the region of groups of professional people and public servants devoted to the task of reviving the economy. This movement culminated in 1949 with the constitution of the 'Comité d'Etude et de Liaison des Intérêts Bretons' (CELIB), designed to coordinate efforts within the region and to exert pressure for government aid. In 1955, the CELIB was recognized by the government as a regional expansion committee and was instrumental in Brittany being the first

★The Paris region absorbed 47 per cent of all Breton emigrants between 1954 and 1962. In 1962 350,000 persons resident in Paris were born in Brittany.

region to secure a 'Programme d'Action Régionale', in 1956.[14]

Since 1964 the internal impetus for development has also been expressed through the CODER,* headed by the regional prefect, which produced its first report in 1965.[15] This report proposed the objective of a reduction in the level of emigration by one third by 1970, leading to a stabilization of the labour force and a 3 per cent increase in the total population over the 1962 level. The report anticipates that structural reform and an increased concentration on livestock will reduce the agricultural labour force by almost 100,000, or 25 per cent, during the course of the period from 1962 to 1970. As a consequence, non-agricultural employment must expand from 574,000 in 1962 to 665,000 by 1970 if successful redeployment is to be achieved and the desired one third reduction in emigration obtained. Taking into account anticipated closures, a net increase of 35,000 jobs must be created in the secondary sector between 1965 and 1970, including 17,000 in manufacturing industry. The attempt to revive the economy of Brittany must be measured against these planned aspirations expressed by the region's own representatives.

Of all the objectives proposed by the CELIB and endorsed by the CODER, that of raising the level of industrial development appears the most difficult to attain. In favour of the movement of industrialization is the allocation of the maximum government assistance, the existence of an abundant, if largely unskilled, labour supply, and an improvement in the provision of energy.[16] The latter has been achieved by the construction of the Rennes refinery, the Rance tidal power scheme,[17] the arrival at Lorient and Rennes of Lacq natural gas and the construction of a nuclear power station at Brennilis†. On the other hand, the severe deficiencies of the transport infrastructure, the high cost of energy resulting from protective limits on coal imports, and the distance from markets, are disincentives to industrial development, especially in interior and western Brittany.

Table 25.2

THE GROWTH OF NEW INDUSTRIAL EMPLOYMENT IN BRITTANY, 1956–1965

	1956–1960	1961	1962	1963	1964	1965
New employment[a]	9,314	7,749	2,864	3,325	1,090	1,341
Employment created with state assistance[b]	10,386	1,947	3,640	5,648	3,127	3,091
Number of decentralizations	44	45	37	57	39	28

[a]Total employment created in new firms of over 10 workers.
[b]Total employment created at the end of decentralization operations.
Source: Op. cit?, p. 85.

*Commission de Développement Economique Régional.
†This is still an experimental reactor.

Adequate statistics concerning the growth of industrial employment are unavailable, but figures are available for new firms of over 10 employees and also for employment created with the help of government funds.

Table 25.2 gives a superficially encouraging picture of over 25,000 new jobs created, including 250 industrial decentralizations benefiting from state assistance. This progress must be qualified by three further observations. The pace of new industrial growth, quite rapid until 1963, has since progressed at a slower rate. Secondly, in large measure new industrial growth has been offset by a decline of established activities, amounting to a loss of 15,000 jobs between 1954 and 1966. Finally, the growth of new industry has been unevenly distributed, affecting especially the accessible portion of Brittany east of a line from St. Malo and Rennes to Lorient.*

While the total level of new industrial employment created falls short of planning targets, certain positive advances have been achieved. The Rennes Citroën plant, creating 8,000 jobs between 1962 and 1968, has given Brittany its first large-scale plant and has been followed by other automobile component decentralizations in the form of Renault at Lorient and Michelin at Vannes. Secondly, the success of the Citroën operation, the nomination of Rennes as a centre of electronic research and the creation of subsidized industrial estates have made Rennes a strong growth pole for industry†.[18] Thirdly, Brittany has acquired a substantial number of light industries, especially in electronics and clothing, which have increased the level of employment in skilled branches and also the participation rate of females in industry. Finally, the strong growth of the food processing industry has brought new employment to several of the smaller towns of eastern and southern Brittany.

The evolution of agriculture during the last decade contains both elements of progress and of unsolved problems. Most progress has been made in modernization leading to increased output and productivity. Although in 1965 only one farm in three owned a tractor, the number of collective machinery organizations (CUMA) has increased from 183 in 1960 to 926 in 1966. Similarly, the use of fertilizers has tripled since 1954 and attained a level equal to the national average. Production of fodder crops and animal products exceeded the national growth rate and an increased proportion of the agricultural output is processed within the region.

The exodus of agricultural workers has continued but has not led to any important reduction in the number of farms or increase in average farm size. Rural exodus has merely removed surplus population without

*Between 1958 and 1967 of over 21,000 jobs created by government aid almost 14,000 were located east of the St. Malo–Rennes–Lorient line.

†In addition to Citroën, Rhône-Poulenc, Kodak and Fairchild have established large factories or laboratories at Rennes and a military electronics research centre is planned.

facilitating major structural reform. The retirement of older farmers under the FASASA arrangements has freed 2 per cent of the agricultural land surface, but taking into account the existence of over 170,000 farms with an average size of only 11·8 hectares, this gives little possibility of increasing farm size on a significant scale. The same problem confronts the region's SAFER organization, which, although controlling 10 per cent of land transactions, had only acquired 9,000 hectares for redistribution by the end of 1965. Progress in remembrement has been slow and irregular, a major difficulty being the high cost of clearing hedgerows and road and drain building in the dominant pattern of dense bocage. By 1965, 188,000 hectares had been consolidated or were in course of consolidation, of which over 105,000 hectares was located in Morbihan,* but the area requiring remembrement exceeds one million hectares. In spite of considerable progress, especially in rural electrification, the condition of the rural habitat remains the worst in France. In 1966, less than half of the rural communes were supplied with running water, almost half of the rural dwellings suffered from serious overcrowding and less than 10 per cent had bathrooms.

While not underestimating the assistance rendered by government and official agencies, much of the progress achieved by Breton farming may be attributed to initiative on the part of the farming community, especially in the form of collective mechanization and cooperative marketing. Brittany has demonstrated its capacity to raise output, but unaccompanied by structural reform, improved marketing and more rigorous specialization this has been insufficient to raise income levels within existing price structures. Public manifestation of this frustration has taken extreme and often spectacular forms over recent years.[19]

If the future of the region depends on the striking of a new balance between agriculture and industry, the complementary role of tourism must nevertheless be expanded. The tourist industry currently yields over 5 per cent of the region's revenue and the CODER plan calls for a doubling of the volume of tourism in the decade 1960 to 1970†. It is considered that yachting will form the basis for the expansion of tourism and considerable investment is necessary to provide appropriate facilities, especially on the northern coast. The major problem is to extend the length of the season and to reduce the present disparity between the littoral and the interior‡. The recent designation of a regional park may aid both problems by attracting tourists to interior Finistère and creating a weekend recreational

---

*At the end of 1967 remembrement had been completed in 174 communes, of which 70 were in Morbihan.

†Rather more than two million tourists per annum visit Britanny, spending 70 million tourist-days—approximately 10 per cent of the national total.

‡Tourist activity is concentrated to the extent of 80 per cent on the littoral.

zone for the population of Brest. The expansion of tourism is unlikely to make a far-reaching impact on the fundamental disequilibrium of the Breton economy. The employment created is highly seasonal and the chief benefits are felt indirectly, through the stimulus to the construction industry and the revenue derived from general tourist spending.

PERSPECTIVES

The determined attempt to revive the Breton economy has now been in force for more than a decade. It cannot be claimed that the basic problem has been more than slightly modified. At first sight the provisional figures of the 1968 census appear favourable in that migration loss has been cut from 11,000 per annum between 1954 and 1962, to 2,000 per annum between 1962 and 1968, a performance which exceeds the target established by the CODER.

Table 25.3

POPULATION CHANGE IN BRETAGNE, 1962–1968

	Total change	Rate of change (per cent)	Natural increase (per cent)	Net migration (per cent)
Côtes-du-Nord	4,179	0·8	2·3	−1·6
Finistère	19,371	2·6	3·0	−0·5
Ille-et-Vilaine	38,454	6·3	4·9	1·4
Morbihan	9,641	1·8	3·6	−1·8
Bretagne	71,645	3·0	3·4	−0·5

Source: Recensement de 1968, Premiers Résultats.

Table 25.3 indicates that the total growth, which occurred at less than half the national rate of increase, was largely a function of the rapid expansion of Ille-et-Vilaine, in turn related in large measure to the growth of the Rennes agglomeration. Elsewhere the population growth was extremely low, although the decrease in migration is a positive advance.

Certain encouraging developments must be acknowledged, especially in the industrial sector. The region has acquired a number of advanced technology industries theoretically capable of exercising a multiplier effect, especially in the electronics and automobile branches. The arrival of these firms has stimulated not only the largest towns, Rennes and Brest, but also some of the smaller centres as Vannes, Redon, Fougères and Lannion. Based on the decentralized Telecommunications Research Centre at Lannion, and supported by the universities of Rennes and Brest, the electronics industry has made remarkable progress in Brittany, the characteristics of this branch making it less inhibited by the region's lack of raw materials and peripheral location.

On the other hand, certain priority needs are as yet unfulfilled. In particular, the transport infrastructure remains skeletal, consisting of the north and south coastal axes which are only weakly interlinked[20] The conversion of the coast roads to dual carriageway and the improvement of roads in central Brittany by 1975 are recognized as being vital to expand industry and tourism. Secondly, the need to expand Brest as a counter-balance to Rennes is desirable, and could be based on its geographical location in relation to sea routes and the deep water characteristics of its port. Dry docking facilities for vessels of up to 200,000 tons are under construction and plans exist for an oil terminal for super-tankers and the creation of a refinery of at least three million tons capacity. Brest also benefits from government aid for tertiary decentralizations previously limited to Rennes.

The revival of the economy of the northern coast is also a matter of priority, especially in view of the excessive rates of depopulation of the Côtes-du-Nord. Funds have recently been granted to improve yachting facilities, to enlarge the port of Roscoff in order to promote the export of vegetables to Britain, and to stimulate industrial growth at St. Brieuc.

Finally, the trend towards greater specialization in agricultural production must be reinforced if agricultural income is to increase. This involves specialization not only in the type of production but also in the methods of farming, with greater emphasis placed on animal selection, rational feeding and greater integration with the food processing industry. This, more scientific, specialization must be accompanied by an adjustment of farm structures to meet the rigorous demands of competitive commercial production[21]

Above all Brittany needs to transform its image as an exporter of population and an economic backwater. On the one hand the region must seek to establish itself as the 'Denmark' of France, in terms of realizing its potential in animal farming and food processing; on the other hand, industry must be seen to be successful in Brittany as a viable location rather than as a result of government subsidization.

By virtue of its privileged communications, its expanding university and applied research institutions, Rennes is now established as a strong growth pole,[22] joining Le Mans, Angers and Nantes in a quadrilateral of active industrial centres. The task during the next decade must be to expand westwards from this bridgehead.

REFERENCES

[1] Pleven, R., *L'Avenir de la Bretagne*, p. 19, 1961, Paris, Calmann-Lévy.

[2] Thompson, I., 'The St. Malo Region, Brittany', pp. 83–93, *Geogr. Field Group Stud.*, No. 12, 1968.

[3] Phlipponneau, M., 'La Bretagne, une expérience de rénovation régionale', *Tendances*, No. 22, 1963, pp. 171–19.

[4] Le Lannou, M., *Géographie de la Bretagne*, Tome 2, pp. 23–70, 1952, Rennes, Plihon.

[5] Simon, M., 'Les fonctions industrielles de St. Brieuc', *Norois*, 1965, pp. 450–2.

[6] 'L'Economie de la Bretagne', *Notes Etud. docum.*, No. 3,502–3,503, 1968, p. 65.

[7] Le Guen, G., 'Les structures sociales et économiques des villes bretonnes', *Norois*, 1961, p. 429.

[8] 'Etudes d'économie urbaine', *Bull. Conjonct. rég.*, Rennes, 1966, No. 4.

[9] Anon., 'Le revenu et le niveau de vie', *Grandes Enquêtes*, No. 16–17, 1966, p. 45.

[10] Le Guen, G., 'Les migrations bretonnes récentes—1954–1962', *Norois*, 1965, p. 277.

[11] Le Guen, G., 'L'évolution récente de la population en Bretagne', *Norois*, 1964, p. 17.

[12] Le Guen, G., 'Les migrations bretonnes', *Econ. Cult.*, Rennes, 1967, p. 57.

[13] Anon., 'Le problème breton', *op. cit?*, pp. 34–39.

[14] Phlipponneau, M., *Le problème breton et le programme d'action regionale*, 1957, Paris, Armand Colin.

[15] 'La Bretagne et le Ve Plan', *Vie bretonne*, No. 87–88, 1965.

[16] Gautier, M., 'L'énergie dans la région de programme dite de Bretagne', *Norois*, 1968, p. 253.

[17] Jones, I., 'The Rance tidal power station', *Geography*, 1968, p. 412.

[18] Meynier, A., and Le Guen, M., 'Rennes', *Notes Etud. docum.*, No. 3,257, 1966, pp. 16–19.

[19] Gervais, M., Servolin, C., and Weil, J., *Une France sans Paysans*, pp. 6–7, 1965, Paris, Seuil.

[20] Bertrand, Y., *Le rôle des transports terrestres dans le développement économique de la Bretagne*, Centre Régional d'Etudes et de Formation Economique, Rennes, 1966.

[21] Henry, J., 'Quelques aspects des structures agraires en Bretagne', *Norois*, 1968, p. 79.

[22] Anon., 'Rennes, métropole de recherche', *Usine nouv.*, September, 1968, p. 161.

26

Pays-de-la-Loire

The Pays-de-la-Loire is one of the least integrated and inappropriately named of the planning regions. Lacking in economic articulation and geographical identity, the region is essentially a broad zone of transition in which the attenuated margins of more distinctive surrounding regions merge, often imperceptibly. The Loire valley is not an economic spine integrating the region, nor does Nantes dominate the social and economic organizations of the entire region. While escaping the problems of chronic underdevelopment, the region suffers from an arrested development and a failure to gain the maximum advantage from its human and material resources.

THE RESOURCE BASE

The material resources of the Pays-de-la-Loire are by no means the most meagre of western France, but their maximum exploitation has been impeded by factors of geographical location and by deficiencies of the infrastructure and organization of economic activity. Land resources are capable of supporting a high level of production; although having only limited areas of first-quality soil, the region has little marginal or totally negative land. The proportion of abandoned and fallow land is the lowest in western France. Climatic conditions must also be considered as being favourable for agriculture. North of the Loire, rainfall totals are slightly below those of Brittany but are adequate to support a luxuriant pasture growth. In the Vendée, however, the dryness and heat of the summer arrests grass growth by up to 40 days. The region enjoys the advantage of an extended thermal growing season as compared with the regions to the north and the introduction of the vine into the crop range. The horti-cultural zone of the Val d'Anjou benefits particularly from early springs, giving a slight advantage over Brittany for the marketing of early vegetables. Given an adequate level of artificial fertilization, even the areas reputedly hostile to agriculture can be made to produce high yields in the context of animal farming, supported by permanent pasture, rotational grasses and fodder crops. The basic problems of farming concern organization rather than the environmental setting. However, the full exploitation of the region's land resources is dependent on processes which will inevitably reduce employment opportunities in agriculture. The substitution of a

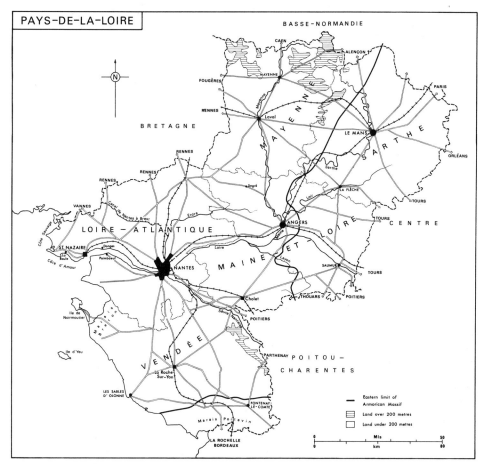

Figure 26.1

capital-intensive farming to replace the traditional labour-intensive system is a prerequisite of the maximum use of the region's agricultural resources.

In the increasingly important sphere of tourism, the resource base is uneven both in quality and distribution. The region is lacking throughout much of its extent in scenic attraction and the tourist industry is overwhelmingly concentrated at the coast. The climate endows the coastal region with certain advantages over northern Brittany and the Normandy coast; particularly the higher temperature and more reliable weather of the summer months. The southern exposure of the 'Côte d'Amour' and the extensive beaches of the Vendée coast are other specific advantages.

It is in the sphere of industrial resources that the Pays-de-la-Loire reveals severe deficiencies. The region has no indigenous power resources and although the enlargement of the Donges petroleum refinery and the pipeline connection to the Lacq gas field now give access to energy sources, the region lacked this impetus to industrialization in the past. Substantial industrial development in the nineteenth and early twentieth centuries occurred only on the Loire estuary, where access to imported coal and waterborne raw materials was possible. Elsewhere manufacturing was limited to the processing of agricultural produce and to craft industries based on local skills and small volumes of raw materials. The recent expansion of Le Mans and Cholet, and the revival of Angers, Laval and Mayenne, reflect the modern technological revolution with its associated changes in location factors, rather than the exploitation of material resources undeveloped in the past.

The mineral wealth of the region is limited to iron, slate and uranium, none of which has given rise to the creation of important industries. The iron ore deposits occur in the Ordovician rocks of the Anjou–Bretagne field, but in spite of substantial reserves and a high iron content,* the Anjou deposits have been little exploited. The lack of local initiative, the absence of coal and the collapse of the Basse-Loire iron and steel industry at Trignac and Nantes, have been cited as factors in this failure.[1] Production of iron ore is at present restricted to the mine of Segré, in Maine-et-Loire, and the output, which has fluctuated between 200,000 and 800,000 tons per annum in recent years, is utilized by USINOR in its Nord steel plants. In view of the trend towards the coastal location of steel plants, using high-grade imported ores, it seems unlikely that the Anjou ores will play any significant economic role in the immediate future†. Slate quarrying is also located in the département of Maine-et-Loire, at Trélazé, near Angers, and at Segré. The production exceeds half the national total but employment in this activity is contracting. Low-grade uranium ores are worked at several points in the Sèvre-Nantaise valley in Vendée. They are concentrated at l'Escarpière but are otherwise of little industrial significance within the region.

The internal resource base is clearly insufficient to sustain the develop-

*The reserves in the whole of the Anjou–Bretagne field have been estimated at 450 million tons iron content; the average iron content of the ore is from 48 to 50 per cent.

†It is significant that in pressing for the location of a coastal steelworks on the Loire estuary, the Comité Régional d'Expansion makes reference to the Anjou deposits only as a supplement to imported ores.

ment of major industrial centres. The dependence on resources derived from outside the region and, to a large extent, on external markets, implies that the geographical location of the region must be evaluated as a resource. As compared with Brittany, the Pays-de-la-Loire is both nearer and more accessible to the principal markets of eastern France. In addition, the Loire port complex assures the provision of imported raw materials. Exception made of the particular case of shipbuilding, there is a tendency for the industries of the Basse-Loire to depend on raw materials from abroad, which sustain metallurgy, food processing, petroleum refining and petrochemicals. By contrast, the eastern centres, such as Le Mans, Angers, Laval and Cholet, derive their impetus from exchange within the nation and particularly with the Paris region.[*] This contrast in orientation also coincides with differences in the stage of industrial activity. Whereas the Basse-Loire has a high proportion of its industrial labour force concerned with the primary stages of processing and refining of raw materials, the other large centres, which have acquired decentralized industries, concentrate on the final assembly or precision finishing of components which have undergone the primary stages of transformation elsewhere.

The population of the Pays-de-la-Loire, 2,461,000 in 1968, is the end-product of a century of demographic stagnation. The total population has increased by less than 100,000 in the course of the last century. This lack of momentum cannot be attributed to an absence of vitality in the rate of natural increase, but rather to the depredations made by a persistent movement of population out of the region.

Table 26.1

POPULATION CHANGE IN THE PAYS-DE-LA-LOIRE, 1962–1968

	Population 1968 (thousands)	Rate of change (per cent)		Total
		Natural increase	Net migration	
Loire-Atlantique	803·4	+5·4	+1·7	+7·1
Mayenne	250·0	+4·2	−3·1	+1·1
Sarthe	443·0	+5·5	−1·2	+4·3
Maine-et-Loire	556·3	+6·2	−1·0	+5·2
Vendée	408·9	+4·6	−1·7	+2·9
Region	2,461·6	+5·4	−0·5	+4·9

Source: Recensement de 1968, Premiers Résultats.

Table 26.1 indicates that the level of natural increase exceeds the national average in all the constituent départements, but, with the exception of Loire-Atlantique, this was offset by migrational losses. In total, the

[*]This has been admirably demonstrated in the case of Laval by Meynier.[2]

regional growth rate since 1962 has been substantially below that of the nation as a whole, and in Mayenne amounted to virtual stagnation. The urban agglomerations of the region have increased their populations at rates close to, or in excess of, the national average, whereas a universal decline has occurred in the purely rural sector. In this respect the Pays-de-la-Loire conforms closely to the national pattern and only in Mayenne does the scale of rural depopulation assume excessive proportions[3]

THE ECONOMIC STRUCTURE

The economic structure of the region is summarized in *Table 26.2*, illustrating the characteristics of employment.

Table 26.2

THE EMPLOYMENT STRUCTURE OF THE PAYS-DE-LA-LOIRE, 1962

| | Employed labour force | | Change (per cent) |
	Total	Per cent	1954–1962
Primary sector			
Fishing	4,675		− 1·5
Agriculture and forestry	369,072		−21·6
Total	373,748	37	−21·6
Secondary sector			
Extractive industry	6,615		−25·9
Building and public works	80,873		+15·3
Manufacturing industry	217,454		+ 6·2
Total	304,942	30	+ 7·4
Tertiary sector			
Transport	24,679		+ 1·5
Commerce, banking, insurance	131,084		+14·5
Personal services	100,795		+ 5·6
Public services[a]	76,604		+27·8
Total	333,162	33	+13·3
Total employed labour force	1,011,852		− 4·0

[a]Including public administration and armed services.
Source: Recensement Exhaustif, 1962.

The dominant position of the primary sector is clearly revealed in *Table 26.2*. In spite of a reduction by over 20 per cent since 1954, agriculture remained the support of over one third of the labour force in 1962, and is the largest single source of employment. By contrast, manufacturing accounted for only 21 per cent of the employed population in 1962, and opportunities in manufacturing increased by less than one per cent per annum in the preceding eight years. The drift from the land has clearly not been absorbed by a commensurate increase in manufacturing employment. The tertiary sector achieved a more rapid growth rate but the overall size of the total labour force diminished by four per cent during the period concerned, whereas the total population increased by over five per cent.

A mixed farming system predominates throughout the region, tenant farming, in various forms, occupying twice the acreage operated by farm owners. Livestock constitutes the main commercial element in the economy, with cereals as the principal cash crop. Apart from localized specializations, the major variations in farming occur in the relative proportions of arable and pasture, and in the degree of evolution of farming methods. On this basis, Flatrès[4] has distinguished three major farming regions: Maine-Anjou, the Loire Valley and Vendée.

Dairy farming predominates in the north of Maine-Anjou, using the 'Normande' breed and stimulated by contact with the Normandy dairy region. South of Laval, the decrease in precipitation and pasture quality is accompanied by an increase in beef production, using the local 'Maine-Anjou' breed. The importance of livestock, including pigs and poultry, in the economy is increasing and has produced a diversion of land from cash crops to rotational grasses and fodder crops, accompanied by a concentration of holdings and a drift of population from the land. Suret-Canale[5] has drawn attention to the intervention of capitalists, often cattle dealers or butchers, who have bought out many small farms and turned them over entirely to pasture for cattle rearing. Remembrement has made slow progress in Maine-Anjou, partly because the problems of fragmentation are less severe than in the case of arable farming.

The Loire valley is a much smaller and more diversified farming region. Viticulture has a widespread distribution but quality production is concentrated in the Val d'Anjou and in the 'Muscadet' area of the Basse-Loire.[6] Cattle farming is located on the low-lying pastures fringing the Loire valley and estuary, while horticulture is important in a zone encircling Nantes and in the Val d'Anjou. The latter area is the more intensive[7] and includes fruit, as well as specialized items as mushrooms,[8] hemp and tobacco.

The Vendée was formerly an area of poor farming with much fallow land. In the nineteenth century, fodder root crops replaced fallow, but recently hybrid maize and rotational grasses have tended to replace root fodders, which are heavy in labour demands, and permanent pasture, which gives too low a yield.[9] The reclaimed coastal marshes of the Marais Breton and the Marais Poitevin have an entirely different landscape. Although animal farming for beef and dairy predominates, some horticulture is present, but the quality of farming varies considerably in relation to water table conditions.[10]

Manufacturing activity is located in one polycentric industrial region—the Basse-Loire—in a small number of isolated centres, and in a diffused pattern of small-scale industries.

Table 26.3

MANUFACTURING EMPLOYMENT IN THE PAYS-DE-LA-LOIRE, 1962

	Total employed (including commuters)		Total employed (including commuters)
Nantes[a]	44,987	Laval	4,830
St. Nazaire[a]	15,607	Saumur	2,075
Le Mans[a]	20,351	Chateaubriant	1,794
Angers[a]	13,941	Mayenne	1,039
Cholet	8,122		

[a]Figure for agglomeration.
Source: Calculated from Recensement Exhaustif, 1962.

It is apparent from *Table 26.3* that the Basse-Loire and the larger industrial centres employed more than half of the region's 217,000 industrial workers in 1962. The Basse-Loire is by far the largest and most varied industrial area of the region, and has several individual features. The situation astride a major estuary is unique in north-western France, and access to ocean navigation enters largely into the development of industry. The status of Nantes–St. Nazaire as a 'métropole d'équilibre' and the immediate access to a populous market* are also unique within the Pays-de-la-Loire.[11] The industrial activity of the Basse-Loire is illustrated by *Figure 26.2*, which demonstrates that the axis is by no means continuous, but rather consists of four areas of development: the city and suburbs of Nantes, the waterfront between Nantes and Couëron, St. Nazaire and Donges.

Within the city of Nantes and the adjacent industrial estates of Carquefou, Bougenais and St. Herblain four branches of manufacturing are dominant: food processing, engineering, shipbuilding and chemicals. Food processing is intimately tied to the port and is one of the oldest activities of the city, dating from the colonial trade. The engineering industry is extremely diverse, ranging from metallic construction materials and heavy cranes to precision engineering. The chemical industry is also represented by heavy branches, such as fertilizers, and by a wide range of lighter chemical-using industries such as photographic and printing materials. The shipbuilding industry is secondary in importance to that of St. Nazaire and employed less than 4,000 workers in 1967. The

*In 1968 the combined population of the Nantes and St. Nazaire agglomerations exceeded 450,000 and the 'Zones de Peuplement Industriel ou Urbain' exceeded 600,000.

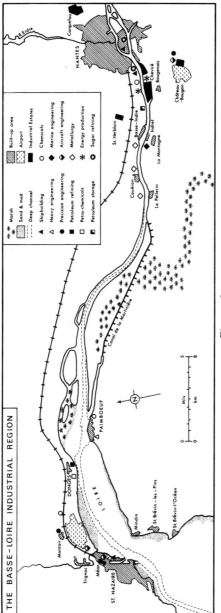

Figure 26.2

two Nantes shipyards concentrate on specialized ships—car ferries, dredgers, naval and fishing vessels—and have recently collaborated in joint production programmes. To the south of Nantes, the industrial estate of Château-Bougon airport is occupied by a branch of the Sud-Aviation aircraft corporation, employing 2,500 workers. Production is of components of advanced civil and military aircraft but some diversification into kitchen appliances has taken place to offset reductions in aircraft engineering. A distinct evolution is taking place in the pattern of location within Nantes. The shipbuilding, bulk-refining and many engineering firms are located close to the port, and their level of activity is stable or declining, whereas the lighter branches of industry are located in new industrial estates on the periphery of the city, and have a higher growth rate. The importance of the port as a specific location factor appears to be weakening in terms of the attraction of new industry.

Immediately downstream from Nantes a significant industrial annexe represents the last vestiges of a once important iron and steel industry. The Basse-Indre works utilized the pig iron of Trignac and Pauillac to establish a steel industry specializing in tin plate production. In spite of the closure of the Trignac blast furnaces during the depression years, steel was produced until 1958. Steel is no longer produced at Basse-Indre but electrolytic rolling and stamping remains and the plant produces approximately one third of the national output of tin plate. The works is linked to its own port installations on the Loire and also to an adjacent factory producing tin cans. In total over 4,000 workers are employed in the Basse-Indre metallurgical complex. To the west of Basse-Indre, Couëron is a centre of non-ferrous metallurgy, producing copper, lead and aluminium pipes and tubing. On the southern shore of the Loire, Indret is the site of an engineering works producing marine motors and furnaces for power generation.

By contrast with the diversified industries of Nantes and its environs, St. Nazaire is dominated by a single activity, shipbuilding. The 'Chantiers de l'Atlantique'* are the largest shipyards in France and in 1967 employed approximately 8,000 workers, including commuters drawn from a 40-kilometre radius around the town.[12] The crisis in the industry in western Europe in the face of Japanese competition was felt severely in St. Nazaire and a large number of redundancies resulted. The situation is now more favourable as a result of the success of the yard in adapting to the pre-fabricated construction of petroleum tankers and bulk carriers†. In addition to shipbuilding, the company also operates a heavy engineering

*Constituted in 1955 by the merging of the Penhoët and Loire shipyards.
†The yard builds tankers in excess of 200,000 tons and since 1968 has had the capacity to construct tankers of 500,000 tons d.w.

section manufacturing a wide range of machinery, from small motors to plant for conventional and nuclear power stations. In an attempt to diversify production, a new precision engineering factory has been built at Montoir. In spite of the improvement in orders and the partial conversion to non-marine activities, the industrial situation at St. Nazaire gives rise to concern. The only other large industry, aircraft engineering, is also experiencing contraction and a quarter of the labour force has been diverted to the production of caravans. Three new industrial estates have been designated in an attempt to attract new firms and create female employment but as yet only a small number of factories have been built. Outside St. Nazaire, the large new chemical works at Montoir and the chemical and engineering works at Paimboeuf on the south bank of the Loire may be considered as annexes of the St. Nazaire industrial zone.

The final element in the Basse-Loire industrial region is the refinery complex at Donges. In 1966, the refinery treated 4·2 million tons of crude oil and also supplied the new refinery at Rennes by pipeline. The postwar rebuilding of the refinery has not created a great addition of employment; only a thousand workers are employed in the refinery. Two companies produce the base products for synthetic textiles and plastics, but the petrochemicals section of the refinery complex must be considered as underdeveloped in relation to its full potential.

The Basse-Loire region employs approximately one third of the manufacturing labour force of the entire planning region and none of the other manufacturing centres approaches it in scale or possesses comparable problems of conversion. The largest individual centre, Le Mans, had a manufacturing labour force of 20,351 in 1962, and owes its growth to the fine communications and the impetus of the Renault works. Built in 1939, the Renault factory produces tractors and car components and its labour force of 8,000 is drawn from a 25-kilometre radius around the town.[13] Recent decentralizations of engineering firms have added over 3,000 jobs and the agglomeration grew by over 14 per cent to almost 150,000 inhabitants between 1962 and 1968. Industry in Angers shows a contrast between long-established activities, such as food processing, cords and steel cables, and such new decentralized industries as television receiver and computer manufacture. While smaller in scale, the recent growth of Cholet has certain outstanding features.[14] The basic activities are textiles and shoe manufacturing, the latter employing 10,000 workers in the town and its vicinity, but recent introductions include clothing, machine tools, electronics and car component industries. These new industries, mostly in small units, are located in and around the town forming a kind of industrial nebula with Cholet at its centre.[15] The towns of Laval[16] and Mayenne have also experienced a change in emphasis from declining staples[17] to engineering industries acquired by decentralization, but unlike Cholet this has not inspired a secondary spread of industry to the surrounding settlements.

URBAN DEVELOPMENT

The Pays-de-la-Loire displays a harmonious pattern of urban development, both in terms of spatial arrangement and hierarchical ordering. The pattern of distribution is extremely regular, no part of the region being more than 50 kilometres from an urban centre of over 25,000 inhabitants. A similar degree of symmetry is present in the hierarchy of urban centres.[18] Angers and Le Mans have direct spheres of influence corresponding approximately to their respective départements, while that of Nantes encompasses much of Vendée and spills over into Brittany in the département of Morbihan. The second level in the hierarchy is occupied by Laval, La Roche-sur-Yon, Cholet and St. Nazaire, controlling spheres of influence approximately 30 kilometres in radius. Chateaubriant, Saumur and Mayenne function as minor centres serving rural areas within a 20 kilometre radius.

The urban centres have increased in population since 1954 at rates double or treble that of the region as a whole. Moreover, the most rapid growth has been experienced by the smaller centres of from 20,000 to 60,000 inhabitants, representing a strengthening of the middle ranks of the hierarchy and the creation of urban centres with a potential capacity to check rural migration close to its source. Bouhier[19] and Renard[20] have drawn attention to this development in the case of La Roche-sur-Yon. The growth of employment in this town of central Vendée is seen by Renard[21] as a change in function from being a filter for transient rural population en route to the major cities, towards a role as an anchor, fixing rural population within the local region.

Nantes is the sole 'métropole d'équilibre' in the north-west quadrant of France, but its direct sphere of influence has been demonstrated by Cabanne[22] to be limited to the western half of the Pays-de-la-Loire. The degree to which Rennes functions as a relay centre transmitting the influence of Nantes must be questioned. Rather must Rennes be considered as a regional capital in its own right, possessing an older and larger university, direct air and rail links with Paris, and a wide range of specialized services and institutions. Only in the sphere of commercial and industrial organization is Rennes notably less well equipped than Nantes*

---

*Nantes employs 10,000 workers in establishments controlled from the city as compared with only 1,800 in the case of Rennes.[23]

The decision to link Nantes with St. Nazaire in the formation of the 'métropole d'équilibre' also appears arbitrary. Linked by 58 kilometres of congested 'route nationale' and by a branch railway line, with no important intervening towns, the connection between the two centres in terms of regional organization seems tenuous.

The next decade is certain to be crucial in the evolution of the region as a result of the contraction of employment in agriculture and the decline in certain staple industries. In recent years, employment in manufacturing has been growing at a net rate of one per cent per annum, which is manifestly insufficient to absorb future needs. In spite of maximum government assistance, the new industrial estates on the Basse-Loire have experienced mixed fortunes. The greatest success has been achieved at Nantes* but St. Nazaire has attracted few firms and two of the estates remain as open fields. Various expansion projects have been proposed by the Comité d'Expansion Régionale, and notably the creation of an iron and steel complex on the Loire.[24] Cabanne[25] has noted the ease of importing raw materials to the proposed site near Donges but admits the small scale of the existing regional market for crude steel. A further project envisages an enlargement of the Donges refinery and the creation of a new deep-water terminal at the mouth of the Loire.

An amalgam rather than an entity, part maritime, part continental, transitional in economy and landscape, the Pays-de-la-Loire has perhaps the weakest personality among French planning regions. It is not entirely typical of the conditions of western France except in the consequences of its peripheral location.

REFERENCES

[1] Prêcheur, C., *La Sidérurgie Française*, pp. 34–35, 1963, Paris, Armand Colin.

[2] Meynier, A., et al., 'Laval' *Norois*, 1964, Fig. 2, p. 159.

[3] Comité Régional d'Expansion Economique, *Données sur la démographie de la région*, 1966.

[4] Flatrés, P., *La Région de l'Ouest*, pp. 61–112, 1964, Paris, Presses Universitaires de France.

[5] Suret-Canale, J., 'Les campagnes françaises au milieu du XXe siecle', *Annls Géogr.*, 1958, p. 97.

[6] Gautier, M., 'La vigne et le vin dans la région Pornicaise', *Norois*, 1965, Fig. I. p. 182.

[7] Ménard, A., 'Angers: centre national d'horticulture', *Norois*, 1956, p. 409.

[8] Lartaut, J., 'La culture des champignons dans l'ouest de la France', *Norois*, 1965, p. 409.

[9] Dumont, R., 'Un schéma de modernisation agricole: Vendée et Loire-Atlantique', *Annls Géogr.*, 1958, p. 206.

[10] Bouhier, A., 'Les communaux de la partie orientale du Marais Poitevin', *Norois*, 1966, p. 5.

[11] Vigarié, A., 'Activités économiques de l'estuaire et métropole régionale', *Norois*, 1967, p. 346.

[12] Vince, A., 'Les courants d'immigration vers la region nazairenne de 1954–1962, et l'émigration apparente', *Norois*, 1966, p. 534.

[13] Dufour, J., 'L'influence de l'usine Renault sur la vie rurale du département de la Sarthe', *Norois*, 1961, p. 452.

[14] INSEE, *La zone industrielle Choletaise*, 1962, Nantes.

[15] Gravier, J., *L'Aménagement du Territoire et l'Avenir des Régions Françaises*, pp. 68–71, 1964, Paris, Flammarion.

*Renault has built a synthetic rubber plant at Nantes, but as a nationalized firm a degree of political impulsion rather than spontaneous choice may be inferred.

[16] Meynier, A., *op. cit*.[2], p. 153.

[17] Suret-Canale, J., 'L'industrie dans le Bas-Maine', *Norois*, 1956, p. 249.

[18] Cabanne, C., 'Nantes–St. Nazaire', *Notes Etud. docum.*, No. 3,362, 1967, p. 11.

[19] Bouhier, A., 'L'évolution récente de la population vendéene', *Norois*, 1967, p. 21.

[20] Renard, J., 'Les migrations alternantes de main-d'oeuvre vers l'agglomération yonnaise', *Norois*, 1967, p. 278.

[21] Renard, J., *op. cit*.[20] p. 284.

[22] Cabanne, C., *op. cit*.[1,8] p. 11.

[23] *Etud. Conjonct.*, 1964, p. 3.

[24] Comité d'Expansion Economique, *Pour le développement économique et social*, pp. 19–20, 1963, Nantes.

[25] Cabanne, C., *op. cit*.[1,8] p. 31.

27

Limousin

Limousin has the smallest population of all the planning regions—736,000 inhabitants in 1968—and the lowest average density—43 persons per square mile. The region also has the dolorous distinction of having experienced the slowest population growth in France in recent years. Between 1954 and 1962, Limousin alone of all the planning regions lost population, while between 1962 and 1968 the population grew by only 0·3 per cent.

Limousin is composed entirely of crystalline rocks and a simple three-fold division of terrain may be proposed. The core of the region is the 'montagne', an elevated granitic plateau above 700 metres, formed by the plateaux of Millevaches and Gentioux. In this mass rise all the major rivers of the region, nourished by abundant rainfall at all seasons. Settlement density is extremely low, in a landscape characterized by moorland, forest and occasional clearings supporting a low-grade polyculture. Urban development is restricted to one or two small centres on the fringe of the montagne. The high plateau is surrounded by an arc of lower plateau, above 500 metres, extending from the Haute-Marche, in Creuse, to the Dordogne valley. The principal towns, Guéret, Aubusson and Tulle are situated at route intersections. Although the higher summits carry patches of moorland and forest, a bocage landscape is dominant and animal farming assumes a more intensive character than on the montagne. The combination of excessive fragmentation, an average farm size of only ten hectares and a rural settlement pattern of isolated hamlets is unconducive to progress and rural depopulation is persistently high. The western half of Limousin constitutes a third type of terrain, a low plateau dissected by steeply incised wooded valleys. A superior basis of land resources supports a dense bocage in which permanent pasture, artificial grasses, cereals and fodder roots are combined with calf rearing, sheep, pig and poultry rearing. Traversed by the main line from Paris to Toulouse, and possessing the region's capital, Limoges, and second largest town, Brive, the low western plateau of Limousin has a more evolved urban and economic development than the remainder of the region.

The natural resource base of Limousin predisposes a pastoral economy and industrial activity was until recently dependent on crafts and traditions rather than on the presence of resources. An exception is the existence of uranium deposits in Haute-Vienne, which are concentrated

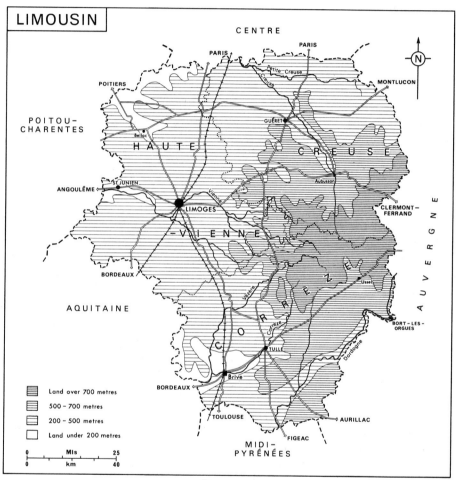

Figure 27.1

at Bessines and account for almost half of the national output.[1] Given the lack of industrial resources and a physique of upland unsuited to intensive land use throughout the eastern half of the region, the central theme of Limousin is depopulation. Since 1891, the census year of maximum population, the region has lost over 25 per cent of its total population. Almost a century of depopulation has led to the ultimate stage where, in addition to migrational losses, the population is failing to replace itself by natural increase. The total population advanced marginally between 1962 and 1968, but this was solely due to the growth of the towns and rural depopulation continues unabated. The demographic future of Limousin is thus dependent on two aspirations: that the natality rate of the rural population will be restored to equilibrium and that the towns will exhibit an unprecedented industrial expansion. Ironically, these two aspirations are contradictory, since any expansion in urban activity must result in a further draining of young people from the countryside, distorting still further the unbalanced age structure of the rural population which is the cause of the low fertility rate.

Limousin is the least urbanized of the planning regions, with only five towns of over 10,000 inhabitants in 1968. The urban proportion of the total population was only 40 per cent in 1968, and when the agglomeration of Limoges is excluded the proportion falls to little more than 20 per cent. The proportion of the total labour force employed in manufacturing industry was 18·9 per cent in 1962 and only two towns can be considered as significant centres of manufacturing activity. Limoges and Brive. Elsewhere, industry is confined to the persistence of traditional crafts in small units, in some towns reinforced by small-scale implantations of modern light industry. The range of traditional industries, for the most part using locally available resources, is very wide, involving principally textiles, tapestry, leather goods, paper manufacturing and furniture making. Such industries are conducted largely on an artisan basis, frequently offering locally important female labour opportunities. In the same manner, food processing is a widespread activity organized on small-scale production units. The durability of artisan and workshop activities in an era of concentration is partly related to the existence of high-grade skills, strong family traditions and the reputation enjoyed by the highly-specialized end products. More often, the persistence of artisan industry must be attributed to the failure of the small towns to attract modern industry, and therefore represents a stage of fossilization based on local skills. In isolated instances, artisan organization has provided the basis for substantial industrial activity, as in the case of the glove industry of St. Junien, which produces almost one quarter of the national putput. The decline of artisan industry would appear to be inevitable, and except where new industries have appeared—for example, the manufacture of electric lamps at Aubusson and the alloying of chrome and aluminium at Guéret—the industrial future of the small towns of Limousin seems compromised.

The agglomeration of Limoges occupies an unchallenged position in the industrial geography of the region, and appropriately grew from origins rooted in artisan and craft activities. The porcelain industry employed over 10,000 workers at the turn of the century and remains the best known, if no longer the dominant industry of the town. Production has turned from enamel and high-quality porcelain towards lower grades of porcelain susceptible to modern methods of factory production. At the present time, less than 3,000 persons are employed in the industry. The remaining industries range from those with a traditional background such as paper manufacture, printing, shoe making and brewing, to new introductions and conversions. The former use of porcelain as an insulator led to the development of electrical engineering concentrating on small electrical fittings, and the military arsenal has been converted to the production of heavy vehicles. Limoges is the centre of a minor industrial region in the middle Vienne valley extending from Eymoutiers to St. Junien, with an overwhelming basis of staple activities in varying degrees of contraction.[3,4] Successively a 'zone critique', a 'zone de conversion', and currently qualifying for state financial assistance, Limoges has so far attracted few major industrial enterprises. The principal exception is the conversion of the arsenal by the SAVIEM division of Renault, which has created almost 3,000 jobs. The growth of the agglomeration by 14 per cent between 1962 and 1968 to a total of 148,000 inhabitants cannot be related to a commensurate increase in manufacturing employment. The tertiary sector has expanded as a result of the establishment of the university, the growth of administrative services and commercial activity. Some decentralization of the administration of postal services has occurred from Paris, and Limoges is one of the 16 regional centres nominated in 1968 for state assistance as a recipient of decentralized tertiary activities from Paris.

By contrast with the modulated industrial growth of Limoges, where new industries merely compensate for the decline of staple activities, the smaller centre of Brive has recently experienced a rapid industrial growth. Situated on a small plain formed by the confluence of the Corrèze and Vézère valleys, the local concentration on primeur cultivation created a conserving industry. Paper carton, clothing and light engineering industries were later established, to which electronics and domestic appliance manufacture have recently been added. As a result, an expansion of the town by 16 per cent occurred between 1954 and 1962 to 44,000 inhabitants. The importance as a road and rail intersection together with the seasonal influx of tourists has reanimated the town and provoked an expansion of the built-up area outside the historic nucleus.

The industrial future of Limousin presents certain problems which affect the future economic balance of the region internally. If certain of the small towns, as Aubusson and Guéret, have been successful in attracting new firms, this merely compensates for the eventual running down of artisan industries already dependent on workers in the middle and older age groups. Similarly, the staple activities of textiles and leather goods are incapable of generating additional employment. The two major industrial centres, Limoges and Brive, do possess certain advantages capable of further exploitation. Both towns have abundant land for industrial development, unlimited water resources, state assistance is available for new firms and industrial estates have been created. Both towns are important route centres where the main electrified line from Paris to Toulouse intersects transverse lines crossing the Massif Central. Both towns have immediate access to areas of high recreational value, while Limoges has the advantages of a university and cultural centre and a civil airport is under construction.

If the industrial and commercial activities of Limoges and Brive are strengthened, this will emphasize still further the economic disparities within the region. Brive, and to a lesser extent Limoges, have a peripheral location within Limousin and are situated in the more favoured agricultural zone of the western low plateau. If the historical and geographical unity of the region is not to be broken, a serious attempt must be made to avert a widening economic and social disparity between western Limousin and the high plateau and montagne of the east. Since large-scale industrial development may be discounted, the economic renovation of eastern Limousin must be founded on alternative bases, notably in the spheres of rural improvement and the expansion of tourism.

The renovation of upland Limousin concerns especially the southern half of Creuse and eastern Corrèze. The problem of checking depopulation and creating new employment is a complex matter, involving the structural reform of holdings, the reorientation of production, an improvement in the physical quality of the rural habitat and the development of tourism. Thus far, two broad patterns of transition are occurring, albeit at a slow pace.

In the zone of intermediate plateau between 500 and 700 metres, especially in Creuse, conditions are favourable for the intervention of the SAFER organization. The high mortality rate in the rural population puts on the land market farms in which the natural successors are uninterested, thus permitting the SAFER to acquire land for consolidation into larger units. Similarly, the high average age of the farming population offers opportunities for the intervention of the FASASA to acquire farms through the retirement of operators. The combined operations of the SAFER, FASASA and Service du Remembrement will permit the consolidation of viable farm units, suitable for livestock production, adjusted both to natural conditions and to the low population densities.

The renovation of the high plateau of Millevaches poses more difficult problems, dependent on high capitalization and new infrastructure works.

This task is being attempted in Corrèze under the auspices of a regional development company, SOMIVAL, and incorporates the reseeding of pasture, the afforestation of degraded mountain pasture, and the construction of tourist villages.[5] The multiple objectives are thus to increase agricultural revenues, to create new forest reserves and to diversify employment by the construction of holiday villages. In the context of very low population densities, such developments are capable of effecting worthwhile improvements in terms of raising income levels and diversifying employment, but are unlikely to generate sufficient employment to reverse the inexorable trend of rural depopulation. The more widespread problem of moderizing the rural habitat through the construction of new buildings, improved roads and improved social amenities poses greater difficulties as a result of the fragmentation of local government into communes with extremely low population totals and feeble public revenues. The existing trend of the decay of outlying hamlets and the concentration of the residual population into the village centres must logically be extended into the amalgamation of communes disposing of increased funds to create centralized services at selected strategically placed villages.

In many respects, the problems of the montagne resemble those of the mountains of Auvergne, and potentially Corrèze may be considered as an annexe of the existing tourist region of Puy-de-Dôme. Faced with the divergent trends and the differing economic structures of eastern and western Limousin it is questionable whether the geographical unity of Limousin accords with present economic realities and the demands of planning. The contrasted economic levels and functions of the two halves of the region suggest a weakening of the historical and geographical integrity of Limousin. The participation of Corrèze in the SOMIVAL scheme, directed from Auvergne, and the attenuation of the influence of Limoges as a regional centre in the montagne as compared with the growing influence of Clermont-Ferrand, suggest a modification of traditional orientations. Gravier has argued that an amalgamation of the regions of Limousin and Auvergne, united by the twin axes of Limoges–Montluçon and Brive–Clermont-Ferrand, would form a more rational framework for integrated planning on the northern flanks of the Massif Central.[6]

REFERENCES

[1] Lacotte, R., 'Le complexe industriel de Bessines', *Norois*, 1966, p. 73.
[2] Perrier, A., 'Saint-Junien. Etude de géographie urbaine', *Norois*, 1965, pp. 340–343.
[3] Anon., *Revue Géogr. Industr. fr.*, No. 37, 1966, pp. 340–343.

[4] Morch, M., 'Economies régionales et planification, le Limousin', *Notes Etud. docum.*, No. 3,118, 1964, pp. 39–40.

[5] Clout, H., 'Rural improvements in Auvergne', *Geography*, 1968, Fig. 1, p. 80.

[6] Gravier, J., *L'Aménagement du Territoire et l'Avenir des Régions Françaises*, p. 303, 1964, Paris, Flammarion.

28

Auvergne

In contrast with the relatively simple physical and economic outlines of Limousin, the neighbouring region of Auvergne presents a complex landscape and a fragmentation of geographical units. The alternation of broad depressions, high volcanic chains, incised valleys, intermontane basins and high plateaux yields a resource base of greater variety than that of Limousin. In spite of these contrasts, the broad disposition of relief is not without some measure of symmetry which gives coherence to the planning region. The general form is that of a central lowland axis, open to the north but surrounded elsewhere by an arc of mountains.

The essential axis, in both physical and economic terms, is the north–south aligned structural depression of the Grande Limagne. Structural accident thus provides an otherwise mountainous region with a lowland heart, below 200 metres in elevation, some 40 kilometres wide and 60 kilometres in length, drained by the Allier. Favoured climatically and edaphically, the Limagne is the site of the region's most prosperous farming, and is bordered by the major towns, including the regional capital of Clermont-Ferrand. The Grande Limagne is projected south-wards by the corridor of the middle Allier valley, a natural communic-ations line with a chain of smaller urban centres. North of Vichy, in the département of Allier, the Grande Limagne opens out on to the broad lowland of the Sologne Bourbonnaise. This zone of alluvial accumulation, drained by the Sioule, Allier, and Loire, has inferior soils and, as compared with the arable and fruit growing systems of the Grande Limagne, a reversion to animal farming takes place. The Sologne Bourbonnaise serves the vital role of providing a natural outlet from Clermont-Ferrand, linking that town to Lyon and, via Montluçon, to Limoges, and giving access to the Paris Basin. The lowland core of Auvergne is surrounded in all other directions by an arc of crystalline upland, generally above 500 metres in elevation, above which distinct mountain ranges appear in diverse forms as volcanic ranges, volcanic masses and horst massifs. To

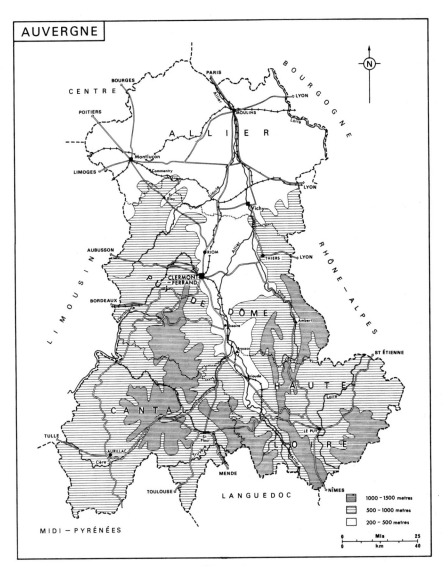

Figure 28.1

the west of Clermont-Ferrand, the Chaîne des Puys, an alignment of 80 volcanic peaks, gives way successively to the volcanic massifs of Mont Dore and Cantal, and the massif of Margeride. To the east of the Allier axis, the mountain barrier is diversified by complex faulting, producing an alternation of crystalline blocks—represented by the mountains of Livradois and Forez—and intervening alluvium filled basins, as the basin of Ambert. In the south-east, the mountain arc is completed by the massif of Velay, isolating the Le Puy basin from the remainder of the region.

The existence of a wide variety of land resources is not of itself indicative of a rich agricultural potential, but rather of a range in quality from first-class land in portions of the Limagne, to degraded summer pasture on the mountain summits. As a result of the variation in the physical constraints on agriculture and in the degree of technical evolution, Auvergne is composed of a mosaic of farming regions.

In general terms, three types of farming occupy the majority of the land area. The Grande Limagne is characterized by intensive mixed farming on holdings of between 10 and 25 hectares in which wheat forms a cash crop while maize, fodder crops and artificial pasture support cattle fattening. On the margins of the plain, and particularly near Clermont-Ferrand, orchards and vineyards occupy small holdings. Formerly a marsh area, the Limagne is now reclaimed and problems arise rather from the lack of moisture resulting from a low summer rainfall. Experiments with irrigation have demonstrated that this, the most evolved farming region in Auvergne, is capable of further increases in output. Secondly, mixed farming of a less intensive character is present on the heavy clays of the Sologne Bourbon-naise and the adjacent plateau of western Allier. In contrast with the open field pattern of the Limagne, the bocage pattern corresponds with a change in emphasis to improved pasture and fodder crops, used especially for the fattening of Charolais beef cattle. It is in the final category, mountain pastoralism, that the greatest variation occurs, in terms of organization, dominant enterprise and the quality of management. The volcanic ranges and the eastern mountain massifs support a pastoral economy based on a modified system of transhumance. The integrated exploitation of the valley floors and lower slopes with the summer grazing of the summits has a traditional basis. The chief element is the raising of cattle for cheese production and the grazing of sheep. Essentially an extensive system, the pastoral economy of Cantal, Haute-Loire and large portions of Puy-de-Dôme has provided only modest employment opportunities and is functionally associated with a history of rural depopulation.

It is clear that over the majority of Auvergne, severe environmental restraints, aggravated by structural defiencies in the farming system, limit the value of the agricultural economy and have acted as an expulsive force, turning population towards the exploitation of other resources or to seek employment by migrating from the region altogether.

The list of non-agricultural resources is comparatively short and marked by changes in the relative importance of various resources with the passage of time. The most obvious material resource is that of coal, the measures being distributed in a discontinuous elongation extending from the basin of Aumance, south of Moulins, to Champagnac, in northern Cantal, and totalling eight separate small basins. In addition, the isolated basin of Brassac is located between Issoire and Brioude, in the middle Allier valley. Exploitation began on the Commentry basin in the mid-nineteenth century and was the basis of the steel industry of Commentry and Montluçon. Elsewhere, the small basins provided thermal energy, nourished the railways and supplied the domestic needs of the towns. In 1938, almost 6,000 workers were employed in mining and over 1·5 million tons per annum were produced. The progressive exhaustion of the best seams, the use of diesel fuel on the railways, the development of hydroelectricity, and, more latterly, the arrival of Lacq natural gas, have reduced the importance of coal drastically. Production has fallen from 1·3 million tons in 1955 to 800,000 tons in 1967. Less than 3,000 workers are employed in the mines and of the original nine basins only three are now in operation. In order of importance these are St. Eloy, Brassac and Messeix. Elsewhere mining activities have ceased and government assistance has been accorded for the introduction of alternative employment. The output amounts to only 1·6 per cent of national production and as an economic resource coal is now of minor and decreasing significance in the regional economy.

The development of hydroelectricity has followed the reverse trend. Lacking the natural falls which initiated hydroelectricity generation in the Alps, production was limited to small-scale schemes, located chiefly in the Sioule valley, serving strictly local needs in the first instance. The development of high-tension transmission, and the advances in engineering permitting the construction of retaining barrages, transformed the situation towards the beginning of the present century. The presence of narrow gorges on the Dordogne and Truyère, the abundance of precipitation on the mountain catchments, and the character of the regime, its winter maximum complementing the summer maxima of the Alps and Pyrénées, stimulated the integral development of these two basins after 1919. The principal barrages are Bort-les-Orgues, Marèges, l'Aigle and Chastang, all on the Dordogne, and Grandval, on the Truyère. The potential of the major rivers is now harnessed but smaller schemes on the tributaries are still under construction. The installed capacity exceeds the present demand of the region and power is fed into the national grid. Unlike the first exploitation of coal, the development of hydroelectricity has not stimulated an equivalent surge of industrialization related to this specific form of power. The production of special steels at Les Ancizes, on the Sioule, and the refinement of aluminium at Issoire are the main exceptions.

The major remaining resource, the suitability of the region for the growth of tourism, is adventitious rather than material, but nevertheless is of growing significance in the region's economy. The tourist industry has its roots in the practice of thermalism and climatic cures, the origins of which go back to the Roman epoch. The reputation of the mineral waters for the treatment of specific illnesses and of mountain resorts for the alleviation of respiratory complaints led to the creation of fashionable resorts at Vichy, La Bourboule, Châtel-Guyon, Mont-Dore, Royat and St. Nectaire. Aided by the eligibility of such cures under the social security system, the practice of thermalism did not remain the province merely of the wealthy. The popularity of the thermal resorts has waned somewhat recently and the number of people taking cures fell from 232,000 in 1957 to 124,000 in 1965.[1] However, the impetus given by thermalism has stimulated a much wider form of tourism which is by no means fully exploited as yet. The attraction of the mountains of the Chaîne-des-Puys, Cantal and Mont-Dore for summer holidays has now been extended to the creation of winter sports and a proliferation of secondary holiday residences. From a specific origin in thermalism, the natural attractions of Auvergne are now the basis of a major tourist industry in full expansion.

While by no means negligible, the resource base of Auvergne is not bountiful and has necessitated continuous reappraisal and highly specific periodical readjustments. The gradual extinction of the coal reserves and the decline of coal-based industries has demanded the introduction of new types of manufacturing, the relative decline of thermalism has necessitated the construction of a broader-based tourist activity, and the depopulation of the mountains has created a need for rural improvement schemes. In total, the resources of Auvergne predispose an uneasy equilibrium which has only been maintained by considerable effort and with varying degrees of success in the different parts of the region. This pattern of resource use is clearly reflected in demographic trends, in the character of industrial and urban development and in the present efforts of planning to shape the future outlines of the region's economy.

DEMOGRAPHIC TRENDS

The demographic history of Auvergne over the last century is one of stagnation at the regional level, but with pronounced variations between the constituent départements.

Table 28.1

POPULATION CHANGE IN AUVERGNE, 1861–1968

	1861	1901	Total population in thousands 1936	1954	1962	1968
Allier	356	422	417	373	379	387
Cantal	241	231	191	177	171	169
Haute-Loire	306	314	245	216	210	208
Puy-de-Dôme	576	544	486	481	509	547
Auvergne	1,479	1,511	1,291	1,247	1,269	1,312

Source: Récensements de 1962 and 1968.

Table 28.1 demonstrates that each département has experienced an individual growth trend. The département of Allier increased during the latter half of the nineteenth century at the height of the mining activity and related industrial expansion. The period from 1901 to 1936 was one of stability resulting from the reduced momentum of industrial growth, the effect of war losses and the continuance of rural exodus. Since 1954, the département has regained equilibrium, mainly through the expansion of the Montlucon agglomeration. The mountainous départements of Cantal and Haute-Loire have both experienced continuous depopulation. This is related to rural exodus, initially on a seasonal basis, but utimately becoming an ingrained and apparently irreversible trend. The département of Puy-de-Dôme has a more complex trend, reflecting the differential trends of the mountain sections, the central plain and the urban centres. In the latter part of the nineteenth century, rural depopulation far exceeded urban development and not until the industrialization of Clermont-Ferrand was the trend reversed. The continued growth of Clermont-Ferrand has maintained the upward trend in recent years, but it is notable that only the département of Allier had a greater population in 1962 than in 1861.[2]

Since 1962, the region has experienced a reversal of the downward trend in population of the previous hundred years. This is explained by the fact that migration has taken the form of internal redistribution within the region rather than a large-scale exodus from Auvergne. Population has moved from the mountains into the agglomerations of the central lowlands, and the drift of population out of the region has been balanced by a compensating migration into the region from the adjoining uplands of Limousin.

URBAN AND INDUSTRIAL DEVELOPMENT

The distribution of urban centres conforms closely to the alignment of relief as affecting the disposition of fertile land resources and the lines of communication. A central axis of urbanization is formed by the chain of small towns in the middle Allier valley—Brioude, Brassac and Issoire—projected northwards by a double line of towns on the margin of the Grande Limagne—Royat, Clermont-Ferrand and Riom on the western margin and Thiers and Vichy to the east. In the mountain zones, the pattern consists of dispersed centres located in agricultural basins, isolated from each other by less productive highland. The principal examples are Le Puy, St. Flour, Aurillac and Ambert. A third distinctive component is the former mining and metallurgical area of western Allier, comprising Montluçon, Commentry and St. Eloy. Finally, Moulins is an individual case, being the marketing, processing and communications centre for the agricultural lowland of the Sologne Bourbonnaise.

In total, the degree of urbanization in Auvergne is modest. In 1962, only Clermont-Ferrand exceeded 100,000 inhabitants and Montluçon had 50,000 inhabitants. This may be accounted for by the lateness and uneven distribution of the development of industry.[3] Although industrial traditions were manifest in the charcoal iron industry of western Allier and the cutlery industry of Thiers, it was not until the latter half of the nineteenth century that large-scale industrial development occurred, and then only along narrow lines and in restricted locations. The substitution of coke for charcoal in iron smelting gave rise to the expansion of Commentry, on a small coal basin, and to the growth of Montluçon as a metallurgical centre. The exhaustion of the coal seams has robbed Commentry of its original raison d'être while the metallurgical industry of Montluçon has been reduced to the finishing of special steels and operates under severe difficulties. An effort of conversion has been carried out and a wider range of manufacturing has been secured for Montluçon involving pneumatic tyres, aeronautical engineering, synthetic textiles, chemicals and precision engineering.

At the close of the nineteenth century it was the turn of Clermont-Ferrand to undergo rapid industrial growth, based in this instance less on locally available resources than a chance element rigorously exploited. The establishment of the Michelin rubber vulcanizing factory coincided with the expansion of the motor car industry and the utilization of pneumatic tyres. The acquisition by Michelin of interests in the manufacture of vehicles* led to the expansion of the Clermont-Ferrand tyre factory and to the creation of a virtual fief dependent on this industry. The tyre

*Michelin controls the Citroën vehicle manufacturing company.

industry still dominates the employment structure of Clermont-Ferrand. Over 17,000 workers are employed by Michelin and labour is drawn from a 20-kilometre radius around the plant.[4] The industrial momentum created by Michelin favoured additional growth and heavy engineering, chemicals and printing works have assumed importance. As a consequence of its industrial growth, Clermont-Ferrand has absorbed the neighbouring settlements of Chamalières and Royat and modern suburbs now sprawl up the lower slopes of the Puy-de-Dôme.

With the exception of the cutlery industry of Thiers[5] and a number of agricultural processing industries, the industrial development of the remaining urban centres of Auvergne is of recent date and has occurred under the influence of the location factors of the modern technological revolution. The importance of access to labour pools, uncongested communications, new sources of power and a pleasant environment, as well as the factor of government assistance, have favoured the industrialization of the smaller centres of the central axis of Auvergne.

PLANNING PROBLEMS IN AUVERGNE

The efforts engaged to solve the problems of Auvergne must be viewed against a background of a century of rural depopulation and a rate of economic and urban growth below that of the nation as a whole. During the last century population has deserted the mountains, the practice of hill farming has stagnated and large areas of former mountain pasture have reverted to mediocre rough grazing. Industrial activity related specifically to coalmining has declined and, with the exception of Clermont-Ferrand and Montluçon, urban development has progressed slowly until the recent phase of expansion. Fundamental to the effort of regional planning is thus the need to raise the level of economic development, especially in the rural areas, and to secure a new and stable balance between population growth and employment opportunities.

Whereas the recent industrial progress has occurred spontaneously in relation to changing location factors, the raising of employment levels and the quality of life in the rural environment is dependent on a total reappraisal of resources and their redeployment towards more productive activities. This involves enormous problems of organization and capital investment and must be accompanied by a change in traditional attitudes. Since 1964, the task of rural renovation has been vested in a mixed economy company, 'La Société pour la Mise en Valeur de la Région Auvergne-Limousin' (SOMIVAL).[6]

SOMIVAL is divided internally into three sections concerned respectively with agriculture, forestry and tourism. Actions undertaken for the amelioration of agriculture centre on the improvement of stock breeding, the expansion of irrigation in the Allier valley and the improvement of upland grazing.[7] By mid-1968, 15 farms* had been established under contract to breed sheep of improved strain to facilitate a revitalizing of sheep rearing throughout the region. Similar measures had been undertaken to improve the quality of Charolais cattle, and 27 farms in the Allier and Sioule valleys had been converted to irrigated production. The object of afforestation is to put to productive use as much as possible of the 400,000 hectares of fallow and abandoned land in the SOMIVAL area. By the end of 1967, 1,429 hectares had been replanted and a forestry school established. The availability of wasteland and the high rate of tree growth in the conditions of heavy rainfall, combined with rising demands for softwood for constructional and chemical uses, make forestry a rational function for land otherwise unproductive†.

In the sphere of tourism, SOMIVAL is attempting to complement the activities of the purely private sector, already in a state of steady expansion. In contrast with the purely commercial forms of tourism, centred for the most part in established resorts, SOMIVAL has attempted to extend tourism into the lesser-known rural areas, where the physical attractions are nevertheless present and unspoilt, and where tourism brings some employment to areas otherwise dependent on agriculture. By mid-1968, 42 developments were completed, under construction, or at the planning stage, with the aim of diffusing tourism throughout wide areas of rural Auvergne. The type of development favoured is that of holiday villages, consisting of individual chalets and secondary homes, in some instances aligned around artificial lakes, possessing communal services. The objective is to afford inexpensive holidays in quiet surroundings as compared with the more animated and expensive established resorts. In this way, tourism is seen as the final stage in integrated rural development, absorbing some of the produce of an improved agriculture and employing a proportion of the labour displaced through agricultural improvement schemes.

The activites of SOMIVAL provide a clear framework of cooperation between the private sector, local authorities and government departments brought to bear upon defined regional objectives. The situation is much less clearly defined in the case of urban and industrial development. The remarkable population growth achieved by most of the towns in the past fifteen years, coupled with the inevitable continuance of rural–urban migration, places the provision of new urban employment at the head of

*Located principally in the canton of Eygurande in Corrèze (Limousin).
†It is estimated that the cost of afforestation may be recouped by the returns from six months of production.

the list of priorities. Lacking a natural resource base capable of inciting new industrial development, and possessing several towns with a narrowly based industrial sector, the problem must be resolved by the introduction of new industry from outside and by an expansion of tertiary activities. In the context of regional planning, it is the role of the regional capital to act as a generator, attracting new growth and, through its function as a commercial, transport and administrative centre, to facilitate the diffusion of economic currents throughout the region. In this respect, Clermont-Ferrand is only partially successful. The road and rail communications to Paris are adequate, but links with Lyon are deficient and communications with the other regional capitals of central France are equally weak. The inauguration of regular air services between Clermont-Ferrand and Lyon and Paris has partially offset the isolation of the regional capital from the other major cities of France. The dramatic increase in the size of the university has confirmed Clermont-Ferrand as the cultural and intellectual capital of Auvergne, but in the realms of commerce and business the city does not yet possess a range and strength of services proportionate to its population size and capable of dominating regional organization throughout Auvergne. In spite of a population approaching 300,000 in its urban-industrial region, Clermont-Ferrand remains above all an industrial city, living in the shadow of Michelin.

In one respect Auvergne has a positive resource, capable of further expansion and assured of permanent exploitation. The region has a natural vocation for tourism compounded of striking mountain scenery, including two large regional natural parks★, relative ease of access as compared with the heart of the Massif Central, and an underdeveloped potential for winter sports. The relative decline of thermalism has been more than balanced by an expansion of family holidays in inexpensive 'gîtes ruraux', well-equipped camping sites, and by an increase in winter sports facilities. The region possesses seven winter sports centres, of which Mont-Dore, La Tour d'Auvergne and Super-Besse, in the département of Puy-de-Dôme, are the best equipped. The future expansion of tourism will not, however. create a large volume of new employment, but its significance in the rural economy in terms of seasonal employment, work in construction and revenue to the commerce of the villages and small towns is of the greatest importance. The ancillary benefits of related road improvements, better water supply and the intrusion of a commercial ethos will have a revivifying effect on settlements too long inured to the process of economic stagnation and demographic decline.

After decades of passivity, Auvergne is now in a period of evolution. The towns are showing an impressive degree of vitality, the rural economy

★The 'Parc des Volcans', in the Chaînes-des-Dômes, and the Massif de Cantal.

is being reformed through efforts emanating from within the region, and tourism is permeating areas hitherto the exclusive province of marginal farming. Elevated to the status of 'métropole d'équilibre assimilée'[*] Clermont-Ferrand has an opportunity to strengthen its role as an effective regional capital.[9]

REFERENCES

[1] Estienne, P., 'L'évolution démographique de la région Auvergne pendant les quinze dernières années', *Fac. Lettres Clermont-Ferrand*, XXX, 1966, p. 169.

[2] INSEE, *Tableaux de l'Economie Régionale Auvergne*, 1966, Table 140, p. 78.

[3] Blanc, J., 'L'Auvergne', *Notes Etud. docum.*, No. 3,003, 1963, pp. 51–63.

[4] Bressolette, R., 'Les migrations journalières de main-d'oeuvre dans le département du Puy-de-Dôme', *Fac. Lettres Clermont-Ferrand*, XXX, 1966, p. 1.

[5] Boeuf, A., 'La coutellerie thiéroise. Une société industrielle en mutation', *Fac. Lettres Clermont-Ferrand*, XXXII, 1967, p. 5.

[6] Clout, H., 'Rural improvements in Auvergne', *Geography*, 1968, p. 79.

[7] SOMIVAL Information, Nos. 1 and 2, Clermont-Ferrand, 1968.

[8] Marty, J., 'Les parcs naturels régionaux', *Auvergne econ.*, No. 1, p. 49.

[9] Montpied, G., 'Clermont-Ferrand, métropole d'équilibre assimilée', *Vie Auvergne*, No. 11, 1966, p. 2.

[*]A status immediately below the eight 'metropoles d'équilibre' and qualifying the town for government assistance to facilitate the decentralization of services from Paris to counterbalance the attraction of the national capital within Auvergne.

29

Poitou-Charentes

The planning region of Poitou-Charentes is not a natural physical unit, but rather the crossroads of four geographical regions—the Massif Central, the Paris Basin, the Armorican Massif and the Basin of Aquitaine. The core of the region is formed by the sedimentary rocks of the Seuil de Poitou and its southern extension, the low plateau of Charentes. The low divide between the rivers draining to the Loire and those draining directly to the Atlantic is an indeterminate feature, presenting no obstacle to communications but rather throughout history having served as a major routeway linking the two major lowland basins of France. In the absence of clearly defined physical limits other than that imposed by the coastline, the definition of Poitou-Charentes must be considered conventional, but nevertheless enclosing an area with certain common traits. The predominance of subdued landforms, the diminished rainfall as compared with adjacent regions, the low level of urban and industrial development and the supremacy of the rural economy give a measure of homogeneity to the planning region.

LAND RESOURCES AND THE RURAL ECONOMY

Poitou-Charentes is an overwhelmingly rural region; 61·7 per cent of the population was rural* in residence and 62 per cent of the labour force was engaged in the primary sector in 1962.[1] Throughout most of the region, contrasts in land resources are comparatively slight. The Jurassic and Cretaceous rocks underlying the greater part of Poitou-Charentes[2] have decomposed into fertile soils, covering an undulating plateau surface traversed by broad, alluvium-filled valleys. It is only at the extremities of the region that some deterioration in environmental conditions is manifest. In Gâtine and the margins of Limousin, the granitic and schistose

*A rural proportion exceeded only by the planning region of Limousin, 62·5 per cent rural in 1962.

385

rocks yield siliceous soils needing liming and occupied predominantly by woodland and pasture. On the coastal margin, the marshes[3] of Poitevin, Aunis and Saintonge require continuous draining in order to support agriculture, and in the east of the region a discontinuous cover of Tertiary sands and clays gives rise to poor soils, the 'brandes', given over to moor-

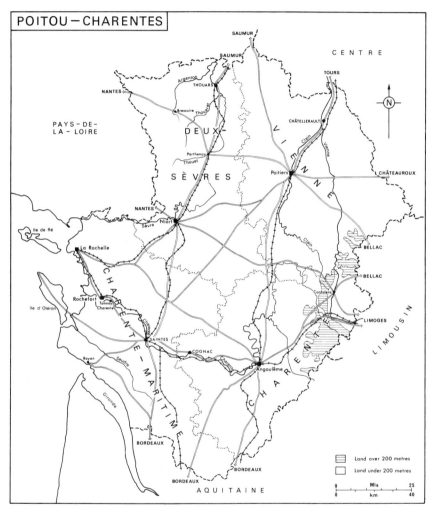

Figure 29.1

land and oak and chestnut woodland.

Within an environment with little exception favourable to agriculture, a system of polyculture has evolved in which the cultivation of cereals, fodder crops and artificial grasses is associated with commercial livestock farming. The basis of production is owner-operated farms, small in size and fragmented in structure, although in Deux-Sèvres tenant farming remains important, while in Charente métayage has survived in significant proportions. As a result of remembrement and the intervention of the SAFER,[4] and partly through spontaneous evolution, the average farm size doubled between 1955 and 1963 from 15 to 30 hectares[5]. Remembrement has progressed actively and, in 1965, had been completed in 293 communes. This, however, amounted to only one third of the total area requiring remembrement and was heavily concentrated in two areas, between the Sèvre-Nantaise and Charentes, and in the Seuil of Poitou between Poitiers and Loudon[6]. The leading arable crop by area is wheat but since 1950 the area under maize has been considerably extended due to the introduction of hybrid strains. Maize is used as a feed grain, a green fodder and for the production of maize oil, but production tends to fluctuate annually in response to climatic conditions. Although cereals are a staple element in the polyculture, the prime objective of the system is the provision of feed for the livestock population which represents the leading commercial enterprise. On the crystalline fringe of the region, and in the poorly drained valley floors, permanent pasture is used for grazing and hay making, but elsewhere artificial grasses and roots provide the fodder, supplemented by cattle cake.

The rural economy throughout most of the region is based on high-grade dairy farming involving cooperative organization. Charente-Maritime has played an important part in the evolution of cooperative farming in France; the movement originated there in 1888 and was diffused throughout the region as livestock farming replaced viticulture, devastated by phylloxera. The emphasis is firmly placed on the production of butter, which absorbs over 60 per cent of the total milk yield and amounts to 10 per cent of national butter production. Much of the remainder of the milk is devoted to cheese production, and, to a lesser extent, casein, while the skimmed milk is fed to pigs. The total output of milk is equivalent to between 5 and 6 per cent of national production in most years and has been steadily increasing as a result of improved stock and husbandry rather than an increase in the number of cattle. The success of the dairy industry is undoubtedly related to the cooperative basis of processing and marketing, and in order to meet competition within the Common Market, the smaller and less well equipped dairies are being eliminated and processing concentrated on larger factory-style establishments.

The major exception to the dairy farming economy, other than sheep rearing on the poorer grazing, is the viticulture of the Charente valley. Reconstituted after the phylloxera epidemic, the vineyards of the middle Charente valley support the brandy distillation industry controlled by the important firms at Cognac and Jarnac. Approximately 70 per cent of the output of brandy is exported.

INDUSTRIAL ACTIVITY

Poitou-Charentes has one of the lowest levels of industrial development of all the planning regions; the proportion of the labour force engaged in manufacturing is only 20 per cent. This lowly industrial status reflects a mediocre resource base devoid of indigenous power resource or industrial minerals. The principal towns are now served by Lacq natural gas but all raw materials, with the exception of building stone and brick clay, either emanate from the agricultural sector or are derived from outside the region, especially from overseas.

Robert[7] has defined three categories of industry in Poitou-Charentes; those dependent on the product of agriculture, forestry and fishing; industries originating from past artisan activities; and industry based on resources derived from outside. The processing of agricultural produce is the most widespread industrial activity, ranging from flour milling, brewing and distilling to fish conserving, but chiefly the processing of dairy produce. The industries descended from an artisan background are more diversified and are experiencing mixed fortunes at present. The textiles, clothing and tanning industries are stable or declining, whereas wood products, agricultural machinery and metallurgical engineering are growing branches. Finally, industries based on resources derived from outside the region tend to be the later established branches, chemicals, plastics, rubber, fertilizers and light engineering. In many instances, not only the raw materials have an external origin but the firms are recent decentralizations from Paris or new branches of national firms. It is notable that absent from the list of industries is any major activity capable of exerting growth tendencies within the region, such as petroleum refining or iron and steel production.

The location pattern of industry[8] demonstrates an even scattering throughout the region, within which four concentrations, one in each of the constituent départements, are clearly defined. Between Poitiers and Châtellerault, an axial industrial zone lines the valleys of the Clain and Vienne in the département of Vienne. The two principal centres differ markedly in character, Poitiers being primarily an administrative and university centre which has only recently received industry, while in Châtellerault industry is more important, longer established and presently experiencing problems of conversion and rejuvenation. The staple activity of Châtellerault is metallurgical engineering, formerly producing armaments but now orientated towards machine components. Both towns have established industrial estates on which decentralized industries have been constructed, often in the high technology category, as aeronautical engineering at Châtellerault. In total, the two major centres, and the intervening smaller towns of the Clain Valley, employed approximately 15,000 workers in manufacturing in 1962.

In the département of Deux-Sèvres industry is also aligned along a valley axis, the Sèvre-Niortaise, between the towns of Niort and Saint-Maixent. The principal branches represented are leatherware, timber, chemicals and mechanical engineering. In Charente, industrial activity is concentrated in the centre and suburbs of Angoulême.[9,10] Metallurgical, electrical and mechanical engineering are the most important sources of employment, followed by paper making, textiles and chemicals. Finally, in Charente-Maritime, over 60 per cent of the industrial labour force is located in the twin port complexes of La Pallice–La Rochelle and Rochefort–Tonnay–Charente. Most industries reflect the influence of maritime activity and access to imported raw materials—for example, shipbuilding and fish processing at La Rochelle and La Pallice, and non ferrous metallurgy, chemicals and tropical woodworking at Rochefort and Tonnay–Charente. Other important industries represented are the manufacture of rolling stock near La Rochelle, aeronautical engineering at Rochefort, and the newly-decentralized SIMCA vehicle plant at La Rochelle.

The low level of industrial development cannot be imputed solely to the absence of a suitable resource base, but also to the remoteness from major markets, the small size of the regional market and difficulties of communications; factors making for high operating costs and particularly adverse for the installation of modern highly-capitalized industries. The entire region is eligible for priority aid to industry, which in the case of La Rochelle and Rochefort is accorded at the maximum rate. Some degree of success has been achieved by the larger centres, as Poitiers, which possesses a university and spacious new industrial estates and is a focus of routes, and as Châtellerault, which disposes of a skilled labour pool released by the running down of the large armaments factory. It seems improbable, however, that new firms can be attracted to each of the dispersed smaller centres, where the decline of the traditional industries and the trend towards rationalization of the dairy processing industry leave a serious vacuum.

URBAN DEVELOPMENT

In 1962, only 38·3 per cent of the total population of Poitou-Charentes of 1·4 million resided in urban centres. Poitou-Charentes has no single large city capable of dominating the entire region, but rather each département has one large centre at the head of its hierarchy. Angoulême, La

Rochelle and Poitiers, each of approximately the same population size*, have direct spheres of influence restricted to their respective départements,[11] while Niort, although smaller in size, has an equivalent status in Deux-Sèvres. This fragmentation at the top of the hierarchy leaves the region without an undisputed capital. Poitiers, the smaller of the three largest towns, has the greatest concentration of high-order services, a growing university and is the seat of the regional préfet, but is overshadowed industrially by its smaller neighbour, Châtellerault. The industrial growth of Poitiers is recent and as yet the town is not equipped to direct economic life in the region. Below the level of département capital, a number of towns in the size category 20,000 to 40,000 inhabitants have achieved importance by virtue of specific functions rather than as centres of extensive hinterlands. Thus, Rochefort and Châtellerault are industrial centres but are too close to La Rochelle and Poitiers respectively to exercise control over large hinterlands. Saintes[12] is specifically a railway centre, Royan a tourist resort and Cognac is equally specialized in the distillation and commercialization of brandy.

It is noticeable that both the large towns and the smaller centres tend to have a peripheral location, leaving the centre of the region devoid of urban development and a reservoir of rural exodus.[13] Central Poitou-Charentes is 'par excellence' an area controlled by small rural service centres. Characteristically, such centres possess a market, food processing industries, secondary schools, and serve a rural area of between 10 and 30 kilometres in radius.[14]

REGIONAL PROBLEMS

Poitou-Charentes affords an excellent illustration of the problems of western France attendant on the dependence on the primary economy at a time when all economic forces are directed towards a contraction of agricultural employment. The inevitable result of the rationalization of farming accompanied by a low level of industrialization is a slow rate of population growth. Between 1954 and 1962 the population increased by only 48,000, at a rate of 3·9 per cent as compared with the national average of 8·8 per cent. Only Limousin and Auvergne experienced lower rates of increase. This was related to a heavy migrational loss of over 30,000 inhabitants. The recent publication of the preliminary results of the 1968 census[15] reveals that further slowing down in population growth has occurred.

*In 1968, Angoulême had 95,000 inhabitants, La Rochelle 92,000 and Poitiers 84,000 in their agglomerations.

Table 29.1

POPULATION CHANGE IN POITOU-CHARENTES, 1962–1968

| | Total population | | Population change | |
	1962	1968	Absolute	Per cent
Charente	327,658	330,000	+ 2,342	+0·8
Charente-Maritime	470,897	485,600	+14,703	+3·1
Deux-Sèvres	321,118	326,600	+ 5,482	+1·7
Vienne	331,619	338,000	+ 6,381	+1·7
Poitou-Charentes	1,451,292	1,480,200	+28,908	+2·0

Source: Recensements de 1962 and 1968.

A clear deceleration of population growth is indicated in *Table 29.1*, related to a reduction in fertility, the tendency for the population to age and a continuation of losses by migration[*]. The reduction in growth was not restricted to the rural centres but was shared by many of the towns. Whereas between 1954 and 1962 a general increase in urban population occurred, only Poitiers, Châtellerault, La Rochelle, Bressuire, Parthenay and Niort achieved a growth of over ten per cent in their agglomerations between 1962 and 1968. Angoulême, Cognac and Royan experienced only modest growth, while Saintes and Thouars remained stagnant. The demographic trend is partly due to a fall in urban birth rates but also reflects a slowing down of the arrival of decentralized firms and the lack of growth in the traditional staple industries.

The scale of rural depopulation is heaviest in the poorer farming land of the crystalline margins of north-west Deux-Sèvres and eastern Charentes; moreover, from these areas the dominant movement is out of the region and particularly to Paris.[16] Depopulation is also high in central Poitou-Charentes, where agricultural reform has made most progress but where little urban employment within easy commuting distance of rural dwellers is to be found. In an agricultural economy geared to the commercial production of high-value products for a competitive market, further rationalization is both inevitable and desirable. The problem of retaining surplus rural population within the region appears to be intractable, unless a large volume of new industry can be created. Thus far large-scale decentralizations have only been attracted to the major urban centres and it seems likely that a further polarization of economic activity on the four largest towns will occur, with adverse effects on the provision of services and quality of opportunity in the rural areas and small towns.

The littoral zone[17] has proved more resistant to rural depopulation

[*]Between 1962 and 1968 net migration amounted to −21,642, as compared with −33,824 in the longer period 1954–1962.

and may possess a greater capacity for growth. The outport of La Pallice is presently being extended[18] and La Rochelle is well represented in the more elaborate forms of manufacturing. Similarly, the tourist industry, centred on La Rochelle, Royan[19] and the offshore islands,[20] is capable of further expansion. The future of port activity is less certain in view of the lack of a developed hinterland, the lack of export cargoes and the inability of Rochefort and Tonnay-Charente to handle large vessels. Similarly, the aeronautical industry of Rochefort is subject to reductions in employment. The decision to build a west coast petroleum refinery at Brest may prejudice the choice of La Pallice for such a development, and without such a 'motor' for growth, the creation of self-sustaining industrial linkages, as opposed to piecemeal decentralizations, is unlikely to occur.

Destined by physical geography to be a region of passage, Poitou-Charentes has thus far failed to intercept fully the lines of movement traversing the region. The main electrified line from Paris to Bordeaux and Spain bisects the region but has brought no economic life into the heart of the region.[21] A paradox exists between the outward appearance of a successful rural economy, based on principles of cooperative organization inherited from the past century and adapted to the changing needs of the present, and an underlying structural weakness in the regional economy as exposed by the demographic trends of the last three census enumerations.

REFERENCES

[1] Pinard, J., 'La population active de la région Poitou-Charentes en 1962', *Norois*, 1968, p. 43.
[2] Robert, J., *Atlas de la Région Poitou-Charentes*, Plate 2, 1964, Poitiers, CESCO.
[3] Chabot, G., *Géographie Régionale de la France*, pp. 45–50, 1966, Paris, Masson.
[4] Gardner, de N., 'Les sociétés d'aménagement foncier et d'établissement rural. Un exemple: la SAFER Poitou-Charentes', *Revue fr. Agric.*, Vol. 12, 1966, p. 65.
[5] *Poitou-Charentes, Economie Régionale*, No. 4, 1968, fasc. 11, p. 27.
[6] Robert, J., *op. cit.*, Plate 20.
[7] Robert, J., 'L'industrie dans la Région de Programme Poitou-Charentes', *Norois*, 1965, p. 540.
[8] Robert, J., *op. cit.*, Plates 16–19.
[9] Comby, J., 'Les quartiers et les faubourgs d'Angoulême', *Norois*, 1964, p. 171.
[10] Comby, J., 'Les faubourgs d'Angoulême', *Norois*, 1965, p. 297.
[11] Robert, J., *op. cit.*, Plate 28.
[12] Blier, G., 'Saintes, centre ferroviaire', *Norois*, 1963, p. 133.
[13] Robert, J., *op. cit.*, Plate 14.
[14] Parrat, L., 'Lezay, centre rural', *Norois*, 1967, p. 211.
[15] *Poitou-Charentes, Economie Régionale*, No. 4, 1968, fasc. I, pp. 53–54.
[16] Robert, J., *op. cit.*, Plate 15.
[17] Robert, J., *op. cit.*, Plate 31.
[18] *Poitou-Charentes, Economie Régionale*, No. 4, 1968, fasc. III, pp. 3–8.
[19] Cotard, S., 'Royan, centre touristique', *Norois*, 1957, p. 333.
[20] Bordarier, 'Le tourisme dans l'Ile de Ré', *Norois*, 1966, p. 453.
[21] Gravier, J., *L'Aménagement du Territoire et l'Avenir des Régions Françaises*, p. 315, 1964, Paris, Flammarion.

30

Aquitaine

For purposes of regional planning, the Basin of Aquitaine, together with its mountain and upland fringe, is divided into two components— Aquitaine and Midi-Pyrénées. On the basis of physical geography, such a division appears arbitrary, but in terms of economic organization it corresponds approximately with the zones of influence of Bordeaux and Toulouse, and with the distinction between a zone orientated towards the Atlantic maritime façade, and an interior zone, where the influence of the Mediterranean competes with the Atlantic in both an economic and climatic sense. Nevertheless, both areas have many problems in common, stemming from the underdevelopment of the Basin of Aquitaine, the history of rural depopulation, the persistence of polyculture and the low overall density of population. The contrast with the level of development in the Paris Basin is striking and it is not inappropriate to consider the Basin of Aquitaine as the epitome of the 'désert français'. Nor is it entirely unrealistic to consider the basin as a future California, based on its viti- culture, fruit growing, market-gardening, oil, natural gas, hydroelectricity and the aeronautical industry. The paradox of Aquitaine has been its inability to capitalize on a favourable physical environment for com- mercial agriculture and by no means negligible resource base for industry.

The planning region of Aquitaine comprises the five départements of Dordogne, Gironde, Lot-et-Garonne, Landes and Basses-Pyrénées. Third largest of the planning regions, Aquitaine occupies 7·7 per cent of the national land area but possesses only 5 per cent of the national population. The core of the region is the middle and lower Garonne Valley, which bisects the planning region and separates totally different geographical units to the north-west and south-east.

To the north-east, the limestone plateau of Périgord is drained by the right bank tributaries of the Dordogne and the Garonne. The limestone has a cover of sands and ferruginous clays, and a third of the area is under woodland. Traditionally an area of depopulation, productive agriculture

393

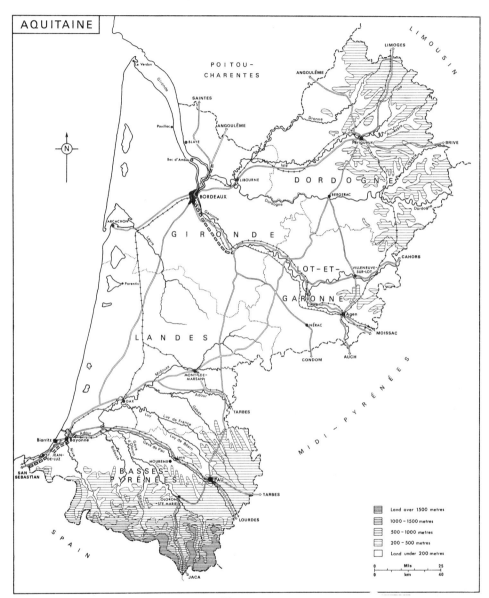

Figure 30.1

is restricted to the alluvial floors of the principal rivers, while the dry
plateau surface affords mediocre grazing. The major town, Périgueux,
owes its development to the convergence of road and rail routes, in
particular the intersection of the main Paris–Limoges–Bordeaux railway
line with the lateral line to Brive and Clermont-Ferrand, and the branch
line to Agen.

To the south-west of the Garonne Valley are three units; the Landes,
the Pays de l'Adour and the western extension of the Pyrénées. The
Landes is one of the most distinctive units of western Europe; an immense
sheet of blown sand, 14,000 square kilometres in area and covered by
France's largest forest. An impermeable hardpan has transformed large
areas into marshland and intense leaching results in soils of poor agricultural quality. The reclamation of the Landes dates from the nineteenth
century, when, after extensive drainage, pine forests were planted and
supported a prosperous forestry economy. This prosperity was under-
minded in the present century by the competition of American and
Scandinavian timber, synthetic dyes and varnishes, and by a succession of
catastrophic fires between 1937 and 1950. In recent years much replanting
has been undertaken, and a regional development company, 'La Compagnie
d'Aménagement des Landes de Gascogne', has reclaimed areas of negative
land and is installing new farms of from 50 to 75 hectares[1]. In spite of the
history of decline, the Landes is not unproductive. Lignite is mined and
supports a thermal power station, petroleum is extracted at Parentis-en-
Born and transported by pipeline to Bordeaux for refining, and the Bay
of Arcachon is the site of a thriving tourist industry.

The Pays de l'Adour is an extensive foothill zone, drained directly to
the Atlantic. Until recently it was an area of polyculture, dominated by
vines and cereals and involved in the transhumant movement of cattle
and sheep from the Pyrénées. In the last decade, the economy of the area
has been transformed by two events: the extension of hybrid maize[2]
sufficiently remunerative to permit mechanization, which now amounts
to one quarter of national production, and the exploitation of the natural
gas at Lacq. Bayonne is the natural port of the area, thriving in the past
on the export of timber and metallurgical products and importing coal
and ore for the steelworks at Le Boucau. The steelworks are now closed
and the timber trade has declined, but new industry has been attracted and
the port has gained impetus from the export of sulphur from Lacq.

The western ranges of the Pyrénées form the southern boundary of
Aquitaine. Much reduced in height and open to moisture-laden winds, a
bocage landscape penetrates the valleys while the mountain slopes support
a pastoral economy. Hydroelectric development in the Gave d'Oloron
has given rise to light industries, while at the coast Biarritz is the centre

of a reputed tourist zone.

The units mentioned briefly above are disposed on either side of the axis of the Garonne Valley, which for a number of reasons is the economic spine of the region. In the first instance, representing the shortest distance between the Atlantic and Mediterranean seas, the Garonne valley is a natural routeway, followed by road, rail and canal. Secondly, forsaking the past pattern of polyculture, the Garonne valley has fulfilled the role of the test ground of specialized commercial agriculture. The orchards and market gardens of the Middle Garonne support food processing industries at Agen and Marmande, while the Bordelais area of the lower Garonne, the Gironde and the lower Dordogne is the leading area of high-quality wine production in France. Finally, in the city and port of Bordeaux, the Garonne axis has an unrivalled focus, and a projection of the valley route to the shipping lanes of the world. Since the principal theme of Aquitaine is the retarded character of economic development at the regional level, it is instructive to elaborate the problems facing the region and to assess the implications of recent trends.

THE PROBLEM OF UNDERDEVELOPMENT

DEMOGRAPHIC WEAKNESS

In relation to the provident character of the resource base, the region of Aquitaine may be considered underpopulated, and in turn the demographic weakness of the region is directly related to the underdeveloped character of the economy. The population of 2·5 millions in 1968 yielded an average density of 55 per square kilometre as compared with a national average of 87 per square kilometre. In fact, Aquitaine was one of the first regions of France to experience a downward trend in fertility, in large measure related to age-selective migration. A century of depopulation has led to an aging population and a depressed birth rate. The population of the region did not regain its level of 1861 until the census of 1962, whereas the national population increased by almost 20 per cent during the same period. The causes of emigration do not appear to have been related to the expulsive forces of an overpopulated rural sector as in Brittany, but rather the attraction of urban living and employment, and Paris has been the major destination of migrants. The factor of improved opportunity applied not only to emigrants leaving the region, but also to a reciprocal current of immigrants entering the region from poorer areas, as interior

Brittany,[3] Italy and Spain, taking up opportunities in agriculture abandoned by the indigenous population.

Between 1954 and 1962 demographic equilibrium was restored to the region, although in a less dramatic fashion than at the national level. Between 1962 and 1968, the population increased by 6·4 per cent as compared with the national trend of over seven per cent. This growth was achieved by an upturn in fertility, a reduction in the rate of rural depopulation, a significant increase in urban growth and a favourable migrational balance. During the same period an important redistribution of population occurred through internal migration. Depopulation has been most severe in the north-east between the Isle and Dordogne valleys, to the north of the lower Dordogne valley, and in certain regions of the piedmont of the Pyrénées and the high mountain valleys. By contrast, the Garonne axis, Bordeaux, the Lacq complex and the coastal tourist areas have gained population, as have almost all the urban centres.

The demographic problems of Aquitaine may be summarized as a low population total, taking into account the size of the area, representing a small and slow-growing internal market, a tendency towards an elderly age structure, especially in the rural sector, and a tendency for the younger and better qualified labour to leave the region, being replaced by an unskilled and in part foreign element in the labour force and by a substantial influx of retired persons.

INDUSTRIAL UNDERDEVELOPMENT

In the sphere of industrial development Aquitaine can justifiably claim to have suffered misfortune, in that the discovery of her substantial wealth of power and raw materials was not made until after the formative stages of the industrial revolution had conferred insuperable advantages on the northern and eastern regions of France. Heavy basic industry took root at only two locations: Le Boucau at the mouth of the Adour, using imported coal and Spanish ore, and Fumel, in Périgord, founded on local small deposits of ore and coal. The blast furnaces of Fumel have survived the rationalization of the iron and steel industry, and the iron is used for the production of tubes, heavy machinery and brake drums. Apart from these isolated cases, industry in Aquitaine was until recently predominantly in two categories: activities related to the agricultural economy, both in the processing of foodstuffs and the manufacture of farm machinery, and, secondly, industries related to the entry of raw materials via the port of Bordeaux. In the latter category may be placed a variety of refining and processing industries, involving especially tropical produce.

The dependence on agriculture and port-based industries persisted until 1930, since when some elaboration of the industrial structure has occurred. The introduction of modern industry has taken place by stages in response to specific events. The first stage occurred in the early years of the decade 1930 to 1940 with the strategic decentralization of the aircraft industry to south-west France.[4] The industry is now of major importance at Bordeaux, where a Dassault plant is located, and in the Basses-Pyrénées at Bayonne, Aire-sur-l'Adour and Bordes. The establishment of a rocket test range in the Landes has given further impetus to the aerospace industry at Bordeaux. Secondly, the development of hydroelectricity in the Pyrénées brought indigenous power to an area previously dependent on imported sources, permitting industrial development and railway electrification in the Pyrénées foothill zones. Thirdly, the discovery of petroleum at Lacq Superieur in 1949, and in more substantial quantities at Parentis in 1954, gave an impetus to the embryonic petroleum refining industry on the Gironde. A small refinery was built at Ambès in 1931 and a second at Pauillac in 1932, producing bitumen, but both were badly damaged during the war. The Parentis field was linked by pipeline to a new refinery built by Esso at Ambès in 1959 and, together with the improvement in terminal facilities for imported crude oil, has stimulated the expansion of refining and the petrochemical industry. The discovery of oil was soon outstripped in importance by the natural gas deposits of Lacq, discovered in 1949. The exploitation of the gas now supports an industrial complex in the vicinity of Lacq[5] and supplies gas to all the major towns of the region. The refining of the gas yields 1·4 million tons of sulphur per annum, the gas field supports one of the largest thermal power stations in France at Artix, and nourishes raw materials for a major petrochemicals complex. In addition, the electricity generated on the gas field is used by a new aluminium plant at Noguères, producing 90,000 tons per annum. The annual production of gas amounts to 7 million tons of coal equivalent but only 25 per cent is consumed in the south-west.

Finally, the introduction of government fiscal measures to aid the industrial development of western France has borne some fruits, particularly in the effort of reconversion carried out at Le Boucau with the closure of the steelworks and the consequent loss of over 1,000 jobs. State aid, and assistance from the iron and steel community of the Common Market, has aided the introduction of a number of new firms in the Bayonne area and a successful redeployment of labour.[6]

The new conditions listed above have reinvigorated industry in Aquitaine but have not transformed the situation. The general level of industrial development remains comparatively low; only 30 per cent of the labour force is employed in manufacturing compared with approximately 40 per cent in agriculture.[7] Moreover, the recent growth of manufacturing has tended to promote a disequilibrium between the new industries of Bordeaux and the Lacq complex and the relative void in central Aquitaine and the eastern portions of the region. The creation of industrial estates in almost all the towns of the region has not yet led to any substantial diffusion of industry. The inability of the smaller centres to expand rapidly in spite of natural gas, new estates and state assistance, may be attributed partly to the regional setting. The small size of the internal market, together with the peripheral location in France and the Common Market, tends to offset the factor of the natural gas supply, which in any case is distributed throughout a large part of the nation. In these conditions Bordeaux, with its large agglomeration and superior communications, and Lacq, with its specific vocation for petrochemical and electro-metallurgical industries, exert an attraction unequalled elsewhere in the region.

THE INFRASTRUCTURE OF COMMUNICATIONS

For long a region of passage, the network of communications is in certain respects the most adequate of western France. In particular the high proportion of electrified rail, the airline network based on Bordeaux, Biarritz and Pau, and the port complex of Bordeaux represent important assets.

The situation is less satisfactory in the case of road transport and inland navigation. The region possesses only a short stretch of motorway, to the north-east of Bordeaux. Particularly serious are the lack of an adequate rapid road connection with Toulouse and the Mediterranean coast and the need for major improvements in the road system of the Basque coast tourist zone. The principal inland waterway, the Canal latéral à la Garonne, gives access via the Canal du Midi to the Mediterranean, but is only accessible to through traffic by barges of 150 tons. The level of traffic has increased substantially in recent years to approximately 500,000 tons per annum, especially due to the transport of cereals from the Garonne valley to the port of Bordeaux.[8] A plan exists to improve this link between the Atlantic and Mediterranean to accept 350 ton barges[9] but the chances of this materializing are prejudiced by the priority given to the Rhône–Rhine link. The canal network, while of significance for the movement of timber, wine and grain, imposes a limitation on the hinterland of the port of Bordeaux.

At first sight the port of Bordeaux, handling 12·8 million tons of traffic in 1967,[10] would not appear to be a manifestation of underdevelopment. Nevertheless, certain severe problems face the port, since, as it is essentially a regional port, the growth of activity is in large measure related to the progress of the regional economy. The most obvious problem is the limitation of the hinterland to the predominantly agricultural region of the Basin of Aquitaine, a hinterland of low population density and modest industrial development. Moreover, the Pays de l'Adour and the southern Landes find a natural outlet in Bayonne, while in the upper Garonne basin the port of Sète enters into competition with Bordeaux. To the east, the hinterland is sealed off by the low population density and underdeveloped economy of the western Massif Central. The weakness of the hinterland is revealed most clearly in the low export component of the port traffic. Only 36 per cent of the cargo handled in 1967 was destined for export. This reflects the low level of industrialization in Aquitaine and particularly the weak representation of the heavy branches. The absence of a prolongation of the port system by a modern high-capacity canal on the Garonne axis is a further limitation on the port's link with the most productive section of its hinterland. Finally, the inland location of Bordeaux, although advantageous in terms of penetration by ocean-going ships, limits the size of vessels able to enter the port at a time when the ability to handle very large bulk carriers and container vessels is becoming increasingly vital.

The character of the port and related industrial development is illustrated by *Figure 30.2*. The port consists of two main components: the river port of Bordeaux, comprising waterfront quays accessible to vessels of up to 25,000 tons and an enclosed basin used by smaller vessels, and a group of four outports downstream from Bordeaux. At the confluence of the Garonne and the Dordogne, some 25 kilometres from Bordeaux, is the Ambès port and industrial complex. The oil terminals are used by small trans-shipment tankers of up to 5,000 tons, and nourish the refineries of Bordeaux (Esso) and Bec d'Ambès (U.I.P.). The small port of Blaye, 36 kilometres from Bordeaux, is used chiefly for the handling of building materials. Pauillac, 50 kilometres from Bordeaux, has a tanker terminal supplying crude oil to the Shell Berre refinery, which produces bitumen. Finally, at the mouth of the Gironde, the outport of Le Verdon, destroyed during the war, has been rebuilt to discharge crude oil. The terminal can now be used by tankers of 110,000 tons for trans-shipment to smaller vessels for the journey upstream to Pauillac and Ambès. The prime function of the outports is thus the reception of crude petroleum and this item of trade accounted for 60 per cent of the total tonnage of maritime trade in 1967.

The trade of Bordeaux has increased steadily over the last decade and certain changes in its characteristics have taken place. The position of coal,

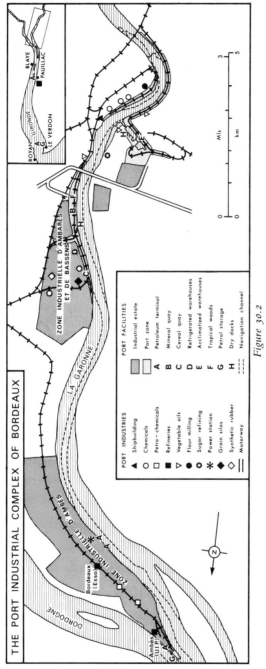

THE PORT INDUSTRIAL COMPLEX OF BORDEAUX

DORDOGNE

ZONE INDUSTRIELLE D'AMBÈS

Bordeaux
(Esso)

Ambès
(U.I.P.)

LA GARONNE

ZONE INDUSTRIELLE D'AMBARÈS
ET DE BASSENS

ROYAN
GIRONDE
LE VERDON
BLAYE
PAUILLAC

PORT INDUSTRIES

▲ Shipbuilding
○ Chemicals
□ Petro - chemicals
■ Refineries
▽ Vegetable oils
● Flour milling
◉ Sugar refining
✳ Power station
◆ Grain silos
◇ Synthetic rubber
‖ Motorway

PORT FACILITIES

        Industrial estate
        Port zone
A Petroleum terminal
B Mineral quay
C Cereal quay
D Refrigerated warehouses
E Acclimatized warehouses
F Tropical woods
G Petrol storage
H Dry docks
---- Navigation channel

0   3 Mls
0   km   5

Figure 30.2

for long a staple import, has now declined before the rise of petroleum. Imports in 1967 totalled 103,000 tons as compared with 2 million tons in 1924. In turn the volume of petroleum traffic has reached a plateau, since the refineries are working at full capacity, and as their output is now absorbed by the regional market the export of refined products has been replaced by imports. The trade in phosphates, ores, tobacco and tropical foodstuffs is increasing, while in the sphere of exports, fertilizers, maize and barley have gained ground. In total, the trend of cargo other than petroleum has been relatively stable in recent years and it is the growth of refining which gives the port an appearance of rapid growth.

The future of trade is dependent on continued improvements in port facilities. In this respect, great efforts are being made by the authority of the 'port autonome' to adjust to the changing patterns of sea transport. The improvement of the deep channel is critical to the future of the port.[11] Dredging enabled the oil terminal of Le Verdon to be reached by 110,000 ton tankers in 1968 and further dredging will raise the limit to 200,000 tons. The industrial quay of Bassens can now be reached by 25,000 ton vessels and by the close of the Fifth Plan this will be increased to 30,000 tons. A further aspect of modernization is the provision of bulk cargo handling quays at Bassens for grain, ores, coal and chemicals and the installation of container berths.

In addition to the improvements in navigation and handling, expansion is dependent on an increase in industrial growth in Aquitaine. Here the port is making a major effort by the creation of waterfront industrial estates,[12] at Bassens, Ambès, and on the left bank, directly connected to the port facilities. A number of major new industries have already been attracted, especially in the petrochemicals and chemical branches. It is clear that the growth of trade is due in large measure to the industrialization of the Bordeaux agglomeration, and especially the expansion of refining and related industries,[13] but as a regional port Bordeaux has remained stable and the extent of the hinterland stubbornly static. The evolution of the Common Market has affected Bordeaux least of the major ports, but the peripheral location could be redressed if Spain ultimately becomes a member country.[14]

THE PRIMARY SECTOR

In 1962, 33 per cent of the labour force was employed in the primary sector and thus approximately half of the total population was dependent on the agricultural economy for its livelihood. Although the conditions and quality of farming are highly variable, in general the problem of retarded development weighs heavily on the agricultural sector and particularly with respect to the level of farm income.

The largest single cause of the inadaptation of farming to modern conditions is undoubtedly the background history of autarchic polyculture. The traditional polyculture involved holdings averaging 10 hectares or less and was based on cereals and vines supplemented by poultry, pigs and cattle. The wintering of sheep from the Pyrénées was a further widespread activity and the contact with the mountain pastoralists fostered commercial exchanges. Although basically designed for self-sufficiency, the system of polyculture included some production to secure a small cash income, such as fruit, quality vines, tobacco, wool, honey, veal, foie gras or meat preserves. During the past century, this stable pattern of polyculture has been subject to a slow evolution in favour of a more commercial system of production.

The breakdown of polyculture was initiated by the growing problem of rural exodus, leaving the countryside short of labour for a system of farming exigent of manual labour. The result was a tendency to simplify the system through a greater degree of specialization, by resort to hired labour and thus to a need of an increased cash income. The decrease in the agricultural labour force has been massive; in 1962 the number of workers employed in farming was 310,000 compared with over 700,000 at the beginning of the century. In the decade preceding the Second World War and more especially since the war, the decrease in manpower has been matched by a pronounced growth in mechanization, but it seems likely that if the present rate of drift from the land continues, the agricultural sector will be left with insufficient labour to realize the maximum potential of the land resources of Aquitaine.

In addition to rural exodus, a second factor modifying the traditional polyculture was the introduction of hybrid maize. Initiated in the Pays de l'Adour, the cultivation of maize has spread throughout the départements of Landes, Gironde and Lot-et-Garonne, where summer rainfall is adequate for the maturing of the plant. The cultivation of maize has effected a revolution in the level of cereal production, in that it has doubled the value of the cereal crop. As a result maize has replaced wheat in the rotation and now accounts for over 80 per cent of the cereal acreage. Moreover, whereas in the traditional polyculture wheat was a subsistence crop, maize yields a profitable cash crop justifying the cost of mechanization. Although maize has had a revolutionary effect it has not fundamentally disturbed the arable-pastoral balance; it has merely replaced other grains and introduced a commercial element, but has not become the basis of a rigorous specialization. In recent years, specialized commercial agriculture has increased in importance in the Garonne and Lot valleys with the establishment of fruit and vegetable growing and livestock rearing.

Some evolution has thus taken· place in the agricultural economy but the process is far from complete and the agricultural resources of the region are by no means fully exploited. The region is among the most retarded in France in the matter of the reform of land holdings. In 1965, remembrement had been completed in only 36 communes, and only 118,000 hectares had been consolidated out of a total of 1·4 million hectares requiring remembrement. The regional development plan[15] cites this as a major obstacle to the solution of the principal problem, that of raising the level of productivity and thus farm incomes. Maximization of productivity is dependent on larger consolidated farm units, permitting mechanization and specialized production.

Productivity is also very low in relation to livestock farming. The practice of keeping a few head of cattle per farm within the polyculture system is unconducive to progress in breeding, while the quality of grassland management is reflected in poor yields per animal. The regional plan foresees improved animal farming, based on fodder crops and irrigated pasture, as one of the most promising specializations open to the region. Low productivity is also a consequence of the small average farm size and the high average age of farm operators. In this respect, the activities of the regional SAFER, farm cooperatives and the 'service du remembrement' must be combined to permit the appearance of large units, amenable to mechanization, amortized through increased revenue from specialized production orientated towards market demands. The work of experimental farms, pilot schemes, and the 'Compagnie d'Aménagement des Landes de Gascogne', has demonstrated the capacity of Aquitaine to increase agricultural output, and especially the advantages to be gained from irrigation. With the exception of the dry limestone plateau of Périgord and the higher slopes of the Pyrénées, the potential of the agricultural economy is far from attained and natural conditions will permit a considerable intensification of production. The essence of underdevelopment is the maladjustment of the operational structure to the task of making the best use of generous land and water resources.

URBAN DEVELOPMENT

The theme of underdevelopment may be pursued in the context of urbanization, for the level of urban development is low; 50 per cent of the total population and almost half the urban population is concentrated in the single agglomeration of Bordeaux. With the exception of the Landes area, the size and spacing of urban centres is remarkably consistent.

A regular network of towns, generally in the size category of 10,000 to 25,000 inhabitants, extends in an arc from Périgueux to Bayonne, with a specific arrangement of from one to three towns in each of the river valleys of the Dordogne, Garonne and Adour basins. The largest agglomerations are those of Périgueux (57,000), Agen (53,000) and Pau (110,000), which combine the function of département capital, commercial centre and route focus, with some industrial development. It is noticeable that the rate of urban growth between 1962 and 1968 decreased from the south northwards, from rates of 27·7 per cent in the agglomeration of Pau, 14·1 per cent at Bayonne, to 11·4 per cent in the Bordeaux agglomeration and 4·4 per cent at Périgueux.

Within an overall regular pattern of urban distribution, three concentrations are sufficiently large and complex as to be distinctive: Pau–Lacq, the Basque conurbation and Bordeaux. Pau is the largest town in a linear urban-industrial zone extending through Lacq to Orthez, with over 100,000 inhabitants. Stimulated in part by the natural gas discoveries and partly by its own industrial and cultural evolution, Pau has grown dramatically since 1954. Distant from the influence of Bordeaux and located on routes orientated east–west, Pau is the dominant centre of the Adour basin. The creation of a direct air link to Paris emphasizes the degree of independence from the regional capital. The new town of Mourenx, built to house the workers of the Lacq complex, has a population of approximately 20,000 inhabitants, but the concentration on capital intensive industries suggests that after the initial surge a period of more moderate population growth may be anticipated.[16] Bayonne is the centre of a conurbation of 110,000 inhabitants on the Basque coast, extending from Hendaye to Le Boucau, based on tourism, fishing, industry and port activity.

The importance of the Pau and Bayonne urban-industrial zones is dwarfed by that of the regional capital, Bordeaux. With 555,000 inhabitants in its agglomeration in 1968, Bordeaux ranked as the fourth city of France and the largest city of western France. The city is sited predominantly on the left bank of the Garonne and has expanded radially in conformity with the meander form of the river. The recent growth of the agglomeration has been modelled by a development plan designed to harmonize land uses and improve circulation.[17] Thus there are contrasts between the older industrial locations, lining the river port in the heart of the city, and the modern estates created upstream at Bègles, downstream at Bassens and Ambès, and on the periphery of the agglomeration at Blanquefort and at Merignac airport. Similarly, the older residential extension is punctuated by 'grands ensembles' while entirely new suburbs are being built on the right bank of Lornon and Cenon. The development plan also includes a relocation of the university in the suburb of Talence, and the construction of a new civic, residential and recreational complex on the northern fringe of the agglomeration. The original external boulevard has long since been absorbed by the built-up area, and a new peripheral motorway encircling the agglomeration and crossing the river by new bridges is under construction. This system has already improved access to the port and will ultimately ease congestion in the business district of the city. The planned development of the city involves a considerable expansion of the built-up area, but with provision for a coherent zoning of functions, inter-linked by intra-urban motorways. Less original in concept than the Toulouse master plan, the plan for Bordeaux provides for a rational expansion of the existing agglomeration rather than the creation of satellites.

Within Aquitaine, Bordeaux occupies an unchallenged position as a regional centre and shares with Toulouse the function of counterbalancing Paris within south-west France. The dominance of Bordeaux within the region rests on three functions: the activity of the port, the importance of industry, related in large measure to the port function, and commercial activity, also animated by maritime trade. The university, founded in 1441, serves the entire region and houses many advanced research institutions of national importance, while the wine trade and shipping activities have fostered the development of important financial institutions. Geographically distant from Paris, unrivalled in the region by any other city and enjoying world-wide trading connections, Bordeaux would appear admirably equipped to discharge its intended role as a 'métropole d'équilibre', but as yet this remains an aspiration rather than a reality. The major industries are controlled by national and international companies, the city lacks the dynamic growth recently experienced by Toulouse, and in the south of the region the influence of Bordeaux is subordinated to that of Pau and of the Bayonne conurbation.

AQUITAINE AT THE CROSSROADS

The regional plan for Aquitaine judges that the region has reached a crossroads in its economic history.[18] Additions to the resource base, advances in technology and the changed political atmosphere resulting from the recognition of the specific problems of western France, present Aquitaine with a new opportunity to emerge from its economic and demographic lethargy. In the last 20 years, the energy situation has been transformed, Bordeaux has become the oil-refining capital of the south-west, Lacq has emerged as a new pole of development and the agricultural economy has been revitalized by the introduction of hybrid maize. As yet, these advances are isolated symptoms of a new potential but have not fostered a general economic resurgence. The central problem of the future is to transform the recent experience of growth at a limited number of points into a broadly based uplift in the level of economic activity. The resources for such an evolution do exist, in the form of power, chemicals, under-used agricultural land, vast forests and large reserves of water for irrigation and industrial use. The difficulty is encountered in creating the appropriate economic climate for the realization of the region's potential. The analogy between Aquitaine and a miniature California is not extravagant, but beneath this vision lies an alternative analogy with Algeria, an economy exporting resources for use by others and the victim of underdevelopment.

REFERENCES

[1] Lerat, S., 'L'installation des agriculteurs par la Compagnie d'Aménagement des Landes de Gascogne', *Revue Géogr. Pyrénées S.-Ouest*, 1964, p. 436.

[2] Lerat, S., 'L'introduction du maïs hybride dans les Pays de l'Adour', *Revue Géogr. Pyrénées S.-Ouest*, 1961, p. 97.

[3] Pinède, C., 'L'immigration Bretonne en Aquitaine', *Revue Géogr. Pyrénées S.-Ouest*, 1960, p. 5.

[4] Guichard, O., *Aménager la France*, pp. 16–17, 1965, Paris, Laffont-Gonthier.

[5] Barrère, P., Heisch, R., and Lerat, S., *La Région du Sud-Ouest*, Fig. 20, p. 84, 1962, Paris, Presses Universitaires de France.

[6] Taillefer, F., 'La reconversion des forges du Boucau', *Revue Géogr. Pyrénées S.-Ouest*, 1966, p. 425.

[7] La Documentation Française, 'L'Economie d'Aquitaine', *Notes Etud. docum.*, No. 3,082, 1964, pp. 46–62.

[8] Brunet, R., 'Expansion et problèmes des canaux du Midi', *Revue Géogr. Pyrénées S.-Ouest*, 1963, p. 207.

[9] Pelletier, E., *Les canaux du Midi*, Le Port de Bordeaux en 1967, 1968, p. 39.

[10] Port Autonome de Bordeaux, *Rapport Annuel*, 1967.

[11] Anon., 'Amélioration du chenal de navigation de la Gironde', *Gaz. Port*, No. 16, 1968, p. 2.

[12] Dumas, J., 'Les zones industrielles de l'agglomération Bordelaise' *Revue Géogr. Pyrénées S.-Ouest*, 1965, p. 415.

[13] Saint-Gaudens, A., *Bordeaux, Métropole Pétrolière du Sud-Ouest*, Le Port de Bordeaux en 1967, 1968, p. 53.

[14] Pages, M., *Le Port de Bordeaux*, Communication faite à l'Association des Grands Ports Français, 1968, p. 13.

[15] 'Aquitaine. Plan régional de développement et d'aménagement', *Journal Officiel*, No. 1,263, 1965, p. 73.

[16] George, P., *La France*, p. 215, 1967, Paris, Presses Universitaires de France.

[17] *Documn Photogr.*, 'Problèmes de la France d'aujourd'hui, "Métropoles Régionales"', 1964, Fig. 111.

[18] Reference 15, p. 45.

31

Midi-Pyrénées

The Midi-Pyrénées is the nation's largest planning region, but shares with Limousin the lowest average population density of approximately 45 persons per square kilometre. The region may be characterized as having generally difficult environmental conditions, a retarded economic structure and a depressing history of chronic rural depopulation.

THE RESOURCE BASE

In broad outline, Midi-Pyrénées is an amalgam of three provinces; the eastern portion of the basin of Aquitaine, the central Pyrénées, and the south-western Massif Central. The heartland of the planning region is the 'molasse' hill and plain zone surrounding the middle Garonne.[1] This area has the region's best land resources and is given over to a traditional polyculture which until recently had remained static, retarded in both structure and technique, provoking heavy depopulation. The molasse hills are traversed by the broad valleys of the Garonne, Tarn and Lot, in which alluvial soils support more intensive polyculture, fruit farming, commercial viticulture and market gardening. North and west of the molasse zone, some deterioration of land resources occurs on the plateau margin of the basin of Aquitaine. In the north, the limestone plateau of Quercy is a karstic area in which agricultural activity is concentrated on the valley floors, where livestock rearing is orientated towards veal and lamb production. The western plateaux of Lannemezan and Armagnac are constituted of detrital material, dissected by powerful streams. The more elevated Lannemezan plateau is formed of coarse free-draining gravels, supporting dry soils and degraded vegetation. The deeper soils of the valley floors are irrigated and support veal production. The lower plateau of Armagnac has finer alluvial deposits and polyculture similar to that of the Garonne hill zone is practised, in which viticulture is the basis of Armagnac brandy production.

408

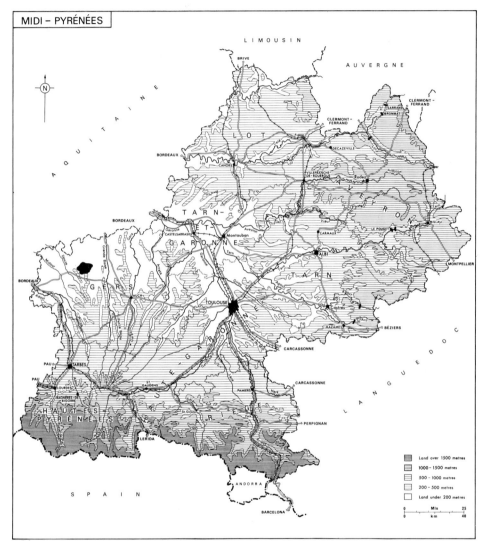

MIDI – PYRÉNÉES

Figure 31.1

To the south of this heartland, the chains of the central Pyrénées attain the maximum elevations of the entire system, at over 3,000 metres. A pastoral economy is practised with transhumance including movement to winter feeding in lowland Aquitaine. The numbers of livestock have declined greatly in the last half century, accompanied by a proportionate reduction in the rural population? The portion of the Massif Central falling within the region consists of two contrasted zones. The western component is an elevated crystalline plateau, with mediocre, siliceous soils and a background of severe depopulation. Between the middle Tarn and the Aveyron, the Segalas stands out as a zone of improvement where cooperative organization of sheep and dairy farming has raised the level of agricultural activity. To the east, limestones are preserved in a downwarp of the crystalline basement, producing the high plateau of the Causses. These bleak, karstic uplands support rough grazing, with small basins given over to more intensive farming. The basin of Roquefort is specialized in the processing of ewe's milk into cheese, the local supplies being supplemented by unprocessed cheese imported from the Pyrénées and Corsica.

The exploitation of land resources encounters certain physical constraints. Open to Atlantic air masses, the region escapes the full rigour of the Mediterranean summer drought, but the large areas of limestone bedrock and gravel detritus reduce the effectiveness of precipitation and the quality of natural pasture throughout much of the region, while in the major valleys damaging floods can occur. Although high summer temperatures permit a wide crop range, including maize, tobacco and soft fruit, damaging spring frosts commonly occur, while a high proportion of the region is sufficiently elevated to experience bleak conditions throughout much of the year. Even the lower land is not free from hazard; the molasse hills have a broken relief where intense rainfall can produce severe soil erosion. In these conditions, successful commercial farming is dependent on rational farm structures, artificial improvement through drainage, fertilization and supplementary irrigation, and thus on a high degree of initiative and capitalization. Until recently, traditional practices characterized farming, and only on the best soils and in the vicinity of the largest towns did agriculture assume a rational and progressive character.

The endowment of energy sources is similarly characterized by both positive assets and serious limitations. In 1966 the hydroelectric schemes of the Pyrénées and the Massif Central yielded just over 17 per cent of the nation's hydraulic electricity, but the coalbasins of Decazeville and Carmaux produced only 3·3 per cent of the national coal output. The 'Houillères du Bassin d' Aquitaine' is constituted by two separate fields, in the Lot valley at Decazeville, and the Carmaux field near Albi in the département of Tarn[3]. The two fields produced 1·6 million tons in 1966, most of which is consumed on the fields in the power and chemical industries. The single mine at Decazeville has now been closed and output is based solely on open-cast mining, with a consequent reduction in manpower[4]. The Carmaux basin is exploited by inclined shafts, and the construction of a new power station at Albi, which entered service in 1969, will maintain output at its present level. Employment in coalmining totalled just over 4,000 in 1966, as compared with over 6,000 workers in 1962.

By contrast, the production of hydroelectricity is both more important and more widely distributed. The principal sites are located on the upper Tarn and Lot, the Agout and Thore in the Massif Central, and on virtually every river draining from the central Pyrénées. Although the contribution made by the two mountain systems is comparable*, the basis of production is different. The long courses and narrow defiles of the Tarn and Lot offer sites for major barrages with huge storage reservoirs and high installed capacity. By contrast, the shorter length and limited catchments of the Pyrenean streams has led to harnessing by smaller stations exploiting the frequent breaks of profile[5].

The region does possess an abundant potential for tourism and this resource has been widely exploited[6] on the basis of summer holidays and winter sports in the Pyrénées[7,8] and rural holidays in the Massif Central. To this must be added the 'en passant' tourist trade of towns of historical and architectural interest like Toulouse and Albi, and the pilgrimage centre of Lourdes.

PROBLEMS OF ECONOMIC AND SOCIAL DEVELOPMENT

Midi-Pyrénées has not always been a problem region of France; until the late eighteenth century the Garonne axis was a major routeway linking the Mediterranean and Atlantic, and the towns were animated by commerce and artisan industries. Possessing only modest industrial resources, the industrial revolution imposed a relative decline on the region. Situated at a maximum distance from the national capital and the industrial towns of eastern France, the region became a cul-de-sac, marked by heavy rural depopulation and urban stagnation. At the turn of the last century, the development of hydroelectricity stimulated the growth of electrochemical and electro-metallurgical industries in the Pyrenean valleys, but little

*In 1966, the Pyrénées contributed 55 per cent of the region's output, and the Massif Central 44 per cent.

progress was made in the rural economy and only the arrival of foreign agriculturalists prevented depopulation from reaching catastrophic proportions. The industrial economy received some stimulus from the strategic decentralization of the aircraft industry before the outbreak of the Second World War, and since the war by the arrival of natural gas from Lacq. In the last 15 years the economy of Midi-Pyrénées has experienced some revival, but the weight of inherited problems and the handicap of a peripheral location still burden the region. A trilogy of problems is of central importance; a chronic loss of population through the combined effect of emigration and reduced fertility, in turn related to the high dependence on a retarded agricultural economy and a low level of industrial and urban development.

Midi-Pyrénées has the dolorous distinction of having sustained the heaviest losses of population during the past hundred years of all the French planning regions. During the latter half of the nineteenth century the region experienced a net loss of a quarter of a million inhabitants, followed by a further loss of the same amount between 1901 and 1936. During the war the influx of refugees caused a slight increase in total population and since 1946 a more pronounced growth has occurred. This recent growth must be attributed to the expansion of Toulouse and the resettlement of French Algerians rather than to any significant reversal of the trend of rural depopulation.

Tabel 31.1

POPULATION CHANGE IN AQUITAINE FROM YEAR OF MAXIMUM POPULATION[a] TO 1968

Département	Year of maximum	Percentage change	Total change (1,000)
Haute-Garonne	1968	–	–
Hautes-Pyrénées	1861	− 5·8	− 14
Gers	1861	−39·4	−118
Ariège	1861	−45·3	−114
Tarn-et-Garonne	1881	−21·4	− 50
Tarn	1881	− 7·5	− 27
Aveyron	1881	−32·4	−134
Lot	1861	−49·0	−135

[a]Since 1861.
Source: Recensements de 1962 and 1968.

It is seen from *Table 31.1* that only Haute-Garonne, dominated by Toulouse, has escaped loss of population. The département of Hautes-Pyrénées owes the slightness of its loss of population to the development of industry based on hydroelectricity, the growth of tourism, and the recent industrial expansion of Tarbes. Similarly, the small-scale industrial and commercial growth of Carmaux, Albi, Castres and Mazamet has retained population in western Tarn. Elsewhere the pattern is of unrelieved and heavy depopulation over the past century, corresponding with an exodus from impoverished mountain areas lacking in urban centres to stem the tide of rural depopulation. Thus the population of Lot has been halved and those of Gers and Ariège reduced by 40 per cent. To the heavy migrational losses of the nineteenth centuries must be added the subsequent losses by natural change sustained by an increasingly elderly population. Although migration to Paris and abroad accounts for much of the reduction in population, not all the losses indicated in *Table 31.1* were due to emigration from the region. There has been considerable internal redistribution within the region in the form of a drift from the mountains to the central agricultural belt and the city of Toulouse.[9] Underlying population loss is the high agricultural dependence and the inability of the urban network to absorb the inevitable efflux of population as agriculture sheds its autarchic basis and adjusts to commercial conditions.

A measure of the dependence on agriculture is afforded by the fact that in 1962 45·6 per cent of the labour force was employed in farming. With the exception of sheep and cattle grazing on the plateaux of the Massif Central, and the pastoral economy of the high Pyrenean valleys, the dominant agricultural system is polyculture, in which wheat is the leading crop. Until quite recently polyculture persisted on an autarchic basis, tolerant of low yields and with a high concentration of elderly operators as a result of depopulation. Between 1955 and 1963, the number of farms declined by over 40,000, accompanied by a 20 per cent reduction in the farm labour force. Family operation is almost universal and 85 per cent of all farms are owner-operated. In 1965 less than 6 per cent of the farms hired three or more permanent workers, but recourse to seasonal immigrant labour is widespread* The average farm size is 15 hectares and only two per cent of all the farms exceed 50 hectares. The basic problem of the polyculture system is to integrate a structure traditionally oriented towards self-sufficiency, and thus paying little attention to labour costs and productivity, into a viable commercial system.

Considerable progress towards achieving this transformation has been achieved since the Second World War. The introduction of hybrid maize as a high-yielding alternative to soft wheat has made spectacular progress, the more so since mechanization has permitted its introduction without increase in labour demand. By 1965, maize production was almost half that of wheat and amounted to over 17 per cent of the national output.

*In 1966, 123,000 seasonal foreign workers were employed in the region, largely in agriculture and chiefly Spaniards and Italians.

Brunet[10] has, however, indicated that the introduction of maize has created certain difficulties. The late harvesting period conflicts with the sowing time of wheat, while the association of the two grains is handicapped by the fact that a good climate season for maize is a poor one for wheat yields and vice versa. In recent years, the extension of maize has slowed down as a result of favourable wheat prices in the Common Market arrangements, and it is likely that an increasing proportion of the crop will be ensilaged for cattle feeding.

The introduction of maize has been followed by other new cash crops, especially colza, sorghum and sunflowers. Extraordinary progress has also been made in mechanization; from being one of the least equipped regions at the close of the war, the region possessed over 115,000 tractors in 1965—11·5 per cent of the national total. This rapid mechanization has, to a large degree, been irrational leading to serious over-capitalization. Brunet[11] has drawn attention to the distinction between 'motorization'—the purchase of powerful and expensive tractors—and 'mechanization'—the rational application of machinery appropriate to the size, character and cash turnover of a farm. In opting for the former, many farmers have ignored the logic imposed by fragmented holdings of 15 hectares, on which a substantial proportion of the produce is still consumed on the farm and thus not available for amortizing machinery.

The progress made in introducing new crops and machinery has not been matched by the structural reforms necessary to permit their rational utilization. At the beginning of 1966, only 158,000 hectares had been consolidated or were in process of remembrement—only 2·4 per cent of the national total. More impressive is the effort to extend irrigation, sponsored since 1959 by a mixed economy company, the 'Compagnie d'Aménagement des Coteaux de Gascogne'.[12] Completed schemes are concentrated on the Lannemezan plateau but future extensions will include the right bank of the Garonne, the Ariège and the valleys of the Lot, Tarn and Aveyron.[13] A further stimulus to modernization and to structural improvement has been provided by the resettlement of repatriates from North Africa. The first arrival of 'colons' dates from the independence of Morocco and Tunisia and involved the creation of large farms, a heavy investment in machinery and an emphasis on cereal cultivation. By contrast, the return of repatriates from Algeria has been more substantial and their preference has been for more intensive farming, especially of fruit and vines.[14] Partly under the impetus of the repatriates, the Garonne valley is now a major fruit growing area, and over-production of peaches, apples and pears may become a serious problem.

The progress outlined thus far applied particularly to the predominantly arable polyculture system of the lowland portion of the region. The pastoral economy of the mountain zones has of necessity experienced a more gradual evolution. The major effort has been placed on improvement of livestock breeds, an increase in the output of more valuable animal produce, such as lamb, veal and dairy items, and an increase in cooperative organization. This has been accompanied by an effort to improve the rural environment through electrification and water supply schemes, in these, the most depopulated and desolate parts of the region.

The high degree of agricultural dependence has its counterpart in the third central problem of the region, the low degree of urban and industrial development. The labour force of 157,000 employed in manufacturing industry in 1962 accounted for only 19 per cent of the region's total work force. With 4·4 per cent of the national population, Midi-Pyrénées employed only 2·9 per cent of the French manufacturing labour force. As a consequence, the urban proportion of the total population was only 48·4 per cent. The secondary importance of manufacturing may be demonstrated by reference to location quotients for specific industries★ (*Table 31.2*).

Table 31.2

LOCATION QUOTIENTS OF SELECTED INDUSTRIES IN MIDI-PYRÉNÉES, 1962

Aircraft engineering	3·14	Clothing	0·77
Leather and skins	1·58	Chemicals	0·64
Tobacco and matches	1·25	Metallurgy	0·64
Textiles	0·83	Mechanical engineering	0·50
Food industries	0·79	Printing and publishing	0·44
Wood and furniture	0·79	Electrical engineering	0·32

Source: INSEE, 'Tableaux de l'Economie Midi-Pyrénées', 1968, p. 126.

Only three industrial activities are shown by *Table 31.2* to have an above normal concentration in the region. The tobacco industry reflects the importance of this crop in the region, but leather industries, originally supported by local resources, are now sustained by imported hides. By contrast, the aeronautical industry has little relationship to the region's resources but springs from the chance development of a Toulouse company, reinforced by strategic decentralizations. Outside the Toulouse agglomeration, industry is marked by small scale of operation and a dispersed location.[15] The most widespread industries are those with a traditional basis, such as textiles, tanning and leather working, and food processing. With the exception of food processing, the traditional industries are currently experiencing contraction. Superimposed on this background are a number

★A quotient of 1·0 indicates an average concentration compared with the national pattern.

of specialized industrial centres related to particular past or present conditions. In this category may be placed the development of electrometallurgy and electrochemicals in the Pyrenean sections of the Adour, Garonne, Ariège and Gave de Pau valleys, nourished by hydroelectricity.[16] Thus aluminium is produced at Lannemezan and Auzat, special and alloy steels at Pamiers, and magnesium near Bagnères-de-Bigorre. The task of equipping the hydroelectric plants and the electrification of the railways stimulated electrical engineering and locomotive construction at Tarbes. The coal deposits of the Tarn basin nourish a chemical industry at Carmaux producing fertilizers, while chemicals, zinc and special steels are produced on the Decazeville coal basin. The production of electro-steels at St. Juéry, on the Tarn, is a survival of the past utilization of local ores. The amount of employment created by these industries was comparatively small, and only Tarbes, stimulated in the past decade by the arrival of Lacq natural gas, has developed into an industrial agglomeration of importance, with 73,000 inhabitants in 1968.[17]

The dispersed pattern of industrial development is overshadowed in scale and variety by the growth of Toulouse. Based on the twin pillars of the aircraft industry and the chemical plant of the 'Office National Industriel de l'Azote' (ONIA), Toulouse nevertheless has a diversified industrial background consisting of both traditional and advanced technology branches. Together with the growth of cultural, educational and commercial importance, industrial expansion has established Toulouse as the sixth largest city of France. In view of this rapid post-war growth and the nomination of the city as a 'métropole d'équilibre', some elaboration of the changing structure of the agglomeration is warranted.

The agglomeration had a population of 365,000 in 1968, an increase by 20 per cent over the 1962 figure* and a growth rate greater than that of any other agglomeration of over 300,000 inhabitants. The site of the Gallo-Roman settlement was a terrace on the right bank of the Garonne, and from this core the medieval town extended to a line now enclosed within an 'enceinte' of boulevards, the majority of the settlement remaining on the right bank. This medieval nucleus now forms the commercial and cultural core of the city (*Figure 31.2*), but contains less than 17 per cent of the total population.

The agglomeration has expanded from this core in concentric fashion in a number of clearly defined stages.[18,19] A first expansion occurred between the seventeenth and late nineteenth centuries, extending as far as the line of the Canal du Midi. Towards the end of the nineteenth century, rapid tentacular development occurred along the major routes, absorbing a number of small settlements, followed by a period during which the

*Between 1954 and 1962 the population increased by 21 per cent.

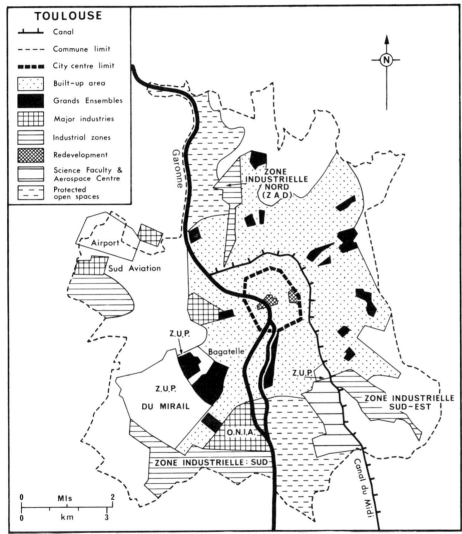

TOULOUSE

⊢⊢	Canal
- - -	Commune limit
■■■■	City centre limit
⠿	Built-up area
■	Grands Ensembles
⊞	Major industries
≡	Industrial zones
⊠	Redevelopment
☰	Science Faculty & Aerospace Centre
⊡	Protected open spaces

Garonne

ZONE INDUSTRIELLE NORD (Z A D)

Airport

Sud Aviation

Z.U.P.

Bagatelle

Z.U.P.

Z.U.P. DU MIRAIL

Z.U.P.

ZONE INDUSTRIELLE SUD-EST

O.N.I.A.

ZONE INDUSTRIELLE: SUD

Canal du Midi

N

0	Mls	2
0	km	3

Figure 31.2

lacuna between the arteries was infilled haphazardly on the basis of small building plots. Thus a second concentric zone was created, within which much of the agglomeration's industry was located. By 1945, Toulouse had begun to suffer the problems of a growth that had been too rapid and uncontrolled, precisely at the moment when its demographic expansion was to reach new heights.

Since 1945, and more particularly since 1950, the development of the agglomeration has been subject to the intervention of planning, and the form of construction has changed.[20] A large number of apartment complexes was built on the periphery of the agglomeration, forming yet another concentric zone of 'grands ensembles' of H.L.M. and similar types. Between 1954 and 1960, 224 apartment blocks were built containing 15,000 dwelling units housing approximately one fifth of the total population. The result was the creation of a virtual wall of concrete round the city, contrasting sharply with the low, mellow pantiled roofs and brick façades of the old centre.[21] Some measure of separation of industry and housing has been achieved by the creation of industrial zones. In some instances, as in the case of the chemical plants of the ONIA company, this involved an extension of existing industrial terrains while others represent new creations, scheduled for specific types of manufacturing.

The construction of 'grands ensembles' has eased the housing problem and has permitted redevelopment of old housing in the city centre. However, they remained essentially residential units, inadequately equipped with services and social amenities. This has placed additional strains on the city centre and has stimulated journey to work movements, adding to the congestion resulting from commuting from surrounding settlements outside the agglomeration.[22] Faced with unabated population growth since 1960, the city has invoked the new powers permitting the creation of 'zones à urbaniser en priorité' in order to establish areas of comprehensive planned development. Of these, the Bagatelle Z.U.P. (see *Figure 31.2*) is completed but will be overshadowed in the future by the ambitious Z.U.P. of Le Mirail.

Situated on the left bank of the Garonne, occupying a site of 1,750 acres, the Le Mirail scheme is planned to receive 100,000 inabitants.* In comparison with the uniformity of the existing 'grands ensembles', Le Mirail will have diversified housing forms, complete educational facilities and recreational facilities including a sports stadium. It will be neither a new town, in the British sense, nor a satellite city, but will depend on Toulouse for its municipal administration and for high-order commercial services. Sufficient employment is planned for approximately a third of

---

*The plan adopted was the outcome of a competition in which architects had to incorporate specific principles of urban design and sociology.

the resident labour force, chiefly located in a new light industrial zone to the south of the residential section. However, Le Mirail is situated at a convenient distance from the city's two largest industrial complexes, the Sud-Aviation aircraft works and the O.N.I.A. chemical plant. In addition to the adherence to sociological principles, generally absent from the 'grands ensembles', the Mirail plan has great originality in its relationship to the existing agglomeration and to the region served by Toulouse. By virtue of its anticipated size and large population, Le Mirail has been termed 'Toulouse II' and 'Toulouse Parallel'. The latter term is an allusion to its location on the relatively underdeveloped left bank of the Garonne, and the long-term prospect of an axis from the aerospace complex of Sud-Aviation, through Le Mirail, to the Zone Industriel Sud, forming virtually a new city, parallel to the present agglomeration. Such a dichotomy is not countenanced by the planners, who envisage a symbiotic relationship between the new and old structures. More challenging is the intended role of Le Mirail within the region of Midi-Pyrénées. Consonant with the selection of Toulouse as a 'métropole d'équilibre', it is intended to concentrate in Le Mirail those social and administrative institutions which have a regional significance. The projected location, in Le Mirail, of the Faculty of Letters and Social Sciences of the University of Toulouse is a first step in this direction.

As yet it is premature to judge the success of the scheme and several problems remain.[23,24] A pilot stage of construction is in operation and a major firm has started to build a new factory on the industrial estate* The significance of the plan is the degree to which it departs from the uncontrolled growth prior to 1945 and the post-war rash of apartment complexes, which have neither enhanced the aesthetic allure of the city nor provided a long-term solution to the general problems of city planning.

In addition to the Mirail scheme, the advent of long-term integrated planning in the context of a 'métropole d'équilibre' is also manifest in the birth of a scientific complex situated in the south-east of the agglomeration. This is constituted by the new university Faculty of Science and by the National Aeronautical College and the National Institute of Applied Science, both recently decentralized from Paris, together with the newly-created National Centre for Space Studies. An adjacent new industrial zone is scheduled to receive industries utilizing advanced technology. The overall plan is completed by a contiguous Z.U.P. providing housing for workers in the science complex and by the provision of a zone of protected open countryside to the west.

Toulouse dominates the urban network of Midi-Pyrénées to an extreme

---

*The American firm of Motorola, which is building a factory manufacturing semi-conductors, employing 2,000 workers by 1970.

degree,[25] being five times larger than the second largest centre, Tarbes. The pattern of urban distribution shows a marked irregularity. A line of towns, including Mazamet, Castres, Albi and Cahors, coincides with the contact between the central lowland zone and the uplands of the Massif Central, while a second line, from Pamiers, Foix, St. Gaudens and Lannemezan to Tarbes, coincides with the strong communications line of the Pyrenean foothills. Between these two lines the dominance of Toulouse is absolute, Montauban being too close to the regional capital to exert a strong independent influence. The eastern portion of the region is a virtual urban vacuum, in which Rodez and Millau, both with approximately 25,000 inhabitants, preside over hinterlands of extremely low population density.

It is difficult to escape the conclusion that Midi-Pyrénées is a region possessing elements of both strength and fragility. It undoubtedly has an agricultural potential which, despite recent progress, is underexploited. However, lacking a large internal demand for high-value produce, the region must seek to compete successfully in the context of the Common Market price structure. In the aerospace industry of Toulouse, the region is participating in advanced technology manufacturing, but the vulnerability of the aircraft industry to contracting sales is a familiar danger. It is likely also that the buoyant growth of Toulouse, the improvement of agriculture in the middle Garonne basin and the expansion of tourism in the Pyrénées, as compared with the continued depopulation and lack of urban expansion in the Massif Central, will distort still further the internal lack of equilibrium in the region. Unless a comparable revival to that achieved by Tarbes can be emulated by such towns as Rodez, Millau or Decazeville, of which there is as yet little indication, there seems little likelihood of reversing the present trend of depopulation or increasing substantially the contribution of the Massif Central to the regional economy.

REFERENCES

[1] Brunet, R., Les Campagnes Toulousaines, 1965, Toulouse, Faculté des Lettres et Sciences Humaines.

[2] Chevalier, M., La Vie Humaine dans les Pyrénées Ariégoises, 1956, Paris, Génin.

[3] Boudou, A., 'L'évolution récente des Houillères du Bassin d'Aquitaine', Revue Géogr. Pyrénées S.-Ouest, 1965, p. 193.

[4] Assie, J., 'Les Houillères du Bassin d'Aquitaine et leurs difficultés', Inf. géogr., No. 5, 1967, p. 232.

[5] Viers, G., Les Pyrénées, Fig. 2, p. 106, 1962, Paris, Presses Universitaires de France.

[6] Coppolani, J., 'Les stations touristiques de Midi-Pyrénées en 1964', Revue Géogr. Pyrénées S.-Ouest, 1966, p. 59.

[7] Bertrand, A., 'Le développement des sports d'hiver dans les Pyrénées', Revue Géogr. Pyrénées S.-Ouest, 1965, p. 65.

[8] Cazes, G., 'Nouveaux aspects du tourisme d'hiver dans les Pyrénées', Revue Géogr. Pyrénées S.-Ouest, 1967, p. 69.

[9] Toujas-Pinède, C., 'Une émigration traditionelle: Les Aveyronnais en Aquitaine', Revue Géogr. Pyrénées S.-Ouest, 1961, p. 141.

[10] Brunet, R., *op. cit.*[1], pp. 594–7.

[11] Brunet, R., *op. cit.*[1], pp. 435–454.

[12] Ministry of Agriculture, 'L'aménagement hydraulique des Coteaux de Gascogne', *Notes Etud. docum.*, No. 2,740, 1961.

[13] Barraud, P., 'L'aménagement agricole des Coteaux de Gascogne', *Grands Aménagement rég.*, No. 3, 1964, p. 46.

[14] Toujas-Pinède, C., 'Les rapatriés d'Algérie dans la région Midi-Pyrénées', *Revue Géogr. Pyrénées S.-Ouest*, 1965, p. 321.

[15] Deveaud, J., 'L'évolution économique et sociale de la région Midi-Pyrénées, *Notes Etud. docum.*, No. 3,166, 1965, pp. 53–66.

[16] Doumergue, Y., 'Electro-chimie et électro-métallurgie dans les Hautes-Pyrénées', *Revue Géogr. Pyrénées S.-Ouest*, 1965, p. 373.

[17] Doumergue, Y., 'Les grandes industries de Tarbes', *Inf. géogr.*, 1965, p. 21.

[18] Coppolani, J., 'Esquisse géographique de la banlieue de Toulouse', *Revue Géogr. Pyrénées S.-Ouest*, 1963, p. 217.

[19] Pechoux, P., *et al.*, 'Les Grandes Villes Françaises, Toulouse', *Notes Etud. docum.*, No. 3,262, 1966, pp. 6–11.

[20] Beringuier, C., 'L'aménagement de l'espace toulousain', *Revue Géogr. Pyrénées S.-Ouest*, 1967, p. 145.

[21] Kayser, B., 'Le nouveau visage de Toulouse', *Revue Géogr. Pyrénées S.-Ouest*, 1961, p. 225.

[22] Coppolani, J., 'Les migrations alternantes vers Toulouse en 1954 et 1962', *Revue Géogr. Pyrénées S.-Ouest*, 1967, p. 165.

[23] Brunet-le Rouzic, L., 'Où en est Toulouse-Mirail', *Revue Géogr. Pyrénées S.-Ouest*, 1964, p. 200.

[24] Lednut, R., and Roy, C., 'Toulouse, sociologie et planification urbaine', *Urbanisme*, No. 93, 1966, p. 51.

[25] Coppolani, J., 'L'armature urbaine du Sud-Ouest', *Revue Géogr. Pyrénées S.-Ouest*, 1967, p. 131.

32

Languedoc

The region of Languedoc is endowed with ingrained problems and seductive possibilities in almost equal proportions. Spoken of as a future California or Florida, the region nevertheless has suffered catastrophic depopulation in certain of its areas, has one of the lowest industrial levels in France, and, on the plain of Bas-Languedoc, has suffered from an inert and monolithic concentration on viticulture, prone to the vicissitudes of climate and market alike.[1] The central problem of Languedoc is therefore not merely to raise the level of economic development, a problem shared by the whole of western France, but rather to effect a total conversion of the economic structure in order to realize the region's undoubted potential. The theme of this essay is the effort of regional reconstruction now being engaged, which is calculated to transform the landscape and economy of Languedoc within the next decade.

The planning region consists of the five départements of Aude, Gard, Hérault, Lozère and Pyrénées-Orientales, having a total population of 1·7 million inhabitants in 1968. Four of these départements share a position on the Mediterranean façade, an orientation of drainage towards that littoral, a contrast between lowland coastal plain and an interior mountain zone, and an environment dominated by Mediterranean climatic influences. The fifth departement, Lozère, occupies an anomalous position, having an interior location, with drainage via the Lot and Tarn towards the Atlantic, and being essentially an integral part of the Massif Central. Ideally, Lozère would be subdivided between the planning regions of Midi-Pyrénées, Rhône-Alpes, Auvergne and Languedoc, and its attachment to the latter is a matter of administrative convenience rather than a strict reality.

The fundamental physical distinction within the region is that between the coastal lowlands and the mountain interior, but conditions are far from uniform within these two zones. The coastal lowland is dominated by the plain of Bas-Languedoc, with à coastal fringe festooned by étangs and sandspits. The much smaller lowland, the plain of Roussillon, is entrenched in the eastern extremity of the Pyrénées and is the site of an intensive irrigated 'huerta'-style landscape. In Roussillon, the contact between the plain and mountain is quite abrupt, but in the case of Bas-Languedoc a discontinuous piedmont zone, the 'garrigues', intervenes between the

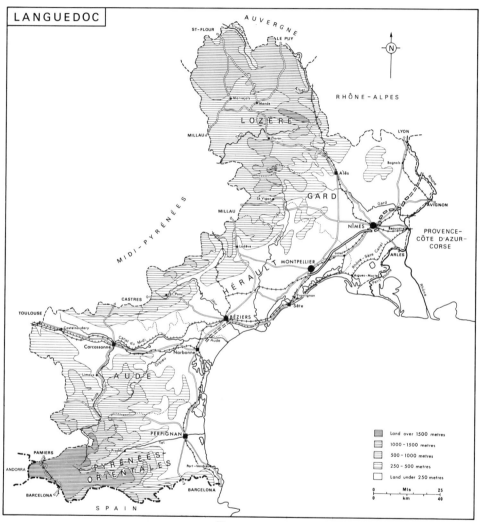

Figure 32.1

plain and the Massif Central. Constituted by folded and fractured Secondary and Tertiary rocks, the 'garrigues' is an area of degraded environment, given over to grazing and supporting low population densities.[2] The mountain zone of Languedoc is formed by two distinct systems. In the south-west, the plain of Roussillon is enclosed by the Pyrenean chains of

Corbières, Canigou and Albères, with crestlines over 1,500 metres and peaks reaching 2,700 metres. To the east of the Gate of Carcassonne, the crystalline basement of the Massif Central constitutes the Montagne Noire in the west and the Cévennes in the east, while the intervening depression has preserved limestones forming an incised karstic plateau.

THE PLANNING PROBLEMS OF LANGUEDOC

After a glorious early history, Languedoc is an area which has slumbered economically and stagnated demographically. The present planning effort is directed towards the removal of archaic structures and a more rational use of resources at present underdeveloped or exploited ineffectively. The most obvious manifestation of underdevelopment is the demographic stagnation during the last hundred years. Although the total population has not declined, this is largely due to the growth of a few large towns while the rural areas have suffered severe depopulation. Of the constituent départements, only Pyrénées-Orientales has experienced sustained growth, whereas the most rural département, Lozère, has lost almost half of its population in the course of the last hundred years. Throughout modern history, population has forsaken the uplands in favour of the towns and fertile lowlands, or has migrated from the region altogether. This represents a rational process of adjustment but the result has been a depopulation of the interior with a consequent atrophying of many of the inland towns and an aging of the rural population. The total population in 1968 of 1·7 millions was only slightly above the total of 1901, and whereas a century ago Languedoc had almost five per cent of the nation's total population, by 1968 the proportion had fallen to under four per cent.

The degree of underdevelopment is most pronounced in the case of the manufacturing industry. In 1962, industry, including public works, employed only 148,500 workers, compared with 178,000 in 1901. The region accounted for only two per cent of the national industrial labour force in 1962: the same proportion as Poitou-Charentes, and only Limousin and Basse-Normandie had lower proportions. The chief industries represented in the region are food processing, which has a widespread distribution, clothing and hosiery, concentrated at Nîmes, Le Vigan and Ganges, steel finishing at St. Chély and l'Ardoise, petroleum refining at Frontignan and chemicals at Sète and Salindres. Until very recently very few industries were in the advanced technology or rapid growth categories while textiles and coalmining are experiencing severe contractions.

In face of the region's apparent inability to industrialize it is pertinent to establish whether this is a reflection of deficiencies in the resource base, or whether structural and locational factors are responsible. Dugrand[3] is of the firm opinion that Languedoc possesses resources capable of supporting a level of industrialization greatly exceeding the present attainment. The region possesses large deposits of bauxite at Villeveyrac and Bédarieux, which are reduced to alumina by the Péchiney plant at Salindres, but the final smelting is carried out in the Alps. Output of bauxite is increasing and in 1966 totalled 617,000 tons. The region also produces a valuable base product for the chemicals industry in the salt yielded by the marine salt pans. Production reached 304,000 tons in 1966 but much of the output leaves the region without elaboration. The energy position is less favourable, the coal reserves of Alès and Graissessac being small, unsuited for metallurgical purposes, and extraction is being rapidly run down. Production of coal totalled 1·8 million tons in 1966 as compared with 3·2 million tons in 1957, and the number of miners has been reduced from 11,000 in 1951 to less than 4,000 at the present time. The region does, however, have access to hydroelectric power from the Rhône schemes, and also to petroleum products refined at Frontignan. In addition to these physical resources, Languedoc has many natural advantages for industrial develop-, ment, which, given the ready transferability of many of the raw materials for light industry, are of growing significance. The region has good water supplies as a consequence of storage and distribution systems built for irrigation purposes. Languedoc is served by the ports of La Nouvelle, Port-Vendres and Sète, the latter disposing of vast areas of waterfront land adjacent to the Etang de Thau. Languedoc is favoured climatically by a temperature regime which reduces factory heating costs and also by an unpolluted atmosphere. Finally, the region benefits from state assistance to industrial investment, has unlimited recreational potential, and, in the university of Montpellier, possesses an institution with a high output of science graduates. Against these advantages must be weighed the problem of isolation and the distance from large markets. In the case of high added-value manufactures and export-orientated industries, the importance of these factors is diminished and Dugrand attributes the low level of industrialization rather to such structural problems as the small size of firms, the lack of capital and of strong initiatives within the region.

A corollary of the low level of industrial development is the high agricultural dependence; in 1962, 35 per cent of the region's labour force was employed in agriculture and forestry. The problem is exacerbated by the fragility of the agricultural sector as a result of the deterioration of pastoral farming in the upland, the existence of unused and under-used land on the plain of Bas-Languedoc, but above all as a result of the monoculture of the vine in Bas-Languedoc. After the phylloxera epidemic, regrafting with American stock has vastly increased the level of output, even though the acreage under vines was halved. The vineyards of Bas-Languedoc produce approximately 30 per cent of the national wine production and almost 15 per cent of the world total. The basic weakness is that of dependence on low-quality wine with a low price elasticity for which demand is falling* The result has been a reduction of income in the farm population, and depopulation in the viticultural areas†, together with costly government purchases of excess production. Viticulture is still the dominant enterprise of approximately 200,000 famers in Bas-Languedoc and almost one million persons depend on the system. The position remained static until recently as a result of the rigidity of climatic conditions. Without irrigation, a diversification of agriculture is impossible, and to irrigate the world's largest vineyard, based on small and fragmented holdings, is a task of forbidding magnitude. The monocultural pattern has also remained static since no alternative dry farming system could absorb the high rural population densities built up under viticulture.

A final major planning problem concerns the underdeveloped and under-equipped state of the tourist industry. Languedoc has a wealth of tourist resources, which the climatic conditions endow with a special privilege, but which are generally under-exploited. In particular, the Languedoc coastline, with 150 kilometres of sandy beach, has remained undeveloped as a result of the undrained state of the coastal lagoons and the consequent mosquito infestation, the poverty of access roads and the lack of sufficient capital investment. The potential pressure of tourism resulting from the saturation of the Côte d'Azur and the consequent risk that unplanned development would disfigure a coastline as yet largely unspoilt, urge the need for a controlled expansion of the industry.

THE EFFORT OF RECONSTRUCTION

The problems cited above, demographic stagnation, industrial under-development, the problem of monoculture and the deficiencies of tourist facilities are still paramount, but during the last decade a major effort of rehabilitation has been made and considerable progress achieved. Since 1954, Languedoc has showed signs of a demographic revival in which gains by net migration have been conspicuous. Whereas in the past, mobility of population has taken the form of a drift of young persons from the region and an influx of retired persons, the present trend reflects a

*Ironically, viticulture has been most profitable in years of poor harvest, when the reduced output has resulted in improved prices.

†Lamour estimates that a drop in real purchasing power of 44 per cent occurred between 1930 and 1951 in the population engaged in viticulture[4] In the last ten years approximately 15,000 workers have left viticulture as a result of the recurrent crises.

genuine mobility of labour. The average age of foreign migrants between 1954 and 1962 was only 29 years, while that of migrants from other regions of France was 32 years.[5] A large proportion of the overseas immigration has consisted of repatriated French Algerians[6] skilled in commercial farming.

The demographic recovery of Languedoc has been paralleled by progress in the industrial sector, helped by government aid to industrial investment. The problem of under-industrialization is most severe in Lozère, where the difficulties are exacerbated by the run-down in agricultural employment. Lozère thus qualifies for the maximum financial assistance. Severe difficulties are also present in towns suffering from a contraction in staple activities, as Graissessac, Alès, Le Vigan, Ganges, Carcassonne and Béziers, all of which qualify for industrial conversion grants. State assistance has been instrumental in establishing new industries in the small centres of the Cévennes and in the coalmining towns, but the most impressive growth has occurred in the towns of the Bas-Languedoc plain. Frontignan has gained a major fertilizer plant, Narbonne has a new factory for treating sulphur, Béziers has a new plant producing metal cans, while the decentralized I.B.M. computer factory at Montpellier has rapidly attracted a number of firms manufacturing electronic components. The progress in irrigated farming has stimulated the processing and preserving of foodstuffs with major new plants at Vauvert and Nîmes in Gard. As a result of these recent developments, the growth of industrial production in Languedoc has exceeded the national rate.[7]

Although the growth of new industry is encouraging, it is in the agricultural sector that the most revolutionary changes are taking place. Since 1955, the 'Compagnie Nationale d'Aménagement du Bas-Rhône-Languedoc' has undertaken the task of converting the viticultural economy of the Languedoc plain to diversified irrigated farming. The company has the status of a mixed economy regional development company, supported by state investment and direction but exploited by private individuals and collective organizations. The details of the scheme have been amply described in English[8,9] and progress on the scheme is illustrated in *Figure 32.2*[10]. The project embraces an area of 625,000 acres in Gard, Hérault and the Aude valley, populated by 650,000 inhabitants. Two perimeters have been designated—east and west of Montpellier—nourished by water taken from the Rhône south of Beaucaire, which is transported across Bas-Languedoc by canal and supplemented in the western perimeter by water from the Hérault, Orb and smaller rivers. Ultimately 225,000 acres of land in the eastern perimeter and 200,000 acres in the western perimeter will be irrigated. In addition to the priority task of converting viticulture to the production of fruit, vegetables, poultry, eggs and dairy

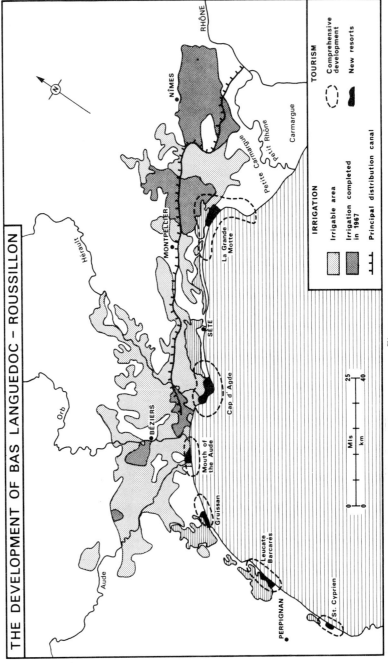

THE DEVELOPMENT OF BAS LANGUEDOC – ROUSSILLON

RHÔNE

NÎMES

MONTPELLIER

Hérault

Orb

Aude

BÉZIERS

PERPIGNAN

SÈTE

Cap d'Agde

La Grande Motte

Petite Camargue

Petit Rhône

Carmargue

Mouth of
the Aude

Gruissan

Leucate
Barcarès

St. Cyprien

| Mls | 0 | | | 25 |
| km | 0 | | | 40 |

IRRIGATION

Irrigable area

Irrigation completed
in 1967

Principal distribution canal

TOURISM

Comprehensive
development

New resorts

Figure 32.2

produce, irrigation will permit the reclamation of land at present under-used and water will be made available for industrial uses.

The essence of the project is the total renewal of agriculture, and with it a profound modification of the rural way of life. Thus the scheme involves remembrement, the construction of new farms and the modernization of existing buildings, the construction of collection, grading and packaging plants, and the building of processing factories. Progress has been most substantial in the eastern perimeter where water was quickly made available from the Rhône, but less transformation has occurred in the western perimeter in view of the extensive engineering works required. By 1967, 40,000 hectares had been placed under irrigation and 20,000 hectares of vines suppressed. Whereas viticulture yielded 60 per cent of the region's total agricultural product in 1954, the proportion had fallen to 49 per cent by 1967 and the proportion yielded by fruit crops had doubled. In 1966, Languedoc became the leading producer of apples, apricots and table grapes in the nation.

The development of coastal tourism has also progressed under the aegis of a government agency,[11] an inter-ministerial mission responsible to the 'Délégation à l'Aménagement du Territoire'. As in the case of the agricultural rehabilitation scheme, the expansion of coastal tourism rests on a mixed economy basis, the state providing overall direction but most of the execution being in the hands of local authorities and private individuals. The intention of the master plan, created in 1962, is the delimitation of six tourist complexes, separated by protected natural zones.[12,13] Development was initiated at St. Cyprien, an established resort 15 kilometres from Perpignan, of which the capacity is to be raised to 130,000 visitors. Completely new resorts have been built at La Grande Motte, on the Etang de l'Or near Montpellier, and at Leucate-Barcarès, on the Etang de Salses, both opened in 1968. Further complexes are being prepared at Cap d'Agde, at the mouth of the Aude and at Gruissan.

In all cases comprehensive improvements are planned, involving the building of yacht marinas, afforestation of the protected zones and the elimination of the mosquito-ridden swamps. The state is responsible for establishing the provision of access roads and has also acquired the necessary land to prevent speculation. The land is then resold at cost price to mixed economy companies created for each of the départements concerned, which are responsible for the provision of internal roads and services. Finally, the actual construction stage is entrusted to private developers in accordance with the specifications laid down in the master plans. It is intended that when the entire project is completed a decade hence provision will have been made for the reception of 450,000 tourists, and a facility of European importance established. The resort area will ultimately be linked to the future Orange–Narbonne motorway and is already accessible from the airports of Nîmes and Montpellier. It is also hoped that the scheme will stimulate the growth of tourism in the hinterland, an area rich in historical and natural attractions.

Agriculture, industry and tourism are thus responding to bold initiatives, and in turn the region has maintained its demographic revival.[14] It would be inaccurate to suggest, however, that the developments now in hand are sufficient to assure a rapid elimination of the region's problems. Certain intransigent problems still await attention while other difficulties may well be aggravated by the present planned developments. The deficiencies of communications are particularly severe in the case of road transport. Although a good rail service links Nîmes and Perpignan, the need for a fast motorway connection becomes increasingly urgent to serve the needs of industry and accommodate the growing tourist traffic. Work has commenced during the Fifth Plan on isolated sections by-passing the main towns but the completion of the entire motorway from Orange to Narbonne is far from being achieved and the equally important branch to Toulouse is still at the projection stage. Similarly, the canal network focusing on Sète is of small gauge, with little immediate prospect of being improved to European standard in spite of the possible attraction of linking the future Rhône–Rhine waterway via Sète and Toulouse to the Atlantic at Bordeaux. The ports of Languedoc have suffered from the loss of staple trade with North Africa and only the possible industrialization of the Sète–Frontignan complex holds out hope of increasing the level of port activity in the region.

A second long-term problem is the degree of rivalry between the larger urban centres, cited by Dugrand,[15] and the absence of an unchallenged regional metropolis capable of acting as a growth pole. A certain degree of specialization exists in the major agglomerations: Nîmes developed as a rail centre and is now assuming importance as the marketing and processing centre of the new irrigated areas; Montpellier is the administrative and cultural centre, until recently shunning industry; Béziers is also an industrial centre and rail junction; while Perpignan has expanded in the specific context of Roussillon, for which it is the natural centre. Montpellier has established a clear lead in population terms, with 171,000 inhabitants in 1968, as compared with 125,000 in the agglomeration of Nîmes, 85,000 in Béziers, 60,000 in Sète–Frontignan and 107,000 in Perpignan. However, Montpellier is far from exercising the kind of direction enjoyed in the neighbouring regions by Toulouse, Clermont-Ferrand, Lyon and Marseille.

The conversion of agriculture has still to prove its commercial viability, for although production is being successfully oriented towards high-value commodities, the scale of production demands a large market and signs of surplus production, especially of fruit, have appeared. The emphasis on the selection of prime varieties, careful grading and packing inevitably results in highly priced products, susceptible to international competition, but more particularly to undercutting by inferior but much cheaper fruit and vegetable produce. It is equally questionable whether the attempt to attract industry to a large number of towns, each aided to establish industrial estates and in many instances benefiting from investment grants, is of necessity the soundest means of achieving long-term expansion. The critical areas affected by the run down of mining are clearly special cases, but it could be argued that in order to yield more substantial long-term advantages state assistance would be better devoted to fostering the growth of large industrial complexes at a limited number of locations rather than to a diffusion of small-scale industries.

A more serious problem is that recent planned developments, while effecting a worthwhile improvement in the total economic structure of the region, seem likely to exaggerate further the internal disparities in economic levels.[16] The contrasts in activity between the plains and mountains must inevitably widen as a result of the work of the regional development companies, as may the divergence between the eastern perimeter—where diversification is well advanced—and the western perimeter—where progress has been slower and viticulture is more firmly entrenched.[17] However, the question of time scale is important, for the reconstruction of Languedoc has been conceived on a European scale in the fields of tourism and agriculture, and if this succeeds a sound springboard will have been built from which to revivify areas at present peripheral to the mainstream of development.

REFERENCES

1 Carrère, P., and Dugrand, R., *La Région Méditerranéenne*, pp. 77–79, 1960, Paris, Presses Universitaires de France.
2 Dugrand, R., *La Garrigue Montpelliéraine*, 1964, Paris, Presses Universitaires de France.
3 Dugrand, R., *Villes et Campagnes en Bas-Languedoc*, p. 16, 1963, Paris, Presses Universitaires de France.
4 Lamour, P., 'Land and Water Development in Southern France', contribution to *Comparisons in Resource Management*, p. 234, 1961, Baltimore, Johns Hopkins.
5 'La région de Languedoc-Roussillon à l'heure européenne', *Usine nouv.*, January 1967, p. 2.
6 Rognant, L., and Schultz, J., 'Les rapatriés d'Afrique du Nord dans l'Hérault 1954–64', *Bull. Soc. languedoc. Géogr.*, 1964, p. 283.
7 INSEE, 'La France Méditerranéene', *Annuaire Statistique*, 1967, p. 13.
8 Lamour, P., *op. cit.*[4]
9 Graves, N., 'Une Californie Française', *Geography*, 1965, p. 71.
10 Dugrand, R., *Atlas Languedoc-Roussillon*, Plate 81–1, 1969, Paris, Berger-Levrault.
11 Racine, P., 'Aménagement touristique du littoral du Languedoc-Roussillon', *Urbanisme*, No. 86, 1965, p. 12.

[12] 'L'aménagement touristique du littoral du Languedoc-Roussillon' *Notes Etud. docum.*, No. 3,326, 1966, pp. 14–29.

[13] Dugrand, R., *op. cit.*[10] Plate 82-1.

[14] Dugrand, R., *op. cit.*[10] Plate 22-2.

[15] Dugrand, R., *op. cit.*[3] pp. 542–548.

[16] Dugrand, R., *op. cit.*[3] pp. 551–552.

[17] Dugrand, R., *op. cit.*[10] Plate 32-2.

33

Corsica

'Parler de la Corse, c'est évoquer un beau corps de léthargie qu'on commence à soigner.'[1] This image of Corsica as an ailing and senile body belatedly receiving treatment is extremely apt. The endemic malaise of economic and demographic decline during the last century has been the ruthless consequence of the failure to adjust traditional patterns of resource use to changing internal and external circumstances. By contrast, the regional plan seeks to establish a new economic structure based on a reappraisal of the resource base. Paradoxically, the insularity at the root of many of the island's economic problems is of advantage to the task of integrated planning. Corsica alone of the planning regions has an unambiguous and meaningful areal definition.

THE ENVIRONMENT AND RESOURCE BASE

At the turn of the century, Ratzel described Corsica as a mountain in the sea. Rondeau[2] has annotated this description by pointing to the greater significance of the mountains as opposed to the sea in the economic life of Corsica, while Bénévent[3] insists on the importance of the Mediterranean context of the sea. Three elements thus form the essential traits of the physical background; the insularity, the predominance of mountainous terrain, and the possession of a Mediterranean climatic régime. The tormented relief, the immense variety of microclimates and the complex patterns of rural economy and sociology defy easy generalization. The major landscape contrasts occur between the crystalline mass forming the western and central mountains, the schistose north-eastern mountain chain, the discontinuous central furrow separating these systems, and the fragmentary fringe of coastal lowland. In terms of land resources, it is more meaningful to differentiate between three altitudinal zones; the littoral, the coteaux, and the high valley and mountain (*Figure 33.2*).

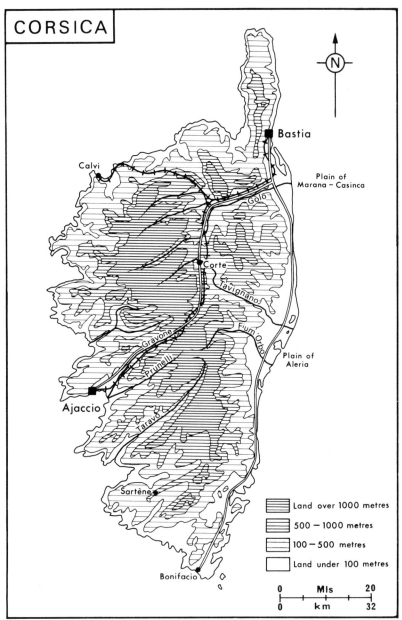

CORSICA

Bastia

Calvi

Plain of
Marana – Casinca

Golo

Corte

Tavignano

Gravone

Fium Orbo

Prunelli

Plain of
Aleria

Ajaccio

Taravo

Sartène

Bonifacio

Land over 1000 metres
500 – 1000 metres
100 – 500 metres
Land under 100 metres

0	Mls	20
0	k m	32

Figure 33.1

Although based on the altitude and terrain, in the context of the Mediterranean setting this division implies contrasts in climate, vegetation and soils, and thus in resource potential.

The littoral zone, below 100 metres, has a discontinuous distribution, consisting of small pockets of alluvial lowland, enlarged at the mouth of the major rivers. The largest area, the eastern coastal plain, extends from Bastia to Solenzara, a distance of 140 kilometres, but has a maximum width of two to ten kilometres. The surface of this plain is accidented and edaphic conditions are far from uniform. A distinction exists between the high terraces, formed by a glacis of debris deposited in the late Quaternary, and the lower deposits of recent alluvium.[4] The high terraces, composed of boulders and pebbles and much dissected by the rivers and ephemeral streams traversing the plain, have a mediocre clay-rich soil and are difficult to irrigate. The alluvial soils of the Marana-Casinca lowlands and the plain of Aleria are of higher fertility, given adequate drainage and irrigation.

The littoral zone affords the optimum conditions for intensive agriculture to be found in the island, but is by no means an easy environment to develop. The smaller plains of the western littoral have been reclaimed and support polyculture of vines, cereals and vegetables, but until recently the eastern coastal plain was virtually unexploited except as seasonal grazing for transhumant sheep and goats. The reasons for the neglect of the island's only extensive area of lowland are related to the combination of physical, historical and social conditions. The absence of settlement on the plain is linked to the history of warfare, siege and internal strife. Open to attack from the sea, the plain was abandoned for the greater security offered by the hill-tops and mountain slopes. To the factor of security from attack was added security from disease; malaria was endemic on the plain until after the Second World War. Even given greater security, it is doubtful whether the eastern plain could have been developed in the context of the prevalent traditional forms of agriculture. Alternating seasonally between marshland and semi-aridity, reclamation involves both drainage and irrigation, demanding a degree of cooperative effort, technological ability and scrupulous maintenance not available to past generations of peasant farmers. It is only since 1957 that a serious attempt has been made to reclaim the eastern littoral. It remains the island's greatest unused land resource and a possible means of regenerating agriculture as a whole.

The coteaux zone, between 100 and 350 metres, also has a discontinuous distribution and an unmodified Mediterranean climate, but in all other respects contrasts sharply with the littoral. It is a zone of dissected hill land flanking the central mountainous core, and degraded in terms of its

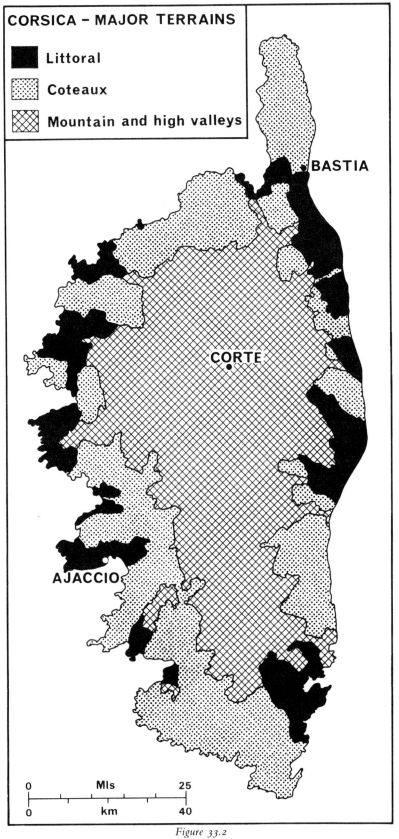

CORSICA – MAJOR TERRAINS

Littoral

Coteaux

Mountain and high valleys

BASTIA

CORTE

AJACCIO

0   Mls   25

0   km   40

Figure 33.2

resource base. The forest cover, removed for cultivation, has been replaced by a dense maquis vegetation. Slopes are everywhere steep, soils unstable, and terracing is essential for field crops. In spite of the hostility of the environment, it was in the coteaux zone that the traditional sedentary agriculture evolved. It offers optimum climatic conditions for the vine and olive, which, together with dry-farmed cereals, were the base of traditional farming. The coteaux zone remains the most densely populated rural zone, but the collapse of arable farming at the beginning of this century initiated depopulation and massive land abandonment. The former fields have been invaded by maquis, which now covers 75 per cent of the coteaux zone. An atmosphere of dereliction and decay pervades the landscape—the inevitable result of irrational resource use.

The vast majority of the island is constituted by the mountain core, which is penetrated by a radial network of high valleys. A general effect of hostility is given by the rugged mountains and deep gorges, but the influence of altitude on climate provides a variety of resources not available elsewhere in the island. Between 600 and 1,100 metres is the chestnut zone, epitomized in the Castigniccia of the eastern schistose range. At this altitude, the chestnut replaced cereals in the traditional economy as the food staple. Above 1,100 metres, the forest cover is composed of beech, larico and maritime pine and firs, giving way at approximately 1,500 metres to stunted grasses. The high valleys, occasionally widening into small basins, are the focus of settlement and the only routeways. Throughout the mountain zone, animal farming is dominant. Cattle are reared in the valleys and large flocks of sheep and goats graze the forest and mountain pasture, following complex patterns of transhumance. The mountain forests are a potential resource, as yet inadequately exploited, but are hindered by a slow rate of growth. Finally, in nourishing the island's rivers, the mountain core supplies the indispensable resource on which the renaissance of Corsican agriculture depends: water for irrigation on the plains.

The resources of the island are thus not negligible, but have been irrationally exploited. On the eastern plain, 40,000 hectares of potentially productive land, including 30,000 hectares suitable for irrigation, is unused. The climate permits an extremely wide crop range and an almost continuous thermal growing season. The island disposes of adequate water supplies for irrigation and suitable sites for the generation of hydro-electricity. Above all, Corsica has a wealth of tourist resources. Against these assets must be set three deficiencies: the island is totally lacking in industrial resources, the factor of insularity has a retarding effect on economic growth[5] and the demographic decline results in a limited internal market and a numerically weak labour force as compared with the other Mediterranean islands[6] The theme of this final essay is the effort now being made, both spontaneous and planned, to reconstruct the economy and to reverse the trends of the past hundred years. It is necessary to refer to the background of decline in order to appreciate the magnitude of this task.

THE DEGENERATION OF TRADITIONAL AGRICULTURE

Internal isolation and weak external contacts enforced an essentially self-sufficient agricultural system on the past generations of farmers. After the collapse of Roman control, the formerly cultivated plains were abandoned in favour of the more secure and healthy mountains. Over the course of ensuing centuries a traditional pattern of farming evolved in which three principal elements were associated: cereals, tree crops and livestock. The coteaux slopes supported vines and olives, and by virtue of laborious terracing extensive areas were devoted to dry-farmed cereals with long fallow periods. At higher altitudes, the chestnut replaced cereals as a staple foodstuff, also supporting livestock and craft industries[7] Above the tree line, mountain pasture offered seasonal rough grazing for sheep and goats.

The collapse of the traditional pattern during this century resulted from its rigidity, imposed in part by the mountain environment and in part by social stagnation. The location of agriculture in the mountains implied a lack of possibilities of intensification, which, combined with archaic methods of production, made resistance to competition from more efficient mainland producers impossible. The collapse of dry-farming was precipitated by improvements in transport, facilitating the import of cheap foodstuffs, especially grains. In addition, the economic expansion of France, the acquisition of a colonial empire, and the widening appreciation of superior opportunities outside the island, attracted young Corsicans from a hazardous existence on the land to seek their fortunes abroad. The inevitable result of exposure to modern commercial competition was massive land abandonment and associated rural depopulation. The cause and effect relationship between these two phenomena is complex; on the one hand, the collapse of arable farming and increase in pastoralism provoked depopulation, while the spontaneous migration of young people resulted in an insufficient labour force to maintain the cultivated area.

The decadence of agriculture by the close of the Second World War has been well described by Kolodny[8] Between 1913 and 1948, the arable proportion of the island fell from 37 to eight per cent, the island lost half of its rural population and came to depend on imports for over half of its food supplies. The arable proportion of eight per cent under-represents the true scale of the decline, since the figure included olive groves and orchards in varying stages of decay. It is doubtful whether the actual proportion devoted to field crops exceeded three per cent. By 1960, the combined total of cropland, vines, orchards and market gardens amounted to only 3·3 per cent of the total land area.

The decadence of agriculture is manifest not only in the abandonment of land, but also in the persistence of archaic structures. Fragmented holdings, uncontrolled grazing, a negligible use of fertilizers and a lack of investment in buildings and machinery are obstacles to a renovation of farming. Of the 10,000 holdings in the island in 1963, 8,000 were smaller than five hectares and only 800 possessed a tractor. Equally limiting is the inbred conservatism of the peasant farmer, for the most part advanced in years and thus impervious to suggestions of reform which cannot be materialized during his lifetime. In these conditions the prime function of the farm becomes the provision of basic foodstuffs for domestic consumption, supplemented by remissions from family earnings on the mainland and by the state pension.

The condition of livestock farming is equally retarded, and the yields per animal are low. The main commercial enterprise is sheep rearing for ewe's milk used in the manufacture of Roquefort cheese. The annual production of pâté is approximately 1,800 tons, 15 per cent of French production. As in the case of arable farming, the best prospects for animal farming exist on the lowland rather than the interior. The utilization of irrigated pasture and fodder crops could increase meat and milk yields immeasurably. At present, the survival of pastoralism in the mountains is based on the low labour requirement and the assured market for ewe's milk. The improvement of pasture and of livestock breeds are thus ignored and preclude advances in dairy and meat production.

Undismayed by the spectre of decay, the Corsican remains attached to his land. Even the rural emigrant returns annually to his village, maintains the farm house and garden and ultimately retires there. A large proportion of the holdings is in the hands of retired persons, cultivating just sufficient of the farm to supply everydays needs and deriving their cash income from pensions, while the majority of the farm lies idle under a cover of maquis. This attachment to the land suggests that the Corsican has not turned his back on the land and that the idea of a renaissance of agriculture is not entirely vain. However, a complete break with the traditional pattern is essential if farming is to be placed on a competitive commercial basis. This depends on a rational system of holdings, a change in location to lowland areas capable of intensive production, and a level of remuneration sufficient to retain the interest and efforts of young Corsicans, who have thus far found greater rewards and security outside the island.

THE DEMOGRAPHIC DECLINE

The demographic history of Corsica is shrouded in uncertainty as a result of the fragmentary and contradictory records relating to the historical past and the unreliability of census data during the last century and a half. Recent research by Rondeau,[9] Lefèbvre[10] and Kolodny[11] has cast much new light on the scale of depopulation. It is widely accepted that in 1890 the population of Corsica was approximately 280,000, and that this, the latest reliable census figure, represents the maximum population achieved by the island. The official census data published during this century are entirely inaccurate due to the falsification of returns as a result of electoral considerations and the attempt to gain additional fiscal subventions. Elaborate research by Lefèbvre, utilizing data on vital statistics, passenger traffic movements, ration cards and school enrolment, gives the following trend.

Table 33.1

THE POPULATION OF CORSICA, 1881–1954

1881	273,000	1921	221,000
1891	259,000	1931	205,000
1901	245,000	1941	185,000
1911	238,000	1954	159,000

Source: Lefèbvre, *op. cit*.,[10] p. 574.

Parallel research by Kolodny suggests a slightly higher figure for 1954, and a census estimate placed the total for that date at 170,000, as compared with the published figure of 247,000. The official 1962 census figure of 275,000 is equally inflated and has recently been revised to an estimate of 176,000.

Whatever the exact figure may be, it is certain that the population has declined by at least 100,000 since 1880; a decline of over 35 per cent. It is also established that the depopulation is almost entirely a rural phenomenon. The principal towns, with the exception of Sartène, have continued to expand their populations. The basis of demographic decline is thus rural depopulation on a massive scale and has been age-selective in character, involving chiefly the younger age groups. Despite this exodus, the island has maintained a positive natural increase, sustained especially by the towns. There is evidence to suggest that far from diminishing, the rate of emigration has accelerated during the last decade. However, the influx of repatriates from Algeria after 1962, which amounted to almost 10,000, has helped to improve the migratory balance. It must also be realized that the statistics quoted refer only to permanent residents and do not include persons who have left the island to work but who return periodically and still play a significant role in the life of Corsica. An important, but unknown, number of Corsicans leave the island, but maintain their village homes, returning during holidays to vote in elections, and ultimately for retirement. This practice has a double significance; the return of Corsicans employed in France injects a certain amount of money, often in the form of assistance to relatives and dependants, and the practice of retirement to the island helps to offset the effects of emigration on total population growth.

The trend in population growth since 1962 has been studied by INSEE[12] and shows a slight improvement over the preceding decade. Between 1961 and 1964 the population increased by 3·8 per cent, but this modest growth was very unevenly distributed. Out of a total of 336 communes, 252 experienced a continued decline in population. In the case of the north of Cap Corse, the mountainous interior and the south, the scale of this decline was very high. By contrast, 110 communes registered an increase in population. In addition to the towns, this growth was shared by every commune of the eastern littoral, from north of Bastia to Bonifacio.

It is premature to suggest that the demographic decline has been checked but recent trends point to a further important evolution: the internal redistribution of population within the island. This redistribution of population is not being achieved by internal migration, although the coastal towns of Bastia, Ajaccio and Calvi are nourished by rural migrants, but rather by the greater capacity of the coastal zones to resist depopulation. The development of tourism, the reclamation of sectors of the eastern coastal plain, the persistence of viticulture on the hill slopes and of market gardening on the patches of coastal lowland are factors in the greater viability of the littoral.

This changing balance in the distribution of population, effected by the expansion of the towns and differential migration rates between the interior and the littoral, reflects a change in resource evaluation of the greatest importance. The security of the interior, the forest and pastoral resources of the mountains esteemed in the past are now exposed as anachronisms, while the littoral zone, disdained until recently, is now seen as the fulcrum of economic revival. The objective of regional planning in Corsica is to provide an impetus to this change in the location and character of economic activity.

THE EFFORT OF RECONSTRUCTION

Although the existence of a 'Corsican Problem' had long been appreciated, determined efforts to solve it awaited the recognition of the broader problem of regional social and economic disparities within France which led to the creation of regional development programmes after 1956. In the first instance, Corsica was included in the planning region encompassing Provence and the Côte d'Azur, and although until 1970 it remained in this circumscription, the island was accorded a separate 'programme d'action régionale' in 1957.[13] This was in recognition of the specific problems of the island, and it has subsequently become a test-bed of integrated regional planning.[14]

The regional plan defined two central objectives: the expansion of tourism and the rehabilitation of agriculture. Tourism was selected as a branch of activity already in full expansion in which the potential development was considered adequate to become the backbone of the island's economy. The rehabilitation of agriculture was seen above all as a process of rationalization; a diversion of activity from the mountains to the potentially productive plains, in an attempt to remove the burden of food imports for the permanent population and growing tourist influx, and, in the longer term, to create an export surplus of certain products.

In addition to the above priority objectives, the plan also contained proposals over a wide field including the improvement of communications, the reform of livestock farming, expansions in agricultural training, programmes of soil conservation and the rationalization of forest exploitation. While these ancillary developments could be achieved within the existing financial and administrative structures, the two priority developments posed problems of organization, administration, technical assistance and financial backing beyond the resources of the island. To meet the problem the legislation of the early 1950s, regulating the establishment of regional development companies, was invoked. Two development companies were created in 1957: 'La Société pour l'Equipement Touristique de la Corse' (SETCO), charged with the responsibility of expanding tourism, and 'La Société pour la Mise en Valeur Agricole de la Corse' (SOMIVAC), responsible for the reconstruction of agriculture.[15] These companies were founded on a mixed economy basis, combining elements of the public and private sector. The participants in both companies are private individuals and business interests, but the administration is in the hands of the public sector. The schemes thus have the external characteristics of private enterprise but benefit from certain advantages normally reserved for the public sector, notably in the case of legal powers, technical resources and, above all, investment funds. The success of the regional plan depends on the activities of the two development companies in their role as instigators of growth as well as by their direct actions. A decade has now passed since their inauguration and it is appropriate to review the results achieved thus far.

THE EXPANSION OF TOURISM

The task of SETCO was to some extent simplified by its involvement in the only sector of the Corsican economy in an active state of expansion. From a pre-war level of 49,000 tourists in 1939, the total had increased to 67,000 in 1955 and 110,000 in 1957, when the regional plan was published. Robinson[16] drew attention, however, to the limited number of tourist centres in the island and the failure of tourist development to benefit the vast majority of Corsicans most in need of additional employment and income, in the interior. SETCO was charged with the task of promoting the creation of 3,000 additional hotel rooms together with holiday villages and tourist complexes. The company intervenes both directly in hotel construction and indirectly as a sponsor of private developments. *Figure 33.3* illustrates the construction achieved by SETCO by 1968. A chain of new high-quality hotels on picturesque coastal sites has been established, but work on more elaborate tourist complexes, consisting of hotels, villas, and sports facilities, has been held up through lack of capital.[17] As a promoter of development, through the guaranteeing of loans and technical assistance, SETCO aided private development worth more than £9 million in its first five years of existence.

In spite of the inadequacy of the infrastructure, tourism has continued to expand rapidly. In the period from June to September 1967, approximately 300,000 visitors entered the island, an increase of 13 per cent over the previous season. Between 1961 and 1967 the number of visitors increased by 90 per cent. The reasons for the increase are manifold and by no means all attributable to the activities of SETCO. The general increase in prosperity and the increase in the number of French families taking holidays make tourism a growth activity in all major holiday areas in France. The improvement in links with the mainland by the inauguration of new car ferries has promoted expansion, particularly of camping and caravan holidays. Similarly, the improvement of air services to Ajaccio,

Bastia* and Calvi and the development of inclusive air tours has stimulated holiday traffic, especially of foreign visitors. The congestion of the Côte d'Azur and the guarantee of fine weather are adventitious factors aiding the growth of summer visitors.

Tourism remains a growth sector and certainly SETCO has played an

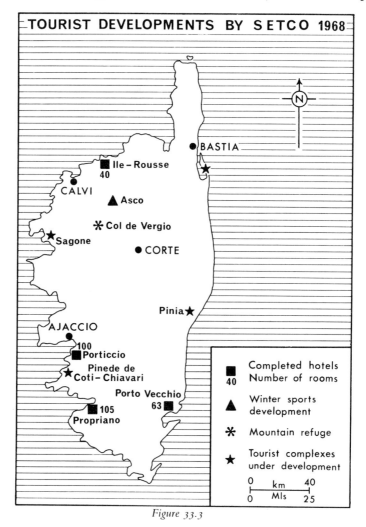

TOURIST DEVELOPMENTS BY SETCO 1968

- ● BASTIA
- ■ Ile–Rousse
  40
- ● CALVI
- ▲ Asco
- ✳ Col de Vergio
- ★ Sagone
- ● CORTE
- Pinia ★
- ● AJACCIO
  - ■ 100
    Porticcio
  - Pinede de
    ★ Coti–Chiavari
  - Porto Vecchio
    63 ■
  - ■ 105
    Propriano

Legend:
- ■ / 40 Completed hotels / Number of rooms
- ▲ Winter sports development
- ✳ Mountain refuge
- ★ Tourist complexes under development

0 — km — 40
0 — Mls — 25

N

Figure 33.3

important role, but the balance sheet of the past decade is not entirely favourable, as Renucci[18] has demonstrated. The internal transport system and road network are entirely inadequate and present an obstacle to the opening up of the interior. Much of the tourist development is in the hands of outside interests and has not aided capital formation within the

*Bastia is now the sixth busiest airport of France.

island. The location of tourist centres still has a limited, and essentially coastal, distribution,[19] so that seasonal labour is often brought in from outside in view of local shortages. There is also a tendency for the cost of holidays to be higher than on the mainland; a factor contributing to the rapid growth of camping, a form of tourism which brings little revenue and even less employment to the island. Finally, the basic equipment in terms of accommodation remains inadequate, and SETCO has established an objective of an increase in bed accommodation from 50,000 at present, to 175,000 in the next 15 years.

Tourism has thus not yet fulfilled its planned role as the lever of the economy. The prevalence of outside interests in holiday camp and hotel development has channeled activity into existing centres rather than to new areas. While the expansion has generated activity in the building industry, and the increased spending has aided the commercial centres, these benefits have not been evenly distributed. Nor has tourism as yet generated a substantial amount of new employment. The objectives of the regional plan are thus unfulfilled and will remain so until the appropriate infrastructure of good communications and varied accommodation has been achieved. Two problems are likely to remain particularly intransigent: the seasonal fluctuation in activity and the opening up of the interior. The creation of a regional park and the establishment of a winter sports centre may help in the latter respect. Corsica does possess outstanding advantages for tourism, but it is a highly competitive industry and the vulnerability to contraction during periods of economic recession adds to the importance of the second development project—agricultural reconstruction—as a means of achieving a balanced structure.

THE REHABILITATION OF AGRICULTURE

Whereas the expansion of tourism was planned to yield immediate economic benefits, the rehabilitation of agriculture involves the reconstruction of a sector which has stagnated, and therefore requires a sustained long-term effort. In this context, the intervention of the development company, SOMIVAC, has been much more direct than that of SETCO in the field of tourism. By its constitution, SOMIVAC was assigned a triple role: research into the physical and economic background of agricultural improvement, the reclamation of 20,000 hectares of the eastern coastal plain, and the construction of an irrigation network serving the new farms.

The immediate task of research was to establish the detailed character of physical conditions on the coastal plain. Soil, micro-climatic and

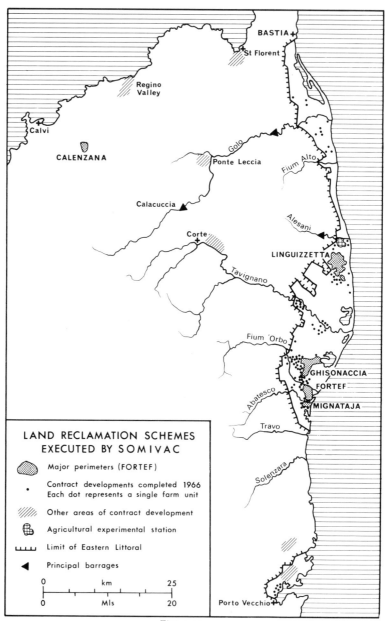

LAND RECLAMATION SCHEMES
EXECUTED BY SOMIVAC

⬮ Major perimeters (FORTEF)

. Contract developments completed 1966
Each dot represents a single farm unit

▨ Other areas of contract development

⊞ Agricultural experimental station

⊔⊔⊔ Limit of Eastern Littoral

◀ Principal barrages

```
0           km           25
|_|_|_|_|_|_|_|_|_|_|_|
0          Mls          20
```

Figure 33.4

hydrological conditions were surveyed in order to determine the extent of cultivable land, the areas amenable to irrigation and the suitability for various types of crop. Parallel research at an experimental centre on the Alesani concentrated on the selection of species of fruit trees adapted to the physical conditions of the plain and resistant to virus diseases. Finally, economic research was devoted to the task of defining the necessary size of farm and the commercial prospects for various types of enterprise. This body of research made possible the task of defining the first perimeters for reclamation and established that physical and commercial considerations favoured specialization in citrus fruit.

Land was acquired by SOMIVAC by the lease of unproductive common-land, subsequently enlarged by the purchase of adjacent land, to form the three main perimeters of Ghisonaccia, Linguizzetta and Fortef.[20] The maquis cover of these perimeters was bulldozed clear and new farms, varying in size between 50 and 100 acres according to their irrigable area, were created. The company builds access roads, farm buildings and installs the irrigation system.[21] The first perimeter, Ghisonaccia was completed in 1960, followed by Linguizzetta in 1966 and Fortef. Outside the coastal plain, a small perimeter at Calenzana has been developed in the same fashion. In total, approximately 4,000 hectares have been reclaimed and over 100 new farms created on the four perimeters. The occupying farmers pay the cost of the reclamation and construction on an annuity basis once the farm has come into production* The farmer must find capital for the stocking of the farm, the establishment of plantations and for the cost of living until the farm produces. Similarly, the cost of the installation of irrigation must be amortized by payments for the water consumed. In these conditions, only farmers with a considerable amount of capital or access to cheap loans were able to take up the new farms.

In order to meet this problem and to accelerate the pace of reclamation, SOMIVAC extended its activities to include the development under contract of existing farms in varying stages of decay. Under this system SOMIVAC undertakes the construction of new roads, buildings, irrigation and drainage works. Payment is made on an annuity basis and in addition the farmer accepts certain conditions with respect to the choice of crops and farming methods. Under this arrangement a further 2,000 hectares had been reclaimed by 1967 involving 151 farmers, chiefly close to the existing perimeters on the Tavignano plain and in the Marana-Casinca plain, but also at a number of locations in the interior valleys and around Porto Vecchio in the south (*Figure 33.4*).

The task of completing an irrigation network totalling 25,000 hectares on the coastal plain is being carried out jointly by SOMIVAC and the

*The level of annuities has been fixed at a sum equivalent to the average price of renting farmland.

'Génie Rural'. At present over 5,000 hectares are irrigated by the use of storage reservoirs on the plain, supplied by pumping from the rivers.[22] The construction of barrages on the Golo and Alesani is nearing completion, and with the future barrage on the Fium' Orbo will permit adequate water storage for the needs of the entire plain.*

After a decade of implementation the achievements of SOMIVAC contain both positive and negative aspects. The work of reclamation must be considered advantageous in that it reverses the trends of the past century. However, the choice of installing large highly-capitalized commercial farms has been criticized. In the first instance, an insufficient number of Corsican farmers with adequate financial means were available to take up the new farms. The evolution of political events in Algeria and the influx of repatriates benefiting from resettlement grants introduced an unexpected element. Experienced in the use of irrigation and versed in commercial production, the repatriates were quick to seize the opportunities offered by SOMIVAC, thereby causing considerable hostility among the indigenous population who lacked the means to benefit from the reclamation programme. Kolodny has argued that in opting for a plantation style of production, foreign to the experience of Corsican farmers and demanding a level of investment exceeding the possibilities of the traditional farmer, the vast majority of Corsicans were virtually excluded from their own development plan.[23] It is arguable that the vast amount of money spent on reclamation could have been devoted to a more widely diffused modernization, involving much smaller intensive polyculture farms on the plain and the renovation of livestock farming and forestry in the interior. Such a programme, Kolodny claims, would at least have the merit of benefiting Corsicans rather than outsiders.

Problems have also been encountered in achieving the choice of cropping desired by SOMIVAC. The selection of citrus fruit, and especially clementines, as the principal specialization on irrigated land, was seen as the best long-term enterprise in terms of marketing opportunities while viticulture was specifically relegated to the unirrigated portions of the plain. Under the impulsion of the repatriates, this stipulation has been ignored. The plantation of citrus fruit has been limited and in spite of the illegality, large areas equipped for irrigation have been planted to vines. Renuci[24] attributes this to the fact that the repatriates were viticulteurs in Algeria and also that vines reach production more rapidly than fruit trees and shorten the period without cash income. As compared with the fragmented parcels of the traditional vineyards, large compact plantations now mantle the perimeters of the plain.[25] In view of the problems associated with this type of monoculture in Languedoc, this development is of some concern.[26]

*The barrage of Calacuccia, on the Golo river, is also equipped to produce hydroelectricity.

Reluctance to adopt the crop range planned by SOMIVAC may also be attributed to the uncertainty surrounding the commercial outlets for citrus fruit, soft fruit and fresh vegetables. The potential cultivable area of the coastal plain is 40,000 hectares, of which over 30,000 is suitable for irrigation. The production from this area will greatly exceed the island's internal demand and it must find export markets. The high cost of Corsican produce delivered on the mainland market makes the task of successful competition difficult. The organization of cooperative marketing and the construction of a small conserving factory at Cassamozza mark the first steps to overcome this problem.

AN APPRAISAL OF CHANGING RESOURCE USE

Implicit in the regional plan is a re-evaluation of the island's resources. In an assessment of progress, the author[27] has suggested that in choosing tourism and the reclamation of the eastern coastal plain as priority developments, the planners have selected a growth sector and a growth point in the economy. Tourism is a potential growth sector not only because of the island's outstanding natural attractions, but also in relation to the rising tide of affluence in western Europe. Given appropriate investment in the infrastructure, and following the precedent of other Mediterranean islands, there seems no reason to doubt the capacity of this sector for growth.

The reclamation of the eastern coastal plain may be viewed as establishing a growth point in the agricultural economy, capable of sustained rather than rapid growth, but from which ideas, experience and capital may ultimately be diffused. The remaining activities may be considered a sector of residual growth in the interior, incapable of adding greatly to employment opportunities but, through rationalization, capable of making a greater contribution to the economy. The reorganization of livestock farming and forestry will be accompanied by the introduction of new functions, largely passive, such as water storage and nature reserves, together with an increase in outdoor tourism.

This shift in the economic centre of gravity from the interior to the littoral, with Bastia and the coastal plain as the fulcrum and Ajaccio and Calvi as secondary poles, has been occurring spontaneously and will be intensified as a result of the plan. It is an entirely rational trend given the existing disposition of resources. Bastia (55,000) and Ajaccio (45,000) are the largest urban markets, the centres of administration and further education, the hubs of tourist circulation and the sites of international ports and airports. The northern coastal arc from Ajaccio to Bastia is the most accessible zone for tourist development, while the eastern coastal plain has proven reserves of agricultural land at present underused. Only the south-western littoral, remote, and lacking areas of fertile lowland, has a development potential that is not appreciably superior to that of the interior. If an acceleration in the trend towards a new balance between the littoral and the interior is rational, it will not be accomplished without problems. These problems, which summarize the dilemma of Corsica, form a fitting conclusion to this chapter.

The changes in the distribution and character of economic activity called for in the plan demand an adjustment of the infrastructure to fulfil new functions. Specifically, the expansion of such highly commercial activities as tourism and intensive irrigated farming must repose on an efficient network of communications. Ease of access to Corsica, freedom of circulation within the island and the possibility of the transfer of export produce to the mainland with the minimum of delay and handling cost are vital. Despite certain recent improvements, severe deficiencies persist. Improvements in air services and the introduction of new car ferries have greatly improved links with the mainland and roll on–roll off facilities have speeded cargo transit in the ports. Movement within the island is, however, impeded by bad roads, an inadequate and uneconomic rail service and by a skeletal system of bus services.

Not only must the planning effort achieve soundly based development; it must also stimulate growth at a rapid pace if the ingrained pattern of exodus is to be halted. Moreover, the creation of new employment must be related to the aspirations and capacities of the indigenous population. The chosen sectors—tourism and intensive irrigated agriculture—are competitive activities, which labour under the burden of high levels of initial investment cost. In these conditions, a premium is placed on commercial experience and access to capital, attributes lacking in the young rural migrant but readily available in the form of outside interests. Not surprisingly, therefore, the achievements thus far in the development plans have been attained in no small measure through the participation of outside skills, capital and management. It is possible to argue that in seeking to establish modern, competitive structures, the plans have created a vacuum which is largely being filled from the outside.

REFERENCES

[1] Dacharry, M., *Tourisme et Transport en Méditerranée Occidentale*, p. 12, 1964, Paris, Presses Universitaires de France.
[2] Rondeau, A., *La Corse*, p. 9, 1964, Paris, Armand Colin.

[3] Cited in Kolodny, Y., *L'utilisation du sol en Corse: sur la décadence d'un terroir insulaire*, UNESCO report on Land Use in Semi-Arid Mediterranean Climates, p. 82, 1962, Paris.

[4] Renucci, J., 'Tentatives de mise en valeur agricole en Corse', *Revue Géogr. Lyon*, 1961, pp. 142–144.

[5] Cerutti, J., 'Quelques aspects du problème des transports entre la Corse et le continent', *Bull. SOMIVAC SETCO*, No. 44, 1967, p. 18.

[6] Kolodny, Y., 'La population des îles en Méditerranée', *Méditerranée*, 1966, p. 3.

[7] Perry, P., 'Economy, Landscape and Society in La Castigniccia (Corsica) since the Late Eighteenth Century', *Trans. Inst. Br. Geogr.*, 1967, p. 209.

[8] Kolodny, Y., *op. cit*.[3]

[9] Rondeau, A., *op. cit*.[2], pp. 74–85.

[10] Lefèbvre, P., 'La population de la Corse', *Revue Géogr. alp.*, 1957, p. 557.

[11] Kolodny, Y., *Géographie urbaine de la Corse*, pp. 115–134, 1962, Paris, SEDES.

[12] Anon., 'Statistique démographique de la Corse', *Bull. SOMIVAC SETCO*, No. 40, 1966, p. 32.

[13] *Journal Officiel*, 'Corse, Programme d'Action Régional', Paris, April 19, 1957.

[14] Thompson, I., 'The Revival of Corsica; regional planning in action', *Geogrl Mag.*, 1966, p. 898.

[15] *Notes Etud. docum.*, No. 2,852, 'La Mise en Valeur de la Corse', 1962, pp. 10–12.

[16] Robinson, G., 'Tourists in Corsica', *Econ. Geogr.*, 1957, p. 337.

[17] Anon., 'Moyens et Action de la Société pour l'Equipement Touristique de la Corse', *Bull. SOMIVAC SETCO*, No. 45, 1968, p. 36.

[18] Renucci, J., 'La Corse et le tourisme', *Revue Géogr. Lyon*, 1962, p. 207.

[19] Dacharry, M., *op. cit*.[1], Fig. 1, p. 27.

[20] Thompson, I., 'Land reclamation in eastern Corsica', *Geography*, 1962, p. 181.

[21] Renucci, J., *op. cit*.[4], pp. 145–149.

[22] Thompson, I., 'Land reclamation in eastern Corsica', *Reclamation in the Seventies*, 1967, Fig. 1, p. 132.

[23] Kolodny, Y., *op. cit*.[3], p. 87.

[24] Renucci, J., 'Problèmes d'aménagement de la plaine orientale en Corse', *Revue Géogr. Lyon*, 1964, pp. 279–284.

[25] Isnard, M., 'Structure des vignobles méditerranéens français: la Corse', *Méditerranée*, 1963, p. 79.

[26] Grelou, C., 'La 48ᵉ excursion géographique interuniversitaire, Corse', *Annls Géogr.*, 1966, p. 437.

[27] Thompson, I., 'Some problems of regional planning in predominantly rural environments. The French experience in Corsica', *Scott. Geogrl Mag.*, 1966, pp. 127–128.

Postscript

In a referendum held in April 1969, the French electorate rejected a series of proposals which included measures of regional reform. It would be erroneous to consider this as a rebuttal of the movement towards regional autonomy and the specific regional proposals received popular approval and the official support of the main political parties. The referendum was rejected on wider political issues beyond the scope of this book. It seems unlikely that the defeat of the referendum proposals will halt the momentum of regionalization but some ambiguity of necessity remains until French internal policies solidify after the period of intense national debate since the disturbances of the summer of 1968.

In analysing rapidly changing situations, certain ambiguity must also attach to some of the recurrent themes of this book. The use of terminology derived from the theory and practice of planning has been unavoidable but this does not imply a conviction on the part of the author of the validity of all the concepts and plans described. Several examples may serve to caution the reader of the need to distinguish between concepts and aspirations on the one hand, and realization and achievement on the other. Frequent reference has been made to 'axes of growth', based on transport alignments. It may be suggested that the existence of such transport axes, however strong, does not of necessity imply the inevitability of growth along their entire length. Thus the creation of a motorway through a zone of depressed economic activity may serve the function of connecting two external highly active regions, using the depressed zone as a region of transit but not of necessity reviving its economy. Similarly, the construction of motorways to outlying regions, although reducing the isolation which has inhibited their industrial expansion, also has the effect of increasing their accessibility as markets for existing centres of manufacturing activity.

A second example is the concept of 'growth poles'. Although many larger towns and cities are firmly established as centres of self-sustaining economic growth, having crossed a critical threshold where strong multiplier effects become evident, this may not as yet apply to many of the smaller towns so designated in planning reports and other publications. It may be suggested that the undeniable demographic expansion of many towns towards the base of the urban hierarchy owes more to their increased importance as service centres than to intense economic forces. The centralization of formerly dispersed rural services on to towns and the redeployment of agricultural population into tertiary functions and small-scale industries has sustained impressive rates of population increase in many of the smaller towns of France. It is not yet clear that this constitutes a sufficient economic base for continued rapid growth once rationalization of rural services has been achieved and a stable demographic balance attained between urban centres and tributary rural areas.

In similar vein, the need expressed by all regions for further decentralized industry must be viewed with a certain amount of reserve for two reasons. Clearly the amount of further industrial employment which can be shed by the Paris region is not limitless, and it is rather the general rate of growth in the French economy and the level of new investment possible which will determine the scale and speed of industrial implantation in the provinces. Equally important, realism dictates that all locations are not of equivalent economic merit, whatever the social imperatives and regional aspirations. The evolution of the Common Market must inevitably confirm the industrial vocation of certain regions, as measured by the opportunity for profitable operation, while other regions must seek their rational vocations in other predominant enterprises.

Finally, this book has approached the geography of modern France as expressed through contemporary economic and social problems. This has posed two intractable difficulties. In seeking to portray rapidly changing situations there is a tendency to be overtaken by events. As problems evolve, new legislation is introduced, plans are revised and a constant stream of data appears. Thus, for instance, the development plan for the Paris region has, predictably, been reviewed, and the disappearance of the Paris District envisaged. Secondly, in stressing problems the author may have appeared unduly critical of French efforts to modernize their nation. This is far from the intention, but rather does the presentation of problems offer a meaningful framework against which to measure achievements, both accomplished and in the future.

At present, the economic geography of western Europe is in a state of flux, resulting successively from post-war reconstruction, modernization of production, changing trading patterns and the impact of technology, which have reacted on the relative advantages of given locations and regions. The possible adherence of other nations, and notably Britain, to an enlarged European Community may be expected to prolong this period of transition. This stage of flux is unlikely to continue indefinitely as new economic structures crystallize into a stable pattern. This book has attempted to interpret the geography of France at an interim, but highly active, stage within this wider evolution.

Bibliography

The relevant literature is so voluminous that only a selection may be listed. This includes general reference works containing comprehensive bibliographies, important statistical sources and series, and books and articles of recent date of relevance to particular themes in the text. Articles cited in the text are not repeated. The bibliography is in no sense complete, but is intended as a guide to further reading. For a complete bibliography the reader should refer to *La Bibliographie Géographique Internationale*, published annually by the Association de Géographes Français, Section B II.

GENERAL REFERENCE WORKS

Pinchemel, P., *Géographie de la France*, 2 vols., 1964, Paris, Armand Colin.

Chabot, G., *Géographie Régionale de la France*, 1966, Paris, Masson.

George, P., *La France*, 1967, Paris, Presses Universitaires de France.

Gravier, J., *L'Aménagement du Territoire et l'Avenir des Régions Françaises*, 1964, Paris, Flammarion.

Guichard, O., *Aménager la France*, 1965, Paris, Laffont-Gonthier.

Le Lannou, M., *Les Régions Géographiques de la France*, 2 vols., 1963, Paris, C.D.U.

Chardonnet, J., *L'Economie Française. Etude Géographique d'une Décadence et des Possibilités de Redressement*, 2 vols., 1958, 1959, Paris, Dalloz.

Monkhouse, F., *A Regional Geography of Western Europe*, 2nd edn., 1964, London, Longmans.

Scargill, I., *Economic Geography of France*, 1968, London, Macmillan.

Atlas Historique de la France Contemporaine, 1800–1965, 1966, Paris, Armand Colin.

Deffontaines, P., and Delamarre, M., *Atlas Aérien*, 5 vols., 1955–1964, Paris, Gallimard.

Atlas de l'Industrie Française, Conseil National du Patronat Français, 1959, Paris.

STATISTICAL SOURCES

INSEE, *Annuaire Statistique*, Annual digest of statistics.

INSEE, Etudes et Conjoncture, *L'Espace Economique Français* (Fasc. 1: *Démographie Générale*, 1965; Fasc. 2: *Population Active*, 1967).

INSEE, *Population de la France; Départements, Arrondissements, Cantons et Communes. Recensement de 1968*, 1969.

La Documentation Française, *Panorama de la France*, Réimpression, 1969.

Rapports de Gestion: Gaz de France, Electricité de France, Charbonnages de France.

Ministère de l'Agriculture, *La Statistique Agricole Annuelle*.

IMPORTANT SERIALS AND JOURNALS

Annales de Géographie.

Bulletin de l'Association de Géographes Français.

Information Géographique.

INSEE, *Etudes et Conjonctures.*
La Documentation Française, *Notes et Etudes Documentaires.*
Population.
Urbanisme.
La Vie Urbaine.
Expansion Régionale.
Bulletin d'Information, Comité National pour l'Aménagement du Territoire.
La Revue Française de l'Energie.
Paysans.
Etudes Rurales.

PART ONE:
PATTERNS OF SOCIAL ORGANIZATIONS

Huber, M., Bunle, H., and Boverat, F., *La Population de la France, son Evolution et ses Perspectives*,
   4th edn., 1965, Paris, Hachette.
Armengaud, A., *La Population Française au XXe Siècle*, 1965, Paris, Presses Universitaires de France.
Benoît, J., 'Evolution démographique de la population française, 1954–1965', *Inf. géogr.*, 1965,
   p. 196.
Pressat, R., 'La population active en France, premiers résultats du recensement de 1962', *Population*,
   1963, p. 472.
L'Evolution de la Vie Rurale en France, Ecole Normale Supérieure Agronomique, Rennes, 1966.
Blache, J., 'Aperçu du problème rural français', *Revue Géogr. alp.*, 1964, p. 573.
Chatelain, A., 'La population agricole française dans la société rurale', *Paysans*, 1964–65, p. 30.
Meynier, A., 'Départements et communes de France, sont-ils trop petits?', *Mélanges offerts à O.
   Tulippe*, p. 30, 1967, Gembloux, Duculot.
Wright, G., *Rural Revolution in France, the Peasantry in the Twentieth Century*, Stanford University
   Press, 1964.
Leroy, L., *Exode—ou Mise en Valeur des Campagnes*, 1958, Paris, Flammarion.
Carrière, F., and Pinchemel, P., *Le Fait Urbain en France*, 1963, Paris, Armand Colin.
L'Urbanisation Française, Centre de Recherche d'Urbanisme, 1964, Paris.
'Métropoles d'Equilibre', special edition of *Urbanisme*, No. 89, 1965.
Prost, M., *La Hiérarchie des Villes en fonction de leur Activités de Commerce et Service*, 1965, Paris,
   Gauthier-Villars.

PART TWO:
PATTERNS OF ECONOMIC ACTIVITY

Bauchet, P., *Economic Planning. The French Experience*, 1962, New York, Praeger.
Hackett, J., and Hackett, A., *Economic Planning in France*, 1963, London, Allen and Unwin.
Fourastie, J., and Courtheoux, J., *La Planification Economique en France*, 1963, Paris, Presses
   Universitaires de France.
Delmas, C., *L'Aménagement du Territoire*, 1962, Paris, Presses Universitaires de France.
Gamblin, A., *L'Energie en France; étude de géographie*, 1963, Paris, C.D.U.
Chardonnet, J., *Géographie Industrielle*, Tome 1: *Les Sources d'Energie*, 1962, Paris, Sirey.
Wolkowitsch, M., 'La consommation d'électricité en France', *Mélanges offerts à O. Tulippe*, p. 123,
   1967, Gembloux, Duculot.
Despicht, N., *Policies for Transport in the Common Market*, 1964, Sidcup, Lombarde Press.
Boyer, A., 'Les Ports Maritimes de Commerce en France', *Notes Etud. docum.*, 1966, No. 3290.
Caralp, R., 'L'évolution de l'exploitation ferroviaire en France', *Annls Géogr.*, 1951, p. 321.
Schofield, G., 'The canalization of the Moselle', *Geography*, 1965, p. 161.
Bloch, M., *Les Caractères Originaux de l'Histoire Rurale Française*, 1952, Paris, Armand Colin.
Klatzmann, J., *La Localisation des Cultures et des Productions Animales en France*, 1955, Paris, INSEE.
Gervais, M., Servolin, C., and Weil, J., *Une France sans Paysans*, 1965, Paris, Seuil.
Pautard, J., *Les Disparités Régionales dans la Croissance de l'Agriculture*, 1965, Paris, Gauthier-Villars.
Gay, F., 'Problèmes de l'étendue et de la structure dans les régions céréalières', *Norois*, 1966, p. 220.

Lavetre, J., 'Premiers résultats du fonctionnement des SAFER', *Paysans*, 1955, p. 27.

Higbee, E., 'Farmers in France', *Geogrl Rev.*, 1965, p. 589.

Rambaud, P., 'Les agriculteurs et la planification régionale', *Etud. rur.*, 1966, p. 5.

Loussiaux, J., and Amoy, C., 'Quelques aspects de la concentration dans les industries françaises: l'exemple de l'industrie textile', *Rev. Econ. politique*, 1965, p. 405.

Prêcheur, C., *La Sidérurgie Française*, 1963, Paris, Armand Colin.

Wolkowitsch, M., 'Les industries de biens d'équipement en France', *Annls Géogr.*, 1964, p. 431.

Bienfait, J., 'L'industrie française de la machine-outil', *Revue Géogr. Lyon*, 1966, p. 11.

Jalabert, G., 'Les industries aéronautiques et aérospatiales en France', *Inf. Géogr.*, 1966, p. 95.

Dezert, B., 'L'industrie automobile française en 1964', *Inf. géogr.*, 1965, p. 124.

Ginier, J., *Géographie Touristique de la France*, 1965, Paris, SEDES.

Burnet, L., *Tourisme et Villégiature sur les Côtes de France*, 1963, Paris,

Cribier, F., '300,000 résidences secondaires', *Urbanisme*, 1966, p. 96.

'Nouveaux résultats des enquêtes sur les vacances des Français', *Etud. Conjoncture*, May, 1966.

Cribier, F., 'Variations de la consommation de farine et migration touristique d'été en France', *Bull. Ass. Géogr. fr.*, 1961, p. 170.

Sister Mary Annette, 'The Changing French region', *Prof. Geogr.*, 1965, p. 1.

Faucher, D., 'Des provinces aux régions de programme. L'aménagement économique de la France moderne', *Mélanges offerts à O. Tulippe*, Tome I, p. 541, 1967, Gembloux, Duculot.

PART THREE: REGIONAL ESSAYS

THE PARIS REGION

Les Cahiers de l'Institut d'Aménagement et d'Urbanisme de la Région Parisienne.

George, P., and Randet, P., *La Région Parisienne*, 1964, Paris, Presses Universitaires de France.

Juillard, E., 'La notion de ville mondiale et le problème de l'avenir de Paris', *Mélanges offert à O. Tulippe*, Tome II, p. 293, 1967, Gembloux, Duculot.

Bastié, J., 'Le bassin parisien existe-t-il?', *Urbanisme*, 1966, p. 54.

Bastié, J., *La Croissance de la Banlieue Parisienne*, 1964, Paris, Presses Universitaires de France.

Bastié, J., *Paris en l'An 2,000*, 1964, Paris, SEDIMO.

Beaujeu-Garnier, J., 'La spécialisation des arrondissements parisiens', *Mélanges offerts à O. Tulippe*, Tome I, p. 444, 1967, Gembloux, Duculot.

Beaujeu-Garnier, J., *Atlas de la Région Parisienne*, 1967, Paris, Berger-Levrault.

Delouvrier, P., 'Bassin Parisien et Schéma Directeur de la Région parisienne', *Urbanisme*, 1966, p. 12.

THE REGIONS OF EASTERN FRANCE

Hommes et Terres du Nord.

Revue Géographique de l'Est.

Revue de Géographie Alpine.

Méditerranée.

Revue de Géographie de Lyon.

Nistri, R., and Prêcheur, C., *La Région du Nord et du Nord-Est*, 1959, Paris, Presses Universitaires de France.

Deligny, H., *Le Nord Demain*, 1964, Paris, Gamma-Presse.

Atlas du Nord, 1961, Berger-Levrault.

C.E.R.E.S., *Atlas des Industries du Nord et du Pas-de-Calais*, 1956, Lille.

Flatrès, P., 'Les structures agraires du Nord de la France', *Mélanges offerts à O. Tulippe*, Tome I, p. 309, 1967, Gembloux, Duculot.

Delsaut, P., 'Population active et emploi dans la conurbation de Lille–Roubaix–Tourcoing–Armentières', *Hommes et Terres du Nord*, 1967, p. 37.

Boitel, F., 'L'industrie textile dans le Nord, son évolution', *Hommes et Terres du Nord*, 1968, p. 19.

Atlas de l'Est, 1959, Strasbourg, Istra, and Nancy, Berger-Levrault.

Prêcheur, C., *La Lorraine Sidérurgique*, 1959, Paris, SABRI.

Frécaut, R., *et al.*, 'Les agglomérations de Metz et de Thionville. Contribution à la géographie urbaine de la Lorraine', *Revue Géogr. l'Est*, 1968, p. 89.

Alix, P., *Vers une Nouvelle Lorraine*, 1967, Paris, Médicis.

Josse, R., 'L'expansion d'Amiens, réalisations et perspectives', *Inf. géogr.*, 1967, p. 63.

Atlas de Normandie, Caen, 1966, Association pour l'Atlas de Normandie.

Gay, J., *et al.*, *Le Littoral du Pays de Caux*, Association des Géographes de Haute-Normandie, Rouen, 1969.

Blanc, A., Juillard, E., Ray, J., and Rochefort, M., *Les Régions de l'Est*, 1960, Paris, Presses Universitaires de France.

Juillard, E., 'L'Alsace, terre rhénane. Passé, présent et avenir', *Inf. géogr.*, 1965, p. 1.

'Etudes comtoises et bourguignonnes offertes à Georges Chabot pour son 75ᵉ anniversiare', *Revue Géogr. l'Est*, 1963, pp. 371, 401.

Dietrich, G., and Garenc, P., 'Le paysage rural en Franche-Comté', *Revue Géogr. l'Est*, 1963, p. 371.

Labasse, J., and Laferrère, M., *La Région Lyonnaise*, 2nd edn., 1966, Paris, Presses Universitaires de France.

Lefèbvre, J., *L'Evolution des Localisations Industrielles. L'exemple des Alpes françaises*, 1960, Paris, Dalloz.

Veyret, P., and Veyret, G., 'Les paysans montagnards devant le tourisme. L'exemple des Alpes françaises du Nord', *Mélanges offerts à O. Tulippe*, Tome II, p. 209, 1967, Gembloux, Duculot.

Labasse, J., 'Interdépendences et armatures urbaines dans la région lyonnaise', *Mélanges offerts à O. Tulippe*, Tome II, 1967, Gembloux, Duculot.

Schnetzler, J., 'La main-d'oeuvre industrielle dans la région stéphanoise', *Revue Géogr. Lyon*, 1965, p. 235.

Faucher, D., *L'Homme et le Rhône*, 1968, Paris, Gallimard.

Carrère, P., and Dugrand, M., *La Région Méditerranéenne*, 1960, Paris, Presses Universitaires de France.

Hermitte, J., *L'Economie Industrielle des Rivages Méditerranéens entre Toulon et la Spezia*, 1967, Gap, Ophrys.

Carrère, P., 'Le contexte démographique et économique de la région marseillaise', *Urbanisme*, 1966, p. 16.

Barbier, B., 'Irrigation et développement agricole en Moyenne et Basse-Durance alpestres', *Méditerranée*, 1962, p. 65.

Delenne, M., 'Les agriculteurs du Sud-Est face au progrès technique', *Revue Géogr. Lyon*, 1966, p. 177.

THE REGIONS OF WESTERN FRANCE

Norois.

Revue Géographique des Pyrénées et du Sud-Ouest.

Bachelard, P., 'Orléans et sa banlieue-problèmes d'agglomération', *Norois*, 1967, p. 439.

Estienne, P., and Joly, R., *La Région du Centre*, 1961, Paris, Presses Universitaires de France.

Musset, R., *La Normandie*, 1960, Paris, Armand Colin.

Elhaï, H., 'La 47ᵉ excursion géographique interuniversitaire. Normandie', *Annls Géogr.*, 1967, p. 458.

Bertrand, Y., *Le Rôle des Transports Terrestres dans le Développement Economique de la Bretagne*, Centre Régional d'Etudes et de Formation Economique, 1966, Rennes.

Pleven, R., *L'Avenir de la Bretagne*, 1961, Paris, Calmann-Lévy.

Gautier, M., 'L'évolution récente des principaux ports de pêche bretons', *Norois*, 1966, p. 59.

Flatrès, P., *La Région de l'Ouest*, 1964, Paris, Presses Universitaires de France.

Gras, J., 'La 49ᵉ excursion géographique interuniversitaire. Pays-de-la-Loire', *Annls Géogr.*, 1968, p. 154.

Fel, A., *Les Hautes Terres du Massif Central. Tradition paysanne et économie rurale*, 1962, Paris, Presses Universitaires de France.

Bonnaud, P., 'Les problèmes du peuplement du Massif Central vus par un géographe', *Revue d'Auvergne*, 1969, p. 1.

Derruau-Boniols, S., and Fel, A., *Le Massif Central*, 1963, Paris, Presses Universitaires de France.

Derruau, S., and Estienne, P., 'Evolution récente du Massif Central français', *Inf. géogr.*, 1965, p. 148.

Clout, H., 'Problems of rural planning in the Auvergne', *Plann. Outl.*, 1969, p. 29.

Robert, J., *Atlas de la région Poitou-Charentes*, Comité d'Expansion Economique et Sociale du Centre-Ouest, Poitiers, 1964.

Robert, J., 'L'économie agricole dans la région de programme Poitou-Charentes', *Mélanges offerts à O. Tulippe*, Tome II, p. 5, 1967, Gembloux, Duculot.

Pinard, J., 'Aléas et atouts de la région Poitou-Charentes', *Norois*, 1969, p. 47.

Barrère, P., Heisch, R., and Lerat, S., *La Région du Sud-Ouest*, 1962, Paris, Presses Universitaires de France.

Atlas de la Région Midi-Pyrénées, 1969, Paris, Berger-Levrault.

Coppolani, J., 'L'armature urbaine du Sud-Ouest', *Revue Géogr. Pyrénées S.-Ouest*, 1967, p. 131.

Kayser, B., 'Les processus de l'urbanisation dans la région Midi-Pyrénées', *Revue Géogr. Pyrénées S.-Ouest*, 1967, p. 113.

Atlas de Languedoc-Roussillon, 1969, Paris, Berger-Levrault.

Milhau, J., 'Connaissance du Languedoc', *Urbanisme*, 1965, p. 16.

Simi, P., *L'Adaptation Humaine dans la Dépression Centrale de la Corse*, 1967, Gap, Ophrys.

Lenquette, P., 'Le problème corse', *Inf. géogr.*, 1967, p. 151.

Index

References to figures and plates are distinguished by italic type. References in bold type relate to important points.